"Coming Canadians"

A History of Canada's Peoples

"Coming Canadians"

An Introduction to a History of
Canada's Peoples

Jean R. Burnet
with Howard Palmer

Published by McClelland and Stewart in association
with the Multiculturalism Program,
Department of the Secretary of State
and the Canadian Government Publishing Centre,
Supply and Services, Canada

Catalogue No. Ci44-14/1988E

Canadian Cataloguing in Publication Data
Burnet, Jean R., 1920–
    "Coming Canadians": An introduction to a history
    of Canada's peoples

(Generations, a history of Canada's peoples)
Co-published by the Multiculturalism Directorate.
Bibliography: p.
Includes index.
ISBN 0-7710-1783-9

1. Canada – Population – Ethnic groups – History.
2. Canada – Emigration and immigration – History.
I. Canada. Multiculturalism Directorate.
II. Title. III. Series.

FC104.B87 1988   971'.004   C87-095160-2
F1035.A1B87 1988

Printed and bound in Canada

McClelland and Stewart
The Canadian Publishers
481 University Avenue
Toronto, Ontario
M5G 2E9

Contents

Editors' Introduction / *vi*
Preface / *1*

ONE: Introduction / *3*

Part One: Immigration and Settlement
TWO: Settlement to 1880 / *11*
THREE: Settlement, 1880–1980 / *25*

Part Two: Major Institutions
FOUR: The Economic Structure / *57*
FIVE: Kinship, Marriage, and the Family / *81*
SIX: Education / *103*
SEVEN: Religious Institutions / *125*
EIGHT: Ethnicity and Politics / *151*

Part Three: Other Institutions and the Maintenance of Identity
NINE: Ethnic Voluntary Associations / *185*
TEN: The Media / *197*
ELEVEN: Ethnic Identity / *212*
TWELVE: Multicultural Canada / *223*

Bibliography / *229*
Index / *241*

Editors' Introduction

Canadians, like many other people, have recently been changing their attitude toward the ethnic dimension in society. Instead of thinking of the many distinctive heritages and identities to be found among them as constituting a problem, though one that time would solve, they have begun to recognize the ethnic diversity of their country as a rich resource. They have begun to take pride in the fact that people have come and are coming here from all parts of the world, bringing with them varied outlooks, knowledge, skills, and traditions, to the great benefit of all.

It is for this reason that Book IV of the *Report of the Royal Commission on Bilingualism and Biculturalism* dealt with the cultural contributions of the ethnic groups other than the British, the French, and the Native peoples to Canada, and that the federal government in its response to Book IV announced that the Citizenship Branch of the Department of the Secretary of State would commission "histories specifically directed to the background, contributions and problems of various cultural groups in Canada." This series presents the histories that have resulted from that mandate. Although commissioned by the government, they are not intended as definitive or official, but rather as the efforts of scholars to bring together much of what is known about the ethnic groups studied, to indicate what remains to be learned, and thus to stimulate further research concerning the ethnic dimension in Canadian society. The histories are to be objective, analytical, and readable, and directed toward the general reading public, as well as students at the senior high school and the college and university levels, and teachers in the elementary schools.

Most Canadians belong to an ethnic group, since to do so is simply to have "a sense of identity rooted in a common origin . . . whether this common origin is real or imaginary."[1] The Native peoples, the British and French (referred to as charter groups because they were the first Europeans to take possession of the land), the groups such as the Germans and Dutch who have been established in Canada for over a hundred years, and those who began to arrive only yesterday all have traditions and values they cherish and that now are part of the cultural riches Canadians share. The groups vary widely in numbers, geographical location and distribution, and degree of social and economic power. The stories of their struggles, failures, and triumphs will be told in this series.

As the Royal Commission on Bilingualism and Biculturalism pointed out, this sense of ethnic origin or identity "is much keener in certain individuals than in others."[2] In contemporary Canadian society, with the increasing number of intermarriages across ethnic lines, and hence the growing diversity of people's ancestors, many are coming to identify themselves simply as Canadian, without reference to their ancestral origins. In focusing on the ethnic dimension of Canadian society, past and present, the series does not assume that everyone should be categorized into one particular group, or that ethnicity is always the most important dimension of people's lives. It is, however, one dimension that needs examination if we are to understand fully the contours and nature of Canadian society and identity.

Professional Canadian historians have in the past emphasized political and economic history, and since the country's economic and political institutions have been controlled largely by people of British and French origin, the role of those of other origins in the development of Canada has been neglected. Also, Canadian historians in the past have been almost exclusively of British and French origin and have lacked the interest and the linguistic skills necessary to explore the history of other ethnic groups. Indeed, there has rarely even been an examination of the part played by specifically British – or, better, specifically English, Irish, Scottish, and Welsh – traditions and values in Canadian development because of the lack of recognition of pluralism in the society. The part played by French traditions and values, and particular varieties of French traditions and values, has for a number of reasons been more carefully scrutinized.

This series is an indication of growing interest in Canadian social history, which includes immigration and ethnic history. This may partially be a reflection of an increasing number of scholars whose origins and ethnic identities are other than British or French. Because such trends are recent, many of the authors of the histories in this series have not had a large body of published writing to work from. It is true that some histories have already been written of particular groups other than the British and French; but these have often been characterized by filiopietism, a narrow perspective, and a dearth of scholarly analysis.

Despite the scarcity of secondary sources, the authors have been asked to be as comprehensive as possible and to give balanced coverage to a number of themes: historical background, settlement patterns, ethnic identity and assimilation, ethnic associations, population trends, religion, values, occupations and social class, the family, the ethnic press, language patterns, political behaviour, education, inter-ethnic relations, the arts, and recreation. They have also been asked to give a sense of the way the group differs in various parts of the country. Finally, they have been asked to give, as much as possible, an insider's view of what the immigrant and ethnic experiences were like at different periods of time, but yet at the same time to be as objective as possible and not simply to present the group as it sees itself or as it would like to be seen.

The authors have thus been faced with a herculean task. To the extent that they have succeeded, they provide us with new glimpses into many aspects of Canadian society of the past and the present. To the extent that they have fallen short of their goal, they challenge other historians, sociologists, and social anthropologists to continue the work begun here.

Jean Burnet
Howard Palmer

[1] *Report of the Royal Commission on Bilingualism and Biculturalism.*
[2] *Ibid.*, Paragraph 8.

Preface

The initial plans for the Generations series included an introductory volume, in which the histories of particular ethnic groups would be woven together. The general editors of the series seemed to be the appropriate people to prepare such a volume. However, when the time came to begin, Howard Palmer was busily engaged in a number of other projects. I therefore set out on my own. Later, Howard was able to join me, writing Chapter Eight and assisting in the revision of Chapter Six. Since I met him in 1970, much of what I have written concerning ethnic groups and multiculturalism has been part of a continuing dialogue between us.

I have borrowed the title for the book from one of the earliest works on Canada's immigrant peoples. *Strangers Within Our Gates or Coming Canadians*, by J.S. Woodsworth, was first published in 1909. It embodied the views of the educated and compassionate of its time. The present volume shows how our knowledge has increased and our attitudes have changed regarding immigrant peoples in the last eighty years.

This volume is based on the work of others, rather than on original historical research. I first had an opportunity to integrate and synthesize studies of immigration and ethnic history and social organization in the 1960's as a research associate of the Royal Commission on Bilingualism and Biculturalism, working on the preparation of Book IV, *The Cultural Contributions of the Other Ethnic Groups*. Echoes of that work probably can be heard in the present volume. I am grateful to the commissioners for the chance I was given and to the researchers with whom I worked, including Harlan Brown, Peter Findlay, and the late T.M. Krukowski.

In the 1970's and 1980's tremendous advances have been made in Canadian ethnic studies from which I have profited. I have relied heavily on the authors in the Generations series, of which fourteen volumes have now appeared and a number are in various stages of preparation. In many cases the authors have had to be pioneers, seeking for scattered letters, memoirs, and newspapers, sifting group myths and legends, weaving a coherent account from unlikely materials. In a few cases the authors, on the contrary, have

1

been submerged in masses of primary and secondary documentation. They have all shown themselves to be dedicated scholars.

I have also profited from the work of colleagues, including among others Raymond Breton, Robert Harney, Sev Isajiw, Cornelius Jaenen, Danielle Juteau-Lee, Lilian Petroff, and Harold Troper. The late Michel Laferrière was one of a number of people who read and commented on part of the manuscript. I have always received kind and generous assistance from members of the Multiculturalism Directorate. Over the years they have included Yok Leng Chang, Helen Eriks, Steve Jaworsky, Myron Momryk, Adrian Papanek, André Rousseau, Roberta Russell, Monique Shoblom, Nadia Slejskova, Maria Tiley, and Judy Young. I have been helped by a sabbatical leave and a research leave granted by Glendon College, and by the support of colleagues and friends there, including Mildred Brown, Helen Goldman, Florence Knight, and Lorna Lampkin.

A skilled literary editor comes as close as anyone can to making silk purses out of sows' ears. I was fortunate, as some of the authors of particular ethnic histories in the Generations series have been, in having as literary editor Diane Mew. She combines great skill in her craft with perceptions going above and beyond it. I am grateful to her as editor and friend.

ONE

Introduction

Ethnic diversity, until recently ignored in Canada both as a dimension of society and as a topic of research for scholars, is now recognized as one of the country's invaluable resources. For thousands of years a variety of peoples have dwelt here, bringing many distinctive outlooks, ideas, talents, experiences, and traditions to help shape Canada's response to the challenges of its environment. Yet the country's history and social science have been written largely in terms of the French and the British, the successive colonizers, with occasional notice of the Indians and the Inuit. It is time to add to the account the other Canadians who, although they were not native and did not share the ethnic identity of the military conquerors or the political rulers of the land, shared in the exploration, settlement, and building of our society.

This book will deal with those other Canadians, as immigrants to Canada and as members of ethnic groups. It will attempt to show some of their common experiences and some of their distinctive histories, against the backdrop of a large and regionally diverse country. The particular stories of many of the groups have been or are being told; this book will bring together such accounts. It will also deal where possible with relations between ethnic groups, which often are ignored or slighted in histories of individual groups.

The French and the British, while not central to the study, will nonetheless be significant parts of it. They have been the chief builders of the institutions and the communities in which the others have played their part. They are the charter-member groups in Canadian society and have expected others to assimilate to them.

Neither the British nor the French group is ethnically homogeneous. The French Canadians in North America became differentiated early into Acadians and *Canadiens*. Later, the mating of French Canadians and Amerindians gave birth to the Métis people. However unified politically, the British were divided in identity and culture into English, Scottish, Irish, and Welsh components, and even within such ethnic groups as the Scottish there were subgroups with a strong sense of peoplehood. The distinction between Highlanders and Lowlanders has been marked; in addition, Elaine Allen Mitchell

3

has said of the inhabitants of the Orkney Islands, who were a mainstay of the Hudson's Bay Company:

> Even today, despite centuries of patriotic adherence to the rest of Scotland, Orcadians (their proper connotation, although the Hudson's Bay records invariably refer to them as Orkneymen) are inclined to regard themselves as a separate people. And in a manner of speaking they are, for the Norse invasions obliterated every trace of Celtic peoples who formerly inhabited the islands.[1]

One very important and variegated story will be omitted: that of the oldest inhabitants of Canada, its Native peoples. For a long time they were pushed to the fringes of society, and some of them are still isolated on reserves and in yet unexploited parts of the North. More and more, however, they have been entering the industrial economy and the city, and in doing so they have been sharing experiences and problems with newcomers to the country and adapting certain concepts and forms of organization used by others to their own purposes. Nonetheless, their history and their situation are so special as to require separate treatment.

There is no satisfactory designation for the Canadians who will be the focus of this study. It is logical to distinguish between the Native or indigenous peoples (the Indians and Inuit), the colonizers (the French and the British), and those ethnic groups who came to Canada in the main as immigrants to an already established society. To speak of immigrant ethnic groups seems to imply, however, that most members of the groups in question were born abroad; in fact, in some of the groups as many as 85 per cent are now Canadian-born. Even to speak of immigrants and their descendants[2] seems to minimize the length of the stay in Canada of those referred to. It might seem possible to distinguish between the British and French groups and other groups in terms of size, but so far as it is possible to determine the size of ethnic groups, small groups would include the Welsh as well as, among others, Estonians, Latvians, and Lithuanians. The term "minority ethnic groups" may be applied differently depending on whether numerical strength or power, or Canada as a whole or a particular region, is being considered. Hence, the term employed in the terms of reference of the Royal Commission on Bilingualism and Biculturalism – "other ethnic groups" – will be used, although with some regret since it relegates those to whom it refers to a residual category and minimizes both the differences among them and their significance for Canadian society. It has the advantage, of course, of implying that the French and British are also ethnic groups, a fact sometimes denied when the term ethnic is given a pejorative meaning.

An ethnic group has been described by R.A. Schermerhorn as "a collectivity within a larger society having real or putative common ancestry, memories of a shared historical past, and a cultural focus on one or more symbolic elements defined as the epitome of their peoplehood. . . . A necessary accompaniment is some consciousness of kind among members of the group."[3] The same view has been put in its most succinct form by Milton Gordon, who talks of an ethnic group as being characterized by a sense of peoplehood.[4] So defined, the essence of an ethnic group is a sense of identity. Thus, it is not wholly definable in objective terms, although it may have objective markers.

An ethnic group is not a tightly closed group, although it sometimes has been considered to be, nor is it a group from which it is impossible to resign. Because of intermarriages, boundary changes, and political redefinitions, many people have some degree of choice of ethnic allegiance. It is well known that some members even of those ethnic groups that have physical markers "resign" from one group and join another by "passing." For groups that mark their ethnic boundaries not by physical but by cultural traits, switching is easier. Norman Ryder gives abundant Canadian evidence of changes of ethnic identity;[5] and recently, Rudolf Kogler and Benedykt Heydenkorn have accounted for the decrease in the number of Canadians of Polish origin between the 1961 and 1971 censuses by changes in affiliation from Polish to Jewish, Ukrainian, British, and other groups.[6]

It is difficult, then, to estimate the numbers belonging to particular ethnic groups. The closest the Canadian census has come to ascertaining membership in ethnic groups is to ask the question: "To what ethnic or cultural group did you or your ancestor belong on coming to this continent?" The resulting figures are usually employed as the best available index of the ethnic affiliations of the Canadian people. It must be kept in mind, however, that they concern *origin* rather than *identity*. Many people, whether their ancestors came to this continent twelve generations ago or two, simply consider themselves to be Canadians; when asked to choose an ethnic category they may name one with which they feel no real affinity. Until 1981 people were directed to respond concerning ancestors on the male side; in the census of that year the reference to the male side was dropped and multiple origins were recorded. It should be noted also that the questions by means of which ethnic origins have been gauged have varied over the years; that many people have been unable to answer the question "properly" as far as the census is concerned; and that at various times, especially when their homeland has been at war with the land of their adoption, people have tried to conceal or change their ethnic origins.[7] In addition to the census, official records of immigration until 1967 included information about ethnic origin, but since then they have not done so: rather, they have classified people by country of last permanent residence and by country of citizenship.

While it was available, the information in the immigration records offered some check on the census figures. However, considerable numbers of immigrants have always either returned home or moved on, in greatest numbers to the United States, so that the change in the numbers of a particular origin category between two censuses has resulted not only from natural increase, immigration, and change of identity within Canada, but also from emigration. There are no official Canadian records of emigration, merely estimates based on official reports of immigrants entering the United States who give Canada as their birthplace or their last place of permanent residence. In addition, the official records of immigration have not included those who have entered the country illegally, or as visitors, until they have obtained official immigrant status; some people have done so only after having been in the country for many years.

Ethnicity is intimately linked with culture. However, the two cannot be equated. A keen sense of ethnic identity can exist where there are few distinguishing cultural traits. In the second half of the twentieth century, ethnicity has become salient throughout much of the world, while cultural differences have diminished to such a point that some students have heralded their disappearance.[8]

Two aspects of culture are frequently of special significance as ethnic boundary markers: language and religion. Language has been described as a determinant of culture,[9] an essential expression of culture, the most typical expression of culture, and the natural vehicle for other elements of culture.[10] It is frequently the most cherished cultural symbol of identity. It is currently of great importance for the two ethnic groups, British and French, that were parties to the bargains out of which Canada grew. However, many ethnic groups, the West Indians among them, do not have distinctive languages; there are many groups, such as the Italian, in which people from different regions of the country speak in dialects that are not mutually comprehensible; and in some instances language has become especially treasured as an ethnic boundary marker only as other cultural distinctions have dwindled and disappeared, as in French Canada. In Canada the use of language as a marker by scholars is facilitated by the recognition given to language by the census. It has indicated that the language a person or his ancestor spoke at the time of coming to North America should be used as an aid in determining his or her ethnic origin, and it makes available statistics concerning mother tongue, knowledge of official languages, and, since 1971, the language most commonly used at home.

Religion may also be a determinant of culture. It has been the basis for a distinctive identity and way of life for Jews to such an extent that those who no longer profess Judaism may yet maintain their Jewish identity and culture. It has also been the basis for distinctive identities for some Christian sects that have stressed their separation and differences from their neighbours, such as Mennonites, Hutterites, and Doukhobors. However, many religions and many particular denominations cut across ethnic and cultural lines: while most Scandinavians are Lutherans and most Poles and Italians are Roman Catholic, Germans, for example, belong to the Lutheran and the Catholic faiths and a number of others as well.

Like language and religion, nationality is frequently related to ethnicity; indeed, many people equate nationality and ethnicity. However, whereas nationalism usually refers to a sense of ethnic unity, nationality is frequently interpreted as referring simply to membership in a state, and few if any states have been ethnically homogeneous. Ethnic minorities have frequently developed a strong sense of nationalism or unity. Their members have often been numerous among emigrants, fleeing from active or latent oppression. It is notable that immigrants belonging to a minority in their homeland have changed their response to queries concerning ethnic origin as that minority has become self-conscious and declared itself a state-deserving nation: Ukrainians, once known in Canada as Galicians, Bukovynians, and Ruthenians, are an outstanding case in point.

Physical traits are the most obvious and permanent of boundary markers; groups distinguished by them are frequently termed races or visible minorities rather than ethnic groups. Including racial groups among ethnic groups points to the fact that the physical marks are superficial, not necessarily borne by all members of the group, and modifiable by interbreeding, and that there is not complete consensus as to what groups are "non-white" or "visible" in Canadian society.[11] This should not conceal or minimize the fact that racial groups or visible minorities have been and are being singled out for greatest prejudice and discrimination, in Canada as elsewhere.

A number of factors have been important in shaping Canada's ethnic history and composition. One is its situation immediately to the north of the United States. That dynamic country has overshadowed Canada as a receiver of immigrants. It was the goal of "the largest migration of people in all recorded history,"[12] and it pictured itself and was pictured by others as a crucible in which disparate cultures and peoples were blended into a single great new culture and people. Not only did Canada receive fewer immigrants than the United States and serve as a way-station for many of these, but substantial numbers of those it did receive have always been from the British Isles. Further, whereas the United States was looked upon as an exuberant land of opportunity in which all comers were transformed into members of a new and dynamic breed, in its own eyes and those of the world Canada was a country in which disparate cultures and peoples retained their identity while forming parts of a static and not particularly colourful whole.

In other respects, also, Canada has been influenced by the proximity of the United States. Changes in race and ethnic relations in the United States have always been known in Canada and affect attitudes and behaviour here. In the decades since World War II, the rise of black nationalism, the outbreaks of racial violence, including the Watts riots, the increasing part played in the mass media by blacks and Latin Americans, the "ethnic revival" or "new ethnicity" of the 1960's and 1970's – all have had repercussions in Canada. The United States has also been a major source of immigrants to Canada and the chief recipient of emigrants from Canada, both "old Canadians" and transmigrants. There has been virtually no restriction on the movement of Canadians across the border, and no impediment of language or culture has existed for those among them who were English-speaking. The restless, the ambitious, the specially gifted or trained have been able to move into the more populous and more strongly developed country with ease and have made a mark for themselves there. On the other hand, shortages of training and talent in some areas of power and prestige in Canada have been alleviated by importation from the United States, often at premium prices; university faculties in the expansive late 1950's and the 1960's and the oil industry in Alberta during the 1950's offer examples. As in other less developed countries, native-born Canadians have often been at a competitive disadvantage compared to immigrants, temporary or permanent, from a more developed country. Their resentment has found expression from time to time in bitter anti-Americanism.

Another great fact shaping the ethnic composition of Canada has been the Canadian dualism. The existence of both an English-speaking and a French-speaking Canada, each able to be a majority in certain political subdivisions of the country, has from the beginning been fateful. For a long time the view that others held of French Canadians, and to some extent the view that French Canadians held of themselves, was that they were homogeneous, rural in values if not in residence, staunchly Roman Catholic, strongly bound by their distinctive language and culture, and inhospitable to immigrants. Since 1960 the French fact has changed drastically. The French Canadians have become more like their compatriots, even to wanting a monopoly of positions of power and prestige in the areas where they are the majority; the governments of the province of Quebec have been eager to receive immigrants who will accept the French language as their medium of communication in their new country, and the population has begun to lose its xenophobia.

The existence of French and English Canadas has presented a choice to some immigrants. For others, however, whether they settled in Montreal or in Toronto, Winnipeg, or Vancouver has been a matter of chance. Recently, with the increasing adoption of bilingualism as a federal policy and the emergence of a Québécois orientation among French Canadians, a political significance has been given to ethnicity in all groups.

The concentration of French Canadians in Quebec is only one aspect of the strong regionalism of Canada. The vastness of Canada, its geographical and climatic variety, and the length of time over which its settlement has taken place have resulted in marked differences among the parts of the country. Usually the regions are considered to be five: the Atlantic provinces, Quebec, Ontario, the Prairie provinces, and British Columbia. Probably a sixth, the North, consisting of the Yukon and the Northwest Territories, should be added, as its population increases and becomes more and more assertive. The regions – geographical, economic, and cultural – have been settled at different times, have developed at different rates, have exercised different degrees and kinds of attraction on peoples arriving in the country, and have displayed different abilities to retain population. Hence, they are now markedly varied in their ethnic composition and their ethnic attitudes, and their comportment as regions is related to those variations.

Finally, the policies of Canadian governments concerning immigration and ethnic relations have been extremely influential, whether the policies have been explicit or implicit. They have been based on judgements concerning the economic situation, the attitudes of electors, and opinions abroad. They have embodied strong racial discrimination, which has decreased only within the last few decades, and discrimination also among European groups. They have also embodied an encouragement to maintain ethnic identities and cultural heritages, accompanied by some discouragement of bloc settlement and an insistence on participation in the public school system. In the 1970's the policy of multiculturalism within a bilingual framework formalized the underlying notions that the maintenance of ethnic identities and participation in Canadian society were complementary. The policies have not been the sole determinants of immigration and settlement: for example, illegal immigration has often been sizable. They have, however, had a major effect.

In treating together those Canadians who are not British, French, or Native in origin, it is not intended to imply that they constitute a third force in Canadian life. Whatever they share, they differ in many respects. Among their differences are their historical pasts; their values, skills, and aspirations on coming to Canada; their degree of concentration or dispersion; the length of time they have been in Canada; the size of their communities, whether they are decreasing, stable, or increasing in number, and what proportion of the total population they are; the region or regions and the occupation or occupations in which they are concentrated; their degree of similarity to or difference from the charter-member groups. The British subdivide into a number of peoples; so do the French. To look for unity, other than an unstable unity related to shared minority status, among those who have in common little beyond not being British or French is futile.

On another level, of course, this volume is an exploration of the unity of all Canadians. It attempts to trace how over the years people who have come to this country from an ever-widening area of the world have met the challenges of its geography and its society. They have neither conformed entirely to an established pattern nor fused, as nineteenth- and early twentieth-century writers were fond of forecasting, into wholly new models. They have begun to have much in common, in spite of differences of background and region, but they have also kept a sense of distinctiveness, the basis of which has altered with the years. In doing so, they have become Canadian.

NOTES

1. Elaine Allen Mitchell, "The Scot in the Fur Trade," in W. Stanford Reid, ed., *The Scottish Tradition in Canada* (Toronto: McClelland and Stewart, 1976), pp. 28-29.
2. Jeffrey Reitz, "Immigrants, Their Descendants, and the Cohesion of Canada," in Raymond Breton, Jeffrey G. Reitz, and Victor Valentine, *Cultural Boundaries and the Cohesion of Canada* (Montreal: Institute for Research on Public Policy, 1980), pp. 329-417.
3. R.A. Schermerhorn, *Comparative Ethnic Relations* (New York: Random House, 1970), p. 12.
4. Milton Gordon, *Assimilation in American Life* (New York: Oxford University Press, 1964).
5. Norman B. Ryder, "The Interpretation of Origin Statistics," *Canadian Journal of Economics and Political Science*, 21, 4 (November, 1955), pp. 466-79.

6. Rudolf Kogler and Benedykt Heydenkorn, "Poles in Canada 1971," in Benedykt Heydenkorn, ed., *Past and Present* (Toronto: Canadian Polish Research Institute, 1974), pp. 27-36.

7. Ryder, "Origin Statistics"; John Kralt, "Ethnic Origins in the Canadian Census, 1871-1981," in W.R. Petryshyn, ed., *Changing Realities: Social Trends Among Ukrainian Canadians* (Edmonton: Canadian Institute of Ukrainian Studies, 1980), pp. 18-49.

8. John Porter, "Bilingualism and the Myths of Culture," *Canadian Review of Sociology and Anthropology*, 6, 2 (May, 1969), pp. 111-19.

9. Kenneth McRae, "Language Policies as an Aspect of Cultural Policy," working paper prepared for Linguistic and Cultural Diversity, a Canada/Unesco Symposium, Ottawa, September 25-30, 1972.

10. *Report* of the Royal Commission on Bilingualism and Biculturalism, General Introduction (Ottawa: Queen's Printer, 1967), p. xxxiv.

11. Doug Daniels, "The white race is shrinking: perceptions of race in Canada and some speculations on the political economy of race classification," *Ethnic and Racial Studies*, 4, 3 (July, 1981), pp. 353-56; Subhas Ramcharan, *Racism: Nonwhites in Canada* (Toronto: Butterworths, 1982).

12. John F. Kennedy, *A Nation of Immigrants*, revised and enlarged edition (New York: Harper & Row, 1964), p. 3.

PART ONE

Immigration and Settlement

TWO

Settlement to 1880

EXPLORATION AND EARLY SETTLEMENT

From the time of exploration of the coasts of what became Canada, people from many parts of the world have been involved in our history. The colonizing powers have stressed the exploits of those whom they themselves could claim and have been justified in doing so to the extent that the work of French and British explorers and colonizers has had more obvious consequences than that of explorers from other nations. Nonetheless, the claims that can be made, with much or little evidence to support them, indicate the diversity that has characterized the population of what is now Canada.

The Viking voyages around A.D. 1000 are one of the exceptions to the stress on French and British explorers in most Canadian histories. The voyages have been authenticated by much evidence, including the archaeological finds at L'Anse aux Meadows in Newfoundland. Later expeditions from Scandinavia included that of the Dane Jens Munk and his Norwegian seamen who explored Hudson Bay in 1619, within a decade of Henry Hudson and Thomas Button; of a crew of sixty-four, only two men and their commander survived a winter at what is now Churchill, and they took the expedition's two ships home in one of the greatest maritime feats of all time.[1]

A German named Tyrkir, the foster father of Leif Ericson, was part of the Viking expedition of A.D. 1001 and is said to have the dubious distinction of being the first European to get drunk in North America. Two German skippers in the Danish service, Diedrich Pining and Hans Pothorst, may have rediscovered Newfoundland and Labrador between 1471 and 1480, and a German set foot in Newfoundland in 1583 as a member of Sir Humphrey Gilbert's expedition.[2]

The Portuguese can point to considerable activity in the North Atlantic in the latter part of the fifteenth century. The expedition of Diogo de Teive in 1452 is said to have provided information for Christopher Columbus; later expeditions are said to have explored the coasts, named the landmarks – including Labrador, named for an Azorean, João Fernandes, in 1500 – and penetrated into Hudson Bay. There was a Portuguese colony in Cape Breton from 1520 to 1525. Portuguese may have advised the explorer John Cabot, or Giovanni Caboto. Cabot was the symbolic British "discoverer" by virtue of his Bristol backing, but in fact he was Genoese by birth and Venetian by citizenship. The Italians also claim that Verazzano, originally of Florence though later resident in France and in the service of the King of France, explored the coast of Nova Scotia in 1524 and provided knowledge of which Jacques Cartier made use. Spanish Basques built sheds for rendering whale carcasses on the shores of Labrador during the sixteenth century.

Slavs, including Poles and Croats, claim to have participated in early explorations. Croats are said to have been among Venetian explorers of the fifteenth century; more probably they were members of the Cartier-Roberval expedition of 1542-43. Champlain's expedition of 1605-06 included a miner named Jacques, "a native of Sclavonia," who has been identified as a Croat or a Slovene.[3] A Pole is said to have discovered Labrador in 1476.[4]

The Hungarians speculate that a member of Leif Ericson's expedition to Vinland around 1000 may have been Hungarian. With greater certitude they point to Stephen Parmenius, explorer and poet, who accompanied Sir Humphrey Gilbert to Newfoundland in 1583.

A curious incident is told of Joseph de La Penha, head of an old Spanish-Jewish family living in Holland. He claimed the coast of Labrador for England in 1677 and twenty years later was granted the land, as a reward for saving the life of William III, ruler of both England and the Netherlands. He did not take advantage of the grant, but in the 1920's his heirs presented a claim to the Privy Council, and in 1984 the Newfoundland Supreme Court dismissed the case of Daniel S. de La Penha of South Carolina, who had asked to be recognized as lawful owner of half of Labrador.[5]

On the West Coast the Chinese have tales of Buddhist monks who sailed from China on junks or sailing-rafts and went ashore in A.D. 458, of a settlement near the present site of Vancouver in 499, and of a voyage to British Columbia in 594.[6] The Greeks and the Spanish boast of the visit to the West Coast of Juan de Fuca in 1592. The explorer was navigating for the Spanish navy, but was Greek by birth.[7] The Spanish add to their claim the crew of the ship *Tres Reyes*, said to have reached the strait named for Juan de Fuca in 1603.[8]

All these claims are illustrative, and by no means complete. Some of the earliest voyages may well be legendary or mythical, and all of them occurred before the ethnic groups of the present had emerged. Attribution to an ethnic group is often made on the hazardous basis of name, or birth or residence in a locality that later became part of a political unit associated with a particular ethnic group.

The number and variety of the claims serve at least two purposes, however. On the one hand, they are a reminder that contact and co-operation of peoples is an age-old phenomenon. The explorers whose exploits are renowned were not solitary adventurers but part of a considerable maritime activity. On the other hand, the claims underline the importance that Canadian ethnic groups attach to a long Canadian lineage or pedigree. The importance may have been accentuated by the emphasis, since the setting up of the Royal Commission on Bilingualism and Biculturalism in July, 1963, on founding peoples as having special status. The terms "founding peoples" and "charter-member groups," as used by French Canadians and Canadians of British origin, are usually taken to refer to those who set up institutions, especially political institutions, of a kind unknown among the Native peoples. The terms can be given a broader meaning, however; they can be used to signify the first arrivals, and members of the other ethnic groups frequently use them in that way.

ETHNIC GROUPS ON VARIOUS FRONTIERS, 1600-1900

New France

The French and British took possession of the northern parts of North America, and the French established the first permanent settlements. During the 150 years of the French regime, immigration was low, averaging only sixty-six persons a year.[9] It is sometimes considered to have been confined, as the official policy long required, to French Roman Catholics. However, many countries were represented in the colony: sojourners or settlers came in small numbers from Austria, Belgium, England, Germany, Greece, Ireland, Italy, the Netherlands, Poland, Portugal, Scotland, Spain, Switzerland, China,[10] and Africa.[11] The English (especially prisoners and refugees from New England), Irish, and Scots were the most numerous, but little is known of these or other non-French immigrants. One of the most exotic was a young Bengali who had been converted to Christianity in France.[12]

One whose story is known in part is the Italian Jesuit, Father Francesco Giuseppe Bresciani or Bressani. He was born in Rome, educated at the Jesuit College there, and arrived in Quebec City as early as 1642. The following year he became administrator in Trois-Rivières, and in 1644 he made his way into Huronia with six Christian Hurons. Wounded in an Iroquois attack, he returned to France that same year, but in 1645 he returned to Trois-Rivières and remained in Canada until 1650.[13] His description of the Native peoples, written in Italian, has been called one of the best early ethnographic studies. He was followed by other Italians, including officers of the army and the marines, and administrators; the explorer Henri de Tonty, who travelled widely in North America, at first in the service of La Salle and, after the latter's death, on his own account, although born in France was of Neapolitan parentage.

German settlers began to arrive in the late seventeenth century; the first on record was Hans Bernard, who bought two *arpents* of land near Quebec City in 1664. The Germans came chiefly from Alsace-Lorraine, which was occupied by France, and included sailors, craftsmen, and two medical doctors.[14] By 1700 it is estimated that they numbered thirty or forty: the names of three, Andreas Wolf of Danzig (Gdansk), Leonard Crequy of Cologne, and Andreas Spencer of Mayence, found a place in the public records when they

13

married French-Canadian women between 1687 and 1690. In the eighteenth century the number increased, after France in 1717 granted citizenship rights to all Roman Catholic Europeans residing in North America. There were about 200 German families living along the St. Lawrence, and two Germans, Charles Joseph de Feltz, a Montreal surgeon, and Jean Lucas Schmid, a seigneur and captain of the local militia, attained prominence.

The claim of the Poles to early settlement in New France is based on the fact that Dominik Barcz, from Danzig, signed a marriage contract in 1752 at Montreal with Thérèse Filian-Dubois. He may have been wealthy; at any rate his children were, and his grandson, Pierre Dominique Debartch, became a member of Parliament and member of the Legislative Council of Lower Canada.[15]

Africans were present from the early seventeenth century, as servants and slaves. The first to have been brought directly from Africa and the first to have been sold as a slave in New France was Olivier le Jeune, brought to New France from Madagascar by the English as a child and sold to a French clerk. He died a free man in 1654, little more than thirty years of age.[16] Slavery never was of large proportions in New France, and involved more Amerindians than blacks; nonetheless, in a period of about 125 years, the number of Africans seems to have been well over a thousand.[17] The slaves served chiefly as domestics.

It appears that the Roman Catholic Church was successful in keeping Jews out of New France. There are legends of "Juifs bien peu juifs"[18] (very un-Jewish Jews) such as a Jesuit priest, who managed to enter. There is also the well-documented case of Esther Brandeau, a young Jewish woman who went to New France disguised as a boy in 1738 and spent a year there.[19] But Jews were officially excluded from 1615 on, and the beginnings of Jewish settlement were after the Conquest.

Some of the other non-French came not as settlers (though they may have later become such) or as traders but as mercenary soldiers. In the seventeenth and eighteenth centuries, and particularly during the last years of the French regime, soldiers from the South German states and from Austria were enrolled in French regiments. A number of present-day ethnic groups date their Canadian history from such soldiers.

The low rate of immigration into New France and the social organization of the colony led to an unusually homogeneous society. The homogeneity has led to controversy as to whether the French settlers were all from the same part of France or from different and culturally distinct parts. Certainly some of the homogeneity was attributable to the centralized character of the colony and the unifying effect of the St. Lawrence River. The same factors, and the small numbers of those who were not French, prevented the latter from maintaining either isolation or distinctiveness, as the frequency of intermarriage with French Canadians indicates.

If the mercenary soldiers who fought for the French in the Seven Years' War were of diverse backgrounds, they opposed equally diverse mercenaries on the British side, and indeed the change from French to British rule brought people of many origins into the St. Lawrence Valley. Vaugeois lists the declared birthplaces of 130 Protestants of the district of Montreal in November, 1765: Ireland, 37; England, 30; Scotland, 27; Germany, 15; New England, 70; Switzerland, 6; France, Prussia, Italy, Guernsey, and Lapland, one each. To these would have been added Roman Catholics of other than French background, and Jews.[20]

The Conquest led on the one hand to the departure of some of the French population and the end of French immigration, and on the other hand to the beginning of British and other European immigration. The growth of the French-Canadian population was not arrested, inasmuch as the rate of natural increase was high enough to double the population every twenty-five years between 1760 and 1850. Nor did British immigration begin with a rush, except for the merchants who had been poised to take immediate advantage of the change of rulers; the depressed state of agriculture made the province unattractive to many. According to Garon, the number of British was barely 200 when civil government was instituted, and scarcely more than 600 in 1770.[21] In 1780 the Anglophone population was about 3,000. But the arrival of United Empire Loyalists and disbanded soldiers following the American Revolutionary War changed the situation: these immigrants were of many origins, including German, Swiss, Dutch, Indian, and Jewish, but considerable numbers of them were British and even more were Anglophone.

The immigrants extended the populated area of the new British possession far beyond the seigneuries of the St. Lawrence lowlands. The settlement of the Maritime provinces, which had begun in the early seventeenth century and had been built on since the area passed into British hands in 1713, was completed, and Upper Canada was created. Within Quebec, settlement by the British took place in the Gaspé and the Magdalen Islands, the Eastern Townships and the Ottawa Valley, as well as in Montreal and Quebec City. The Eastern Townships "had been occupied at the end of the French regime and [were] settled, from the South, only during the last forty years of the 18th century. After 1783, Loyalists and other New Englanders crossed the border, in large numbers, to take up the lands being offered in the Eastern Townships by the Crown and by private land companies."[22] Only in the 1840's did French Canadians begin to penetrate the Townships in any numbers; at that time many of the British were moving farther west. The Gaspé and the Magdalen Islands were also settled at the end of the eighteenth century by United Empire Loyalists, followed by Irish and by Channel Islanders. Soon after, early in the nineteenth century, the Ottawa Valley's timber resources attracted New Englanders, Scotch settlers, and Irish sawmill and logging camp workers; French Canadians also flocked into the lumber camps.

The British were less exclusionary than the French regarding the Jews. Jews had settled in Halifax soon after it was founded in 1749, and occasionally settled in the Maritimes thereafter. Just as a Jew had participated in provisioning the French during the final struggle for New France, Jewish merchants based in the thirteen colonies contributed to the furnishing of

British troops.[23] And Jews accompanied Amherst's armies to Canada in 1760, though whether some came as officers or all were commissaries is a matter of dispute. Shortly after, a Jewish community began to develop in Montreal, and Jews also settled in Quebec City, Trois-Rivières, and other communities; Aaron Hart, who had probably followed Amherst and the British army to Quebec, became wealthy, influential, and highly regarded in Trois-Rivières and the surrounding district, and was progenitor of an outstanding family. All may not have been, or may not have remained, practitioners of Judaism; some contracted marriages with French Canadians and sent their children to Ursuline schools.

Among disbanded soldiers who had fought on the British side in the campaigns for New France and shortly after in the American Revolution were German mercenaries. A number of them settled in Quebec, and some married French-Canadian women. In Montreal and Quebec City, the former soldiers were joined by skilled craftsmen and tradesmen from Germany. New settlements were also begun by German ex-soldiers in the Eastern Townships, notably in the autumn of 1783 in Missisquoi County. Early in the nineteenth century some wealthy Germans purchased seigneuries.

The German mercenary regiments included members of other ethnic groups. One of the outstanding Polish families of Quebec traced its ancestry back to a surgeon in the Hesse-Heynan Regiment, Auguste France Globensky. He came to Canada in 1776, left the regiment in 1783, married a French Canadian, and settled in St. Eustache. His three sons served in the War of 1812, and one of them also in the Rebellion of 1837.

Several hundred Italian soldiers from the Watteville and de Meuron regiments settled in Quebec and were joined by other Italians. Like other early settlers who came without wives and families, many married French Canadians. Among them were Giovanni and Francesco Donegani and their families, who entered the hotel business in Montreal. Giovanni returned to Italy, where he died in 1809, but his three sons and daughter remained in Montreal. The eldest, John, a merchant and innkeeper, became the first Italian to serve as a municipal councillor (1833-35) and the first to serve as a judge (1836-40); the third son, William, became the first Italian doctor in Canada.[24] Other early Italian settlers were musicians, shoemakers, gardeners or farmers, carpenters, and even fur traders.[25]

The Atlantic Provinces

The Atlantic provinces are generally considered to be the least ethnic part of Canada, largely because the most prominent groups in their population – of Amerindian, British, and French origins – have been there for a long time and have for the past century and a half received little substantial immigration. Nonetheless, at least in the province of Nova Scotia, ethnic structures persist, there is a considerable degree of physical and social isolation of the various ethnic groups, there are indications of an ethnic class structure, and important cultural traits have been maintained.[26]

In pre-Confederation days, at least two ethnic groups other than the British, French, and Amerindians played an important part in Maritime history: blacks and Germans. Germans were first brought to the Maritimes from the Palatinate, that is, from southwestern Germany. They were Protestants, intended by the British government to be settled among and to serve as a counterweight to the Roman Catholic Acadians. The first organized group arrived in Halifax in 1750 aboard the *Ann*. About 2,400 settlers came in three years. In Halifax the Germans settled close to the Citadel, and it was in Halifax that the first German printing in Canada was done. In 1853, in accordance with a resolution of the Colonial Council, about 1,500 of them moved to Lunenburg, south of Halifax. There they cleared the land, set up their own municipal government, and built their houses and a school. At first they were content to accept the services of the Church of England, but when they became sufficiently affluent to support Calvinist and Lutheran churches, these were built. Having been farmers and craftsmen, they made a remarkable adaptation to life by the sea, their specialties being fishing and the building of the Lunenburg schooners.

During the American Revolutionary War some of the German mercenaries who fought on the British side sojourned in Halifax and, on being disbanded, settled in Nova Scotia and New Brunswick. At about the same time other Germans joined the settlements, coming from Europe and from Pennsylvania.

Blacks had been in Nova Scotia from the beginnings of European settlement. A black died of scurvy at Port Royal in 1606; another was a servant of Port Royal's governor, Sieur de Monts; there were black slaves in Acadia, black defenders of Louisbourg in 1745, and black free men among the labourers on the French side in the fighting with the English. The British from 1713 on brought in slaves, some blacks took part in the construction of Halifax in 1749, and free blacks were given the same opportunities as whites during the New England migration after 1759 to settle the lands vacated when the Acadians were expelled. Before the Loyalist migration, the number of black slaves has been estimated to be from a few hundred to as high as 500, between 3 and 5 per cent of the population.

Loyalist migration brought a considerable increase of the black population. Between 1,000 and 1,500 blacks were brought as slaves, and about 3,000 as free people. During the revolution the British had proclaimed that freedom, land, and provisions would be granted to slaves who would desert their masters and join the British. Many took advantage of the proclamation, and they and several hundred free-born and previously freed blacks were shipped to Nova Scotia. There, however,

> Despite British promises, black loyalists did not receive the same treatment as white loyalists. Many did not obtain land; those who did obtained usually inadequate and inferior land and when their land was adequate, it was not secure. Their participation with whites in schools and churches was obstructed. In some cases, their indentured status was manipulated and they were sold as slaves.[27]

17

Some blacks, like some of the white Loyalists, later returned to the United States. Others, almost 1,200 in number, went to Sierra Leone in 1791-92. Jamaican Maroons, descendants of slaves who fought the British for a century after Jamaica was conquered from the Spanish, were deported to Nova Scotia after their last revolt was crushed in 1796; they also departed for Sierra Leone in 1800.

In spite of the discrimination against blacks, slavery was never specifically recognized by statute in Nova Scotia, and from 1800 on slaves could easily obtain freedom. After 1808 no attempts were made to have slavery recognized by the courts.

During the War of 1812 the British made promises to American blacks similar to those they had made during the Revolutionary War. As a result, between 1813 and 1816 more than 2,000 blacks settled in Nova Scotia. Called Refugee Negroes to distinguish them from the Black Pioneers and the Maroons, they were treated somewhat better than their predecessors, but nonetheless they did not quickly receive title to their land and were so poor as to require relief for thirty years. This was the last large-scale movement of blacks into Nova Scotia.

In time the differences between the descendants of the Black Pioneers and the descendants of the Refugee Negroes disappeared, but the blacks remained a segregated and neglected part of the Maritime population. Their number was small, but they and the blacks of Upper Canada were the two major concentrations of blacks in Canada. In contrast to the isolation of the blacks was the public involvement of the Germans, who quickly began to take an active part in the economic, political, and social life of the Maritimes.

Few other ethnic groups entered the Maritimes. By the 1881 census, only 3.5 per cent of the population of the three Maritime provinces was other than British, French, or German in ethnic origin. On the other hand, distinctions among both the British and the French remained, with Gaelic-speaking Highland Scots and Acadians being outstanding.

Upper Canada

Until the late nineteenth century the history of what is now Ontario was, like the history of the Maritimes, largely a matter of the relations between those of Amerindian, British, and French origin. But as in the Maritimes, there was a variety of additional elements. William Lyon Mackenzie described the heterogeneity of an election crowd at Niagara in 1824:

> There were Christians and Heathens, Menonists and Dunkards, Quakers and Universalists, Presbyterians and Baptists, Roman Catholics and American Methodists; there were Frenchmen and Yankees, Irishmen, and Mulattoes, Scotchmen and Indians, Englishmen, Canadians, Americans and Negroes, Dutchmen and Germans, Welshmen and Swedes, Highlanders and Lowlanders, poetical as well as most prosaical phises, horsemen and footmen, fiddlers and dancers, honourables and reverends, captains and colonels, beaux and belles, waggons and bilburies, coaches

and chaises, gigs and carts; in short, Europe, Asia, Africa, and America had there each its representative among the loyal subjects of our good King George, the fourth of the name.[28]

By all odds, British ethnic groups – English, Scottish Lowlanders and Highlanders, Northern Irish (Scotch Irish) and southern Irish – and Americans dominated the social scene, and the relations between them shaped the economic, political, educational, and religious institutions of the province. Much of the development of the province can be interpreted in terms of the differences between the Americans and the British settlers, with class lines to some extent modifying the picture. The French Canadians tended to be isolated in rural communities or to be competitors of Catholic Irish lumbermen and construction workers as members of the emerging proletariat. The Indians were permitted little participation in the life of the province.

As in the Maritimes, in Upper Canada Germans, Swiss, and Dutch were among the earliest and most numerous settlers of other origins. They were among the military settlers along the St. Lawrence River and on the shores of the Great Lakes, among the pacifist sectarians – Mennonites, Amish, Dunkards, and Moravians – who moved from Pennsylvania, and among the other United Empire Loyalists and non-Loyalists who came into the area before the province was created and in its early decades. Some also came directly from Europe after the War of 1812.

Blacks came in small numbers as slaves with early settlers, and later in larger numbers as fugitives and as free men. Lieutenant-Governor John Graves Simcoe was an opponent of slavery, and in 1793 had a bill for the gradual abolition of slavery introduced in the Assembly, where it received unanimous passage. From then on slavery declined steadily, and Upper Canada became the goal of many American blacks. The reception accorded those who arrived varied from time to time and place to place, depending in part on the ethnicity of their neighbours. Segregation and discrimination were common. Organized attempts at black settlement either failed fairly quickly or suffered slow decline. The total number of blacks in Canada West by 1860 may have been as high as 40,000, but the number dwindled during and after the American Civil War.

One of the first Italians to settle in what is now Toronto was Philip de Grassi. He had been captured while an officer in Napoleon's army and transferred to England. There he had received a commission in the British army, married an English woman, and taught languages in Chichester for sixteen years before migrating to Canada in 1831. He held a land grant in the Don Valley, and his daughters played a part in the insurrection of 1837, carrying a message through the rebel lines. De Grassi has left his name on a downtown Toronto street.

The Pole, Casimir Gzowski, took part in the insurrection of 1830-31 in his homeland, after which he was interned and eventually shipped to America. There he learned English, worked in a law office and as an engineer in canal and railway construction, and married an American girl. In 1842 he moved to Canada, where he supervised the construction of railways, canals, harbours, and bridges, including the International Bridge over the Niagara River between Fort Erie and Buffalo, and took part in the organization of the Canadian engineering profession. In addition, Gzowski took an outstanding part in military, educational, and religious activities.

A group of Kashubs from Poland arrived from 1858 on and established an enduring community in the Renfrew area. Most became farmers, although their land was stony. Others worked in lumber camps, on the roads, or as labourers.

Jewish settlers appeared at least as early as the 1830's, although the first comers often stayed for only a few years. They were in the main merchants of English or German background. The first Jewish settler in Toronto was Arthur Wellington Hart, grandson of Aaron Hart of Trois-Rivières, who in 1832 occupied a two-storey shop in King Street. In 1836 he left for England; later he went to Scranton, Pennsylvania. He died in Montreal in 1894.[29]

The Prairie West

Like earlier areas of settlement, the vast territory between the Great Lakes and the Rockies attracted from the start an ethnically diverse population. The Indians, the French, the British, and the Plains-born ethnic group, the Métis, were joined, from the first decades of the nineteenth century, by individuals and groups of many ethnic origins. Some stayed only a short time; the descendants of others are part of the present Canadian population.

Lord Selkirk brought some Europeans to the Red River area, along with the Scots in the interests of whom he carried out his ventures in colonization. He recruited fifteen Norwegians to build roads from York Factory to his settlement in 1814, and although at least one Norwegian, the leader of the group, was killed in the battle of Seven Oaks in 1816, it appears that a few remained, one of them, Peter Dahl, becoming a land-owning farmer.[30] Just before Seven Oaks, Selkirk signed on about eighty mercenaries from the Swiss de Meuron regiment, which had fought in the War of 1812, as Red River guards and settlers. While mostly Swiss, the men included Germans, Poles, Italians, and others; Croatian, Ukrainian, and Byelorussian scholars have found grounds for claiming that members of their ethnic groups may have been among them. An agent of Lord Selkirk recruited about a hundred Swiss, including a number of women, to join the soldiers. However, most of the de Meurons and the Swiss left for more hospitable regions, some after a grasshopper infestation ravaged crops from 1818 to 1821, the rest after floods in the winter of 1825-26.

British Columbia

In the last quarter of the eighteenth century the Spanish were very active on the West Coast, but by 1795 they had withdrawn. From then until the discovery of gold, British Columbia's population was composed chiefly of Indians and British. The gold rushes of the Pacific area exerted a powerful attraction on men of all conditions of life and all ethnic backgrounds. The most heterogeneous of Canadian frontier societies in the nineteenth century were the mining camps of the Fraser Valley and the Cariboo from 1858 to 1862 and of the Yukon at the turn of the century. The majority of the newcomers were American and eastern and central Canadian, but many other ethnic groups were also represented, including blacks, Chileans, Chinese, Hawaiians (who had earlier been active in the fur trade), Mexicans, and various European groups.

Chinese came in 1858 from California and, beginning in the spring of 1859, from Hong Kong, on chartered ships. Their numbers may have reached 6,000 or 7,000 in what is now British Columbia in the early 1860's. They were almost all men and they engaged not only in prospecting for gold but in various other enterprises: prospecting for jade, importing, transporting, fishing, gardening, and serving as laundrymen, restaurateurs, and labourers. They won a reputation as satisfactory workers among contractors for road-building and stringing telegraph wires. In 1864 they moved into domestic service. The departure of Chinese from Vancouver Island and British Columbia in the middle and late 1860's, inevitable because of the end of the gold rush, was heightened by discrimination against them, manifest by the early 1860's although not yet embodied in legislation. In the 1880's, however, new immigration of Chinese began from both the United States and Hong Kong as Andrew Onderdonk, who received the contract for the British Columbia portion of the Canadian Pacific Railway, employed Chinese labourers to build some of the most difficult sections of the railroad.

The Chinese were not the only people to seek occupational niches that offered surer wealth than prospecting for gold. Croats, who like the Chinese had settled in California before the rushes to British Columbia, had become saloon-keepers, storekeepers, traders, and speculators, and it was in such occupations that they engaged in Victoria and in the Cariboo. With the decline of the mining communities, they disappeared.

Germans also, chiefly from southwest Germany, came north from California with the gold miners but themselves tended to serve as grocers, shop-keepers, brewers, and even as dance-hall girls.[31] Many were transient, but some, who entered farming and ranching or urban trades and professions, became influential in the economic, political, and social life of British Columbia. Such men as Frank Laumeister, who imported camels to carry freight up the Cariboo Trail, Augustus Schubert and Theodore Kruger, pioneers in the Spallumcheen Valley and Osoyoos respectively, Dr. John Sebastian Helmcken, first medical officer for the Hudson's Bay Company and an important political figure, and Jacob Grauer, dairy farmer and father of outstandingly successful sons, were only a few of the Germans who played leading roles.

Blacks first came to Vancouver Island in 1858, not because of the gold rush but because of increasingly restrictive legislation against them in California. There in 1850 blacks were disqualified from giving evidence against white men, in 1852 legislation was discussed that would permit slave-holders to retain their property, and in 1858 a number of other measures, including restriction of black immigration, were under consideration. The intention of those who came north was to settle permanently. Some became farmers and ranchers; a few became miners, and later bakers, restaurant-keepers, merchants and outfitters, draymen and barbers. They encountered racism, but it was usually less violent and less organized than in the United States. However, the rise of prejudice and economic depression in British Columbia, and the abolition of slavery in the United States, led most to return to the United States before the end of the 1860's.

The first Jewish immigrant to British Columbia, Frank Sylvester, arrived in Victoria in July, 1858, and after some time in the gold fields entered the hardware business in that city. Later he became an accountant and a prosperous feed merchant. In 1860 Selim Franklin, a Jewish auctioneer and real estate dealer in Victoria, was elected to the Vancouver Island legislature. Another Victorian, Henry Nathan, Jr., was elected to the Legislative Council of British Columbia in 1867 and to the House of Commons in 1871. David Oppenheimer, one of a remarkable group of five brothers prominent in business, served with his brother, Isaac, on the Vancouver City Council and later as mayor. The early generation of Jews was almost entirely from western Europe and from the United States, and found the atmosphere in British Columbia friendly.

Among the other ethnic groups of European background, the first Belgians were Oblate missionaries who arrived even before the discovery of gold, and the first Czechs included Brother Peter Pandosy, a Bohemian Oblate who founded Okanagan Mission, the first permanent settlement in the Okanagan, in 1858. However, many other groups date their entrance into the province to a miner or prospector or to someone who came to fill the wants of the miners. A Norwegian, Hans Helgesen, came up to Victoria from California during the gold rush and was an early member of the legislature. Austrians also entered at the time of the gold rush, some going into business supplying the miners and one, Francis Xavier Richter, becoming a successful pioneer cattle-rancher. Likewise there were Swiss gold miners, including George Stelli, who arrived in 1858 and later opened a contracting and transfer business in Victoria, and the Dutch Volkert Veddar settled in Hope district in 1860.

Of those who came to British North America before Confederation, many did not stay. Explorers came and went; others, whether they intended to sojourn or to settle, also were transient. By the first Canadian census in 1871 and the more complete one of 1881 (when Canada had been extended from sea to sea), those of British, French, and Native origins constituted over 90 per cent of the population; the only other group of any size was the German. Soon, however, a massive and diversified wave of immigration was to inaugurate change.

NOTES

1. Gulbrand Loken, *From Fjord to Frontier: A History of the Norwegians in Canada* (Toronto: McClelland and Stewart, 1980), pp. 7-12.

2. Gerhard P. Bassler, "Heinz Lehmann and German-Canadian History," introduction to *The German Canadians, 1750-1937: Immigration, Settlement and Culture*, by Heinz Lehmann, ed. and trans. by Gerhard P. Bassler (St. John's, Newfoundland: Jesperson Press, 1986), p. xxix.

3. Anthony W. Rasporich, *For a Better Life: A History of the Croations in Canada* (Toronto: McClelland and Stewart, 1982), p. 11.

4. L. Kos-Rabcewicz-Zubkowski, "Contribution Made by the Polish Ethnic Group to the Cultural Enrichment of Canada," an essay prepared for the Royal Commission on Bilingualism and Biculturalism.

5. B.G. Sack, *History of the Jews in Canada*, vol. I (Montreal: Canadian Jewish Congress, 1945); *Globe and Mail*, 26 January 1984.

6. John Norris, *Strangers Entertained: A History of the Ethnic Groups of British Columbia* (Vancouver: British Columbia Centennial '71 Committee, 1971), p. 209.

7. Peter D. Chimbos, *The Canadian Odyssey: The Greek Experience in Canada* (Toronto: McClelland and Stewart, 1980), p. 22.

8. Norris, *Strangers Entertained*, pp. 202-03.

9. Jacques Henripin, "From Acceptance of Nature to Control: The Demography of the French Canadians Since the Seventeenth Century," in Marcel Rioux and Yves Martin, eds., *French-Canadian Society*, volume 1 (Toronto: McClelland and Stewart, 1964), p. 206.

10. Henry B.M. Best, " 'The Auld Alliance' in New France," in Reid, ed., *The Scottish Tradition in Canada*, p. 16.

11. Marcel Trudel, *L'Esclavage au Canada français, Histoire et conditions de l'esclavage* (Québec: Les Presses Universitaires Laval, 1960); Robin W. Winks, *The Blacks in Canada: A History* (Montreal: McGill-Queen's University Press, 1971), pp. 1-23.

12. Marcel Trudel, *Initiation à la Nouvelle-France, Histoire et institutions* (Montréal: Holt, Rinehart and Winston, 1968), p. 147; Morris Bishop, *Champlain: The Life of Fortitude* (Toronto: McClelland and Stewart, 1963), pp. 82, 265, 285.

13. A.V. Spada, *The Italians in Canada*, Canada Ethnica VI (Ottawa: Riviera Printers and Publishers, 1969), pp. 29-31.

14. H.W. Debor, "The Cultural Contribution of the German Ethnic Group to Canada," an essay prepared for the Royal Commission on Bilingualism and Biculturalism, pp. 2, 5, 10.

15. William Boleslaus Makowski, *History and Integration of Poles in Canada* (Niagara Peninsula, Canada: The Canadian Polish Congress, 1967), pp. 4-5.

16. Winks, *The Blacks in Canada*, pp. 1-2.

17. Trudel, *L'Esclavage au Canada français*, p. 317.

18. Denis Vaugeois, *Les Juifs et la Nouvelle France* (Trois-Rivières: Boréal Express, 1968), p. 54.

19. *Ibid.*, pp. 55-57. Abraham Gradis, a Jew, had complicated commercial relations with New France and with François Bigot, intendant from 1748 to 1760. *Ibid.*, pp. 63-84.

20. Vaugeois, *Les Juifs et la Nouvelle France*, pp. 138-39.

21. André Garon, "La Britannization (1763-1791)," in Jean Hamelin, ed., *Histoire du Québec* (Toulouse: Privat, 1976), p. 258.

22. Richard J. Joy, *Languages in Conflict* (Toronto: McClelland and Stewart, 1972), p. 98.

23. Vaugeois, *Les Juifs et la Nouvelle France*, pp. 87-104; Sack, *History of the Jews in Canada*, 1, p. 40.

24. Spada, *The Italians in Canada*, pp. 54-55.

25. Robert F. Harney, *Italians in North America* (Toronto: Multicultural History Society of Ontario, 1978), p. 4.

26. Douglas F. Campbell, "The Ethnic Literature and the Nova Scotia Experience," in Douglas F. Campbell, ed., *Banked Fires: The Ethnics of Nova Scotia* (Port Credit: The Scribblers' Press, 1978), pp. 240-44.

27. Donald Clairmont and Fred Wein, "The Blacks: A 'White' Problem," in *ibid.*, p. 150.

28. William Lyon Mackenzie, *Sketches of Canada and the United States* (London, 1833), p. 89.

29. Stephen A. Speisman, *The Jews of Toronto: A History to 1973* (Toronto: McClelland and Stewart, 1979), pp. 11-12.

30. Loken, *From Fjord to Frontier*, p. 51.

31. Norris, *Strangers Entertained*, pp. 98-99. The material on British Columbia has been drawn largely from Norris.

THREE

Settlement, 1880-1980

THE SETTLING OF THE PRAIRIES, 1880-1920

Until the late nineteenth century, settlement of the West was slow and consisted in the main of people from eastern and central Canada and Great Britain. Americans played a role, but primarily as traders rather than settlers. Not until Confederation, the building of the Canadian Pacific Railway, and the ending of Métis resistance under Riel did the pace of settlement accelerate and the population begin to diversify ethnically.

In 1870, the Red River settlement, the most important in the West, had 11,963 inhabitants, of whom about 575 were Indians and 9,700 were Métis. The 1,700 whites were made up of 750 native-born Red Riverites and 290 Canadians, some of whom may have been of other ethnic origins than British and French; 240 from Scotland; 125 from England; 70 from America; 47 from Ireland; 15 from France; and a scattering of others.[1]

By then the new Canadian government wanted to promote settlement of Manitoba and the Northwest Territories. It thought settlement necessary to safeguard the forty-ninth parallel against American encroachment: the legislature of Minnesota had passed a resolution for the annexation of the Red River district, and the governor of the Hudson's Bay Company had both prophesied and advocated annexation shortly before the Company surrendered its rule. Also, only through settlement could the projected transcontinental railway be made economically possible. In 1871 the first of a series of conferences on immigration was held in Ottawa, and in the following years surveys were made and legislation passed to encourage settlement. However, results were meagre, in part because of the depression of 1873-78 and strong competition from the United States, Brazil, Argentina, Australia, and New Zealand.

Two notable settlements of the 1870's brought Mennonites and Icelanders to Manitoba. The former made the first group settlement in the West. The Mennonites were an Anabaptist sect that emerged in the sixteenth century in various European countries, chiefly Holland, Switzerland, and Germany.

25

They spoke a Low German dialect and were characterized by a simple lifestyle, pacifism, and separation from the world. One group had gone to Pennsylvania, and a part of it, after the American Revolutionary War, settled in Upper Canada; another had gone to Russia. In Ukraine changing conditions and changing attitudes after the liberation of the peasants in 1861 had threatened the peace and prosperity of the Mennonites, and withdrawal of total exemption from military service in the 1870's had precipitated a search for a new home. About a third of the Russian Mennonites emigrated, and of these the majority went to the United States. However, land was cheaper in Canada and, unlike the American government, the Canadian government was willing to grant military exemption, bloc settlement, and the "fullest privilege of exercising their religious principles"[2] and educating their children. Four delegates of the Mennonites in southern Russia signed an agreement with the Dominion government in 1873, and in the next three years more than 6,000 Mennonites settled in Manitoba. By 1880 some 7,500 had arrived. They were provided with two tracts of land, the East Reserve and the West Reserve, where, after initial hardships, they prospered greatly.

Ukrainians were neighbours of the Mennonites in Europe, and some Ukrainians may have come with the Mennonites to avoid Tsarist persecution or at the invitation of Mennonites, and settled near them. Other than the Mennonites, few Germans arrived, but there were enough to organize a German Society in Winnipeg in 1871, and in the early 1870's Germans were among that city's hotelkeepers and saloon owners. Colonies were created in the Northwest, some of them by Germans from Romania and Russia and others by Germans from the United States.

Meanwhile, Icelanders, wearied of the struggle against a harsh climate and poverty and afflicted in 1875 by volcanic eruptions that destroyed farmlands and made much of their homeland uninhabitable, had begun to come to Canada. They were first directed to Kinmount and Rosseau in Ontario and to Nova Scotia, where they endured many hardships. Eventually they settled on the southwest shore of Lake Winnipeg, founding the village of Gimli. Again they were beset by hardships, this time including wet weather, floods, severe cold, and smallpox; by 1880-81 more than half left for North Dakota. However, new arrivals in the 1880's brought the total number to about 7,000 by 1890. Needing and at the outset receiving more government aid than some other immigrants, the Icelanders eventually succeeded outstandingly. From 1876 on, some immigrants decided to stay in Winnipeg, and in the 1880's Icelandic settlement took place in what became Saskatchewan and Alberta and in British Columbia.

The Icelanders were among the earliest Scandinavians to settle on the Prairies. The Swedes and the Norwegians were courted by Canadian authorities, but although they were emigrating in large numbers they tended at most to sojourn in Canada on their way to the United States. New Scandinavia, north of Minnedosa, was the only land set aside as a reserve for them. In the late 1880's Swedes, Danes, and Norwegians settled in small numbers. Norwegians from Eau Claire, Wisconsin, helped to establish a lumber mill at

Calgary in 1885 to begin the lumber industry there.[3] They soon entered into other activities and spread out to other areas of the Northwest, although Alberta retained the largest share of them. Most Scandinavians came to western Canada indirectly, by way of Scandinavian settlements in the American Midwest.

Individual Jews and Jewish families had begun to trickle into the West at least as early as the 1850's as fur traders, gold miners, farmers, and merchants. In the 1880's groups of Jews, fleeing deplorable conditions in Poland and Russia, were taken to the Northwest as an experiment, sponsored by associations in London, Berlin, and New York, to test their abilities as farmers; the first colony was on Pipestone Creek, south of Moosomin. The experiment failed. A similar experiment in the next decade, supported by the Hebrew Society of Montreal and the Jewish Colonization Association of Baron de Hirsch, resulted in successful Jewish colonies at Hirsch, Wapella, Qu'Appelle, and Oxbow, in what was later to become Saskatchewan.

In the late 1880's and the 1890's the tide of immigration turned toward Canada. The completion of the Canadian Pacific Railway, to be followed by two other transcontinental lines, the closing of the American frontier, the gold rush to the Yukon, developments in dry-land farming, and bumper wheat crops, combined with high prices in the markets of the world, were some of the factors that caused the acceleration of development. Although the influx began under a Conservative government, the man who has given his name to the era is Clifford Sifton, Minister of the Interior in the Liberal government of Sir Wilfrid Laurier from 1896 to 1905.

Sifton, a Manitoban, was determined to "settle the empty West with producing farmers,"[4] and he directed a vigorous recruitment campaign in the countries whence he considered promising agricultural immigrants might be drawn. Britain no longer figured prominently as a source of farmers; nonetheless, it continued to be the leading supplier of immigrants. Between 1901 and 1911, the number of immigrants from the United Kingdom was one and a quarter million.

The United States, where farmers no longer found it easy to establish their sons on farms, was a prime target for Sifton. In the years 1901 to 1914, nearly a million immigrants came into Canada from south of the border, some of them returning Canadians, others from various European countries. In particular, Austrians, German-Russians, Slovaks, Czechs, Hungarians, Estonians, Dutch, Belgians, Germans, Swedes, Danes, Finns, Norwegians, Mennonites, and Welsh came to establish group settlements, and several hundred blacks moved into the region of Edmonton. Many of the newcomers brought capital; all of them brought experience in dealing with North American conditions and were able to provide advice and support to neighbours.

In addition to those of European origin who came by way of the United States, thousands came directly from continental Europe. These immigrants may have been drawn less by the propaganda of the government and the railways than by the letters and the visits home of those who had preceded them and the tangible evidence of North American wealth offered by money

27

sent home by emigrants. Between the 1901 and 1911 censuses there was an increase of well over 800,000 in the Canadian population of ethnic origins other than British and French.

The groups already established in the West greatly increased in numbers during this period. In the three Prairie provinces the number of Germans, for example, increased from 46,844 in 1901 to 147,638 in 1911, many of the newcomers being sponsored by German Catholic church organizations. Only a small proportion came directly from Germany: many came from German settlements in eastern Europe. In 1921 the numbers of those of German origin had decreased, according to the census, to 122,979; but, especially since they increased to 241,760 in 1931, it seems safe to attribute the decline to temporary denial of an ethnic origin that had become an object of hatred and suspicion during World War I.

The Scandinavians also increased greatly in numbers. Many Norwegian, Swedish, and Danish farmers and farmers' sons migrated from the United States as homesteaders, and many Swedes came as railway workers. The census gives 17,316 persons of Scandinavian origin in the three Prairie provinces in 1901, and 129,625 in 1921.

Dutch immigrants, aided by emigration societies, went to all three western provinces. Mostly single young men with agricultural experience, they found Canadian homesteading a difficult and lonely pursuit. Many gravitated to Winnipeg, where growing and peddling fresh vegetables provided a means of livelihood and where Dutch institutions were established early. Others located in Edmonton. More successful were the rural Dutch settlements in which some people at least had had farming experience in the United States.

Even more spectacular, however, was the growth of groups from central and eastern Europe, such as those of Ukrainian, Polish, Hungarian, Romanian, and Russian origins. So fluid had been national boundaries in eastern Europe, and so unversed were the peasants who immigrated in ethnic designations, that the census is a very uncertain guide to the numbers in any one of these groups. It is particularly unreliable regarding Ukrainians, since a Ukrainian state existed only between 1917 and 1921. However, between 1901 and 1921 the census recorded an increase in Ukrainians from 5,622 to 96,055 in the three Prairie provinces and from thirty-seven to 9,483 in Ontario and Quebec.

Although it is probable that Ukrainians arrived in Canada much earlier, the symbolic first Ukrainian immigrants are Wasyl Eleniak and Ivan Pylypiew from the province of Galicia, who arrived in 1891. They were said to have been enticed by German-speaking neighbours from Galicia who had immigrated earlier to Alberta.[5] Five years later the mass movement of Ukrainians to Canada began under the inspiration of Dr. Joseph Oleskiw, who had negotiated with the Conservative government before its defeat in June, 1896. Oleskiw was an agriculturalist who had been disturbed by the plight of Ukrainian immigrants in Brazil and other South American countries and therefore had begun to study the problems of migration. He felt that

Canada was extremely promising and was able to confirm his impressions when he toured the country under the aegis of the Department of the Interior in 1895. His contacts and correspondence with officials were also encouraging. On his return to Lviv, he published a brochure that made a tremendous impact on Ukrainian peasants, and he also organized groups of immigrants. The first of these, 107 in number, arrived in Quebec on May 1, 1896. Thus began a flow of immigrants that continued until the outbreak of war in 1914. At its peak in 1913 it brought 22,363 Ukrainians to Canada, chiefly from Galicia and Bukovyna. The total for the period was 171,386. They settled in the more northerly parkland rather than the prairie, both because the prime prairie lands had already been taken up by British, American, Scandinavian, and German settlers and because they wanted wood for building materials and for fuel.

Among the Russians who immigrated to western Canada were 7,000-8,000 Doukhobors, who first arrived in 1899 and took up land in what became Saskatchewan. Because of the Doukhobors, only residents of British, native Indian and Inuit, and German origins surpassed the Russians in numbers in Saskatchewan in 1901. By 1911 the number of Russians in Saskatchewan had declined because some Doukhobors had lost their land there after refusing to comply with the authorities' interpretation of the Dominion Lands Act and had gone to British Columbia. They comprised a substantial part of the rise of those of Russian origin in that province from 227 in 1901 to 4,392 in 1911 and 7,773 in 1921.[6]

Hungarian settlement on the Prairies began in 1885 and 1886 through the activities of Count Paul Esterhazy. Esterhazy, a colourful adventurer, at first won the support of the Canadian Pacific Railway and the Department of Agriculture for grandiose settlement schemes, but he soon lost their confidence. However, he was responsible for several hundred Hungarian families moving to the Canadian West from the United States and a smaller number directly from Hungary, who settled near Minnedosa in Manitoba and at Esterhazy and Kaposvar in Saskatchewan. Having been peasants in Hungary, the heads of families had worked in mines and foundries in Pennsylvania doing the hardest, most dangerous, and worst paid jobs; consequently, the idea of returning to the land was alluring. The settlers were not all Hungarians: they included "Slavs, Bohemians, Russians, Germans, Roumanians."[7] The early Hungarian settlers were joined by others, particularly in what became Saskatchewan, where eight Hungarian colonies developed. The number has been estimated to be 5,000 by 1914.

Poles were fewer in number than Ukrainians, but from the mid-1890's until World War I some 116,000 entered Canada, chiefly small farmers, farmers' sons, and farm labourers from Galicia. They were escaping from severe economic and cultural poverty and from compulsory military service. Some were settlers; others intended only to find work, save to pay off debts and buy land in their homelands, and then return home. Having co-existed with Ukrainians in Europe, many of them settled in small groups among

Ukrainians in the Canadian West. Some eventually considered themselves as Ukrainians, as they intermarried with Ukrainians and changed their names to Ukrainian forms.

Winnipeg was the gateway to the West through which thousands of immigrants passed. The peopling of the Prairies was reflected in Winnipeg's growth between 1881 and 1911 and its increasing ethnic heterogeneity. During this period the population of Winnipeg increased from 7,985 to 136,035 and the proportion of Anglo-Saxon ethnic origin declined from 83.6 to 58.6 per cent. In 1921, 67.3 per cent of the population of 176,087 reported Anglo-Saxon ethnic origin. The proportion was probably inflated, as a result of strong anti-alien sentiments after World War I and the General Strike of 1919; in 1931 the Anglo-Saxon proportion dropped to 60.5 per cent, and it has declined at each succeeding census.[8]

Because of the homestead laws that interspersed free homesteads with government lands, few areas were settled entirely by one ethnic group. Only where special arrangements were made, as with the Mennonites, or in the case of such small colonies as those of the Hutterites, were there solid bloc settlements.

Sometimes proximity to members of another ethnic group, whom one had known in the homeland and who spoke one's language, was a criterion in choosing where to locate. Mennonites, other Germans from Eastern Europe, and Ukrainians, for example, in a few cases chose to be near each other; Ukrainians, Romanians, and Poles had an affinity; Norwegians and Swedes were sometimes found in the same settlements.

IMMIGRATION TO CENTRAL CANADA AND BRITISH COLUMBIA, 1900-1920

The immigrants drawn to the industrial towns and cities of central Canada included many from the United Kingdom and the United States, but also many from other countries. They were of a great variety of ethnic origins. The number of Italians recorded by the census rose between 1901 and 1911 from 10,834 to 45,963 and by 1921 to 66,796. The Italians, forced to immigrate by the unsettled economic and political conditions at home but discouraged from agricultural settlement by Sifton, were attracted by the demand of the railways and other construction enterprises for labour. The number of Jews grew from 16,131 in 1901 to 76,199 in 1911 and 126,196 in 1921. The Jews were largely refugees from pogroms in Russia and Romania. In both cases, the bulk of the immigrants located in Ontario and Quebec, although some Italian labourers worked on western railway construction and some Jews settled in Winnipeg and in pioneer farming communities in the West. In 1921 about two-thirds of Canadian Jews lived in the three largest cities of Montreal, Toronto, and Winnipeg: in Toronto the Jews were second only to the British in numbers. The Greeks, Macedonians, Syrians, Lebanese, and Armenians were much fewer in numbers than the Italians and Jews, but, like them, they entered trade rather than farming; hence, they settled in the towns and cities of central Canada, especially Montreal, rather than on the Prairies.

Sifton disapproved of the immigration of Asians,[9] but on the West Coast the Chinese continued to increase in spite of discriminatory regulations and mob violence directed against them. In view of the importance of their labour on the Canadian Pacific Railway, it is ironic that, because of pressure from anti-Asian groups, the charter granted to the Grand Trunk Pacific Railway forbade hiring Chinese for construction work. Few were in fact employed on that railway and those only because of a shortage of labour.[10] By 1921, the number of Chinese in Canada was 39,587; of these, 23,533 were in British Columbia.

From the turn of the century, Japanese began to immigrate in large numbers. In the first ten months of 1907, over 8,000 came to Canada. After the violent anti-Asian riots in Vancouver in 1907, their entry was impeded by a series of "gentlemen's agreements" between the Japanese and Canadian governments, by which Japan voluntarily limited the number of passports issued to male labourers and domestic servants to 400 per year. From 1908 on, most Japanese immigrants were women. The Japanese were rural settlers, engaging in farming, fishing, logging, boat-building, and mining, and they stayed near the West Coast. The number of Japanese in Canada in 1921 was 15,868, the number in British Columbia, 15,066.

Among those listed in immigration statistics as Japanese were Okinawans, who in Japan were considered to constitute a distinct ethnic minority and were subject to discrimination. In Canada Okinawans tended at first to live apart from other Japanese, in southern Alberta, where they farmed or mined coal, rather than in British Columbia, but in time their distinctiveness vanished.

In addition, about 5,000 South Asians came to British Columbia between 1905 and 1908. Although chiefly Sikhs, they were usually referred to as Hindus. They found work mainly as unskilled labour in railroad construction and in the logging and lumbering industry. After 1908 the movement of Indians was halted by an order-in-council, requiring "a continuous journey from the country of origin." Since it was impossible to come from India by a continuous journey, the measure was an ingenious attempt to restrict immigration of "coloured" British subjects, some of whom were actively engaged in efforts to drive the British out of India. There was also an attempt to persuade the South Asians to move from British Columbia to British Honduras, but it failed when delegates reported on the condition of South Asians there. In 1914, 376 East Indians arrived in Vancouver on the *Komagata Maru*, a Japanese steamer that an enterprising Sikh, Gurdit Singh, had hired to test the requirement for a continuous journey. They were refused entry and eventually returned to the Orient after the Supreme Court had ruled against their admission.

The number who entered Canada from any country, though large compared to earlier and later periods, was often small compared to the total number of emigrants from that country. Canada was not a popular target for many Europeans. Germans were inclined to choose the United States rather than Canada in the years just before and after the Boer War and in the years before World War I; Italians came to Canada in greater numbers, but while there were more than two million Italian immigrants and their children in the United States in 1910, there were but 46,000 people of Italian origin in Canada.

Many of the men were sojourners rather than settlers, who left their families behind and travelled back and forth to the Old World a number of times. This was true of Italians at Montreal until about 1911, of Hungarians, and of many others.[11] On the other hand, there were small numbers of people from many countries who could not return, however harsh their experience in Canada. Having been politically active, they fled their homelands, and they knew that unless great changes occurred they would face persecution if they returned.

During the years of massive immigration there was not a warm welcome for immigrants of other than British origin. It was generally accepted at the time that ethnic and racial groups varied greatly in intellectual ability and in character; the best informed and most humane, including E.W. Bradwin of Frontier College and J.S. Woodsworth of the All People's Mission in Winnipeg, found in the science of the day and in Social Darwinism descriptions of group differences that now seem ludicrous. Hence, hostility against settlers from many countries found ready expression.

Prejudice and discrimination against Asians in British Columbia culminated for the Chinese and Japanese in the Vancouver riots of 1907 and for the South Asians in the *Komagata Maru* incident. Blacks who wished to flee the United States, where their position was deteriorating after the collapse of Reconstruction, found that the promises of the immigration pamphlets were withheld from them: the Immigration Branch and its agents managed to discourage all but a few intending settlers.[12] Southern Europeans also suffered.[13] That many immigrants returned home in disappointment is reflected in the fact that between 1901 and 1911 immigration was 1,759,000 while emigration is estimated at 1,043,000, and during the next decade immigration was 1,612,000 and emigration is estimated at 1,381,000. Some of the emigration, of course, was of sojourners who had never intended to stay and of Canadians moving to the United States.

BETWEEN THE WARS, 1920-1940

World War I cut short the movement of peoples to Canada. The number of immigrants dropped precipitously; only 36,665 entered in 1915, three-quarters of them from the United States, and some reverse flow occurred. Those who had entered and taken up land in the last decade of the nineteenth century and the first decade of the twentieth had been threatened by depression in 1913, but they prospered during the war because of the growing demand for food. The city-dwellers also prospered as commerce and industry developed and their numbers increased considerably. But wartime hostilities created difficulties for many, not only for Germans, previously among the most welcome of immigrants, but also for other "enemy aliens," who had been part, however much against their will, of Germany or of the Austro-Hungarian Empire. Romanians, Slovaks, Czechs, Hungarians, Poles, and Ukrainians were among those interned, chiefly in camps in western Canada. Farmers were not interned but had to register, be fingerprinted, surrender their firearms, and lose the right to vote. Naturalization was suspended for all aliens, and Ukrainians in particular have a deep sense of having been treated unjustly as a people because of this. Poles were divided: those from the Congress Kingdom or the Russian part of Poland were highly regarded Canadian friends and allies, but those from Germany and Austria were subject to internment as enemy aliens. Pacifist sects such as the Mennonites and Doukhobors also suffered.

The Canadian government had found itself in a difficult situation at the beginning of the war. The presence in the population, especially in the West, of large numbers of aliens born in countries with which Canada was at war, incautious statements immediately before the outbreak of war by the Austrian consul at Montreal and the Uniate (Ruthenian Greek Catholic) Bishop of Winnipeg, the circulation of both indigenous and imported newspapers favourable to the German and Austrian cause, and the haste of Austrian army reservists to try to escape to the United States and back to Europe all occasioned fears that were not entirely hysterical or baseless. The government also was responding to public opinion, and public opinion was fearful of and hostile toward enemy aliens.

Although it was not to be expected that Canadians could make fine distinctions among non-English-speaking immigrants, they may have been less sweeping in their hostility than Americans. For example, Norwegians in Wisconsin and Minnesota were the object of considerable hostility during the war, in spite of their country's neutrality, but immigration of Norwegians from the United States and development of Norwegian communal institutions in the Canadian West proceeded unchecked. For Finns, a peak period of migration from the United States to Canada occurred during World War I, as several hundred crossed the border to avoid imprisonment for their political activities or military service.[14]

After the war, there was pressure to have "enemy aliens" fired to create employment for returning veterans. The situation was exacerbated the year after the end of the war by the Winnipeg General Strike, in which European immigrant workers played a prominent part. Ukrainians, Finns, Russians, and Jews were among the ethnic groups represented in left-wing labour ranks. The strike led to fears of a Bolshevik revolution in Canada and to repressive measures, including the enactment of Section 41 of the Immigration Act, which gave federal authorities power to deport "dangerous" aliens. Although Section 41 was not used at this time, a number of deportations of non-British immigrant radicals did take place; others were annulled only because of unsettled political and economic conditions in the homelands of the immigrants.[15]

Among post-war manifestations of nativism was a hardening of attitudes against pacifist sects such as the Mennonites. The Mennonites had tried to show their loyalty by contributing generously to relief funds and buying large quantities of war bonds, but as the war progressed they were unable to avert resentment and abuse. In 1919 an order-in-council, which would remain in effect until 1922, barred Mennonite, Hutterite, and Doukhobor immigration.

In 1918 there was an economic slump, which did not begin to lift until 1922, and former enemy aliens were not permitted to immigrate until 1923. However, the social and economic changes that occurred in Europe during and after the war increased the restlessness of many people, who circumvented new obstacles to free movement from country to country. The United States from 1917 on was developing a policy that reduced the total number of immigrants permitted entry each year, restricting particularly the number from southern and eastern Europe and excluding the Japanese. Canada therefore replaced its southern neighbour as the favoured destination for people from many countries. Canada also restricted immigration, supplementing prohibitive clauses of earlier years by a list of "preferred" and "non-preferred" countries from which to select immigrants, excluding Chinese and less explicitly some other peoples, and severely limiting other Asians; but it did not adopt formal quotas for Europeans. The result was that immigration to Canada from 1919 to 1931 fell below 100,000 per annum only in 1921, 1922, and 1925, and the proportion of the population that was not of British, French, or native Indian or Inuit origin rose to more than 18 per cent by 1931.

Under the Railway Agreement of 1925, which stayed in force until 1931, the railway companies played a leading role in promoting immigration to fill the lands they held in the West. On the whole, however, fewer immigrants went west than in the pre-war years; the wheat lands were filled, the wheat boom was faltering, cities were beginning to burgeon, and the new arrivals were more urban in their outlook than their predecessors. The immigrants of the "second wave" stayed in the industrial and commercial centres of Ontario and Quebec or went to the construction camps in the North or to the booming mining and pulp and paper towns in central Canada and British Columbia. The industrial towns and cities also grew because of migration from farms to urban areas. A committee of the House of Commons voiced consternation that immigrants who had been intended to provide a labour force for agriculture were instead accumulating in the cities, often in slum areas,[16] but no effective means of changing the situation were found.

As in the previous period, among the non-British and non-French, the Ukrainians made the greatest gains. Between 1920 and 1939 the number of new arrivals giving their origin as Ukrainian was 67,000. In addition, awakening ethnic consciousness led earlier immigrants who had not previously identified themselves as Ukrainian to do so. As a result, those of Ukrainian origin moved between 1921 and 1941 from eighth to fourth place among the ethnic-origin categories represented in the Canadian population.

The Ukrainian immigrants differed in education and skills from their predecessors, and settled in urban centres in much greater numbers. Woycenko wrote:

> Although the reasons for their coming to Canada were basically the same as those of the first settlers (economic and political), they had the advantage of some form of schooling, and many had high school or more advanced education. The war and technological progress had equipped them with more knowledge and skills. Many of them had served with the Ukrainian armies. The rise and fall of the independent Ukrainian State (1917-1921) had developed in them a deep national consciousness; they were well versed in the historical past of their country. Nor were they confused as to their identity, a state of mind not shared by earlier immigrants. They were inclined to urban living, and only a small number settled permanently on farms. Many looked on agricultural work as a temporary occupation for the transitional period until jobs in cities were available. Others, as soon as some capital had been accumulated, opened their own business establishments.[17]

Ukrainians began to spread out from the Prairies, with the number in Ontario virtually doubling and the number in British Columbia almost tripling between 1931 and 1941.

The Poles also came in considerable numbers. The Polish government discouraged the emigration of skilled, trained, and professional people who could contribute to the rebuilding of the war-shattered country, and the Canadian government in any event did not want such immigrants. But peasants and farm workers, excluded from the United States by the small Polish quota, entered: between 1919 and 1931, the number of Polish immigrants was 51,847, with 1927 and 1928 the peak years. As a result of compulsory education, fewer were illiterate; many had had the experience of belonging to voluntary organizations; a considerable number had even travelled in North America to towns and cities, mines, and construction and lumber camps. More than half went to Ontario and Quebec.[18] Some went west as farm labourers, and of these a number later returned to central Canada.

The friendly relations Ukrainians and Poles had enjoyed in the first years of settlement had begun to cool before the outbreak of World War I, and during and after the war turned to outright hostility. The roots of the hostility lay in the rise of a nationalist movement among Ukrainians and the political conflicts in Europe following the rebirth of the Polish state in 1918. In Canada, members of the Ukrainian intelligentsia, particularly priests, worked to strengthen and discipline ethnic awareness among Ukrainian immigrants. Lacking numbers and an intelligentsia, the Poles were forced into a defensive posture.[19]

Between 1921 and 1931, the population of Hungarian origin increased to 40,600, with almost 28,000 entering as immigrants. It also scattered. Saskatchewan's Hungarian population increased by 48 per cent, but Manitoba's more than doubled. Alberta's increased five times, Ontario's eight times, and Quebec's went from fewer than 100 to more than 4,000. As a result, Saskatchewan, which had included more than two-thirds of Hungarian Canadians in 1921, had less than one-third ten years later.

Equally notable is the urbanization of the Hungarian population. In 1921 only 11 per cent lived in cities; by 1931, the percentage had increased to 30. Montreal emerged as a centre of Hungarian life; in Ontario, Hamilton, Welland, Toronto, and Windsor also had large Hungarian communities.[20]

The census records 100,000 persons of Russian origin in 1921, the large increases all being in the Prairie provinces. Since there were only 44,400 persons of Russian origin in 1911 and 88,150 in 1931, it is likely that members of German-speaking groups that had lived in Russia, such as the Mennonites, claimed Russian ethnic origin because of antagonisms toward Germans engendered by the war. However, some Russians did enter Canada after the Russian Revolution, coming either directly or by way of China and Manchuria.[21]

In the 1920's groups of Mennonites, of German origin, left Manitoba and Saskatchewan for Mexico. In all, approximately 6,500, chiefly Old Colony Mennonites, emigrated to avoid what they considered to be the encroachment of Canadian culture on their way of life. But in the same period the Mennonite Colonization Association brought to Canada almost 20,000 people, and other immigration organizations brought additional thousands of Mennonites from Russia to the West. In the Mennonite group, as in others, the new arrivals were more urban than their predecessors.[22]

One new and wholly rural group was the Hutterite sect, which, like the Mennonites, had originated in central Europe and migrated by stages to Russia. Hutterite representatives had accompanied Mennonites to North America in 1873 to investigate conditions, but while only a portion of the Mennonites migrated, virtually all of the Hutterites, about 13,000, did so; also, some of the Mennonites came to Canada, but the Hutterites went to the Dakota territory in the United States. A colony moved to Manitoba in 1898, fearing conscription during the Spanish-American War, but they returned to South Dakota in 1905. During World War I, however, Hutterites were brutally treated, and a migration to Canada was decided upon. In 1918, a total of fifteen colonies were founded, six in Manitoba and nine in Alberta. During the depression some Manitoba colonies began to move back to South Dakota while some Dakota colonies came to Alberta. Legislative restrictions on the purchase of land by Hutterites were imposed in Alberta from 1942 to 1972, and the threat of similar restrictions in Manitoba was met by an informal agreement. Nonetheless, the Hutterites prospered. By 1982 there were sixty-seven colonies in Manitoba, thirty-seven in Saskatchewan, and ninety-nine in Alberta.[23]

In the interwar period the Scandinavians continued to settle in the farming areas of the West. About 20,000 Swedes, 19,500 Norwegians, and 17,000 Danes entered the country from 1923 to 1930, coming directly from Europe rather than from the United States as their predecessors had. These later Scandinavian immigrants were impelled by a severe depression in their homelands. The number of people of Scandinavian origin increased between the 1921 and 1931 censuses from 167,350 to 228,500.

Many Finns were among the immigrants who settled in the mining and mill towns of northern Ontario and British Columbia. They were from the peasant and working classes, fleeing severe economic difficulties, avoiding compulsory military service in the Russian army and Russification in Finland, or seeking religious freedom.[24] Some Finns had settled earlier in the Port Arthur area; the newcomers joined them and also gravitated to Sault Ste. Marie, Timmins, Sudbury, Toronto, Montreal, and Vancouver. At the 1921 census there were 21,500 Finns in Canada; by 1931 there were 43,900.

Between 1918 and 1930 more than 15,000 Dutch settled in Canada. They were escaping from worsening economic conditions at home and were sped on their way by agreements between the Dutch and Canadian governments, the colonization activities of the railways, and the care of the various emigration societies in Holland. Like others, they were attracted primarily to Ontario rather than to the West.

For the Italians the second wave of immigration to Canada was of short duration. From 1925 on the Fascist government discouraged emigration from Italy except to North Africa; Canadian economic conditions and restrictions on immigration reinforced its policy.[25] Migration and natural increase combined were not quite enough to double the population of Italian origin between 1921 and 1941: according to the census it rose from 66,769 to 112,625. In this period Montreal and Toronto continued to be the main centres of the Italian population; in 1941, Montreal was listed as having 23,800 persons of Italian origin, Toronto, 14,200.

Jewish immigration continued during the interwar period, with 20,200 Jewish immigrants settling in Canada. Regardless of citizenship, Jews were treated separately from their fellow countrymen by Canadian immigration authorities: other Europeans could simply buy a ticket at the nearest steamship office, but a Jew could not obtain a ticket until he could produce a letter of admission from the Department of Immigration.[26] As before, Jewish immigrants preferred the urban centres as places of residence.

Asian groups increased slowly in this period: the restrictive policies of the United States in the 1920's lent weight to the campaigns in Canada for tighter restrictions against them. From 1923 on, the Canadian government adopted the principle of excluding Chinese, except for certain extremely limited classes; and the "gentlemen's agreement" of 1928 restricted the entry of Japanese to 150 a year. So successful were the campaigns against the "yellow peril" that the census listed only 84,548 of Asian ethnic origin in 1931, an increase of fewer than 19,000 in the decade, and the census of 1941 showed a decrease to 74,064. The decrease was especially marked among the Chinese and reflected the dying out of a group with a strong tradition of returning home in old age, very few women, and a lack of reinforcement through immigration.

Blacks also suffered from discriminatory measures. After 1923 the term

"British subject" was limited to citizens of Commonwealth countries with predominantly white populations. Thus, West Indians were deprived of preferential status to which they had in theory been entitled previously. In practice, of course, they had never had easy entry because of racism in the application of immigration regulations.

The depression of the 1930's led the government to cut off the flow of immigrants into Canada. An order-in-council was passed in August, 1930, restricting immigrants to members of the immediate families of men already established in Canada and farmers with enough money to start farming at once. The view began to be expressed, in fact, that Canada was fully settled and never again would need or be able to absorb immigrants, especially non-British immigrants.[27] Deportation was resorted to, both to help British immigrants to return home and to rid the country of non-British immigrants who were indigent or considered to be dangerous radicals. Voluntary repatriation also occurred: as many as 3,000 Finnish radicals left for Soviet Karelia. Immigrant arrivals had totalled 1,782,000 between the 1911 and 1921 censuses, and 1,198,000 between the 1921 and 1931 censuses. In the next decade the number dwindled to 149,000. In 1935, only 11,300 people entered, two-thirds of them from the United Kingdom or the United States. Net migration was negative for the decade. Between 1931 and 1941 the number of people of German ethnic origin fell by almost 9,000, of Russian origin by almost 4,500, and of Asian origin by 10,500; the proportion of the population that was of other than French, British, or native Indian or Inuit origin held steady in Canada as a whole, declined in Nova Scotia, remained the same in Prince Edward Island, New Brunswick, and Quebec, and increased in the five other provinces.

During the depression the drift to the cities was slowed, but it did continue. Small urban concentrations of particular ethnic groups were augmented as people moved away from the drought areas of the West. The Romanian community in Montreal, for example, which had existed since the turn of the century, grew considerably, and Hungarian communities in Toronto and Calgary throve.[28]

A small proportion of the immigration after 1935, and especially in 1939, was composed of Jewish refugees, but economic recovery was slow in Canada and the government was reluctant to admit even the victims of Nazi Germany.[29] The decision to give economic considerations priority over humanitarianism was buttressed by the anti-Semitism expressed by small but noisy and even violent minorities in various parts of Canada in the 1930's. The most notorious was led by Adrien Arcand in Quebec, but others existed in Ontario and in western Canada. During World War II, by agreement between British and Canadian authorities, a number of highly educated German Jews who had been in Great Britain when the war broke out were sent to Canada for internment; many of them proved to be extremely gifted intellectually and artistically. About a thousand elected to remain in Canada, and they have made signal contributions to Canadian arts and letters.[30]

Probably no other people in Canada suffered such upheavals because of the war as the Japanese. At the outbreak of war they were some 23,000 in number; 22,000 lived in British Columbia; of those in British Columbia, 13,300 were Canadian-born, 2,900 were naturalized Canadians, and most of the rest had been Canadian residents for from twenty-five to forty years. After Japan entered the war, much of their property was confiscated and they were uprooted from the West Coast and placed in relocation centres. At the war's end about 4,000, over half of them Canadian-born and two-thirds of them Canadian citizens, left the country under the governmental "repatriation" scheme, which was intended to rid the country of as many Japanese as possible.

THE "THIRD WAVE" AFTER WORLD WAR II

The next wave of immigration began soon after the end of World War II. By 1961 2,500,000 people had come to Canada; between 1961 and 1971 almost 1,500,000 entered. Of the post-war immigrants, by 1971 approximately 1,200,000 had died or emigrated. Although many of those were of origins other than British and French, and although in addition many pre-war immigrants returned to Europe after the war, nonetheless by the 1971 census 25 per cent of the Canadian population claimed ethnic origins other than British, French, or native Indian and Inuit. Since 1971 immigration has faltered somewhat, but the proportion of the population belonging to the other ethnic groups has continued to rise. This third wave of immigration has continued longer than either the first or second and has included a wider variety of ethnic groups, social classes, and occupations than previous waves of immigration.

The third wave had hardly begun when Prime Minister W.L. Mackenzie King stated in the House of Commons, in May, 1947, that the policy of the government was "to foster the growth of the population of Canada by the encouragement of immigration."[31] Immigrants were to be carefully selected, and admitted only in such numbers as could be absorbed by the economy. The principles of selection were to include preservation of "the fundamental composition of the Canadian population." For many years, the principles enunciated by Prime Minister King were cited as governing immigration policy. However, an exception was made for refugees and later recruitment of immigrants was broadened in response to public opinion.

The vast majority of the post-war immigrants settled in towns and cities, largely because Canada was becoming increasingly urban and industrial during the period. A substantial number settled in Montreal. Toronto, however, became the immigrant metropolis of Canada. In the 1960's the proportion going to Montreal fell off slightly because of the turbulent situation there, but there was no diminution in the flow to Toronto. In the 1970's immigration as a whole declined, and its destinations became more varied: Toronto, Montreal, and Vancouver remained popular, while Edmonton and Calgary advanced.

The ethnic origins most strongly represented among the immigrants from

TABLE 1

Immigration to Canada
by Calendar Year, 1852–1986

1852	29,307	1886	69,152	1920	138,824	1954	154,227
1853	29,464	1887	84,525	1921	91,728	1955	109,946
1854	37,263	1888	88,766	1922	64,224	1956	164,857
1855	25,296	1889	91,600	1923	133,729	1957	282,164
1856	22,544	1890	75,067	1924	124,164	1958	124,851
1857	33,854	1891	82,165	1925	84,907	1959	106,928
1858	12,339	1892	30,996	1926	135,982	1960	104,111
1859	6,300	1893	29,633	1927	158,886	1961	71,689
1860	6,276	1894	20,829	1928	166,783	1962	74,586
1861	13,589	1895	18,790	1929	164,993	1963	93,151
1862	18,294	1896	16,835	1930	104,806	1964	112,606
1863	21,000	1897	21,716	1931	27,530	1965	146,758
1864	24,779	1898	31,900	1932	20,591	1966	194,743
1865	18,958	1899	44,543	1933	14,382	1967	222,876
1866	11,427	1900	41,681	1934	12,476	1968	183,974
1867	10,666	1901	55,747	1935	11,277	1969	161,531
1868	12,765	1902	89,102	1936	11,643	1970	147,713
1869	18,630	1903	138,660	1937	15,101	1971	121,900
1870	24,706	1904	131,252	1938	17,244	1972	122,006
1871	27,773	1905	141,465	1939	16,994	1973	184,200
1872	36,578	1906	211,653	1940	11,324	1974	218,465
1873	50,050	1907	272,409	1941	9,329	1975	187,881
1874	39,373	1908	143,326	1942	7,576	1976	149,429
1875	27,382	1909	173,694	1943	8,504	1977	114,914
1876	25,633	1910	286,839	1944	12,801	1978	86,313
1877	27,082	1911	331,288	1945	22,722	1979	112,096
1878	29,807	1912	375,756	1946	71,719	1980	143,117
1879	40,492	1913	400,870	1947	64,127	1981	128,618
1880	38,505	1914	150,484	1948	125,414	1982	121,147
1881	47,991	1915	36,665	1949	95,217	1983	89,157
1882	112,458	1916	55,914	1950	73,912	1984	88,239
1883	133,624	1917	72,910	1951	194,391	1985	84,302
1884	103,824	1918	41,845	1952	164,498	1986	99,219
1885	79,169	1919	107,698	1953	168,868		

SOURCE: Canada Employment and Immigration Commission.

1945 to 1967 were British, Italian, German, Dutch, Polish, and Jewish. A major revision of the regulations concerning immigration came into effect in 1962, a new system of calculating admissibility was introduced in 1967, and a new Immigration Act became law in 1976. These had the effect of eliminating discrimination on racial and ethnic grounds and emphasized education, training, and skills. Almost immediately, considerable increases in the numbers of immigrants from China, India and Pakistan, and the West Indies occurred, so that some of the traditional donor countries were eclipsed by them.

One important element of the post-war immigration was made up of displaced persons and refugees. Almost 100,000 entered between April, 1947, and March, 1950: Poles, Ukrainians, Jews, and Balts – Estonians, Latvians, and Lithuanians – were most numerous among them. Including the refugees from the Hungarian revolution of 1956 and from Czechoslovakia in 1968, by 1971 they numbered over 300,000. In the 1970's they included Asians from Uganda, Chileans, and Vietnamese. The political catastrophes that led to their migration had at least as great an impact on the well-to-do and well-educated as on the poor; refugees therefore included numbers of the skilled and highly educated.

In the immediate post-war years the government tended to favour farmers, domestics, and industrial labourers rather than skilled technicians and professionals, but as time went on those who came to Canada were drawn increasingly from the lower-middle and upper-middle classes. They were urban and generally well educated, people with professional training, trades training, artistic talents, linguistic skills, and/or experience in business, government, or the military. They saw the greatest opportunities to exercise their abilities in the expanding economy of Ontario, and about half of them chose to settle there. They included Poles, Ukrainians, Lithuanians, Estonians, Latvians, and Jews. Among the Poles were a group of approximately 4,500 ex-soldiers who entered under a special scheme just after the war.

Jewish refugees after the war were mainly from Poland, but there were also Jews among the immigrants from Hungary after the revolution of 1956 and among the immigrants from Egypt and North Africa after the Algerian crisis. Toronto and Montreal were favoured destinations; for the French-speaking North Africans, Montreal was especially attractive. The wartime and post-war additions to the Jewish communities were especially noteworthy because they added variety to what had previously been a remarkably homogeneous Jewish group.

The refugees were a well-educated group but other immigrants also included larger numbers of the educated and the skilled, partly because economic and social development made Canada more attractive to middle-class migrants and partly because government policy made admission easier for those with education, training, and skills. Because of their middle-class and upper-class background and their familiarity with urban life, the immigrants did not establish heavily concentrated settlements. They quickly spread out

TABLE 2

Population by Ethnic Origins Other than British Isles and French for Canada, 1871, 1881, and 1901–1971

(1,000s)

Ethnic Group	1871	1881	1901	1911	1921	1931	1941	1951	1961	1971
Other European	240	299	458	945	1,247	1,825	2,044	2,554	4,117	4,960
Austrian, n.o.s.	—	—	11	44	108	49	38	32	107	42
Belgian	—	—	3	10	20	28	30	35	61	51
Czech-Slovak	—	—	—	—	9	30	43	64	73	82
Finnish[1]	—	—	3	16	21	44	42	44	59	59
German	203	254	311	403	295	474	465	620	1,050	1,317
Greek	—	—	—	4	6	9	12	14	56	124
Hungarian[2]	—	—	2	12	13	41	55	60	126	132
Italian	1	2	11	46	67	98	113	152	450	731
Jewish	—	1	16	76	126	157	170	182	173	297
Lithuanian	—	—	—	—	2	6	8	16	28	25
Netherlands	30	30	34	56	118	149	213	264	430	426
Polish	—	—	6	34	53	146	167	220	324	316
Romanian[3]	—	—	—	6	13	29	25	24	44	27
Russian[4]	1	1	20	44	100	88	84	91	119	64
Scandinavian	2	5	31	113	167	228	245	283	387	385
Ukrainian	—	—	6	75	107	225	306	395	473	581
Yugoslavic	—	—	—	—	4	16	21	21	69	105
Other	4	6	5	7	18	9	10	36	88	195

Ethnic Group	1871	1881	1901	1911	1921	1931	1941	1951	1961	1971
				(1,000s)						
Asiatic	—	4	24	43	66	85	74	73	122	286
Chinese	—	4	17	28	40	47	35	33	58	119
Japanese	—	—	5	9	16	23	23	22	29	37
Other	—	—	2	6	10	15	16	19	34	129
Other	52	174	177	158	153	158	190	354	463	519

1. Includes Estonian prior to 1951.
2. Includes Lithuanian and Moravian in 1901 and 1911.
3. Includes Bulgarian in 1901 and 1911.
4. Includes Finnish and Polish in 1871 and 1881.
SOURCE: Warren E. Kalbach and Wayne W. McVey, *The Demographic Bases of Canadian Society*, second ed. (Toronto: McGraw-Hill Ryerson, 1971), pp. 198-99.

into parts of urban areas where others of their occupation, educational level, and tastes were located.

From several countries, however, immigrants continued to come in large measure from rural areas and country villages and towns. Immigrants from Italy, Greece, Portugal, and Malta were to a large extent sponsored by relatives in Canada rather than selected on the basis of education and skills. The Italian immigration was the most spectacular of the post-war period, especially between 1951 and 1960, when over 250,000 Italians entered the country. By 1971 the Italian ethnic origin category was considerably larger than any other non-British and non-French category except the German. Persons of Greek and Portuguese origin had always been few in Canada, but in the early 1950's immigration from these countries increased sharply, and the increase has since been maintained. Italians, Greeks, Portuguese, and Maltese have settled predominantly in cities, especially in Toronto, Montreal, and Vancouver. In Toronto, by the 1960's the Italians were second only to the British in numbers and the Greeks were one of the ten largest groups by origin.

The restrictions on the immigration of Asians and blacks were greatly eased. Members of these visible minorities became an accustomed part of the Canadian population, not only in British Columbia but in urban areas throughout the country. By 1981 Chinese ranked next to Italians in number in Metropolitan Toronto and other Asians there exceeded 150,000.

Most Japanese Canadians who remained in Canada after the war did not return to British Columbia but continued the dispersal that relocation had begun. Several thousand went to southern Alberta, about a thousand to Manitoba, and considerable numbers to Ontario. Many went to Toronto, which, like many other Canadian cities, had been closed to Japanese during part of the war.[32] There, they became part of that city's spectacular expansion of the 1950's and 1960's. By 1961 there were around 8,000 Japanese in the metropolitan area, and by 1971 there were 15,000. When Japanese Canadians celebrated the centenary in 1977 of the arrival of the first Japanese in Canada, they numbered approximately 40,000 throughout Canada.

Immigration from Japan did not resume in any volume after the war. Immigration of those of Chinese origin, however, which had been virtually non-existent since 1923, revived with the removal of some of the restrictive measures in 1947, and about 21,000 people of Chinese origin entered between 1949 and the end of 1961. Immigration from India, Pakistan, and Ceylon also resumed, and began to increase in the late 1950's. With the changes in immigration regulations in the 1960's, these groups became major constituents of Canadian immigration.

According to the census, the number of blacks in Canada fell from 22,174 in 1941 to 18,020 ten years later, but by the census of 1961 it had risen again to 32,127, and by 1971 to 62,470. The fall in the war and early post-war years, so far as it represented a real decline in population and not under-enumeration in the 1951 census, probably reflected the tendency of young Canadian blacks to emigrate to the United States for higher education and for employment. A rise in immigration began in 1954 and has been maintained since. Coloured West Indian immigrants, hampered by discriminatory regulations, increased from 1,000 to 2,000 a year before 1962 to between 2,200 and 3,700 from 1963 to 1966, and with the introduction of the point system to almost 8,000 in 1967 and 1968, 14,250 in 1969, and 13,600 in 1970. In 1980, West Indians were estimated to number 200,000 in the Metropolitan Toronto area, to which most were drawn, except for Haitians, who in greatest numbers flocked to Montreal.

THE SITUATION IN THE 1970's AND 1980's

By 1971 one-quarter of the Canadian population claimed an ethnic origin other than British, French, or native Indian and Inuit. The increase in the proportion of other origins was related to a decrease in those of British origin from 60.5 per cent in 1871 to 44.6 per cent in 1971. British immigration had always been high: in most years the number of immigrants of British origin, chiefly from the United Kingdom and the United States, was highest or second highest. French immigration had been a slow trickle until 1951, when it showed a slight increase. The natural increase of the French Canadians enabled them to maintain their proportion of the population, however, while the British proportion steadily declined, except between 1961 and 1971, when it increased slightly.

In 1981 the ethnic origins of Canadians were as shown in Table 3. The 1981 census was the first to accept more than one ethnic origin for an individual. Of the total population, 40.2 per cent gave the single response British and 5.8 per cent gave a multiple response that included British; 26.7 per cent gave the single response French and 2.7 per cent a multiple response that included French; 1.7 per cent gave the single response Native peoples and 0.3 per cent a multiple response that included Native peoples; 31.4 per cent gave other single responses and 5.8 per cent a multiple response including other origins.

In spite of the volume of post-war immigration, a large proportion of those of non-British, non-French, and non-Native origins were Canadian-born. By the 1971 census, 82 per cent of those of Ukrainian origin, 78 per cent of those of Scandinavian origin, and 75 per cent of those of German origin were born in Canada. Only such groups as the Italians, Hungarians, Greeks, and Portuguese, among the larger ethnic groups, and Indians and Pakistani among the smaller, were predominantly foreign-born. Moreover, the Canadian-born in some origin categories included not only first-generation and second-generation Canadians but ninth-generation and tenth-generation Canadians as well.

The history of Canadian ethnic groups is reflected in their spatial distribution. Their time of arrival, their entrance status and the speed with which they moved out of it, the effects on them of cataclysmic events such as wars and economic crises, and their changing culture and social organization have all influenced their location. In turn, their location within the country and within

45

TABLE 3

Population by Selected Ethnic Origins,[1] Canada, Provinces, and Territories, 1981

	Canada	Nfld.	P.E.I.	N.S.	N.B.	Quebec
Total Population[1]	24,083,500	563,750	121,225	839,805	689,375	6,369,065
Single origins	22,244,885	547,640	112,545	767,205	649,420	6,241,115
African	45,215	85	20	3,900	240	6,220
Armenian	21,155	5	—	20	5	10,385
Asian Arab	60,140	190	245	2,880	705	16,850
Austrian	40,630	30	15	250	105	2,275
Balkans	129,075	115	10	360	150	6,875
Baltic	50,300	45	20	425	100	4,665
Belgian and Luxembourg	43,000	10	145	465	235	6,585
British	9,674,245	519,620	93,345	608,685	369,125	487,385
Czech and Slovak	67,695	40	25	410	185	4,845
Chinese	289,245	635	165	1,545	880	19,255
Dutch	408,240	675	1,340	13,495	4,400	8,055
Finnish	52,315	70	5	260	95	1,140
French	6,439,100	15,355	14,770	71,350	251,070	5,105,665
German	1,142,365	1,640	820	33,145	6,490	33,770
Greek	154,365	30	—	1,695	360	49,420
Magyar (Hungarian)	116,390	15	50	470	360	9,745
Indochinese	43,725	75	45	400	525	15,130
Indo-Pakistani	121,445	520	55	940	540	12,195
Italian	747,970	410	100	3,235	1,145	163,735

Japanese	40,995	25	5	40	30	1,395
Jewish	264,025	285	80	2,090	720	90,355
Latin American	117,555	85	20	690	125	26,315
Native Peoples	413,380	3,225	435	6,305	4,605	46,855
North African Arab	10,545	5	—	20	35	6,090
Pacific Islands	155,290	530	25	1,060	360	6,490
Polish	254,485	180	90	2,455	425	19,755
Portuguese	188,105	245	50	490	315	27,370
Romanian	22,485	—	—	155	50	2,790
Russian	49,435	35	10	155	65	2,940
Scandinavian	282,795	640	250	2,175	2,345	4,225
Spanish	53,540	180	5	400	255	15,460
Swiss	29,805	10	15	440	95	4,320
Ukrainian	529,615	135	105	1,965	635	14,640
West Asian	10,055	15	—	135	—	1,605
Other single origins	176,160	2,455	280	4,690	2,660	6,315
Multiple origins	1,838,615	16,110	8,680	72,595	39,950	127,960
British and French	430,255	10,245	5,305	27,650	22,820	62,270
British and other	859,800	3,485	2,440	29,995	11,170	20,645
French and other	124,940	350	225	3,570	1,910	21,790
British, French, and other	107,080	500	370	4,735	2,100	7,120
European and other[3]	238,455	330	145	5,160	1,040	10,585
Native Peoples and other[4]	78,085	1,200	190	1,485	910	5,540

TABLE 3 (Continued)

	Ont.	Man.	Sask.	Alta.	B.C.	Yukon	N.W.T.
Total Population²	8,534,265	1,013,705	956,440	2,213,650	2,713,615	23,075	45,540
Single origins	7,751,615	912,360	853,315	1,940,915	2,407,045	19,580	42,125
African	24,895	1,590	500	4,285	3,445	20	25
Armenian	9,665	10	10	215	840	—	—
Asian Arab	26,330	885	785	8,285	2,970	15	15
Austrian	15,145	3,155	4,115	6,400	9,025	60	45
Balkans	90,975	3,315	1,880	9,340	15,910	60	85
Baltic	35,600	1,275	435	3,020	4,580	90	30
Belgian and Luxembourg	18,035	6,500	2,830	4,305	3,830	20	35
British	4,487,800	373,995	366,080	962,785	1,385,165	10,060	10,200
Czech and Slovak	33,025	3,590	3,725	11,195	10,470	110	75
Chinese	118,640	7,065	6,970	36,770	96,915	215	200
Dutch	191,125	33,875	17,215	65,060	72,280	400	315
Finnish	33,395	1,060	1,275	4,135	10,810	30	45
French	652,900	74,050	46,915	111,865	92,310	1,080	1,765
German	373,390	108,140	161,700	233,175	187,630	1,300	1,160
Greek	85,960	2,380	1,220	4,820	8,390	30	65
Magyar (Hungarian)	59,135	4,160	11,080	15,170	15,920	190	100
Indochinese	12,815	2,020	1,865	6,385	4,410	15	35
Indo-Pakistani	60,375	2,960	1,140	13,225	29,425	45	30
Italian	487,310	9,595	2,755	26,605	52,760	95	220
Japanese	16,685	1,300	205	5,225	16,040	30	10

Jewish	131,320	14,950	1,515	9,460	13,170	25	55
Latin American	74,250	3,695	975	6,845	4,525	10	25
Native Peoples	83,860	59,925	54,720	60,010	64,690	3,415	25,325
North African Arab	3,535	125	60	490	185	—	5
Pacific Islands	70,220	13,835	2,100	16,645	43,840	50	145
Polish	122,945	28,445	18,335	37,655	23,795	190	205
Portuguese	129,005	7,830	515	6,125	16,125	5	30
Romanian	8,170	900	3,905	3,805	2,650	35	25
Russian	8,715	3,765	6,290	7,715	19,605	50	75
Scandinavian	40,335	25,170	42,720	78,565	85,035	745	595
Spanish	25,185	1,470	730	4,945	4,845	25	40
Swiss	11,755	870	1,225	4,680	6,335	25	40
Ukrainian	133,995	99,795	76,815	136,710	63,605	635	580
West Asian	5,445	120	65	895	1,770	—	10
Other single origins	69,700	10,545	10,645	34,105	33,740	520	515
Multiple origins	782,650	101,345	103,120	272,735	306,570	3,490	3,415
British and French	201,415	12,400	9,095	34,995	42,955	540	565
British and other	375,800	46,485	52,985	142,930	171,195	1,560	1,110
French and other	45,145	8,820	8,325	19,185	15,290	165	175
British, French, and other	50,110	4,320	4,425	15,585	17,475	210	135
European and other[3]	83,985	22,965	23,820	48,005	41,705	385	325
Native Peoples and other[4]	26,200	6,355	4,480	12,045	17,950	630	1,100

NOTE: Totals may not equal the sum of components due to rounding.

1. The 1981 Census is the first to accept more than one ethnic origin for an individual. Therefore, this table includes counts of single and multiple origins.

2. Excludes inmates.

3. Includes multiple origins involving European, Jewish, and Other origins not included elsewhere.

4. Includes multiple origins involving Native Peoples and British, French, European, Jewish, or Other origins.

SOURCE: *Census of Canada*, 1981.

TABLE 4

Population Born Outside Canada by Province or Territory of Residence, Showing Place of Birth, 1981 and 1971[1]

Province of residence:	Population Born Outside Canada			Place of Birth								
				Europe			Southeast Asia			Other Asia		
	1981	1971	% Change	1981	1971	% Change	1981	1971	% Change	1981	1971	% Change
Canada	3,876,160	3,295,530	17.3	2,586,080	2,626,790	-1.5	152,590	26,025	486.3	390,905	139,720	179.8
Nfld.	9,785	8,945	—	5,660	5,775	—	425	175	—	900	640	—
P.E.I.	4,550	3,705	—	2,400	2,165	—	105	15	—	185	175	—
N.S.	41,710	37,190	—	23,880	24,385	—	940	250	—	3,415	2,105	—
N.B.	27,580	23,735	—	13,820	14,210	—	815	200	—	1,140	760	—
Quebec	525,955	468,925	—	325,495	350,415	—	22,400	4,180	—	42,010	21,170	—
Ont.	2,025,750	1,707,400	—	1,444,020	1,436,785	—	62,925	13,520	—	179,985	57,595	—
Man.	146,055	151,250	—	99,160	126,310	—	14,200	1,565	—	7,545	3,495	—
Sask.	83,655	110,690	—	53,820	80,775	—	4,215	395	—	5,430	3,560	—
Alta.	364,825	282,260	—	225,115	211,625	—	20,035	1,930	—	42,425	11,670	—
B.C.	631,620	496,660	—	389,095	370,775	—	26,300	3,745	—	107,510	38,385	—
Yukon	2,885	2,525	—	1,785	1,875	—	50	5	—	185	70	—
N.W.T.	2,780	2,245	—	1,830	1,690	—	180	45	—	175	95	—

Place of Birth

Province of residence:	U.S.A.			Caribbean Islands			South and Central America			Other Countries		
	1981	1971	% Change	1981	1971	% Change	1981	1971	% Change	1981	1971	% Change
Canada	312,015	309,640	0.8	172,245	67,980	153.4	107,960	36,150	198.6	145,370	89,225	62.9
Nfld.	2,255	1,890	—	125	75	—	80	55	—	335	335	—
P.E.I.	1,740	1,295	—	15	15	—	35	10	—	80	30	—
N.S.	11,335	8,780	—	735	560	—	260	155	—	1,150	955	—
N.B.	11,005	7,950	—	200	130	—	105	150	—	490	330	—
Quebec	40,420	46,480	—	43,770	15,195	—	16,290	5,200	—	35,570	26,280	—
Ont.	109,325	101,440	—	110,120	44,550	—	64,505	20,720	—	54,875	32,795	—
Man.	11,405	12,090	—	3,535	2,170	—	7,515	3,575	—	2,700	2,050	—
Sask.	16,555	23,785	—	895	435	—	1,305	395	—	1,425	1,340	—
Alta.	43,820	47,515	—	7,315	2,205	—	8,755	1,580	—	17,355	5,740	—
B.C.	63,110	57,720	—	5,480	2,595	—	9,035	4,270	—	31,100	19,170	—
Yukon	660	430	—	25	25	—	30	15	—	150	125	—
N.W.T.	380	270	—	35	25	—	45	25	—	135	95	—

1. 1981 figures exclude inmates.
SOURCE: *Census of Canada*, 1981.

51

particular communities, their concentration or dispersion, and their relations with their neighbours have vitally affected their participation in society and the maintenance or loss of their sense of identity, their language, and their culture.

As time has passed the population has tended to be recruited more and more widely, and consequently the longest settled parts of the country have the lowest proportion of population of origins other than French, British, and native Indian and Inuit; they also have the lowest proportion of foreign-born of such origins. In 1981, 92.2 per cent of Newfoundland's population reported British as their sole ethnic heritage, 2.7 per cent French, and 1.8 per cent British and French. Quebec outside of Montreal, Prince Edward Island, and New Brunswick also have less than 7 per cent of their population of other ethnic origins and negligible proportions of foreign-born. In Nova Scotia, 14 per cent of the population is of other origins, but only 1.5 per cent is foreign-born of other origins.

In the Atlantic provinces, the bulk of the population of other ethnic origins is composed of Germans and Dutch, many of them descended from very early settlers, with Scandinavians ranking third and blacks as a small but important group in Nova Scotia. Others, such as Chinese and Lebanese, have recently won a place in some centres. The most prominent groups seeking to preserve their cultural heritage in this region are of British Isles and French origin: Newfoundlanders, Highland Scots, and Acadian French. The first named, long part of a separate British colony, have felt menaced by the breakdown of their isolation that followed their entry into Confederation and economic development; they have also felt discriminated against by other Canadians. The Scots have been concerned about the preservation of the Gaelic language and Gaelic folklore. Seeking to gain a greater measure of equality than they have enjoyed in the past are the Acadians and the blacks.

In Quebec, economic developments such as mines and the James Bay project employed some workers of non-British, non-French, and non-Native origins, but still, in 1971, 90 per cent of those of other ethnic origins and of the foreign-born of such origins lived in the Metropolitan Montreal area. Italians and Jews were the largest of the other ethnic groups in Quebec, and the numbers of these groups were greater in that province than in any other except Ontario. The Italian and Jewish groups also occupied interesting positions in relation to the changing balance of power between English and French. Italians were culturally and linguistically close to the French, yet until the late 1970's they insisted that their children learn the English language in Canada. Jews, formerly oriented toward the Anglophone community, recently have included both people who spoke English as mother tongue or as second language and people from North Africa who spoke French as mother tongue, as well as a considerable proportion of bilinguals or multilinguals. In addition to the location and the commercial and financial importance of Montreal, some groups have been attracted to Quebec because they found its inhabitants more sympathetic than English Canadians.

While in the 1970's the number of immigrants attracted to Quebec was not great enough to balance the number of migrants who left, Quebec received a large share of Chilean and Vietnamese refugees and was also a favoured destination for Haitians, whose claim to refugee status was generally not conceded by the Canadian government. The Vietnamese who came to Quebec in 1975 were French-speaking, as were the educated among the Haitians. The linguistic factor, as well as a desire to maintain the population, led the government of the province to offer a welcome. The much greater numbers of Vietnamese who came to Canada in 1979 were not French-speaking to the same degree and did not concentrate in Quebec.

In Ontario, 30 per cent of the population is of ethnic origins other than British, French, or native Indian, and 14 per cent of the population is of foreign birth and other ethnic origins. Of the 14 per cent, the vast majority, 86.5 per cent, immigrated after 1946. Ontario has by far the greatest number and greatest proportion of post-war immigrants of other ethnic origins. Most ethnic groups that have received immigrants since the war have more members in Ontario than in any other region of Canada.

Toronto, long considered to be among the most British of Canadian cities, had by the late 1970's become extremely cosmopolitan. Its economy was dependent on the labour and the buying power of immigrants, and its social life was enlivened by its many ethnic groups. In 1971 those of British origin constituted 57 per cent of the population of Metropolitan Toronto and 46 per cent of the population of the city of Toronto. By 1981 those of British origin were 43 per cent of the population of Metropolitan Toronto; in the total of about 2,200,000 were approximately 232,000 Italians, 98,000 Jews, 78,000 Chinese, 70,000 Portuguese, 59,000 Greeks, 53,000 Germans, 39,000 Ukrainians, and 37,000 Poles.

However, in sharp contrast to Quebec, those of other ethnic origins and of foreign birth in Ontario were by no means concentrated in the province's largest metropolitan area but were found throughout the province. In Hamilton, for example, approximately 38 per cent of the population were of other ethnic origins, and in Thunder Bay almost 50 per cent.

The Prairie region is usually considered to be the most ethnically heterogeneous part of Canada. It does in fact have the highest proportion of population of other ethnic origins, in 1971 just over 45 per cent, in 1981 about 48 per cent. Except for Alberta, though, large-scale immigration into the region was virtually over by 1931 so it is largely a native-born population. It includes many members of the ethnic groups that predominated among immigrants from 1900 to 1914: Germans, Scandinavians, Ukrainians, and Poles.

Among the three provinces of the region, Alberta prospered most in the post-war period. In the 1950's and 1960's it attracted a considerable number of Dutch and German immigrants, and during the oil boom of the 1970's it drew migrants from other parts of Canada as well as from abroad. It drew members of some of the new ethnic groups to arrive in Canada, such as South Asians, West Indians, Koreans, Filipinos, Chileans, and Vietnamese.

British Columbia ranks behind the Prairie provinces and ahead of Ontario in the proportion of the population that is of other ethnic origins: just over one-third of its population falls in this category. It has a lower proportion of pre-war immigrants than any of the Prairie provinces, but its proportion of post-war immigrants is second only to Ontario's, and its total immigrant population of other ethnic origins than British and French is 12 per cent. British Columbia for long had the highest concentration of people of Asian origin; by 1971 it had been superseded by Ontario but was in second place. It also was second in the number of people of Scandinavian origin, being surpassed only by the Prairie region.

Within provinces and within communities, not only are concentrations found of various ethnic groups but also individuals and families from a particular village or region of the homeland have tended to cluster together. However, it is no longer the case that areas of first immigrant settlement are near the heart of the city and as immigrants prosper and become more at home in Canada they move farther from the city centre into less concentrated areas. Recent middle-class and upper-class immigrants, of whatever ethnic group, have tended to settle immediately, or after a brief period in a down-town area, in the same areas as other Canadians of similar occupations and incomes; frequently these are suburban areas. Even business people who have set up office or shop in a downtown area have frequently located their homes elsewhere. Workers have gone to working-class suburbs near their workplaces or with convenient transportation to their workplaces. The chronic shortages of accommodation have forced people of various income levels to locate where they could rather than where they would. Sometimes this has been with or near their ethnic fellows; sometimes it has been far from them, and connections have been maintained by telephone or by automobile.

In the 1980's the population of Canada is highly diverse. The immigrants from the British Isles and from France and their descendants, the charter-member groups or founding peoples, no longer dominate to the degree that they did in the past. In terms of ethnic origin, those who are not British, French, or Native now constitute the third of the population that they have claimed since at least 1961. Some of them are old Canadians, others are immigrants and their children. They vary in their wants and aspirations, their fears and hostilities, from group to group, within groups, and from region to region within Canada. But everywhere they are significant parts of the population to which attention must be paid.

NOTES

1. Douglas Hill, *The Opening of the Canadian West* (Don Mills, Ontario: Academic Press Canada, 1973), p. 88.
2. E.K. Francis, *In Search of Utopia: The Mennonites in Manitoba* (Altona, Manitoba: D.W. Friesen and Sons, 1955), p. 45.
3. Loken, *From Fjord to Frontier*, pp. 55-61.
4. J.W. Dafoe, *Clifford Sifton in Relation to His Times* (Toronto: Macmillan of Canada, 1931), p. 131.

5. V.J. Kaye, "Three Phases of Ukrainian Immigration," *Slavs in Canada*, vol. 1 (Edmonton: Inter-University Committee on Canadian Slavs, 1966), p. 37.

6. Harry B. Hawthorn, "The Contemporary Picture," in Harry B. Hawthorn, ed., *The Doukhobors of British Columbia* (London: J.M. Dent and Sons, 1955), pp. 7-8.

7. Norman Macdonald, *Canada: Immigration and Colonization 1841-1903* (Toronto: Macmillan of Canada, 1968), p. 227. J.M. Kirschbaum, *Slovaks in Canada* (Toronto: Canadian Ethnic Press Association of Ontario, 1967), pp. 64-66, cites evidence that Slovaks were numerous among the settlers Esterhazy attracted.

8. M.S. Donnelly, "Ethnic Participation in Municipal Government – Winnipeg, St. Boniface, and the Metropolitan Corporation of Greater Winnipeg," a study prepared for the Royal Commission on Bilingualism and Biculturalism, unpublished, p. 50.

9. Mabel F. Timlin, "Canada's Immigration Policy, 1896-1910," *Canadian Journal of Economics and Political Science*, 26, 4 (November, 1960), p. 519.

10. Edmund W. Bradwin, *The Bunkhouse Man: A Study of Work and Pay in the Camps of Canada 1903-1914* (Toronto: University of Toronto Press, 1972), p. 111.

11. Linda Dégh, *People in the Tobacco Belt: Four Lives* (Ottawa: National Museum of Canada, 1975).

12. Harold Troper, *Only Farmers Need Apply* (Toronto: Griffin House, 1972), pp. 121-45.

13. Chimbos, *The Canadian Odyssey*, pp. 24-25.

14. Auvo Kostiainen, "Contacts between the Finnish Labour Movements in the United States and Canada," in Michael G. Karni, ed., *Finnish Diaspora I: Canada, South America, Africa, Australia and Sweden* (Toronto: The Multicultural History Society of Ontario, 1981), p. 37.

15. Donald Avery, *"Dangerous Foreigners": European Immigrant Workers and Labour Radicalism in Canada, 1896-1932* (Toronto: McClelland and Stewart, 1979).

16. Canada, House of Commons, Select Standing Committee, *Report*, 1928.

17. Ol'ha Woycenko, *The Ukrainians in Canada* (Ottawa: Trident Press, 1967), p. 13.

18. Henry Radecki with Benedykt Heydenkorn, *A Member of a Distinguished Family: The Polish Group in Canada* (Toronto: McClelland and Stewart, 1976), pp. 30-32.

19. Victor Turek, *Poles in Manitoba* (Toronto: Polish Alliance Press, 1967), pp. 153-56.

20. N.F. Dreisziger, with M.L. Kovacs, Paul Böldy, Bennett Kovrig, *Struggle and Hope: The Hungarian-Canadian Experience* (Toronto: McClelland and Stewart, 1982), pp. 100-04.

21. Koosma J. Tarasoff, "Russians of the Greater Vancouver Area," *Slavs in Canada*, vol. 1 (Edmonton: Inter-University Committee on Canadian Slavs, 1966), pp. 139-40; Norris, *Strangers Entertained*, pp. 163-64.

22. Francis, *In Search of Utopia*, pp. 190-94, 209-10.

23. John A. Hostetler, *Hutterite Society* (Baltimore: The Johns Hopkins University Press, 1974).

24. Lennard Sillanpaa, "Voting Behaviour of Finns in the Sudbury Area, 1930-1972," in Karni, ed., *Finnish Diaspora I*, p. 103.

25. Jeremy Boissevain, *The Italians of Montreal: Social Adjustment in a Plural Society*, Studies of the Royal Commission on Bilingualism and Biculturalism, No. 7 (Ottawa: Queen's Printer, 1970), p. 1; C.W. Hobart, "Italian Immigrants in Edmonton: Adjustment and Integration," a study prepared for the Royal Commission on Bilingualism and Biculturalism, pp. 23-27.

26. Evidence of M.L. Rosenberg, Research Director, Canadian Jewish Congress, Senate of Canada, *Proceedings of the Standing Committee on Immigration and Labour* (Ottawa: King's Printer, 1946), pp. 172-74.

27. C.A. Dawson, "Introduction," in Lloyd C. Reynolds, *The British Immigrant: His Social and Economic Adjustment in Canada* (Toronto: Oxford University Press, 1935), pp. xvii-xix.

28. John Kosa, *Land of Choice: The Hungarians in Canada* (Toronto: University of Toronto Press, 1957), pp. 22-43; Howard and Tamara Palmer, "The Hungarian Experience in Alberta," in *Peoples of Alberta*.

29. Irving Abella and Harold Troper, *None Is Too Many: Canada and the Jews of Europe, 1933-1948* (Toronto: Lester and Orpen Dennys, 1982).

30. Eric Koch, *Deemed Suspect: A Wartime Blunder* (Toronto: Methuen, 1980).

31. Cited in Freda Hawkins, *Canada and Immigration: Public Policy and Public Concern* (Montreal: McGill-Queen's University Press, 1972), p. 91.

32. Forrest E. LaViolette, *The Canadian Japanese and World War II* (Toronto: University of Toronto Press, 1948), p. 158; Ken Adachi, *The Enemy That Never Was: A History of the Japanese Canadians* (Toronto: McClelland and Stewart, 1976), pp. 287-88.

At the turn of the century Sifton's campaign to settle the West with producing farmers brought thousands of immigrants from continental Europe. (Public Archives Canada/C 75992)

Asians were unwelcome: 376 South Asians brought to Vancouver on the Komagata Maru *in 1914 to test the "continuous journey" requirement were refused entry.*
(Public Archives Canada/C 38613)

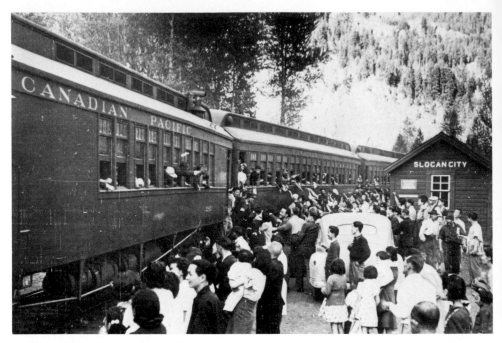

During World War II Japanese Canadians had their property confiscated and were moved to relocation centres away from the West Coast. (Ontario Archives/Multicultural History Society of Ontario Collection)

Refugee scientists, including the Norwegian and the Pole shown, worked in research in Canada during World War II. (Public Archives Canada/PA 129727)

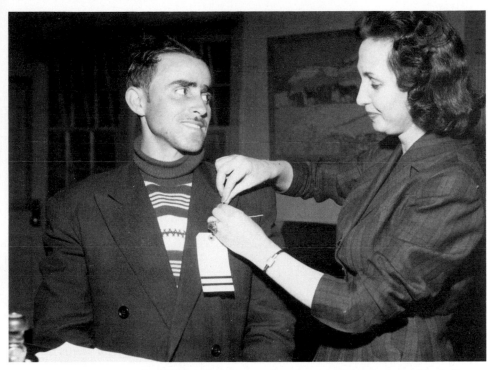

Post-war immigrants in the 1950's included many from "non-traditional sources," including Portuguese. (Photo by Mac Juster/Public Archives Canada/PA 137129)

In 1956 and 1957 Canada received refugees from the Hungarian revolution. (Photo by László Dénes/Multicultural History Society of Ontario)

Vietnamese were among the refugees who added their cultures to Canada's cities in the 1970's and 1980's. (Ontario Archives/Multicultural History Society of Ontario Collection)

Many separate ethnic cultures have become highly visible in Canadian cities. (Photo by David Levine/Ontario Archives/Multicultural History Society of Ontario Collection)

Toronto, once thought of as uniquely British, now boasts of being multiracial, polyethnic, and multilingual. (Photo by David Levine/Ontario Archives/Multicultural History Society of Ontario Collection)

A section of one of Toronto's main streets displays signs in several languages. (Multicultural History Society of Ontario)

For early settlers, such as these Doukhobors in Saskatchewan, moving supplies beyond the end of steel was hard work. (Public Archives Canada/C 09786)

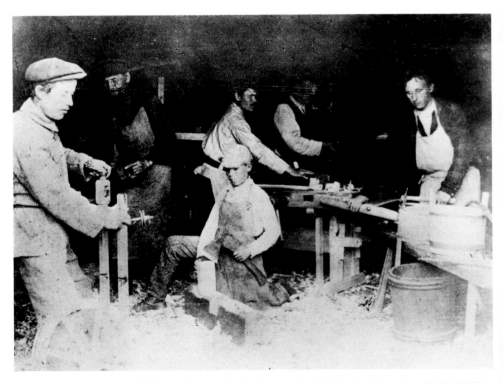

Sects such as the Doukhobors often worked communally. (Public Archives Canada/C 4198)

At the turn of the century, Chinese in British Columbia engaged in many occupations, including storekeeping; those who had moved east mainly operated laundries and restaurants. (Public Archives Canada/PA 122688)

Miners were frequently immigrants: this group at Donkin Mine, Cape Breton, includes Italians and one black. (Photo donated by Len Stephanson/Beaton Institute Archives)

Tobacco farming drew many European immigrants. These farmers were Hungarian. (Ontario Archives/Multicultural History Society of Ontario Collection)

The Dutch, such as these sugarbeet workers in southern Alberta, were among the few immigrants who went into agricultural work after World War II.

Post-war immigrants worked on the railroads, in the factories, and in small businesses. Here Portuguese labourers work on the CNR. (Multicultural History Society of Ontario)

Italian and Greek immigrants work on television cabinets in a Montreal plant. (Public Archives Canada/PA 127037)

An Italian-Canadian clothing store in Montreal advertises in three languages (1962). (Public Archives Canada/PA 133222)

A turbaned shopkeeper displays his wares. (Multicultural History Society of Ontario)

Sifton considered peasant families, such as this one from Galicia, to be ideal settlers for the Canadian West. (Photo by John Woodruff/Public Archives Canada/C 4745)

A Polish immigrant family of the 1920's poses in front of its farmhouse near Winnipeg. (Public Archives Canada/C 85104)

A Slovak family gathers in Toronto, about 1950. (Multicultural History Society of Ontario)

At a country wedding in Saskatchewan in 1917, finery brought from eastern Europe is displayed. (Public Archives Canada/PA 88459)

Guests at a Bulgarian wedding in Toronto in 1949 conform to North American fashions. (Ontario Archives/Multicultural History Society of Ontario Collection)

A Turkish wedding is solemnized in a mosque in Toronto in 1969. (Ontario Archives/ Multicultural History Society of Ontario Collection)

Ukrainian youths and their teacher pose for a class picture at the Presbyterian Mission Boys' Home in Teulon, Manitoba, in 1911. (Public Archives Canada/PA 88412)

Early in this century immigrants wanted the schools to respect their heritages, whereas Departments of Education were bent on Canadianization. Pioneer Ukrainian teachers are pictured at Vegreville, Alberta, 1917. (Public Archives Canada/PA 88497)

Japanese-Canadian children, moved from British Columbia into an internment camp, attend the local school in Picture Butte, Alberta, 1945. (Photo by Jack Long/ Public Archives Canada/C 47100)

Adult education or continuing education has been flourishing in recent years. One form has been the teaching of English to immigrants, in this case an elderly Latvian. (Public Archives Canada/PA 124947)

Supplementary schools have been established by many groups to transmit their language and culture to their children. The picture shows a Lithuanian Saturday school in Toronto, 1958. (Multicultural History Society of Ontario)

A Greek supplementary school celebrates Christmas, 1978. (Ontario Archives/Multicultural History Society of Ontario Collection)

PART TWO

Major Institutions

FOUR

The Economic Structure

Many immigrants have come to Canada chiefly for economic reasons; all immigrants on their arrival have faced the problem of making a living for themselves and their families. Government immigration policy has been based to a considerable extent on economic factors; so has its policy about deportation of illegal or indigent immigrants. It is important, therefore, to examine the part that those of other origins than British or French have played and play now in Canada's economic structure.

Before the era of mass migration at the end of the nineteenth century, those immigrants belonging to the other ethnic groups who came as individuals were hard to characterize occupationally. Adventurers, sailors, soldiers, farmers, fishermen, traders, merchants, of noble or humble rank, they came to take advantage of economic expansion in New France or in British North America, or to avoid economic or political hardships in the homeland. Some, like many of those who came later, had no intention of staying: they intended to get rich and return home. But again, like many of those who came later, they sometimes ended up living out their days in the new land.

Those who became farmers, such as the Mennonites of the Waterloo area of Ontario, or who combined farming with fishing or lumbering, such as the Lunenburg Germans, established the most permanent settlements. The ethnic groups that entered agriculture early are still more numerous in that occupation than would be expected from their representation in the population as a whole. They settled on choice agricultural land, and their ways of life, including their religious beliefs, were appealing enough to keep a substantial portion of succeeding generations on the farms. The Dutch and German Mennonites in both eastern and western Canada provide examples.

There is little to indicate that in the eighteenth and nineteenth centuries those of other than British or French origin constituted a low economic or income stratum. Some individuals among them ranked in the upper levels, and some of the rural group settlements earned a reputation for outstanding prosperity. There was no crystallized social structure for those belonging to the other ethnic groups to enter at the bottom; they entered a fluid situation, and the place they found for themselves depended largely on their skills, attitudes, and ambitions.

BEFORE WORLD WAR I

During the mass influx of immigrants before 1914, the northern Europeans who came to the Prairies either directly or by way of the United States established themselves after initial hardships as prosperous farmers and merchants. Germans and Scandinavians were usually accepted by their neighbours of British origin as literate, skilled, hard-working, and clean. They were thus able to work with and for those neighbours as equals. The eastern and central Europeans fared less well. They were settled, partly by their own choice, on inferior agricultural land;[1] their experience as peasants and migrant labourers did not prepare them for North American agriculture; they brought little capital with them; they were hampered by discrimination from those of British and northern European origin and from some of their former neighbours in their homelands who had brought old quarrels with them to the new country. They had a lowly entrance status, which affected their economic and social future. So did the Asians who became farmers, farm labourers, miners, or lumber workers in British Columbia.

A Ukrainian priest's evaluation of his people's abilities, recorded in 1897 after a tour of Ukrainian settlements in western Canada, was harsh:

> Our individual with his Galician upbringing is at present not adapted for work in America. He is in no position to compete with workers of other nationalities. Lifelong bondage and oppression have made a slave out of him, slothful and unconcerned. Life on the fief in Galicia demoralized him, and his physical weakness makes him incompetent for the kind of work demanded in America. He lacks the necessities of life, but he also lacks the qualities possessed by American workers of other ethnic groups, which are essential for earning money to provide those necessities.[2]

The new arrivals who went to the construction, lumbering, and mining camps strung across the north of Canada in the years before World War I were also sifted and sorted according to their ethnicity. Bradwin described the camps as consisting of the "whites" and the "foreigners":

> Among the whites are included always the Canadian-born, both French-speaking and English-speaking, as well as the new arrivals from the British Isles, and Americans from different states of the Union, engaged on the work. . . . Included with the whites are usually the Scandinavians also, and sometimes the Finns. . . .
> To the white-man falls most of the positions which connote a "stripe" of some kind, officials in one capacity or another – walking-bosses, accountants, inspectors, the various camp foremen, cache-keepers, as

well as clerks who perform the more routine work of checkers and timekeepers. This class also includes the cooks and helpers in the cookery, the tote-teamsters on the hauls, the drivers of scrapers and dump wagons in the mud cuts and on the fills. The white-man, too, does much of the rock work, where more than ordinary skill and practice in the use of powder are essential for effective blasting. . . .

. . . The name foreigner, applied to navvies, is an epithet not necessarily implying a slur at nationality. It is a generic term, used by the supercilious among the English-speaking workers and commonly applied to those campmen, of whatever extraction, who stolidly engage in the mucking and heavier tasks.[3]

Among the "foreigners" in the camps, Slavs predominated: eastern Slavs, especially Ukrainians, western Slavs from Poland and Czechoslovakia, and southern Slavs, including Serbs, Croatians, and others. Hungarians, Bulgarians, and a few Macedonians were found mixed with the Slavs. Italians were also numerous in the camps. There were a few Turks, Syrians, Armenians, and Jews; members of the last three groups commonly engaged not in construction, logging, or mining but in peddling, shopkeeping, and small trading enterprises. The Chinese and the Sikhs were virtually absent from the camps because of prejudice against Asians or "Orientals": the Chinese, in spite of the part they had played in building the Canadian Pacific Railway, were excluded from jobs in construction of the later transcontinental lines.

By 1911 over 57 per cent of all mine workers were immigrants; in Alberta the percentage was 88 and in British Columbia 84.[4] Some were experienced miners; others took work in the mines because, lacking knowledge of English and having only farming experience, they could find no other jobs. A government inquiry in 1918 found that in Alberta 90.5 per cent of mine workers were immigrants. In the Crow's Nest Pass area, 34 per cent were British immigrants, 1 per cent American, 23 per cent Slovak, 7 per cent French and Belgian, 14.5 per cent Italian, 2 per cent Russian, and 8.5 per cent "other European." In other areas for which figures were given, the ethnic mix was similar.[5] Other Europeans represented among Alberta coal miners at various times included Lithuanians, Hungarians, and Ukrainians; there were also Chinese and Japanese miners.

The work in construction and in mining was hard and dangerous. It had been said of the Chinese who worked on the CPR that for every foot of railroad through the Fraser canyon a Chinese worker died, and while this is an exaggeration, more than four Chinese did die for every mile, from explosions, exposure, and malnutrition.[6] White immigrants, though coddled compared to the Chinese, were also exposed to disease and disaster:

The proportion of Croatians killed in industrial accidents was no higher than for other immigrant groups, but their numbers added to the high mortality rate incurred in the building of Canada. The injuries and fatalities in the mines of the Far West reveal similar hazards to life and limb. Among minor incidents reported in the mining districts of British Columbia in 1913 were two involving Croats, the first working at the Granby mine in Phoenix and the second at the Mother Lode mine at Greenwood. One B. Spelac, a mucker, was injured about the shoulders after being struck by a motor, and another, Matt Zellinich, was similarly injured by falling rock in a chute. Two others at the Britannia mines on Howe Sound were less fortunate. Emil Siukovich was instantly killed in 1915 when he drilled into a hole packed with dynamite that had not fired, and John Pradovich was killed when his head was crushed by falling rock. And at the Extension Mine near Ladysmith in 1915, another four Croats were fatally injured: Juraj Berdik, "Bill" Keseric, Janko Bulic, and Loje Jurkas. The Alberta Mines reports reveal the same toll on human lives in the coal mines of the Rocky Mountain range from the Crowsnest coalfields in the south to the Coal Branch mines east of Jasper in the north. Every year at least twenty names of European immigrants would be added to the list of fatalities, and in some years bumps and explosions such as the one at Hillcrest in 1914 claimed hundreds of miners' lives.[7]

Though the wages were low and the conditions were harsh in the camps and the mines, for some immigrants they were better than wages and conditions at home. Hence they were at times accepted with less protest than the trade unions and concerned individuals considered natural or desirable. They were accepted especially by those who regarded themselves as sojourners rather than settlers.[8]

Nonetheless, the men resorted to two types of protest. One was leaving a job without notice when it was rumoured that better wages or conditions existed elsewhere, a practice that contributed little to the immigrants' reputation among employers. When workers were organized as work gangs under natural leaders (as happened, for example, among the Croats), a considerable part of the work force could disappear overnight. A second, often violent, form of protest was the strike. These occurred from time to time in mining communities and in railway construction camps. In the West the CPR strike of 1903, the Canadian Northern Railway strike of 1912, the Rossland hardrock miners' strike of 1901, the Lethbridge coal miners strike of 1906, and the miners' strike in the Rocky Mountain region in 1911 were among those occurring in industries where southern and eastern Europeans were important constituents of the labour force. Among the most bitter in central Canada were the six strikes that took place between 1902 and 1912 among freight handlers in Fort William and Port Arthur, in which the company hired strikebreakers and special police to supplement the local police. Italians, Greeks, Finns, and immigrants from the Austro-Hungarian and Russian empires were involved, as well as British immigrants; the Italians and Greeks were allegedly the most prone to violence.[9]

Those who went to the camps in some instances did so to obtain a stake that would enable them to buy or to improve a farm. Some, however, did not achieve their aim, and either returned home or prolonged their seasonal stays in the cities and towns into permanent residence, along with campmen who had had no agricultural ambitions. There they joined other immigrants who had gone directly to urban centres. Others went to the camps as migrant workers, travelling regularly to North America in search of work rather than to nearby European countries. When they could not afford to return home during the slack season, they, too, went to the urban centres.

In the cities as in the camps, the immigrants from the British Isles were, like the native-born Canadians, most able to enter the higher-ranking occupations, although there were also substantial numbers of working-class British immigrant men in labouring jobs and women in domestic service. Immigrants from northern and western Europe ranked below the British but could win respected positions as artisans and businessmen and as domestics. Immigrants from southern, eastern, and central Europe ranked lower, and Asians lowest of all. Many immigrants had a keen awareness of discrimination and were influenced by it to enter self-employment, as peddlers and later shopkeepers and traders. Syrians, Armenians, Greeks, and Jews were notable for following this course.

In the late nineteenth and early twentieth centuries peddling was for some immigrants the means of gaining an economic foothold in the new country. It was work with which some of them were familiar before migration; it did not involve being hired by someone who had ethnic prejudices or who sought to exploit workers ignorant of Canadian conditions; it required little capital and little literacy; it enabled Jews to observe the Sabbath. Funds and experience gained in peddling could be used to start a small shop or factory, and some peddlers quickly made the transition to stationary independent businesses.

Peddling was sometimes intimately linked with the boarding house, an important immigrant institution. Among Syrians, for example, Abu-Laban found:

> As far back as the mid-1880s, Ameen Lufti, a Syrian wholesaler in Montreal, supplied peddlers not only with goods, but also with accommodation in a rented house, often without charge. Newcomers from Syria were given accommodation while being initiated into the trade. Men roomed with men and women with women, "except in the case of a married couple and their young children who were allotted special accommodation." The arrangement proved to be profitable for all concerned. Hence, it was expanded to the point where "as many as two score or more were living under the same roof." According to knowledgeable respondents, this type of accommodation was also developed in Toronto and it continued well into the second decade of the twentieth century.

The rooming house accommodation arrangement was significant in that it provided structural and community support for a specific occupation. It also nourished an associational need and created a community feeling among Syrian peddlers, both as an ethnic group and an occupational group. Syrian women played a vital role in the success of this type of accommodation, cleaning the premises and looking after the clothing and food needs of the boarders. Thus peddling could, and at least for some, did become almost a total institution, meeting economic as well as social needs.[10]

For Ukrainians,

> The boarding house in Edmonton or Vegreville, owned by a Ukrainian, operated by his Ukrainian wife and specializing in (crowded) accommodation for single men recently arrived from the Ukraine or the farm may have been the first example of independent Ukrainian business in Alberta. A man with disposable capital need not work as a coolie for richer men; he could invest in a business and make a profit from servicing a captive clientele: his fellow Ukrainians. Few others would patronize him but the Ukrainians would be glad of a chance to do business with somebody in their own language and in the style to which both were accustomed.[11]

The boarding house played the same role for Italians, Hungarians, Poles, Macedonians, and many others. It offered an occupation within a quasi-familial setting for women and provided young men, who predominated among the immigrants of the time, with shelter, food of familiar kinds, social ties, and social controls.

The boarding house could also be considered prototypal of ethnic businesses serving ethnic clienteles. Such businesses developed in all or most ethnic groups, depending on the distinctiveness of the group's wants. They included travel agencies, newspapers, grocery stores, restaurants, cafés, shops selling religious objects, and many other enterprises. Those who began the businesses were frequently among the first immigrants to rise to middle-class status.

Jews were commonly impoverished when they arrived, but they were more prepared for urban living and for certain types of industrial employment than most immigrants. A large proportion had been tradesmen in Europe; others had followed various commercial pursuits, and a few had been in professions or in clerical work. In the garment industry, they quickly moved from being operatives into contracting and thence manufacturing in Montreal, Toronto, and Hamilton and, on a smaller scale, in Winnipeg and Vancouver. In some small businesses and some professions they developed clienteles among Slavic immigrants, with whom they had a common language; they had, however, to endure from the same Slavic immigrants an anti-Semitism based on old-country experiences and old-country myths.[12]

Italians, who also moved chiefly into the cities, gravitated to labouring jobs, especially in construction, to cobbling, barbering, street-vending, and the keeping of small fruit and vegetable and grocery stores. The labour demands of such industries as the railways, mines, and steel mills encouraged Italians and other Europeans scorned by the agriculture-oriented immigration policies to flock to Canada, either from the United States or from Europe. They often saw themselves as sojourners; hence, they were slow to learn English, unlikely to acquire skills or press for advancement, and tolerant of (or resigned to) exploitation. A few of their number rose to positions of wealth and influence through their ability to supply labour to Canadian employers. One of the most noted of these intermediaries was Antonio Cordasco, who became Montreal's largest employment agent because he held exclusive hiring rights for Italian labour for the CPR. In January, 1904, Cordasco was honoured by a parade of more than 2,000 men who presented him with a crown and proclaimed him King of the Workers. But he earned the enmity of rivals, including his counterpart with the Grand Trunk Railway, and of the Italian Immigrant Aid Society, and when later in 1904 he was condemned by the Royal Commission to Inquire into the Immigration of Italian Workers to Montreal and Alleged Fraudulent Practices of Employment Agencies, he lost much of his prestige and power. He later recouped some of his loss as a banker.[13]

Other groups not so predominantly urban in some instances established beachheads in certain industries in such cities as Montreal and Toronto. In the latter city, for example, there were in 1905 some fifty tailors in a Finnish co-operative tailors' shop.[14] Such a concentration went far toward making a certain trade an ethnic specialty, in which it was fairly easy for members of the group to find employment and toward which members of the larger community tended to look for goods or services.

Asians by the turn of the century had entered the building trades and secondary manufacturing on the West Coast. The Chinese who had been left without jobs or resources on the completion of the railway played an important part in coal mining and market gardening. Forced by discrimination on the part of unions in a society where women were in short supply, many engaged in what elsewhere would be considered women's work: laundry, restaurants, food-processing, tailoring, and domestic work. They were now well established in small businesses in Victoria and Vancouver, as well as in scattered communities elsewhere. Laundries were the pioneer enterprises in Toronto and Montreal; restaurants, serving Western-style food, were also numerous, in spite of attempts to exclude the Chinese from the restaurant business by law. Import-export businesses began early and throve. Credit associations, based on kinship or locality, were effective means for the Chinese to start or expand a business, since they made sizable amounts of capital available to aspiring entrepreneurs.

WORLD WAR I AND THE INTER-WAR PERIOD

Having entered Canada early and met with little discrimination from the British, Germans by the early twentieth century were well established in most areas of Canadian society. But the war was disastrous for some Germans who had become prosperous businessmen. For example, Gustav Constantin Alvo von Alvensleben, who arrived in Vancouver in 1904 after resigning his commission in the German army and from 1905 on had been an important figure in real estate, was absent from Canada at the beginning of the war and never returned; his many companies either collapsed or were confiscated as enemy property.[15] But less prominent "enemy aliens," though they were frequently dismissed from their jobs early in the war, found themselves courted by employers and even constrained to accept work when the demand for labour mounted. By 1916 many internees were released to take jobs.

For many other Canadians of all origins, the war was a time either of economic prosperity in agriculture or of migration to urban communities to take advantage of industrial development. The war had been preceded by two years of recession, but by 1915 things turned around. In the wheat-growing areas, soaring prices enabled farmers to pay off most of their debts, buy new and better farm implements, buy new land, and put money in the bank. Farm labourers used high wages to become landowners.

Immigrant farmers may have fared better than their English-Canadian neighbours.[16] The years 1918-19 for Ukrainian Canadians were the most prosperous until World War II, and by the mid-1920's Polish immigrants owned nearly 4,000 farms worth over $27 million with total yearly incomes of nearly $7 million.[17] The prosperity of some of the European settlers was due in part to their small operations that used only family labour and to their large families, all of whom from an early age shared in the work of the farm. The children also frequently left school earlier than children of British or "old Canadian" parents.[18] Their sons often did not enlist, and few of them were conscripted. Indeed, those of "enemy alien" origins were prohibited from enlisting: for example, Japanese were not allowed to enlist in British Columbia and had to go to Alberta to join up.

In the cities, immigrants prospered less. While jobs were plentiful, in contrast to high unemployment at the outbreak of the war, wages did not keep pace with inflation, and the spectre of post-war depression was always present. In western cities in particular, the immigrant workers of other than British origin protested vigorously against conditions. Conscription, from which they were not exempted as farm workers were, became the focus for much of their activity.[19] In some communities they joined with British militants and radicals in their protests; in others – Timmins, Ontario, for example – a split developed between the Ukrainians and Finns on the one hand and the British, who suspected their fellow workers of disloyalty, on the other.[20]

By the 1920's the younger children in rural immigrant families were able to complete high school and even in some cases to go beyond. Many became teachers in rural schools serving their ethnic group:

> When Ukrainian-Canadians talk about themselves in the professions, they like to refer to the lawyers, doctors, dentists and academicians among them. But the fact is that the overwhelming majority of Ukrainian-Canadians educated beyond high school were people who had decided to become teachers. In 1941, as in 1961, teachers made up the

largest category of "professionals" in the Dominion census (clergymen were second). One thousand, two hundred and thirteen teachers and two hundred and two public service workers. The disparity in numbers reflects not so much that Ukrainian-Canadians of that generation were uniformly pedagogical zealots or that school-teaching delivered rewards that a post-office job didn't, but that work in the public service (not to mention high status jobs in the private sector) "was considered a privilege reserved for certain nationalities and the access to which for Ukrainians was only accidental." But there was no objection to Ukrainian-Canadians holding a teaching job in a one-room rural school among Ukrainian-Canadian farm families – in 1940 there were exactly two teachers of Ukrainian origin in the Edmonton Public School system – and so inevitably most educated Ukrainian-Canadians became teachers.[21]

After the war, immigration policy continued to favour farmers and farm workers, but it became increasingly difficult for newcomers to establish themselves in agriculture. The success of the earlier arrivals of other ethnic origins had bred resentment among those of British origin: the ethnic immigrants were thought to have profiteered while loyal Canadians were in the army. Land was no longer free or cheap: the available homesteads were in the Peace River district of Alberta.[22] Hence, male immigrants worked as farm labourers, hoping to save enough money to buy land, or took jobs on railroads, in factories, mines, lumber camps, and road-building and construction, or established businesses serving either the community at large, immigrants from the same general area, or their ethnic fellows. Single women, who entered under schemes for admitting domestics, worked as household servants.

Farm labourers later told of working long hours, of being given little food and poor accommodation, of being laid off or forced to work for room and board only in the winter months, and, above all, of being cheated out of their earnings. Sometimes an employer refused to pay the wages that had been agreed upon; sometimes he would borrow from his farm hand and not return the money; sometimes he would allege theft and have the labourer pursued by the police. Although unfamiliarity with English and with Canadian ways played a part in the victimization, such exploitation frequently came from a member of one's own ethnic group, and it was a member of a different group who showed kindness. A Pole who went to western Canada in 1928, for example, was defrauded by more than one Pole but befriended by a Chinese restaurant owner.[23]

Factory workers also had tales of being cheated out of their pay and of having to take dangerous and dirty jobs in heavy industry. Many employers were only willing to hire immigrants for work that the Canadian-born refused. When workers were blinded or maimed as a result of accidents on the job, there was little compensation, and they were thrown back on their ethnic communities for assistance.

Those who protested against exploitation were regarded as dangerous revolutionaries. The association in the public mind of non-British immigrant workers with radicalism had been exacerbated by the opposition of labour militants to conscription during the war and by the Russian Revolution and the Winnipeg General Strike. However, the 1920's were a more prosperous time for labourers, including immigrant labourers, than the previous two decades had been.

Those who had been peddlers in the 1890's and early 1900's had entered other occupations by the 1920's. Abu-Laban suggests three reasons for the decline of peddling: restriction of the immigration of Asians, including those from the Middle East; the fact that those who became peddlers had regarded it as a temporary occupation; and the supplanting of peddling by the mail-order and telephone-order business.[24] Shopkeeping, manufacturing, and, for those (chiefly in the second generation) who had been able to secure advanced education, medicine and law were among favoured occupations.

Some people who had previously worked for others were able to become self-employed. In the 1920's Sikhs in British Columbia were still developing the sale of scrap wood for fuel into an occupational niche. Requiring little capital or skill, it had many of the same advantages as peddling. The fuel business was not to disappear until the late 1950's.

By 1931 the Great Depression was well under way. In addition to cutting off immigration, it dampened the movement out of agriculture: by census criteria the Canadian population was little more urban in 1941 than it had been in 1931. It was the rural farm population (as against the rural non-farm population) that declined during the 1930's; it has continued to decline during each succeeding intercensal period, as Canada has become increasingly industrial.[25]

In the West, the years of depression were also years of drought and other agricultural disasters. Debts cheerfully assumed in the preceding prosperous years became crushing. Mortgages were foreclosed; machinery was repossessed; land was abandoned; even food and clothing were often lacking. Relief supplies were sent from eastern and central Canada, but since the depression afflicted those areas as well as the West, the poor quality of these relief efforts stoked regional resentments among people too preoccupied with their own problems to acknowledge those of others. It was also charged that the authorities in the rural municipalities and small towns, overwhelmingly British and Scandinavian in origin, took the choicest of the relief supplies for themselves and their friends.

Two factors enabled farmers of some ethnic groups to survive: diversified agriculture and mutual aid. Supplementing grain, which could no longer be called a cash crop, with produce from a garden carefully tended by a Polish, Ukrainian, or Romanian farm wife and by game shot by her husband fended off starvation. Mutual aid embodied in the organization of co-operatives and credit unions even led some westerners later to look back on the depression years nostalgically, since never before or after were people so close or so helpful.

For new arrivals who had not yet been able to establish themselves on farms or who had had labouring jobs in the camps and the cities, the depression was shattering. Even the most menial and hardest work was scarce; when it was available, it was given to Canadian citizens or Canadian residents of British stock who once would have scorned it, rather than to immigrants or Canadians of other ethnic origins. James Gray reminisced:

> In my search for employment I was free to range over the whole of commercial Winnipeg and nobody denied me a job from any ulterior motive. This did not hold true for the Ukrainians, Poles, and Jews. For them, Winnipeg was far from being a city of 250,000 in which they too were free to search for work. As much as two-thirds of it was barred and bolted against them.
>
> None of the city's chartered banks, trust companies, or insurance companies would knowingly hire a Jew, and anyone with a Ukrainian or Polish name had almost no chance of employment except rough manual labour. The oil companies, banks, mortgage companies, financial and stock brokers, and most retail and mercantile companies except the Hudson's Bay Company discriminated against all non-Anglo-Saxons. For the young Ukrainians and Poles, there was a possible solution if they could beat the accent handicap. They could change their names. So they changed their names, sometimes formally and legally, but mostly informally and casually. Caroline Czarnecki overnight became Connie Kingston, Mike Drazenovick became Martin Drake, and Steve Dziatkewich became Edward Dawson. But, for the Jews, a name change was not enough. It was not even enough to leave the synagogue, as did many of the young Jews who became Communist converts. In the minds of anti-Semitic Winnipeggers, there was no way in which a Jew could escape from Judaism. In plain truth, the unhappiest Jew in town would have been one who managed to sneak into a job in any of the Anglo-Saxon companies.

Gray described some of the expedients by which members of different ethnic groups in Winnipeg tried to survive:

> . . . racial discrimination was so much a fact of life that it drove the minorities into economic ghettoes. Jews tried to live off the trade of other Jews; and Ukrainians, Poles, and Germans tried to live off other Ukrainians, Poles, and Germans. This drive to survive in a prejudice-ridden community produced the rash of small industry and of bootstrap manufacturing that developed in Winnipeg. . . .
>
> Small-scale garment factories, glove factories, shoe factories, printing plants, and dress plants proliferated. Long-empty warehouse space in the old wholesale district began to fill up with Jews trying to scratch a living in manufacturing. The North End filled up with home-based contractors. When a Ukrainian went into the construction business, he

67

trailed a small army of other Ukrainians behind him – a Ukrainian con-
crete-mixer, a Ukrainian plumber, a Ukrainian carpenter, a Ukrainian
painter, a Ukrainian plasterer. It was the same with the Germans. The
Jews tended more towards commercial enterprises and manufacturing.[26]

Those who could not find work were often ineligible for welfare because of
residential restrictions; in any event, some men feared to ask for aid for fear
of being deported. Many of the indigent and the radical were deported.
Those who had left families in their homelands could no longer send remittances, nor could they hope to bring their wives and children to Canada.
Some returned home, others lacked the fare to do so; some committed sui-
cide.[27] For some the federal relief camps, which paid twenty cents a day or
five dollars a month, offered a recourse. Others roamed from town to town,
on foot or on the top of trains: a Hungarian newspaper editor claimed in
1933 that it was not unusual to find twenty or thirty Hungarians on top of a
freight car, and that on some days as many as three Hungarians died of falls
from the trains.[28]

In some instances misery led the immigrants to organize into labour unions
and to strike. The strike of workers at Noranda mines in 1934, for example,
was known as the foreigners' strike. It resulted in a fall in the percentage of
foreign-born workers employed in the mine from 50 to 25 per cent of the
work force:

> The (foreign-born) naturalized Canadian citizens were 354 in number
> before the strike, now they were only 195.
> Finally, with respect to foreigners who had not obtained Canadian
> citizenship, the newspaper [the *Rouyn Noranda Press*] gave the following
> information, furnished by the general manager of the mine, H.L. Ros-
> coe: Yugoslavs were 149 before the strike, 43 after; Czechoslovaks
> went from 39 to 17; Ukrainians, Poles, and Russians from 91 to 54;
> Austrians from 10 to 4; Serbs from 5 to 2; Finns from 35 to 9; Swedes
> from 15 to 7. There was little change with respect to the relatively small
> number of Hungarians, Romanians, Bulgars, Italians, Norwegians,
> Danes, Montenegrins, Belgians, Swiss, Germans, French and Dutch.[29]

Immigrant workers desperate for employment also on occasion ran the
risk of acting as strikebreakers. A Polish woman reminisced about her
sponsor:

> I can't remember what year it was that there was a strike at the
> factory in Kitchener where Mr. M. worked. The walkout was a real gold
> mine for Mr. M., because he knew how to operate nine machines. He
> would go to work for sixteen hours a day. One morning on his way there
> somebody jumped him and hit him on the back of the head with a piece
> of metal. He was found lying in a pool of blood.[30]

The immigrants joined with other unemployed in protest marches and treks to provincial capitals and to Ottawa, including the On-to-Ottawa Trek of 1935 that started in Vancouver and was broken up by the RCMP in Regina. Finnish men and women were prominent in demonstrations in Sudbury and other northern Ontario cities. Elsewhere, even when the ostensible leaders were British radicals, there were frequently people of other backgrounds – Finns, Ukrainians, Hungarians, Croats – who worked behind the scenes to avoid the risk of deportation.

In towns and cities, as in farming areas, some of the ethnic groups from southern, eastern, and central Europe weathered the depression better than their neighbours. Since many of their members had arrived recently, they were accustomed to meeting hardship with frugality. In addition, they were unconcerned about Canadian symbols of social status: since the symbols were unlike those to which they were accustomed, they did not recognize them and saw Canadian society as classless. They were thus free to practise economies that older Canadians, of British and northern European origin, could not bear, and were well situated to take advantage of the prosperity and expansion of the 1940's.

WORLD WAR II AND THE POST-WAR YEARS

The outbreak of World War II, like the outbreak of the Great War, led to economic hardship for those who were considered to be enemy aliens. Prominent entrepreneurs among Italian Canadians were interned; Italian working-men found that their mates refused to work with them; in the Timmins area, Italians with responsible positions in the mines were replaced by "Canadians" and put on pick-and-shovel duty. Germans fared better than Italians because they were from northern Europe and because fewer of them were recent immigrants.

As the war continued, labour shortages tended to lessen discrimination in the labour market, and the conflict brought high prices for farm produce and rapid industrial expansion. Like other Canadians, those belonging to the other ethnic groups profited from the prosperity, and their occupational distribution moved toward conformity with the distribution of the total population.

One means of economic advance that was used increasingly was the ethnic credit union. Often sponsored by churches, the credit unions made financing available for ventures that banks and other conservative institutions would not consider. Ukrainians, accustomed to institutions resembling credit unions in the Ukraine, began establishing credit unions in Canada in 1939, and by the 1970's counted more than forty that were avowedly Ukrainian and twenty more in which Ukrainians were prominent, the largest being the Ukrainian Credit Union of Toronto. The Polish St. Stanislaus and St. Casimir Credit Union in the mid-1970's had 11,583 members, assets of $22 million, and its own monthly publication.[31] Among the ethnic groups, large and small, that have formed credit unions are the Byelorussians, Croats, Danes, Dutch, Estonians, Germans, Hungarians, Japanese, Lithuanians, Poles, and Slovenes.

69

TABLE 5

**Percentage Foreign Born, by Major Ethnic Groups
for Canada, 1921–1971[1]**

Ethnic Group	1921	1931	1941	1951	1961	1971
British Isles	25.9	25.1	20.2	16.1	14.4	12.4
French	3.0	2.6	2.2	1.6	1.6	1.8
Other European	44.2	44.7	36.2	33.7	37.1	64.7
Austrian, n.o.s.	47.9	46.3	39.5	35.9	41.0	37.6[3]
Czech and Slovak	56.0	72.2	61.4	55.5	45.9	49.1[3]
Finnish	63.0	71.8	59.9	50.1	48.9	40.9[3]
German	28.3	30.5	24.2	20.9	27.4	24.6
Hungarian	50.0	72.2	58.0	51.5	56.9	47.8
Italian	57.0	46.9	38.5	41.0	58.9	54.2
Jewish	59.7	56.2	49.0	43.0	37.8	37.2
Netherlands	17.2	20.1	16.0	24.9	36.2	35.4
Polish	48.2	53.0	42.1	44.4	39.9	33.3
Russian	50.4	46.0	38.2	33.7	27.1	22.9
Scandinavian	62.4	56.4	43.7	33.8	27.1	22.0
Ukrainian	45.8	43.0	34.8	30.4	23.3	18.3
Other	—[2]	60.0	50.3	55.7	57.5	55.9
Asiatic	86.8	71.2	58.5	47.7	46.0	61.1
Chinese	92.5	88.4	80.2	69.4	60.5	62.4[3]
Japanese	72.7	51.5	39.0	27.3	21.8	24.0[3]
Other	—[2]	48.2	40.1	33.4	41.9	69.6[3]
Other and Not Stated	22.6	4.0	3.0	5.3	4.8	12.8

1. Exclusive of Newfoundland in censuses prior to 1951.
2. Included with "Other and Not Stated."
3. Estimates based on Public Use Sample Tape data do not include Prince Edward Island or the Yukon and Northwest Territories.
SOURCE: Warren E. Kalbach and Wayne W. McVey, *The Demographic Bases of Canadian Society*, second ed. (Toronto: McGraw-Hill Ryerson, 1971), p. 202.

By 1961, the occupational shifts out of agriculture and out of primary and unskilled occupations were marked. Only Italians were heavily concentrated in primary and unskilled occupations. Asians and Jews had begun to figure largely in professional and financial occupations.

The concentration of Italians in primary and unskilled occupations is related to the massive influx of Italians in the 1950's. Throughout the decade they ranked either first or second to the British in numbers of arrivals, except for the 1951-54 period, when they were exceeded by those of German ethnic origin. Having low levels of education and few skills, many of the Italian men became labourers in construction and many of the women became garment workers and domestics. Thus they bulked large in entrance-status occupations, through which earlier immigrant groups had passed at varying speeds. The trowel trades in construction were an ethnic specialty of Italians, for which they were thought to have a particular affinity. Unskilled construction work was in general an immigrant occupation, since it did not make linguistic demands or require much skill. It was a "stepping stone," [32] which enabled some to acquire skills and to become subcontractors, contractors, and speculative builders.

The manner in which construction brought Italian workers into association with other ethnic groups is illustrated by a study on the division of labour in the construction industry on the island of Montreal in the 1960's. The Italians ranked with the Anglo-Saxons, French Canadians, and Jews as leading participants in construction. But while the Anglo-Saxons and French Canadians were found among those who carried out the construction, those who designed and supervised it, those who conceived of and planned the projects and arranged the financing, and those who provided the funds, the Italians were found only among those who carried out the construction and among the speculative builders, where they served primarily the Italian market.[33] By the 1980's, however, they had expanded into finance in the Montreal area: there was a trust company entirely owned and managed by Italian Canadians.

During the 1950's there was little immigration from Asia. The advance of Asian ethnic groups into professional and financial occupations thus was comprised mainly of Canadian-born Asians, rising through education acquired in the public schools.

A number of the other groups, such as the Polish and the Ukrainian, increased their representation in clerical and professional occupations in the 1950's, a decade in which they had received few immigrants, although they did not reach the same proportion in those occupations as the total Canadian population. However, during that period the prestige of clerical and professional occupations declined.[34]

During the 1960's the trend toward more even distribution of various ethnic groups throughout the occupational and income structures continued. Those of British origin by 1971 ranked third, behind the Jewish and Asian. To some degree this was a statistical artefact, related to such factors as the age composition and concentration in high-income areas of the different groups; but there is little doubt that a real change in occupational opportunities, in the direction of greater equality, was occurring.

The rise in occupational status of Asians occurred during the heavy immigration following the introduction of the nine-point system in 1967: those of Chinese origin increased from 58,000 to 119,000, those of Japanese origin from 29,000 to 37,000, and those of other Asian origins from 34,000 to 129,000 between 1961 and 1971. The very high average educational level of the Asian immigrants is reflected in their occupational status: in 1971 the

TABLE 6

Occupational Status Index for Ethnic Origin Groups in Canada, 1961 and 1971

Ethnic Origin	1961	1971	Change
Jewish	2.42	1.92	-0.50
British	1.28	1.15	-0.13
Scandinavian	0.91	0.87	-0.04
Asiatic	0.90	1.19	0.29
German	0.85	0.87	0.02
Polish	0.83	0.86	0.06
Dutch	0.82	0.84	0.02
Other European	0.80	0.79	0.01
French	0.79	0.89	0.10
Ukrainian	0.78	0.84	0.06
Italian	0.47	0.57	0.10
Native Peoples	0.15	0.41	0.26

SOURCE: Jeffrey G. Reitz, *The Survival of Ethnic Groups* (Toronto: McGraw-Hill Ryerson, 1980), p. 132; column on change added.

percentage of Chinese and Japanese post-war immigrants with some university training or a university degree was higher than the percentage for any other major ethnic origin category except the French.[35] Nonetheless, it is still possible, as has frequently been alleged, that Asian immigrants experience difficulty in obtaining employment commensurate with their training and experience. To some extent this may be because, in order to get a relatively high return quickly, they, like other immigrants, accept jobs that prove to be dead ends. But difficulty in having their credentials accepted at full value and discrimination are other factors.

Since 1945, Canadians have increasingly introduced legislation with which to fight many forms of discrimination, almost all of which have economic implications. Provincially, human rights codes, equal pay acts, fair employment practices acts, and fair accommodation practices acts proliferated; federally, the Canadian Bill of Rights of 1960 and the Canadian Charter of Rights and Freedoms of 1982 gave support against discrimination. Legislation has, however, not eliminated discriminatory behaviour, and groups have varied in their willingness to resort to legislation to fight against discrimination.

Discrimination is invariably laid at the door of the white Canadians of British origin. That members of the other ethnic groups shared in anti-Semitism or in discrimination against blacks and Asians, or brought with them from Europe age-old rivalries and antagonisms, is quickly forgotten. Nor is the possibility entertained that apparent discrimination may on some occasions be related to objective differences in qualifications. The hard fact remains that because of the dominant position of white Canadians of British origin, they have most frequently been the employers of labour and the leaders of professional associations with control over job opportunities.

To some degree an ethnic group may be able to raise its occupational status if its members gravitate to self-employment to avoid discrimination. Owning a small business, serving either one's ethnic community or the community at large, puts one in a lofty occupational category without necessarily bringing with it a high income or middle- or upper-class lifestyle. Driver-owned taxis, owner-operated dump trucks or long-haul trucks – all small businesses among members of the visible minorities in the late 1970's – need not bring high financial returns and are vulnerable to economic recessions. The owners, however, are frequently flexible enough to start again after encountering failure.

WOMEN IN THE LABOUR FORCE

The statistics presented by most researchers are based on male workers. However, such figures are no longer adequate. The participation of women in the work force has increased markedly in recent years. Before World War I the participation rate for women was under 20 per cent; by 1975 it was 41 per cent. The change was most dramatic among married women: in 1931 only 3.5 per cent of married women were in the labour force, but in 1981 the percentage was 48.9.[36] Immigrant women are more likely to be in the labour force than Canadian-born women; they also engage in paid labour that sometimes escapes official enumeration, such as cleaning and baby-sitting. As a result, the customary measures of occupational distribution by ethnic group, which were based on the male labour force, are increasingly imperfect. The available histories of ethnic groups offer little corrective: most of them, however warmly they pay tribute to women's contribution to the family or to the farm, or even to women's role in encouraging men to migrate or in informing men in the country of immigration about jobs they have heard of in letters from immigrant husbands, say little about women in the labour force.

Paid domestic labour has been a specialty of immigrant women throughout Canadian history. It requires skills that most women possess or readily acquire, makes few linguistic demands, and is almost always in short supply; further, it provides an opportunity, rarely available otherwise, to learn something of the life in Canadian homes. On the other hand, domestic service is an occupation of low prestige, usually of low pay, and open to exploitation. Illegal immigrants in domestic work are especially open to abuse, since if they question their working conditions or their pay they may be threatened with deportation.

During the early decades of the twentieth century, British, Scandinavian, and Finnish maids predominated. Lindström-Best stresses that in the period 1900 to 1940 Finnish women, who were regarded and regarded themselves as among the best domestic servants, chose their occupation because of the advantages it offered compared to such options as camp cook, laundress, rooming-house keeper, bootlegger, and prostitute.[37] Lysenko wrote of Ukrainian women:

> It was the custom for the young girls particularly to go into domestic service in the cities, where in the homes of established Canadian families they came into intimate contact with new ways of living, new social relationships, a new language – in short, a new world. And this world was all the more attractive to them as they compared its social amenities with the harsh, crude ways of life in their pioneering families on the farms. The fare of the settlers was of the plainest (although they might splurge on holidays) – boiled potatoes, dumplings, sour milk with little variety in diet, little to appeal to appetite or sight.
>
> In the city homes, the girls were introduced to a rich, abundant and varied fare. Many of the women for whom they worked took an interest in them, bought them clothing in the English fashion, taught them the language, ways of eating and behaving. . . . Some of the girls even married the sons of the family, and in a few years became almost completely assimilated.[38]

Later, an intention to enter domestic service frequently opened the door to immigration for women not otherwise admissible. Between 1947 and 1952 female displaced persons could come to Canada only as domestic contract workers, and in the 1950's and early 1960's West Indian and Greek women in restricted numbers could enter Canada as domestics.

Those who come as domestics or, once in Canada, find employment as domestics usually seek other work as quickly as possible, even breaking contracts to do so. Factory work in the needle trades or in food-processing, work in hospitals, and work in hotels and restaurants are among choices for the unskilled and little educated. The ethnicity of women in such employment, as well as in domestic labour, is a fairly accurate index of immigrant flows, or at least of the movement of working-class immigrants.

At higher occupational levels are women who have had formal education and professional training in their home country. Among post-war immigrants and refugees have been women who have prepared themselves for highly skilled occupations and professions, in some cases ones that few Canadian women have entered – for example, women dentists from the Baltic countries. They have had to conquer not only linguistic barriers, obstacles erected by professional associations, and discrimination against immigrants, but also discrimination on the part of prospective colleagues and clients against women. When they have managed to establish themselves they have helped to change Canadian notions of what constitutes men's and women's work.

When immigrant women work outside the home it has a favourable effect on family income. Recent arrivals have been able to achieve such goals as home ownership with remarkable speed, and have not been slow to purchase consumer goods, including status symbols. However, part of the family income is often sent home to relatives. In the past, villages in Europe and China depended largely on such remittances; now villages in many parts of the Third World do so.[39]

Where women are heads of households rather than secondary wage-earners, or when they live alone, they tend to be poor. This is true for members of all ethnic groups in the population. Even the group with the highest average income, educational level, and occupational status, the Jewish (which owes its statistical primacy to its age distribution and traditions of self-employment), has a sizable proportion of women with incomes below the current poverty lines as defined by government. For example, in Montreal in 1971 over one-third of the Jewish working poor and 70 per cent of the Jewish poor on welfare were women.[40]

ELITES

In the post-war period there has been growing attention to the top levels of the occupational structure, the elites or holders of power. Members of various ethnic groups have considered access to positions in the elites, and particularly to positions in the economic or corporate elite, to be of crucial importance. They have asserted that they were kept out of such positions, and until recently scholars have confirmed their assertion.

John Porter argued in 1965 that the myth of an ethnic mosaic was used by the elites, members of which were almost exclusively British in origin, to prevent those of other origins from gaining power and influence. Using data for 1951, he defined the economic elite as consisting of members of the boards of directors of 183 dominant corporations. He found them to be largely of British origin, with a small admixture of French - 6.7 per cent, whereas those of French origin were 31 per cent of the population - a very few Jews, and almost no others. Further, he minimized the role of the Jews, saying that they were "associated either with the liquor industry or two of the smaller dominant corporations," and not with banks, insurance companies, or larger corporations.[41] In other elites - labour, political, bureaucratic, and ideological - Porter found few members of the other ethnic groups, the Jews being less underrepresented than the rest.

Ten years after *The Vertical Mosaic* appeared, Wallace Clement compared data for 1972 with Porter's data for the corporate elite and the media elite. Clement constructed an index of representation by dividing the proportion of a given ethnic group in the elite into the proportion of that ethnic group in the total Canadian population. In the corporate elite, he found that the index of representation of those of British origin or, as he called them, "the Anglos," was still exactly what it had been in 1951, that is, 1.93. The French Canadians and the other ethnic groups (taken as a whole) had both made small gains. However, the Jewish group had vaulted into a position far ahead of the Anglos, constituting 4.1 per cent of the economic elite and 1.4 per cent of the population and thus having an index of representation of 2.93.[42]

It is worthwhile examining how Jews have won a place in the corporate elite. The first mass migration of Jews, from the 1880's to World War I, was of impoverished people – as poor as the eastern and central European peasants who went west, or the Italians who, like the Jews, went to Montreal and Toronto. But the Jews had skills adapted to urban living and soon started in trade and industry. Even before 1914 they had become notable as workers, manufacturers, wholesalers, and retailers in the garment industry in Montreal, Toronto, Hamilton, and Winnipeg. In the 1920's the Bronfman dynasty had begun its ascent to power through the family's activities in the liquor trade.[43]

Jews chose self-employment because they faced more direct and rigid discrimination than most other groups, which limited their access to higher education and to many professions; they chose new and high-risk occupations because these were where opportunities were open to them. They prospered, and their corporations by the 1960's, though not the largest in the country, still were extremely successful. Since then they have continued to prosper and have entered fields, such as finance, previously closed to them. They did not – could not – go to the private schools on which Porter and Clement laid stress as training grounds for the elite; on the whole, they used the public schools. They did not – could not – join the national upper-class men's clubs; instead, they built their own communal institutions, including exclusive clubs, such as the Montefiore Club in Montreal and the Primrose Club in Toronto. They built a parallel elite to that of the broader community, which is largely made up of persons of British origin. When, in the late 1960's and the 1970's, they had won elite positions, the exclusive private schools and clubs began to admit them and even to court them. They did not always yield to the courtship.

Individual members of European ethnic groups other than the Jewish have entered the corporate elite because they have achieved wealth and status before immigration to Canada or because they have been successful entrepreneurs in innovative and high-risk enterprises. On the whole, they have not faced the exclusion that the Jews have faced and hence have not had to build parallel structures. However, groups whose occupational status and income are high, and members of which appear either to have entered the corporate elite since 1972 or to be about to do so, include Asians. Early Asians faced discrimination both at entry and later; more recent arrivals have come with high educational levels and with capital and entrepreneurial skills and connections. Like the Jews, they have on occasion taken great business risks that have paid off. For example, South Asians and Chinese took part in the 1970's in explosive real estate development in Vancouver, Edmonton, and Calgary. It is not yet clear how high the barriers to membership in the general elites (or in high-status social circles) will be for them.

Porter's findings for the political, bureaucratic, and media elites in the early 1960's were not too different from his findings for the corporate elite, except for greater representation in them of people of French-Canadian ethnic origin. In the political elite in the period 1940 to 1960, those of other ethnic origins were only 3.2 per cent; in the bureaucratic elite in 1953 they were 2.5 per cent. Clement and Olsen calculated that from 1961 to 1973 they had increased their proportion to 7.6 in the political elite and in 1973 they had risen to 4.5 per cent of the bureaucratic elite.[44] In the political elite, Jews again had won most representation; Jews have held or at present hold such posts as Chief Justice of the Supreme Court (Bora Laskin), chief negotiator in trade talks with the United States (Simon Reisman), leader of a federal political party (David Lewis), and Governor of the Bank of Canada (Louis Rasminsky). Clement indicated that in 1972 the other ethnic groups were 4.8 per cent of the media elite, with Jews being less represented than in the corporate elite.[45]

The success of Jews in entering the elites, the high occupational statuses of Jews and Asians, and the convergence of occupational status indices for all of the major ethnic origin categories indicate that the vertical mosaic is not as permanent as Porter assumed. If such factors as region, industry, educational level, and age distributions were taken into account, the range of occupational status indices would be even further reduced. The technique of Porter and Clement for determining representation in the elites minimizes their openness to the extent that it includes in the various ethnic-origin categories not only the Canadian-born and long-time residents but also newly arrived immigrants, who could hardly be conceived to have the knowledge of Canadian society necessary for membership in the elite.

When members of various Canadian ethnic groups tell their story, in its economic aspects it is almost without exception a story of initial hardship, long struggle, and eventual success, limited, however, by exclusion from the topmost ranks. The duration of the struggle and the degree of prosperity achieved have varied not only from group to group but within groups. They have also varied for the immigrants of different epochs. The immigrants of the 1920's, confronted by the Great Depression soon after their arrival, were slower to establish themselves economically than those of the 1946-1960 period. The latter, by 1971, had moved from lower earnings than the native-born in 1961 to higher total earnings, whether family heads or families are considered; they had done so in most of the larger ethnic-origin categories.[46] Many factors are involved in this: the changing economic structure, immigration policies favouring the educated and enterprising, the concentration of immigrants in high-income metropolitan areas. But that economic success is being achieved, and that even the topmost ranks are beginning to be breached, is undeniable. In the 1980's many of the people whose names are symbolic of wealth and economic power – they may, of course, not in fact be the wealthiest and most powerful people in Canada – are first-generation or second-generation immigrants of other than British or French ethnic origin: the Bronfmans, the Ghermezians, the Belzbergs, the Reichmanns, Thomas Bata, Frank Stronach, and others.

NOTES

1. Clifford Sifton, address to the Westerners Club of Montreal in 1923, quoted

by Paul Yuzyk, *The Ukrainians in Manitoba: A Social History* (Toronto: University of Toronto Press, 1953), p. 40; John Lehr, "The Government and the Immigrant: Perspectives on Ukrainian Block Settlement in the Canadian West," *Canadian Ethnic Studies*, 9, 2 (1977), pp. 42-52.

2. Rev. Nestor Dmytrius, " 'Canadian Ruthenians,' a Traveler's Memoirs," in Harry Piniuta, *Land of Pain, Land of Promise: First Person Accounts by Ukrainian Pioneers 1891-1914* (Saskatoon: Western Producer Prairie Books, reprinted 1981), p. 40.

3. Bradwin, *The Bunkhouse Man*, pp. 92, 104-05.

4. Avery, *"Dangerous Foreigners,"* p. 30.

5. Howard Palmer, *Land of the Second Chance: A History of Ethnic Groups in Southern Alberta* (Lethbridge: The Lethbridge Herald, 1972), pp. 226-27.

6. Edgar Wickberg, ed., *From China to Canada: A History of the Chinese Communities in Canada* (Toronto: McClelland and Stewart, 1982), p. 24.

7. Rasporich, *For a Better Life*, p. 54.

8. Robert F. Harney, "Men Without Women: Italian Immigrants in Canada, 1885-1930," in Betty Boyd Caroli, Robert F. Harney, and Lydio F. Tomasi, eds., *The Italian Immigrant Woman in North America* (Toronto: The Multicultural History Society of Ontario, 1978), pp.79-101; Radecki, *A Member of a Distinguished Family*, p. 174.

9. Jean Morrison, "Ethnicity and Violence: The Lakehead Freight Handlers Before World War I," in Gregory S. Kealey and Peter Warrian, eds., *Essays in Canadian Working Class History* (Toronto: McClelland and Stewart, 1976), pp. 143-60.

10. Baha Abu-Laban, *An Olive Branch on the Family Tree: The Arabs in Canada* (Toronto: McClelland and Stewart, 1980), p. 102.

11. Myrna Kostash, *All of Baba's Children* (Edmonton: Hurtig, 1977), pp. 213-14.

12. *Ibid.*, pp. 153-54.

13. Robert F. Harney, "The Padrone System and Sojourners in the Canadian North, 1885-1920," in George E. Pozzetta, ed., *Pane e Lavoro: The Italian American Working Class* (Toronto: Multicultural History Society of Ontario, 1980), pp. 119-37; Bruno Ramirez and Michele Del Balzo, "The Italians of Montreal: From Sojourning to Settlement, 1900-1921," in Robert F. Harney and J. Vincenza Scarpaci, eds., *Little Italies in North America* (Toronto: Multicultural History Society of Ontario, 1981), pp. 63-84.

14. Varpu Lindström-Best, "The Unbreachable Gulf: The Division in the Finnish Community of Toronto, 1902-1913," in Karni, ed., *Finnish Diaspora I*, p. 12.

15. Rudolf Helling *et al.*, "They, too, Founded Canada: A Socio-Economic History of German-Canadians," unpublished manuscript (n.p., n.d.), p. 66.

16. John Herd Thompson, *The Harvests of War: The Prairie West, 1914-1918*, (Toronto: McClelland and Stewart, 1978), p. 86.

17. Radecki, *A Member of a Distinguished Family*, p. 171.

18. *Ibid.*

19. A. Ross McCormack, *Reformers, Rebels, and Revolutionaries: The Western Canadian Radical Movement 1899-1919* (Toronto: University of Toronto Press, 1977), pp. 118-64.
20. Peter Vasiliadis, " 'The Truth is Sometimes Very Dangerous': Ethnic Workers and the Rise and Fall of the Workers Cooperative in the Porcupine Camp," Ethnic Research Programme, York University, 1983, p. 10.
21. Kostash, *All of Baba's Children*, p. 217.
22. Radecki, *A Member of a Distinguished Family*, p. 53.
23. Benedykt Heydenkorn, ed., *Memoirs of Polish Immigrants in Canada* (Toronto: Canadian-Polish Research Institute, 1979), pp. 63-84.
24. Abu-Laban, *An Olive Branch on the Family Tree*, p. 108.
25. Leroy D. Stone, *Urban Development in Canada* (Ottawa: Dominion Bureau of Statistics, 1967), p. 26.
26. James. H. Gray, *The Winter Years: The Depression on the Prairies* (Toronto: Macmillan of Canada, 1966), pp. 126-27, 134-35.
27. Radecki, *A Member of a Distinguished Family*, pp. 47-48.
28. Dreisziger, *Struggle and Hope*, p. 142.
29. Evelyn Dumas, *The Bitter Thirties in Quebec*, translated by Arnold Bennett (Montreal: Black Rose Books, 1975), pp. 39-40. The Yugoslavs were Croats, who had been radicalized by lowered wages and deteriorating working conditions, and they had been the object of an organizing campaign by the Workers' Unity League.
30. Rasporich, *For A Better Life*, p. 143.
31. Radecki, *A Member of a Distinguished Family*, p. 82.
32. Grace M. Anderson, *Networks of Contact: The Portuguese and Toronto* (Waterloo: Wilfrid Laurier University Press, 1974), pp. 71-82.
33. Peter C. Briant and Daniel Hadekel, "Ethnic Relations in the Construction Industry on the Island of Montreal," report presented to the Royal Commission on Bilingualism and Biculturalism, unpublished (1966).
34. Wsevolod W. Isajiw and Norbert J. Hartmann, "Changes in the Occupational Structure of Ukrainians in Canada: A Methodology for the Study of Changes in Ethnic Studies," in W.E. Mann, ed., *Social and Cultural Change in Canada*, Vol. 1 (Toronto: Copp Clark, 1970), p. 104.
35. Warren F. Kalbach and Wayne W. McVey, *The Demographic Bases of Canadian Society*, second ed. (Toronto: McGraw-Hill Ryerson, 1971), p. 258.
36. S.J. Wilson, *Women, the Family and the Economy* (Toronto: McGraw-Hill Ryerson, 1982), p. 94.
37. Varpu Lindström-Best, " 'I Won't Be a Slave!' - Finnish Domestics in Canada," in Jean Burnet, ed., *Looking into My Sister's Eyes: an Exploration in Women's History* (Toronto: Multicultural Historical Society of Ontario, 1986), pp. 33-35.
38. Vera Lysenko, *Men in Sheepskin Coats: A Study in Assimilation* (Toronto: Ryerson, 1947), pp. 238-39.
39. Norman Buchignani and Doreen Indra, *Continuous Journey: A Social History of South Asians in Canada* (Toronto: McClelland and Stewart, 1985), p. 153.

40. Jim Torczyner, "To Be Poor and Jewish in Canada," in M. Weinfeld, W. Shaffir, and I. Cotler, *The Canadian Jewish Mosaic* (Toronto: John Wiley & Sons, 1981), pp. 177-83.
41. John Porter, *The Vertical Mosaic: An Analysis of Social Class and Power in Canada* (Toronto: University of Toronto Press, 1965), p. 286.
42. Wallace Clement, *The Canadian Corporate Elite: An Analysis of Economic Power* (Toronto: McClelland and Stewart, 1975), pp. 237-39.
43. Peter C. Newman, *Bronfman Dynasty: The Rothschilds of the New World* (Toronto: McClelland and Stewart, 1978).
44. Wallace Clement and Dennis Olsen, "The Ethnic Composition of Canada's Elites 1951 to 1973, A Report for the Secretary of State," unpublished, 1974.
45. Clement, *The Canadian Corporate Elite*, pp. 334-45.
46. Anthony H. Richmond and Warren E. Kalbach, *Factors in the Adjustment of Immigrants and Their Descendants* (Ottawa: Minister of Supply and Services, 1980), pp. 109-22.

FIVE

Kinship, Marriage, and the Family

The family is the agent of primary socialization. Experiences within it are intense and emotional; they remain significant throughout the life of the individual, even after peer groups, neighbourhoods, and the larger community begin to assume importance. It is in the family that children learn their ethnic identity and the cultural traits that symbolize it; the learning is the more profound for beginning early and for being informal and in large part unconscious. It is also in the family that many ethnic rituals, especially those involving feasting or fasting or both, are celebrated. When in adulthood the majority of people found new families, it is of great concern to the ethnic group whether they do so with members of the same or another ethnic group, and whether or not they take pains to transmit their ethnic identity to their offspring.

For most people who have come to Canada, adjustment to Canadian economic life has been easier to achieve than change in family relations. Many of Canada's immigrants were helped by their families to come to Canada. When they arrived, they in turn brought out other members of their families or started new families. Immigrants have tended to consider the family one of their most important institutions. They have been critical of the Canadian family as being less warm and cohesive than the family as an institution in their homelands, and they have been anxious about the changes in their own families that have occurred in North America. Yet changes were going on in their homelands also, and differences and changes were inevitable in Canada because of the different environment, the nature of immigration, and contact with other kinship systems.

THE FAMILY PATTERN IN THE HOMELAND

Each ethnic group tends to regard its family form as unique, but over the century during which most of the non-British, non-French immigration has occurred, there is a similarity in the descriptions of family patterns in the homeland and the effects of immigration and the North American environment on the family. Whether the family was Ukrainian and came to Canada before World War I or Portuguese and came to Canada in the 1950's or 1960's, whether it was European or Asian, Christian, Jewish, Muslim, or Confucian, it appears to have somewhat similar authority structures and divisions of labour. The similarities reflect a common family form in rural and pre-industrial societies. They also suggest that the immigrants may have come from the most conservative classes and regions of their countries, or perhaps that the immigrants, and students of the family after them, have described the traditional rather than the actual form of family, since by the time of the departure industrialization and urbanization were well under way in many of their homelands.

In the societies from which many immigrants came, far more aspects of life were regulated by kinship than in North America and feelings of familial responsibility were stronger. Familial and kinship roles overrode others in much of day-to-day life. The families were patriarchal: the husband and father held authority over both wife and children and had chief responsibility for the economic welfare of the family. He was the breadwinner or provider and the steward of the family's wealth. He was also the disciplinarian and was expected to correct any misbehaviour of wife or children in a stern manner, as evidence of his loving concern. The wife and mother had an obligation to answer to her husband's sexual needs, to bear children, in particular a son, to care for the young, and to perform the myriad tasks of the household. Usually she was considered to be duty-bound to submit to her husband and to subordinate herself to male children who had achieved a certain age. She had little interaction with men outside the family. The family, ideally, was large. Children were considered to be a blessing, in whatever number they came: contraception was frowned upon. Children were expected to obey and honour their parents and to contribute to the economic welfare of the family. Girls were assigned domestic roles, boys economically dominant roles; any money earned by either girls or boys was to be given to the father to be used for the family's benefit. The eldest son wielded authority second only to that of the father. Young men were expected to defend their sisters, and young women were expected to protect their honour and that of their families. Aged parents and grandparents were re-spected for their wisdom and experience and were cared for in the household. They were expected to share in the education of the young, passing on to them the traditions and customs of the group.

In the homelands of many immigrants, the concept of honour was of considerable importance. Honour had to do with the courage and success in providing for the family on the part of men, the chastity of unmarried women, and the fidelity of wives. It was a precious possession, and in guarding it, injuring or even killing might be condoned. Chaperonage was considered essential for the maintenance of women's honour.

Marriages were alliances between families, not simply between individuals, and were arranged by representatives of the families rather than being left to the caprices of the young. Adolescent girls were strictly supervised and dating was unknown. Matchmakers were often involved. Exchanges of goods between families were expected, and not infrequently the goods were of great value. Except among Muslims, divorce was frowned upon and difficult to obtain. Spinsterhood was a disgrace, and widows and widowers were expected to remarry.

Families were rarely looked upon as consisting simply of parents and children: they were extended or joint families, embracing three or more generations and several collateral lines, that is, cousins of several degrees. Marriages between cousins were sometimes welcomed as strengthening the extended family.

The relationship between godparents and godchildren was taken seriously. When the godparents were relatives, the ties between them and the family of the child were thus reinforced. When the godparents were friends of the family, a quasi-familial bond was created.

The descriptions, of course, are of an ideal or pure type of family. They depict what people consider family patterns would be like if nothing interfered. They do not take into account the variations that in fact exist, nor the selection processes which ensure that immigrants are never a cross-section of the society from which they come. Nor are the descriptions by the immigrants themselves free of nostalgic distortions.

FROM 1880 TO 1920

During the first major wave of immigrants of non-British, non-French origins, people were often enabled to migrate to North America by help from the family. It was usually a young man who came first, aided by financial contributions from his father, his uncles, and his cousins. He was expected not only to repay his passage money but also to contribute to the welfare of his kin group. He might do so by remitting funds home or by assisting young relatives to join him; they were usually cousins and nephews rather than brothers, for several ethnic groups considered that "it is enough if one son goes overseas."[1]

Many of the young men were used to leaving home to find work and earn money in another part of Europe - Poles in Germany, for example, and Macedonians in Istanbul. Crossing the ocean was only a slightly more adventurous migration. They may, like the Italians of Cosenza province, have been pushed to go to America by the knowledge that young women considered them more desirable marriage partners if they had been to America,[2] but they did not think of establishing families in the new land.

Nor could they have done so easily. In most ethnic groups women were few. In 1911, for example, when there were 113 men per 100 women in the total population, there were 158 men per 100 women among the foreign-born. The Chinese and South Asian ethnic groups in particular were at that time almost wholly male, and the Japanese had only just begun to move toward a balanced sex ratio, since the "gentlemen's agreement" of 1908 limited the number of male immigrants but did not restrict the entry of wives.

By 1921, after seven years of almost no immigration, there were 106 men per 100 women in the total population and 125 men per 100 women among the foreign-born.[3] The women who did migrate were chiefly wives and fiancées; unattached women came from some European countries, as they did from the British Isles, but they were few and usually they speedily married. Scandinavians and Finns came out to work as domestics and some peasant and working-class women from Ukraine, where there was a shortage of men, used their dowries to pay their fare to Canada.[4] Young men, when they made the decision to reside permanently, sometimes returned home to seek a bride, or, if return was difficult, resorted to mail-order or "picture" brides. Immigrants as different as the Japanese and the Greeks of the late nineteenth and early twentieth centuries developed systems of picture brides. Marriages were arranged through the exchange of photographs with eligible young women in the homeland selected by parents or matchmakers.[5] For want of eligible women in their own ethnic group, some men married members of other groups. However, linguistic and cultural barriers and discrimination made exogamy difficult for some groups, such as the Hungarians and the Asians.

Among some groups, whole families migrated or were quickly established in Canada. These included groups that settled in rural areas, where the labour of wives and children was essential for the success of the farming enterprise. Various ethnic groups that moved into western Canada from the United States before 1920 migrated as families after a few men had acted as scouts or advance agents.

The families that settled in western Canada came by team and wagon or by rail, with their farm equipment and household goods. Those – Norwegians, for example – who came from the United States might be well supplied with livestock, machinery, and furniture; those who crossed the ocean and then undertook a journey overland often brought little except barest necessities and a few family treasures. Sometimes the journey was safe and pleasant; some parties of Ukrainians had "well-heated, well-lit, and uncrowded railway cars; a plentiful fresh water supply; and medical aid in case of illness."[6] At other times, the journey was uncomfortable or even hazardous. Arrival brought shock at the isolation of the homesteads and the rudeness of the log shanties or sod huts that were to provide shelter.

The hazards of travel and settlement were such that some of the families lost members during the voyage or shortly after arrival. If the husband died, there were occasions when the wife assumed the duties of head of the family and proceeded to establish a homestead and to bring up the children. If both parents died, young people sometimes homesteaded together; more frequently they were scattered among their kin and neighbours, made welcome by their capacity for work.

The difficulties of male heads of families in coping with the unfamiliar conditions of the new country and new settlement were manifold. At times, especially among former peasants, they helped to maintain or to shape harsh and uncompromising attitudes toward wives and children, regarded as sub-servient sharers in the immense labours of the homestead. Charles Young wrote of the Ukrainian family in the early years of settlement:

> The Ukrainian family was of a type which has prevailed in the Slav communities from time immemorial, that of the patriarchal family, in which the power of the husband and father, while not the equivalent of the patria potestas of the Roman family, was nevertheless very great. "An Englishman's house is his castle," but that of the Ukrainian was a stamping ground for an uncouth, ill-mannered, and oft-times brutal husband or father. . . .
>
> This Ukrainian tradition has persisted in their Canadian settlements, especially among the members of the older generation. The women "are little better than slaves who toil laboriously at the beck and call of inconsiderate husbands". . . . Wife beating is common, and while we hear that women take advantage of the more favourable laws in this country, in general they submit as to an unalterable law in this best-of-all-possible worlds. It might be humorous were it not so pathetic to hear, as we did, of a big able-bodied Ukrainian woman in one of the settle-ments who could outstrip her husband cutting cordwood, yet submitted to a beating from the rascal when in the house.[7]

The frustrations of the men were relieved to some extent by contacts with their fellows and by satisfactions derived from economic advance. Their wives had few such outlets. They frequently met bitter disillusion when they saw the shanty and the rough land to which they had been brought. They then had to endure fear and loneliness when their spouses went off to earn money in construction camps or to work among more established settlers in order to learn agricultural techniques. To the care of the household, the women had to add many unaccustomed tasks that in the homeland were performed by grandparents, neighbours, priests and pastors, and school teachers. In some groups, such as the Ukrainian, they also laboured in the fields, often contrib-uting more to the work of the farm than the average hired man. They bore many children and frequently endured the grief of children's deaths from disease or accident.

Many mothers regarded as their role "how to keep alive faith, learning, the accustomed practices, how to hold intact the family structure."[8] It was a source of anxiety to them that they had little time for this. Their children also had little time, since they began to take part in the work of the farm and household at a very early age. Nonetheless, in rural settlements language and culture were generally preserved.

For some children the preoccupation of parents with necessary chores, early initiation into the work of farm and household, and absence of schools meant early independence, to which they responded with enterprise and achievement. Others suffered from the harsh environment and the lack of facilities for education and training. Girls had the additional burden of the old-country view of the status of women. The time required by some ethnic groups to move out of their entrance status was lengthened by the deprivations suffered by the second generation.

The family was most easily and strongly established among such sectarian groups as the Mennonites, Doukhobors, and Hutterites. Part of their adaptation to previous migrations had been the development of family forms that could be transferred intact from one agricultural setting to another. The families were the more able to withstand the hardships of adjustment to a new environment since in the sectarian settlements they did not lack the support of neighbours or of familiar visitations. The village communities of the Mennonites mitigated the isolation of the Prairies in the early years and then tended to disappear; among the Doukhobors, some groups fairly soon became individualistic while others remained communal; the Hutterite colonies have remained the principal units of social organization of the sect.

In the West, many single farm labourers had to live with their employers' families. There were also bachelor households, composed of men who had not found wives or had not persuaded their wives to join them on their homesteads. Sojourning single men in the mining and construction camps lived in bunkhouses while working and found substitutes for the family in partnerships or larger groupings in the off-season. Sometimes the groups they formed were based on kinship or locality; sometimes they were composed of members of the same ethnic group who had met first as steerage passengers on immigrant ships or as fellow workmen. They found that they could live more cheaply in pairs or groups and thus save more of their wages to send home; they could work out a division of labour for such household tasks as shopping, cooking, and cleaning; and they could develop controls concerning cleanliness, aggressive behaviour, and the consumption of alcoholic beverages.

Single women worked as hired girls or domestics. The work was heavy, the pay low, and the life lonely. However, so great was the demand for wives that most women married quickly and moved into homes of their own.

Among campmen, according to the long-time worker with Frontier College, E.W. Bradwin, Bulgarians, Macedonians, and Italians were especially given to banding together in the off-season. Of the Italians he wrote:

> Large numbers of Italian nationals, during the long periods between seasonal works, tie-up in some adjacent town in what are really communal stopping places, run by one of their own countrymen. These buildings are large tar-papered structures which for fifteen to twenty cents give the inmate floor space on which to spread his blankets, with the further privilege of cooking meals on one of the half-dozen stoves. As many as forty men are not infrequently roofed over night in such places. Slightly improved houses will be found in the larger towns where the foreign-born natives spend the winter months.[9]

In the cities the men found immigrant boarding houses run by employers of labour or other entrepreneurs. These were frequently extremely congested and lacking in amenities. The Polish-Canadian scholar, Victor Turek, deplored them:

> This disgraceful and harmful phenomenon of the "boarding houses" which existed in all places of the North America to which poor immigrants from Europe were coming in masses, did not spare Poles in Winnipeg, although the local Polish press dispassionately combatted the creation of such houses and letting them to tenants. The large overplus of single persons among immigrants, their scanty earnings, their illiteracy and ignorance of the English language – explain why the immigrants were eagerly taking advantage of the low-rent accommodation provided by the owners of the boarding houses. The operators of these houses were at the beginning, and even up to the War 1914-1918, mostly the non-Polish people, the native Canadians or members of other immigrant groups. Sometimes the boarding houses were owned or run by Poles, who managed, in one way or another, to save money for buying or constructing houses; more often than not in these cases the houses were second-hand structures, rebuilt, or readapted for purposes of keeping in them "the boarders." The possession of boarding houses used to be a source of considerable profits. Preoccupied mostly with saving money immigrants of the first period of economic immigration were very eager to reap benefits from living in the boarding houses, crowding in the primitive conditions and falling prey to the shameless exploitation by bloodsucker landlords.[10]

Woodsworth quoted "an ordinary police court item" from a Winnipeg newspaper, indicating the limits that were imposed on boarding-house keepers:

> M. Simok and M. Selenk endeavored to ascertain how many adults they could crowd into a given space. Selenk managed to accommodate forty-three occupants in five rooms where only fourteen could hope to find sufficient atmosphere for healthy respiration. Simok ran his neighbour close, having twenty-four in one room where only seven should have been. His rooms were too low, and lacked ventilation. In consideration of the immense profits made by such economic means, Magistrate Daly, at this morning's police court, charged Selenk $15 and costs, and Simok $10 and costs.[11]

The boarding houses did not meet the standards of Canadian social workers. Congestion and lack of sanitation often led to disease and death, and doctors and public-health nurses were usually involved only by chance or as a last resort; however, in 1909 Woodsworth noted of Jews that their death rate was low because, although "often housed in crowded tenements . . . [they] yet observe certain sanitary precautions that save them from many of the diseases that attack others."[12] Linguistic, class, and economic barriers all limited access to health services and forced reliance on the folk remedies and the elders within the ethnic group. The boarders were aware of the poor quality of their housing; they accepted it, not as was often said because their standards were low but because they were determined to save as much money as possible as quickly as possible, in order to return home or to establish a family in Canada.

When urban immigrants succeeded in bringing out their families, they frequently paid for the rent of their quarters and helped out fellow immigrants by taking roomers or boarders. When a boarding house was a family enterprise, the wife of the boarding-house keeper sometimes provided the paying guests with some of the services of wives or mothers, such as shopping for food, cooking meals, doing laundry, mending clothes, keeping money in trust, reading letters from home and writing replies, and even giving moral admonitions. Sometimes the woman of the boarding house was called auntie or grandmother or the missus, and took it upon herself to scold her boarders for being late for supper or keeping bad company. The family boarding houses were often as congested as the employer-run or commercial boarding houses, but inasmuch as they frequently brought together people from the same village or district, they served as refuges from the anonymity and *anomie* of the North American city. They also enabled women and children to contribute to the family income without running the risks to family honour that were involved in working outside the home.[13]

BETWEEN THE WARS

In the 1920's, as before, the bulk of immigrants were men; indeed, in the broad categories in Table 7 the only groups other than the British and French to move to more balanced sex ratios between 1921 and 1931 were the Italians, Jews, and Asians. Among Italians, some migrant men did not return to Canada after the war. Among Jews, the circumstances leading to immigration, such as pogroms in eastern Europe, bore as hardly on women as on men. As for the Asians, the Chinese after 1911 and the Japanese after 1908 had brought in wives and children in an effort to build families; South Asians also were able from 1925 on to bring in wives and children more easily than before. In none of the Asian groups, however, was anything like balance achieved among the foreign-born, although the Japanese began to include a sizable proportion of Canadian-born; and Chinese immigration came to an almost complete halt in 1923.

Except in areas afflicted by drought, by the 1920's the families that had settled in the West were well established and prosperous. The high prices for grain in the war years enabled them to pay off mortgages and to face the future with confidence; in some instances the confidence led them to assume new debts for land and machinery. The second generation began to mature, and families began to develop new ambitions regarding education and occupations for the young. Intermarriage increased among youths who had grown up together in Canada: for example, Poles, fewer in number than Ukrainians and living among them, frequently married Ukrainians. In rural Alberta a

TABLE 7

Sex Ratios for the Foreign Born, by Selected Ethnic Origin Groups, Canada, 1921–61

Ethnic origin	1921	1931	1941	1951	1961
British Isles	113.2	112.4	108.1	96.8	92.0
French	103.4	98.1	93.7	89.8	91.4
German	122.0	128.9	123.2	111.5	104.5
Netherlands	126.5	129.2	118.8	110.3	112.2
Scandinavian	151.7	175.0	166.2	158.2	142.0
Central European[1]	146.0	198.9	149.5	141.4	132.3
Eastern European[2]	145.2	154.4	141.6	139.5	128.3
Italian	204.1	171.8	160.0	169.1	123.0
Jewish	106.1	102.0	101.2	102.2	98.7
Chinese	3,297.1	2,775.3	3,601.6	924.8	211.5
Japanese	250.2	181.7	165.2	139.8	103.2
Other Asiatic	165.3	167.5	161.6	144.5	130.9
TOTALS	125.0	128.7	121.2	111.9	107.4

1. Austrian, Czech, Slovak, and Hungarian.
2. Polish, Russian, and Ukrainian only.
SOURCE: Warren E. Kalbach, *The Impact of Immigration on Canada's Population* (Ottawa: Dominion Bureau of Statistics, 1970), p. 46.

Latvian married an Alberta-born Dutch woman; of their two daughters one married a Hungarian and another a Ukrainian, and their son married a girl whose father was Finnish and mother Norwegian.[14] Sharp differences between migrant and Canadian families began to decline.

However, the maintenance of language and culture within the family became of greater concern as the problems of livelihood became less pressing. The "little white schoolhouse on the prairie" became the agent of Canadianization and the enemy of ancestral languages and familial values. To counteract this outside influence, mothers frequently regarded it as part of their special mission to transmit the mother tongue to their children, to maintain old-country ways of cooking and old-country crafts, and to observe important feasts and holy days in traditional fashion. But with the passage of time and with contact with neighbours who had different customs, they became less rigidly retentive of their culture.

During the 1920's the expansion of most ethnic groups occurred in the towns and cities to a greater extent than in rural areas, in spite of the preference in immigration regulations for agriculturalists. For many groups the transition from sojourning to settlement had begun before the war but was completed after it; for a few, events of the immediate post-war years either made the prospect of returning home distinctly unappealing or opened Canada's door more widely than before.

The time that elapsed between the arrival of the sojourner and the coming of his wife meant that those who arrived were "not just more womenfolk, but women who had lived through a further decade of European history, who lacked their husbands' sense of the New World and needed the linguistic and cultural reassurances of an ethnic community." On the other hand, they were women in many instances who had had to make decisions for themselves and their children, had become self-confident and enterprising, and were unwilling to resume a submissive role. They were especially unwilling since they knew or soon learned that North American women had a reputation for independence from, not to say domination of, their husbands – a reputation allegedly summed up by a Macedonian woman, "So this is the country where the men work and the women are bosses!"[15]

In the city the work of a single breadwinner was often insufficient for the maintenance of a family. Women who had been accustomed to sharing in the labour of a farm turned their skills to account by working in the family grocery or bakery, cleaning other people's houses, or taking jobs in the needle trades or food-processing. Others might view such work as degrading; the women took pride in contributing to their families' welfare. When possible, they chose work that could be done in the home, for it allowed them to watch over their children and prepare meals for the family while supplementing the household income. The fact of contributing to income inevitably led to a less submissive stance within the family, particularly as examples of more equalitarian husband-wife relationships were not lacking. The decline in the birthrate also enhanced women's ability to participate in family decision-making.

Immigrant parents in the city considered that they were more concerned about their children than Canadians of British origin: "more warm for the kids," in the words of a Macedonian woman.[16] But the children were subject to the influences of the school, the streets, and in some cities the settlement house, as well as the influences of family and ethnic group. They learned the language and the ways of the new land more rapidly than their parents. As this occurred the parents often became dependent on them for assistance in dealing with Canadians and less able to exercise authority over them. Children who worked in family enterprises remained tied to their families, experiencing guilt if they did not drop in after school to see if they were needed. But children who worked as newsboys, shoeblacks, or messengers, although they did so initially to contribute to the family's welfare, gained an independence that shook the structure of the family.

At the beginning of the 1930's the Great Depression struck with devastating effects. Immigration was quickly restricted. Family income dropped sharply; farms, jobs, and businesses were lost; young people left home to relieve the family of the burden of their support and moved from place to place in search of work or a handout; recent immigrants found themselves unable to repay money borrowed for their fare or to bring out their families, and sometimes returned home or were deported as indigents or radicals. In these circumstances, more women entered the labour market, and sometimes they became the sole supporters of the family. Marriages were postponed, and the birthrate, which had been inclining downward, reached a new low: the fertility index for married Hungarian women between the ages of 15 and 44 went from 150 in 1931 to 90 in 1941.[17] Unemployed young men presented a hazard for families. Advice printed in a Polish paper in the 1930's cautioned:

> 1. Don't keep single boarders in your home, especially those who are unemployed.
>
> 2. Don't allow your wife to go out to the cinema, the park or a picnic with your boarders or other boarders.
>
> 3. Live usually by yourselves, let there be one room less and let it cost a few dollars a month more, but for this you will have peace of mind and certainty in your home, that no one will seduce your wife.[18]

Nonetheless, some survivors of the depression remember it as a time when the members of the family and the ethnic community drew close together for mutual support. "Looking after their own" was a matter of pride. Celebrations of family and community events had a special poignancy because of the sacrifice involved. A Dutch mother on the Prairies in the 1930's wrote in letters home of the observance of St. Nicholas Day, a highlight of Dutch popular culture:

> The fifth of December, we were sitting in the living room . . . round the big table and playing *Ganzebord* with the boys, the old Dutch game that our parents played with us when we were children. And even if we tried to conform to the ways of this country now and celebrated Christmas the way Canadians do it, St. Nicholas evening never passed unheeded in our house. And so here in the midst of our Canadian fields you will still find three little boys who can sing the old well-known songs about the bishop who comes from Spain in the steamboat and the moon that shines through the trees.[19]

The war brought a renewal of prosperity, but it did not end the separation of family members. Wives and mothers continued to enter the labour force. Young people joined the armed services or went to work in war industries. Many immigrants still found themselves unable to bring out their relatives. Like the economic crisis, though, the crisis of war did serve to strengthen the emotional ties between family members.

THE POST-WAR PERIOD

When immigration was renewed after 1945 the trend toward a more balanced sex ratio among the foreign-born and in the population as a whole

TABLE 8

Immigration Population[1] by Place of Birth and Sex, Showing Period of Immigration, Canada, 1981

Place of Birth and Sex		Total	Period of Immigration						
			Before 1945	1945– 1954	1955– 1964	1965– 1969	1970– 1974	1975– 1977	1978– 1981[2]
Immigrant population	t	3,843,335	544,135	676,810	767,455	591,835	576,870	346,850	339,375
	m	1,897,555	247,530	350,255	380,900	299,785	286,725	167,380	164,980
	f	1,945,780	296,605	326,560	386,555	292,060	290,145	179,465	174,390
Europe:	t	2,563,235	426,030	625,990	658,910	395,375	237,815	118,415	100,705
	m	1,281,740	197,280	324,200	330,515	202,870	118,100	59,210	49,565
	f	1,281,495	228,750	301,790	328,400	192,505	119,720	59,200	51,140
United Kingdom		878,985	224,195	174,675	169,560	136,115	80,395	52,095	41,945
Italy		384,780	11,855	84,380	167,755	85,185	22,660	7,445	5,500
West Germany		155,265	7,710	53,095	57,225	18,285	8,820	5,365	4,770
East Germany		34,115	2,745	15,015	12,455	2,500	700	365	345
Poland		148,540	47,195	55,090	23,300	8,765	6,585	3,480	4,130
Other Europe		961,555	132,330	243,745	228,620	144,525	118,655	49,665	44,015
U.S.A.	t	301,525	100,695	18,795	33,240	39,460	55,015	27,610	26,705
	m	133,280	40,890	8,120	14,760	18,980	26,165	12,740	11,620
	f	168,245	59,800	10,680	18,480	20,475	28,850	14,870	15,085
Central and	t	106,855	1,275	2,955	7,960	12,670	35,035	26,760	20,200
South America	m	51,455	595	1,395	3,535	6,070	17,435	12,915	9,515
	f	55,400	680	1,570	4,430	6,600	17,595	13,845	10,680

Caribbean Islands	t	171,435	1,435	3,445	12,205	35,000	62,420	34,985	21,940
	m	77,005	720	1,770	5,195	15,715	27,970	16,015	9,630
	f	94,425	715	1,670	7,010	19,285	34,450	18,975	12,310
Southeast Asia	t	152,165	245	1,360	3,020	11,545	31,190	27,230	77,580
	m	74,505	130	710	1,295	4,505	14,335	13,055	40,485
	f	77,660	110	655	1,735	7,040	16,850	14,180	37,090
Other Asia	t	388,635	8,425	15,815	32,595	67,015	112,100	81,535	71,155
	m	198,740	5,290	9,800	15,870	35,475	60,300	38,105	33,900
	f	189,895	3,130	6,010	16,730	31,540	51,805	43,430	37,255
Africa	t	101,745	1,030	1,650	12,515	19,995	30,490	21,730	14,335
	m	53,310	480	885	6,470	10,900	16,235	11,095	7,235
	f	48,440	550	765	6,040	9,100	14,255	10,635	7,100
Oceania	t	32,995	925	2,115	3,795	7,095	8,345	5,825	4,895
	m	16,395	435	1,190	1,790	3,650	4,095	3,000	2,245
	f	16,600	495	930	2,005	3,445	4,250	2,825	2,650
Other countries and regions	t	24,745	4,075	4,680	3,205	3,690	4,465	2,755	1,865
	m	11,120	1,700	2,185	1,470	1,625	2,100	1,250	780
	f	13,625	2,375	2,495	1,735	2,070	2,360	1,510	1,080

1. Excludes inmates.
2. First five months only of 1981.
SOURCE: *Census of Canada*, 1981.

NOTE: t = total, m = male; f = female.

93

continued. The sex ratio for the foreign-born was 112 in 1951, 107 in 1961, 101 in 1971 and 98 in 1981; the foreign-born included those born in the British Isles and the United States, which have especially high surpluses of women. The sex ratio for the total population was 102 in 1951, 101 in 1961, 100 in 1971, and 93 in 1981.

In the few years immediately after the war the sponsorship system, which had first been introduced in the 1920's, was employed to permit entrance of close relatives and also certain orphan nieces and nephews. However, many families had been disrupted by the war, and reunification was slow. There were many single people among immigrants: displaced persons, army veterans, and the like. The displaced persons included women as well as men, and it was not long before marriages began to take place as people sought for security after a long period of turmoil and in face of the conditions of a new land. Ethnic differences among Europeans were often of little moment, since they were dwarfed by the differences between Europeans and Canadians. A Latvian displaced person working in a hospital and a Polish veteran fulfilling a contract as a farm labourer, for example, found that they had much in common.

During the years just after the war, immigrants also included war brides. Although many came from Great Britain, some came from other countries where Canadian troops had been stationed. The Canadian government identified 1,886 Dutch, 649 Belgian, and 100 French war brides for whom passage to Canada was paid.[20]

In 1947 the Chinese Immigration Act was repealed, and Chinese became eligible to sponsor wives and minor children. To a limited extent it began to be possible to establish families in Canada. However, older children could still not enter, and relatives other than the most immediate could not be brought in.

After the first few years, as immigration to take advantage of Canada's economic expansion set in, many of the phenomena that had occurred during earlier waves of immigration appeared again. For example, the extended family played the same role among Italian immigrants from southern Italy to Toronto in the late 1940's and early 1950's as it had among eastern Europeans a half century earlier:

> The migration process would frequently throw together several kin to make migration possible for any one individual. While an uncle in Toronto might act as "sponsor," dealing with bureaucrats in order to prepare the necessary documents, a second uncle in Chicago would loan the nephew the passage money, while a third in the village would check with Toronto in-laws to see if a job could be made available. If the migrant was married, financial constraints would usually force him to leave his family behind for a year or two until he could send for them. In this case the immigrant's wife and children would be maintained by the male members of his family, the younger, unmarried brothers assuming responsibility for their protection. Female members were instrumental

in giving emotional as well as domestic support to his wife and children.

The migrant would search out kin who were leaving for Toronto at the same time so that they could support each other during the migration. Likewise, when his wife was able to rejoin him, it was imperative that a male kinsman accompany her.[21]

The boarding house also reappeared, as a means of increasing family income and at the same time serving single immigrants until they could bring out their families.

Generally, because of the buoyant economy and also the immigrant regulations that favoured family reunification, wives and children or sweethearts were brought out sooner than they had been during the earlier waves of immigration. Indeed, for Europeans, less immediate relatives could often also be sponsored, as the classes considered admissible were from time to time expanded and differentiation was made among countries; thus, southern Europeans in particular could reconstitute their kin systems in Canada through the process of chain migration.

At least as much as in the 1920's, immigrant women entered the labour force. That women, including married women, had worked during the war had lent respectability to employment outside the home; the labour shortages of the 1950's and 1960's created opportunities. As before, some women worked in family enterprises; some developed cottage industries, knitting, crocheting, tatting, and embroidering; others engaged in domestic service or in factory work. When they had children, they dropped out of the labour force either temporarily or permanently.

In many cases they regarded their work, as had their predecessors, as a contribution to the family. Sometimes they had a specific goal, such as accumulating the down payment for a house or paying off the mortgage; sometimes they worked because their husbands were unemployed. But as had happened among earlier immigrants, the income-earning capacity and the North American ideology led women to assert greater equality with their husbands in decision-making.

The relationship of parents to children also changed. To parents from Europe or Asia, the Canadian family of those of British origin seemed cold and unemotional, with little hugging and kissing, and unnecessarily permissive, with little corporal punishment. Immigrant parents attempted to maintain traditional values. However, both parents frequently worked, often for long hours and sometimes at several jobs, leaving them little time with their children. Contacts were inevitable with members of other ethnic groups, which led to dating, courtship, and marriage outside the ethnic group. Rebellion on the part of children led to conflict, but in time greater equality and independence were conceded to the young.

In the last couple of decades, family reunification has continued to be a principle of immigration policy. Under the nine-point system introduced in 1967, those who cannot accumulate enough points to enter Canada as independent immigrants have been able to come in because they have relatives already in the country willing to assume some responsibility for them. According to the Immigration Act of 1976, those who sponsor close relatives, or family-class immigrants, must undertake to provide them with accommodation and care for ten years, and sponsors of less close relatives, eligible to enter as assisted relatives, must undertake responsibility for them for five years. Even if a relative in Canada is not prepared or not able to assume formal responsibility, if such a person is judged to be willing to help an immigrant to establish himself the immigrant receives points toward the total needed for admission.

Within Canada, many immigrants first locate in the homes of relatives, in the same neighbourhood, or at least in the same city. They thus retain some of the ties of family in the new land. In Edmonton in 1965 among British, German, Italian, and Ukrainian immigrant families, from a half to more than three-quarters of those who did not maintain their own households lived with relatives.[22] In the early 1970's it appeared that among Portuguese in Montreal the intensity of family life and of contacts with the extended family diminished with immigration, but outside Quebec the majority of families had some relatives nearby, and many spent their holidays visiting kin in other parts of Canada and in the United States.[23]

In early years communication with kin in the homeland is frequent. Anderson and Higgs, studying Portuguese Canadians some twenty years after immigration from Portugal began, quoted a Montreal study to the effect that "more than half the families correspond on a weekly or biweekly basis."[24] A particular form of communication, the regular transmission of savings to the family of the emigrant, has been of great economic importance to families in many European and Asian homelands. The money has been used to pay off debts, to purchase additional land, to build new homes, and to provide dowries. The development of air travel has meant that visits back and forth also contribute to the maintenance of family ties.

However, the form of family described as characteristic of the homeland has by no means been reconstituted in Canada. During the last twenty-five years certain trends have been marked in the Canadian family. Wives as well as husbands work outside the home and share in making decisions for the family, although they still do most of the housework. Children are few, usually one or two, and spaced close together. Households are usually limited to the nuclear family of parents and children. Divorces, especially since the Divorce Act of 1968, and separation are relatively frequent and socially acceptable. Single-parent families are increasing in number.

Many post-war immigrants have in fact come from urban and industrial backgrounds and are accustomed to such a family. Those who have not have responded to the less familial society in which they have found themselves. For example, the working of married women, even after the birth of children, has been accepted as a necessity even if it has not been considered ideal, and with the earning of income has come a greater share in making decisions in the family. Among post-war immigrant Poles in Toronto in 1970, for example,

72.2% of fathers shared all important decisions (purchase of a house or automobile, changing his job) with their wives and the remaining 27.8% involved the whole family in such decisions. Fathers are no longer solely responsible for deciding on their children's education. In 58.3% of cases both parents decided, while in 35.0% of instances the children were given the responsibility for this decision. In the remaining 6.7% of cases, the decision was reached through a mutual agreement between the parents and children.[25]

Among South Asians,

> Although men have been reluctant to pick up household tasks, they have been more flexible about sharing decision-making with their wives. For example, everyday household finances are often managed by women and there is usually consultation between husbands and wives prior to major purchases. Extensive husband-wife deliberation in regard to family planning is equally common.[26]

The size of the family has declined in most groups. Among many, two or at most three children have become the ideal and often the actual family size. Family planning has become accepted, even among those whose religion condemns artificial birth control. The decline in family size is often related to a desire to educate the children. It is notable, however, that even the entirely rural Hutterites, with their belief in a guarded education, have since the late 1960's had a declining birthrate because of structural changes in Hutterite society, particularly in the division of labour.[27]

Although many groups have attempted to reconstitute the extended family in Canada, few have succeeded. Some families have maintained the tradition of caring for aged parents, including the South Asian family,[28] but in most cases homes for the aged, senior citizens' residences, and nursing homes have begun to be used. In the homeland the old had been cared for in the home by family members; in the receiving country there were people who had no relatives to look after them, or whose relatives felt unable or unwilling to care for them in their households. There were also the elderly poor, dependent on government pensions that, although they improved over time, were never ample. In the past, allowing such people to enter senior citizens' residences or nursing homes was considered a disgrace to their relatives and to the ethnic community. Now it is becoming accepted. But those who immigrated at an advanced age sometimes were unfamiliar with the language and/or customs of those around them, or were alienated by what seemed cold and formal in the Canadian institutions for the general public. Hence, the ethnic community has taken the responsibility of raising funds and operating homes to care for them. The homes run by ethnic groups have been able to adapt to their clients.

> The simple matter of alcohol is a case in point. Within the homes for the aged operated by Metropolitan Toronto, a resident must obtain special permission to imbibe a small quantity from his or her own bottle of

97

liquor, which is kept carefully locked up in the cupboards of the infirmary. But Villa Colombo [Italian] has a wine cellar, and Baycrest [Jewish] follows the tradition of wine in moderation at the Sabbath dinner.[29]

Fund-raising for a home for the aged within the ethnic community has sometimes become a means of displaying the success of individuals or of the ethnic group as a whole. In these instances the needs and wants of the old may be subordinated to other interests.

In some groups concern for the aged emerged at a very early period. Among Icelanders, for example, the Ladies Aid of the First Icelandic Lutheran Church in Winnipeg discussed the need for a home for the aged in 1901 and began setting aside money for such a home in 1906.[30] But it has been since the 1950's that institutions have multiplied: for the Jews, Maimonides in Montreal, Baycrest Centre in Toronto, and the Jewish Home for the Aged in Vancouver; for the Italians, the Villa Colombo in Toronto; for the Chinese, the Mon Sheung Foundation in Toronto and the Oi Kwan Foundation in Calgary; for the Poles, Polish senior citizens' homes in Montreal, Toronto, Winnipeg, Edmonton, and Vancouver. Many other groups also have special homes for senior citizens. The homes do, of course, receive public funding.

The problem of caring for the old varies from group to group, depending on the proportion of the population in the older age categories, the wealth of the group, and the linguistic and cultural characteristics of the group that affect the adequacy for aging group members of public institutions. In 1971 among the other ethnic groups the Russian, Jewish, Scandinavian, Hungarian, and Ukrainian ethnic groups, in that order, had the highest proportion of people sixty-five years of age and older; the Italians, the Dutch, and the Asians had the lowest proportions.[31] Low fertility, low mortality, and declining immigration are associated with an aging population.

The most important change, however, has been intermarriage in the increasingly polyethnic Canadian population. Most first-generation immigrants have opposed intermarriage, considering that the maintenance of language and culture requires marriage within the group. The strength of opposition to intermarriage has varied from one ethnic group to another and from one time and generation to another. Japanese Canadians, for example, were once strongly opposed, but after the disastrous events of the 1940's their opinions varied. Some began to favour intermarriage as essential for complete assimilation, others opposed it for the time being as likely to present difficulties to the offspring of a mixed marriage, and still others opposed it generally as it would "spoil the purity of the Japanese blood."[32] In a survey in Thunder Bay in 1969, it was found that in a sample of 450, 73 per cent of Greeks, 52 per cent of Slovaks, and 11 per cent of Dutch immigrants were strongly opposed to marriage of their sons to someone outside their group.[33] In a survey of ethnic groups in Metropolitan Toronto, conducted between 1977 and 1979, it was found that of nine groups – German, Italian, Jewish, Ukrainian, English, "Majority Canadian," Chinese, Portuguese, and West Indian – only the Jewish placed a high degree of importance on marrying within the group; the Ukrainians in the first and second generations, but not in the third, gave moderate importance to endogamy.[34]

The Jewish attitude to intermarriage is based on a fear that the Jewish community could disappear. Intermarriage not only may remove a stream of descendants from the future Jewish population, but it may weaken the norm of endogamy and thus lead to even more intermarriage. Further, since Judaism is a highly ethnic religion, even if the non-Jewish partner becomes a religious convert he or she is considered less than a "true" Jew.[35]

Some exogamous marriages are more acceptable than others. Those involving groups that are culturally similar, or groups that share the same religion, are often accepted with resignation. In Thunder Bay, only 56 per cent of the Greeks, 1 per cent of the Slovaks, and 6 per cent of the Dutch in the sample definitely objected to children's marriages outside the ethnic group but within the religion.[36] On the other hand, Anderson and Driedger reported that in rural communities in Saskatchewan that they surveyed, 44.4 per cent of the Hutterites, Mennonites, Scandinavians, French, German Catholics, Ukrainian Orthodox, Ukrainian Catholics, Poles, and Doukhobors in their sample objected to ethnic intermarriage, but 69.8 per cent objected to religious intermarriage.[37]

Marriages between members of the dominant group and members of some of the other ethnic groups are sometimes considered to be the least objectionable of intermarriages, and young men belonging to the dominant group are sometimes attracted by what they see as a greater warmth within the family circle or a submissiveness on the part of wives within the other ethnic groups. In any event, the numbers of Canadians of British origin are so large that many immigrants or children of immigrants of other origins married into the British origin group.

It is almost inevitable that exogamy rates should be fairly high, even for members of the immigrant generation. In Montreal in the 1960's, of a sample of Italians 13 per cent of immigrants had married persons not of Italian descent, and 76 per cent of the Canadian-born had married out.[38] Among Poles, in 1951, 44.3 per cent of marriages of men and 43.3 per cent of marriages of women, and by 1961, 51 per cent of marriages of men and 46.9 per cent of marriages of women were exogamous.[39] In Canada in 1971, 24 per cent of all family heads were married exogamously, including 80.9 per cent of Scandinavians, 75.9 per cent of Poles, 74.2 per cent of Hungarians, 73.1 per cent of Dutch, 69.6 per cent of Italians, 67.1 per cent of Germans, 59 per cent of Russians, and 55 per cent of Ukrainians.[40]

The Jewish group in Canada has maintained a low rate of exogamy. In 1971, 90 per cent of Jewish husbands were married to Jewish wives. However, since the mid-1960's the rate of intermarriage has increased by approximately 1 per cent per year. The rate in the United States, which has also been increasing since the mid-1960's, is about twice that in Canada.[41]

Among the "visible minorities" exogamy has long occurred, in spite of prejudice and discrimination. At present it seems to be increasing. Pakistanis have entered Canada mainly since 1967, yet as early as 1971 20 per cent had married British, Canadian, American, and European wives.[42] Among Japanese in southern Alberta, exogamy rose from negligible rates in the early 1950's to 71.4 per cent in Taber and 82.0 per cent in Lethbridge between 1970 and 1974; it was estimated to be around 60 per cent in Vancouver and 70 per cent in Toronto.[43] Among the *sansei*, the third generation in Canada, it was said to be as high as 85 to 90 per cent. It is not unusual for all the children in large Japanese families to be married to people of European origins. Intermarriage is also fairly common between blacks and whites.

One indication of the acceptance of ethnic intermarriages as a fact of Canadian life, as well as of a more egalitarian attitude to men and women, is the reporting in the 1981 census for the first time of multiple ethnic origins. More than one origin was claimed by 1,838,615 persons, or almost 8 per cent of the population. The Yukon Territory and the four western provinces had the highest proportions of multiple responses.

Many ethnic groups have considered the family to be the bulwark of their ethnic identity. They have counted on it for the transmission of their language and culture to future generations. As the family changes in Canada, under the impact of new social and economic conditions, it will not be able to carry out this mission as before.

NOTES

1. Kosa, *Land of Choice: The Hungarians in Canada*, p. 15.
2. Franc Sturino, "The Role of Women in Italian Immigration to the New World," in Burnet, ed., *Looking into My Sister's Eyes*, pp. 22-23.
3. Warren E. Kalbach, *The Impact of Immigration on Canada's Population* (Ottawa: Dominion Bureau of Statistics, 1970), p. 46.
4. Marusia K. Petryshyn, "The Changing Status of Ukrainian Women in Canada," in Petryshyn, ed., *Realities: Social Trends among Ukrainian Canadians*, p. 196; Varpu Lindström-Best, "Tailor-Maid: the Finnish Immigrant Community of Toronto before the First World War," in Robert F. Harney, ed., *Gathering Place: Peoples and Neighbourhoods of Toronto, 1834-1945* (Toronto: Multicultural History Society of Ontario, 1985), pp. 205-38.
5. Adachi, *The Enemy That Never Was*, pp. 89-91; Chimbos, *The Canadian Odyssey*, p. 27.
6. Vladimir J. Kaye and Frances Swyripa, "Settlement and Colonization," in Lupul, ed., *A Heritage in Transition*, p. 44.
7. Charles H. Young, *The Ukrainian Canadians: A Study in Assimilation* (Toronto: Thomas Nelson and Sons, 1931), pp. 155-56. Young's observations are those of an Anglo-Canadian, but his comment about wife-beating is quoted by Kostash, *All of Baba's Children*, p. 164. See also Helen Potrebenko, *No Streets of Gold: A Social History of Ukrainians in Alberta* (Vancouver: New Star Books, 1977), p. 17.
8. Jorgen Dahlie, "Scandinavian Experiences on the Prairies, 1890-1920: The Frederiksens of Nokomis," in Howard Palmer, ed., *The Settlement of the West* (Calgary: Comprint Publishing Company, 1977), p. 109.

9. Bradwin, *The Bunkhouse Man*, p. 134.

10. Turek, *Poles in Manitoba*, pp. 110-11.

11. James S. Woodsworth, *Strangers Within Our Gates or Coming Canadians* (original ed., 1909; repr. Toronto: University of Toronto Press, 1972), p. 217.

12. *Ibid.*, p. 127.

13. Robert F. Harney, "Boarding and Belonging: Thoughts on Sojourners Institutions," *Urban History Review/Revue d'histoire urbaine*, 2 (1978), pp. 8-37.

14. J. Mezaks, unpublished manuscript on the history of Latvians in Canada.

15. Lillian Petroff, "Contributors to Ethnic Cohesion: Macedonian Women in Toronto to 1940," in Burnet, ed., *Looking into My Sister's Eyes*, pp. 126-27.

16. *Ibid.*, p. 135.

17. Dreisziger, *Struggle and Hope*, p. 148.

18. Apolonia Kojder, "Women and the Polish Alliance," in Burnet, ed., *Looking into My Sister's Eyes*, p. 103.

19. Mark Boekelman, "The Letters of Jane Aberson. Everyday Life on the Prairies during the Depression: How Immigration Turns Conservatives into Social Democrats," in Herman Ganzevoort and Mark Boekelman, eds., *Dutch Immigration to North America* (Toronto: Multicultural History Society of Ontario, 1983), p. 129.

20. Michiel Horn, "Canadian Soldiers and Dutch Women after the Second World War," *ibid.*, p. 192.

21. Franc Sturino, "Family and Kin Cohesion among South Italian Immigrants in Toronto," in Caroli, Harney, and Tomasi, eds., *The Italian Immigrant Woman in North America*, p. 294.

22. Charles W. Hobart, "Italian Immigrants in Edmonton: Adjustment and Integration," unpublished research report prepared for the Royal Commission on Bilingualism and Biculturalism, vol. 1, pp. 80-82.

23. Grace M. Anderson and David Higgs, *A Future to Inherit: The Portuguese Communities of Canada* (Toronto: McClelland and Stewart, 1976), pp. 130-31.

24. *Ibid.*, p. 128.

25. Henry Radecki, "The Polish-Canadian Family: A Study in Historical and Contemporary Perspectives," in Ishwaran, ed., *Canadian Families: Ethnic Variations*, p. 51.

26. Buchignani and Indra, *Continuous Journey*, p. 156.

27. Karl A. Peter, "The Decline of Hutterite Population Growth," *Canadian Ethnic Studies*, 12, 3 (1980), pp. 97-110.

28. Buchignani and Indra, *Continuous Journey*, p. 155.

29. Albert Rose, "The Jewish Elderly: Behind the Myths," in Weinfeld, Shaffir, and Cotler, eds., *The Canadian Jewish Mosaic*, p. 203.

30. Walter J. Lindal, *The Icelanders in Canada* (Ottawa: National Publishers, 1967), p. 304.

31. Kalbach and McVey, *The Demographic Bases of Canadian Society*, p. 212.

32. E.D. Wangenheim, "The Social Organization of the Japanese Community in Toronto – a Product of Crisis" (M.A. thesis, University of Toronto, 1956), p. 52.

33. Peter D. Chimbos, "Immigrants' Attitudes toward their Children's Inter-Ethnic Marriages in a Canadian Community," *International Migration Review*, 5, 1 (1971), p. 8.
34. Wsevolod W. Isajiw, *Ethnic Identity Retention*, Ethnic Pluralism paper no. 5 (Toronto: Centre for Urban and Community Studies, University of Toronto, 1981), pp. 60, 80-82.
35. Morton Weinfeld, "Intermarriage: Agony and Adaptation," in Weinfeld, Shaffir, and Cotler, eds., *The Canadian Jewish Mosaic*, p. 366.
36. Chimbos, "Immigrants' Attitudes toward their Children's Inter-Ethnic Marriages," p. 11.
37. Alan Anderson and Leo Driedger, "The Mennonite Family: Culture and Kin in Rural Saskatchewan," in Ishwaran, ed., *Canadian Families: Ethnic Variations*, pp. 172-74.
38. Jeremy Boissevain, *The Italians of Montreal: Social Adjustment in a Plural Society*, Studies of the Royal Commission on Bilingualism and Biculturalism, 7 (Ottawa: Queen's Printer, 1970), p. 41.
39. Radecki, *A Member of a Distinguished Family*, p. 155.
40. Alan B. Anderson and James S. Frideres, *Ethnicity in Canada: Theoretical Perspectives* (Toronto: Butterworths, 1981), p. 125.
41. Morton Weinfeld, "A Note on Comparing Canadian and American Jewry," *The Journal of Ethnic Studies*, 5, 1 (1977), pp. 96-98.
42. Hugh Johnston, *The East Indians in Canada* (Ottawa: Canadian Historical Association, 1984), p. 19.
43. Gordon Hirabayashi, "Japanese Heritage, Canadian Experience," in Harold Coward and Leslie Kawamura, eds., *Religion and Ethnicity* (Waterloo, Ontario: Wilfrid Laurier University Press, 1977), pp. 63-66.

SIX

Education

The basic values of a society are transmitted by the schools. Thus, the Canadian educational system has usually been given the task of moulding children to conform to the patterns of behaviour that the majority of people find acceptable. The British and French colonizers who first settled Canada naturally set up school systems that attempted to pass on values they felt to be important. As other immigrant groups began arriving, the newcomers found themselves forced to choose whether and how much they wanted to conform to the prevailing British-Canadian or French-Canadian values expressed in the school system.

Canadian educational policy toward non-British and non-French ethnic groups has evolved over time, reflecting variations in prevailing notions of Canadian identity and differences in the historical background and ethnic mix of each province.[1] Under Canada's constitution, education is a provincial responsibility; consequently, each province has formulated its own educational policy toward ethnic groups. The strong regional variations in ethnic concentrations in Canada have been reflected in educational issues. For example, the Jewish "school question" arose in Quebec because of the large numbers of Jews in Montreal and the British-French duality embodied in a denominational Protestant-Catholic school system. Likewise, in Nova Scotia and Ontario the issue of whether or not blacks should have segregated schools or be integrated into white schools was debated throughout the nineteenth century and into the twentieth century, because the vast majority of blacks in the country lived in these two provinces. On the Prairies, the presence of religious minorities such as the Mennonites, Doukhobors, and Hutterites, who had come to Canada specifically to preserve their identity and had been promised a degree of educational autonomy by the federal government, precipitated conflicts for decades, as did the presence of Ukrainian immigrants, as determined to keep alive their language and culture as the educational authorities were to assimilate them.[2] British Columbia faced a unique situation in that over 90 per cent of the Asian immigrants who came to Canada in the late nineteenth and early twentieth centuries settled in that province, and B.C. also dealt most intensely with the problems surrounding the education of Doukhobor children.

In education, pressures for ethnic groups to conform to a pre-existing norm were strong.[3] Two important factors complicated this overall pattern. In some parts of the country, such as Manitoba, the presence of a numerically important, historically powerful, and constitutionally protected French-Canadian minority made it difficult for the British-Canadian majority to impose its language and culture on all other ethnic groups. Racial minorities across the country also complicated the issue: prevailing notions of racial differences led many to regard the assimilation of racial groups such as blacks or Asians as impossible and undesirable.

Before World War II, with these two exceptions, Canadians desired the assimilation of immigrants into either British-Canadian or French-Canadian society, and educational authorities designed the school systems to accomplish this task. Although they doubted whether immigrants could give up their old ways, educational authorities were convinced that the children of the immigrants could and should be moulded to conform to prevailing patterns.

CONFEDERATION TO 1914

While the British North America Act guaranteed the rights of Protestants in Quebec and of Catholics in some other provinces to separate education, it did not stipulate a uniform approach to standards of education or to curriculum. Language rights were not clearly defined, so the language of instruction in schools gave rise to bitter controversy. The issue, involving primarily French Canadians outside Quebec, became inextricably intertwined with the issues surrounding schooling for non-English-speaking immigrants and ethnic groups.

The Prairie Provinces

The Prairie provinces received by far the largest number of non-British immigrants between Confederation and World War I. Since this was a new region where people were trying to come to terms with the question of what type of society should be established, education became a major focal point of political conflict. The questions of French-language rights and rights for other languages were inseparably linked.

The conflicts developed in much the same way in Manitoba and the Northwest Territories, which became the provinces of Alberta and Saskatchewan in 1905. Initially, the strong presence of French Canadians led to the establishment of school systems along denominational Catholic/Protestant lines, as well as the use of French in the courts and the legislature. However, during the 1870's and 1880's English-speaking settlers came quickly to outnumber the French-speaking settlers: in Manitoba, for example, between 1871 and 1891 the proportion of the French-speaking population was reduced from one-half to one-fifth. In both Manitoba and the Northwest Territories, English-speaking newcomers, primarily from Ontario, exerted pressure for a non-sectarian unilingual national school system. They believed that all other ethnic groups, including French Canadians, would have to be assimilated if western Canada was to develop a unified and cohesive society. Consequently, the issues of immigration and the language rights of immigrant groups became intermeshed with the questions of French-language rights and Roman Catholic schools.

In Manitoba, despite constitutional guarantees, in 1890 the Anglo-Canadian majority eliminated the French language and Catholic religion from publicly supported schools. Although there were similar pressures for conformity in the Northwest Territories, the lack of provincial status and continuing government control from Ottawa made it more difficult for the territorial legislature to remove religious guarantees, though it did remove French from the courts and the legislature.[4]

Thus, when new immigrants began flooding into the Prairie provinces in the 1890's, the issue of language had been decided in favour of English, while the issue of separate schools was still being debated. The prevailing cultural ideology on the Prairies was that newcomers had the obligation to conform to the already fixed values and institutions of British-Canadian society.

The focal point for this assimilationist sentiment was the school system. Assimilation of the immigrants through education was seen as the eventual answer to all social problems and as necessary for social integration and for democracy, which presupposed a literate electorate. Between the 1890's and 1916, the predominant aim of the school systems was to inculcate the values of British-Canadian nationalism, individualism, and the Protestant work ethic.[5]

Between 1896 and 1916 Manitoba had the most generous policy toward the languages of new immigrant groups because of the Laurier-Greenway compromise. This compromise, reached in 1896 between the federal and Manitoba governments, attempted to resolve the protracted constitutional and legal battles over French and Catholic education in Manitoba after religious and language rights had been removed in 1890. Under the terms of the compromise, named after the Prime Minister and the Premier of Manitoba, provision was made for bilingual schools, and languages other than English could be used as languages of instruction whenever ten pupils spoke French or other languages as their mother tongue. This compromise had been arrived at before the massive influx of central and eastern European immigrants, and although there were sizable Icelandic and Mennonite minorities in Manitoba, few people anticipated that a variety of groups would take advantage of the provision for bilingual schools. However, German, Ukrainian, and Polish bilingual schools were soon established, and the provincial government set up training schools for non-English teachers. The Conservative government of Premier Roblin, which came to power in 1899, saw the necessity of making an accommodation with ethnic voters, and Roblin supported bilingual schools.[6]

Among those who made use of bilingual schools were the more liberal or progressive of the Mennonites. The Mennonites were committed to separation from the world and believed that their agreement of 1874 with the federal government gave them freedom to educate their own children, although education was under provincial jurisdiction. From 1874 to 1883 they had developed a system of private schools, but the progressive Mennonites were lured into the public system by its financial advantages. The conservative Mennonites resented paying taxes for the public schools, and many Mennonites were repelled by legislation passed in 1907 requiring that the Union Jack be raised daily in public schools. Language then was only one aspect of an extremely disruptive issue in Manitoba's Mennonite communities.[7]

The bilingual schools came under increasing attack after the turn of the century from Anglo-Canadian opinion leaders who believed that they were educationally inferior, did not teach English adequately, and generally prevented assimilation. John W. Dafoe, the editor of the *Manitoba Free Press*, led the attack. Between 1910 and 1914, his paper carried over 100 editorials on the subject. He was joined by many other influential Manitobans in demanding an end to bilingual schools and the introduction of compulsory school laws. Dafoe's view was definite: "We must Canadianize this generation of foreign-born settlers, or this will cease to be a Canadian country in any real sense of the term."[8]

Saskatchewan and Alberta, although they did not experiment with bilingual schools, had to face the question of how non-English-speaking immigrants would fit into the educational system. In Saskatchewan, provision was made for instruction in languages other than English or French between three and four in the afternoon. Saskatchewan's Liberal government, which dominated provincial politics from 1905 onward, attempted to attract support among European immigrants by defending the immigrants' right to such classes in the face of criticism. But teacher training for these classes was sporadic and the politicians' rationale for the classes was that they were a way to get the children of immigrants into the school and thus facilitate assimilation.[9]

Although in Alberta it was possible to teach languages other than English or French after school hours, the government made no provision to train teachers to do this. In 1913 the Alberta Department of Education had a major confrontation with Ukrainian teachers and parents when the government prevented qualified out-of-province teachers of Ukrainian background from teaching in schools in Ukrainian districts at a time when there were no qualified Ukrainian teachers in Alberta. Alberta's Minister of Education took a firm stand, arguing that he wanted no repeat of the Manitoba experience: "This is an English-speaking province . . . and every Alberta boy and girl should receive a sound English education."[10]

With the outbreak of World War I, the provisions that existed for languages other than English and French came under increasing attack across the Prairies. For many western Canadians during the war, loyalty and cultural and linguistic uniformity were synonymous. Languages such as Ukrainian and German were now suspect due to their connection with enemy countries. In the wartime atmosphere, provincial governments enacted measures to ensure linguistic uniformity. When the Liberal government came to power in Manitoba in 1916, one of its first measures was to abolish bilingual schools and to introduce compulsory school attendance. Similarly, in 1918 the Saskatchewan government abolished the provision allowing for the teaching of languages other than English or French in the schools.

By 1918 the provisions for teaching languages other than French or English in the Prairie provinces had been eliminated. The French-Catholic clergy had been ambivalent toward the newcomers from Europe, at times seeing them as potential allies in a struggle against an Anglo-Protestant monolith, but at other times fearing that with so many new immigrant groups the French-Canadian group would lose its unique status and become just one of many. In any case, the French-Catholic clergy no longer had the power to prevent the erosion of the French language, to say nothing of other languages. The new immigrant groups, many of whom were under suspicion as "enemy aliens" and all of whom were without constitutional guarantees, were powerless against the will of the majority of Canadian society.

Over the period from 1870 to 1918 the Prairie region had moved from a policy of French-English bilingualism to a limited multilingualism and then to unilingualism. The Anglo-Canadians were too convinced of the superiority of their own ways and language and too concerned about the overall level of social cohesion in a new frontier society to allow much scope for the languages of others in the school system, or in other realms of society for that matter.

British Columbia

In the Prairie provinces the central and eastern Europeans and the pacifist religious sects were thought to pose the greatest challenges to educational authorities, but in British Columbia the Chinese and Japanese immigrants were considered the greatest problem. Given the prevailing attitudes in British Columbia in the late nineteenth and early twentieth centuries, educational authorities did not perceive the issue as being how to bring about assimilation. They held the view that the Chinese and Japanese, as non-whites, neither could nor should be assimilated. Some school authorities fought a prolonged battle with Chinese and Japanese immigrant parents to keep non-white children out of public schools or at least segregate them in their own classrooms.

Discrimination against the Chinese included deprivation of the right to vote in school board elections, and Chinese parents were often discouraged from sending their children to public schools. Chinese children were few, since few families had been established, but they were considered a potential threat to the morals of white children. Attempts to segregate Chinese children first began in Victoria in 1901, when residents of Rock Bay District petitioned the school trustees for either the withdrawal of Chinese children from the school or their placement in a separate room. During the next three decades there were repeated though only occasionally successful attempts to segregate the Chinese in the public school system. To some extent attempts at segregation reflected the fact that Chinese youths often did not know English and it was felt that they needed separate education, for their own good as well as for that of white children. But the basic factors behind the drive for segregation were the strong racial prejudice in West Coast society and the consequent objection of white children and their parents to racial intermingling in schools.[11] Chinese immigrants did not accept passively the attempts to segregate their children. They initiated school boycotts and other forms of resistance. But segregated classes continued sporadically in Vancouver, Victoria, and other parts of the province.

The Japanese arrived in British Columbia later than the Chinese, and before World War I the number of Japanese children in the province was small. They entered the public school system too slowly to attract great notice, though lack of facility in English was a problem for them. During World War I, opponents of Asian immigration in Vancouver argued that Japanese children were a menace to the health and educational progress of white children and should be removed from the schools, but the school board resisted this pressure.

Educational authorities in British Columbia were also fighting a prolonged battle with the Sons of Freedom sect of the Doukhobors to force them to send their children to public schools. The Community Doukhobors had moved to British Columbia from Saskatchewan after being dispossessed of their land by the federal government in 1907 for failing to comply with regulations. As in Saskatchewan, most of the Doukhobors achieved an accommodation with the provincial authorities and began sending their children to public schools, but the Sons of Freedom objected to the public schools as agents of militarism, materialism, and assimilation. Following incidents of Doukhobor parents withdrawing their children as a form of protest against government regulations, the British Columbia government in 1914 passed a community regulation act obliging the Doukhobors to send their children to school. If an individual failed to pay a fine, the goods and chattels of the rest of the Doukhobors were liable to seizure. This provocative legislation was to lead in the 1920's to repeated confrontations between the Doukhobors and the provincial educational authorities.

The Maritimes and Central Canada

With two exceptions, the education of "other ethnic groups" was not a significant public issue in the Maritimes or in central Canada prior to World War II. The number of immigrants in the Maritimes was negligible. The main issue was the education of blacks. In Nova Scotia, after 1884, blacks had access to public schools, but these were almost entirely segregated even as late as 1918. Many blacks in Nova Scotia also attended private schools established by religious organizations. But whether they attended private schools, separate black schools, or in rare cases integrated schools, blacks generally received an inferior education. Ontario's Common School Act of 1850 allowed for separate schools on the basis of race as well as religion, and while a few black communities chose to establish segregated schools, more had such schools imposed on them. By the end of the nineteenth century most of the segregated schools had disappeared, but the legislation permitting them remained on the books until 1964. James Walker summarizes the situation in both Nova Scotia and Ontario:

> [Segregated black] public schools tended to follow the same curriculum as their white counterparts, but because black school districts were poorer, the salaries for their teachers were correspondingly lower as were their budgets for books and equipment. Inevitably, the education received by blacks was inferior. School buildings were often over-crowded and ramshackle, creating an environment that was not inclined to encourage blacks to attend. Teachers willing to work for low pay in isolated communities tended to be underqualified, and some were barely literate.[12]

The only other non-British, non-French ethnic group in Ontario that was large enough to raise issues related to education and minority rights was composed of German-speaking settlers. German-speaking religious sects had come to Ontario after the American Revolutionary War, and there had been other waves of German immigration during the nineteenth century. German-language schools had been established in rural Ontario to meet their needs: in 1873, thirty schools in Waterloo County alone taught in German. Although a considerable degree of local educational autonomy had facilitated teaching in German, growing centralization and state control with a standardized curriculum and texts, as well as the overwhelmingly English environment, contributed to the gradual disappearance of the German-language schools in the province. In addition, although Egerton Ryerson, the superintendent of public schools from 1844 to 1876, had been sympathetic to the maintenance of the German language as long as English was adequately taught, his successor, George Ross, wanted to eliminate German-language schools. The number of such schools in Ontario declined gradually from the 1850's through to World War I because of changing educational policy and because of the assimilation of the German-speaking minority.[13]

Ontario saw itself as a bastion of British-Canadian nationalism. In the history syllabus of the Ontario Department of Education at the turn of the century, patriotism, the power and responsibility of the British Empire, and its contributions to civilization were focal points. Few references were made to immigrant students in the annual reports of the Minister of Education, except passing mention of their being placed in classes for slow learners or classes for "pupils of foreign tongue," and of a vacation school for teaching the English language and Canadian citizenship. As in western Canada,

Canadianization was the watchword. Harney and Troper have described how central the efforts at Canadianization were to Toronto's schools in the pre-World War II era:

> Canadianization was not a hidden curriculum. Teaching of the Canadian way permeated every facet of the school's program. The three R's proved no exception. The working of a routine mathematics problem sanctified growth, progress and competitive business practices. Through the study of literature, reading materials promoted nationalism and Protestantism, often as if they were one and the same. As late as 1928, Toronto's Chief Inspector of Schools boasted of one institution, "The teachers of this school are teaching English to their students, but they are also not losing sight of the broader aim, the Canadianizing of our foreign population."[14]

In Quebec, the influx of immigrants prior to World War I was to Montreal, and two groups predominated: Italians and Jews. Since the school systems were designated Protestant and Roman Catholic, it is significant that the first of these immigrant groups was Catholic, the second not. As early as 1907-08, the Montreal Catholic School Commission acceded to the request of the Italian community to subsidize three classes in an east-end church, and by 1915 there were, under the auspices of the commission, two schools for Italians, Notre-Dame-de-la-Defense and Notre-Dame-du-Mount-Carmel. In both, the Italian language was taught in addition to English and French. Educational facilities were also provided by the Catholic School Commission for the Poles, Ukrainians, Lithuanians, Syrians, and Chinese.

The Jews were caught between the Roman Catholic and the Protestant systems. From the 1870's on, when Jews began to come to Montreal in sizable numbers, they could pay their school taxes to either the Protestant or the Roman Catholic board. Most chose to pay their taxes to the former and send their children to the Protestant schools, which were English-speaking. They came to constitute a substantial proportion of the total enrolment in the Protestant schools of Montreal, 44 per cent in 1916. There were a number of reasons for their choice of Protestant schools. They were in the main too poor to pay for private schools; they saw the Protestant schools as affording access to the English community and its institutions; and, perhaps more important, they accepted integration as a goal.

However, the Jewish position in the Protestant school system was awkward. A celebrated case in 1902 tackled the question of whether the Protestant School Board had the right to refuse a scholarship to a young Jewish student who had won a high school competition, and the court upheld the right of the school board not to award the scholarship. Following the case an agreement was reached in 1903 between the Jews and the Protestant School Board whereby Jews were classified as Protestants for educational purposes. But Jews could not serve on the school board, Hebrew was not taught, and there were few Jewish teachers.[15]

Private Schools

The efforts of the public schools at Canadianization were abetted by the Canadian churches, which set up schools in all parts of Canada for immigrant children to teach them the English language and Canadian ways. In Manitoba, the Presbyterian Church provided a loan, only part of which was repaid, for the first school among Ukrainians in Canada.[16] Later, the Presbyterian, Methodist, and Roman Catholic churches all attempted to draw to mission schools the children of the central and eastern Europeans in the Prairie provinces, with limited success. In British Columbia, Anglican and Methodist missionaries concerned about the linguistic difficulties of young Chinese Canadians and Japanese Canadians set up kindergartens for them, which improved their performance in the public schools.

The widespread efforts across the country to Canadianize the new immigrants did not go unchallenged. The immigrants valued their languages and traditions and made valiant efforts to pass these on to their children. In some cases, these efforts proceeded within the family: for example, in Winnipeg in the late nineteenth century many Jewish parents could not wait for a community school, and a few engaged private Hebrew instructors to teach their children.[17] Some geographically concentrated groups attempted to secure members of their groups who would teach their own language in addition to the regular curriculum in the public schools. On the Prairies, for instance, Icelandic and Ukrainian school trustees attempted to hire people of their own background so that their language could be taught after school hours.

Each of these means of passing on language and culture had drawbacks: family efforts could be unsystematic, hiring tutors could be expensive, and hiring teachers for public schools from one's own ethnic group often ran afoul of provincial educational authorities. As it became clear that the public school system was indifferent or hostile to their cultural background, ethnic groups began organizing private schools. For a few groups, such as the conservative Mennonites, private schools were full-time and were seen as an alternative to the public school system. This was the exception, however. In addition to the prohibitive cost of establishing their own schools, most newcomers wanted their children to become part of the larger Canadian society while maintaining part of their cultural background. The public schools could provide English-language training and avenues of opportunity into Canadian society. But through their own part-time schools, immigrant groups could keep alive the language and traditions of their homelands. Across the country, then, immigrant groups established their own language and culture classes after school or on weekends.

BETWEEN THE WARS

In the years between the wars, the emphasis on Canadianization continued in the schools. Wartime nationalism had led to a growing anxiety about unassimilated ethnic minorities. Both the numbers and the diversity of the newcomers were causes of concern. By 1921, half of the population of Alberta and Saskatchewan was foreign-born, and Slavic newcomers from central and eastern Europe comprised approximately 18 per cent of the population of Manitoba and Saskatchewan and 15 per cent of the population of Alberta. The central and eastern Europeans were seen as poor, sickly, uneducated, and backward. There were fears that illiterate immigrants would lower the cultural level of the whole country and undermine British governmental institutions. Further, the bloc settlement pattern on the Prairies caused anxiety that the newcomers would not be assimilated. While immigration officials saw the bloc settlement pattern as a way of attracting immigrants to western Canada and of keeping them there and confining them so that they could be both closely supervised and assisted, other western Canadians feared their social impact.[18]

Capturing the mood of the time, J.T.M. Anderson, the director of education among "new Canadians" in Saskatchewan, in 1918 published *The Education of the New Canadian*, which stressed the need for assimilation through education. Anderson concluded that, to solve the problem of unassimilated ethnic minorities in western Canada, parochial schools would have to be subject to stricter government inspection, compulsory school laws would have to be enforced, and better teachers and teaching methods would have to be introduced.

Wartime nationalism had ended the experiments with limited degrees of multilingualism in the Prairie provinces, and this meant English only in the schools. A Ukrainian Canadian described how the schools felt:

> For the ethnic child of my father's and my generation, school could be and often was, a painful place. Everything valued by one's parents, everything that made up one's after-school life, was feared, misunderstood, occasionally ridiculed, and always subtly undermined. Everything associated with the most significant landmarks of human existence, everything that was most sacred, most poignant, most satisfying – all of that was somehow second or third rate.[19]

However, in the 1920's and 1930's school boards in many rural communities in the West were able to hire teachers of the same ethnic background as the majority of the students. When this happened, the regular English-language curriculum was at times regarded as unimportant. A Ukrainian Canadian who taught in a rural community in Saskatchewan from 1935 to 1939 confessed:

> To be honest, I wasn't really equipped to teach anything. . . . I had scratched the surface of history, mathematics, English and so on – at high school level. I could keep ahead of the students. But in a serious sense Normal School had only just equipped us with the rudiments for teaching. We were glorified baby-sitters. But in Ukrainian cultural

terms we had a little more background in music, choir, folk-dancing (all self-taught), and the people wanted that more than anything else. They weren't interested in the academic side of school as much as what you were going to do with the children after school and on the weekends. The government prescribed what was taught between 9 a.m. and 4 p.m., after 4 p.m. it was expected that we'd dedicate ourselves to Ukrainian work.

When an inspector criticized the teacher for speaking with an accent that was non-British and for devoting too much time to affairs that were not Canadian – presumably between nine and four – the secretary of the school board said, "Well, let him go fly a kite! We want you. As long as you're happy, we want you here." [20]

The major issues concerning the education of ethnic and racial groups during the 1920's and 1930's were simply an extension of those that had arisen prior to 1920. The immigrant influx of the 1920's did not compare in size with the massive wave of immigration prior to 1914, and there were no significant shifts in the ethnic composition of the newcomers. On the Prairies, the conflict between the conservative Old Colony Mennonites and the provincial governments about schools was a major cause of the exodus of about 4,000 Mennonites from Manitoba and 1,000 from Saskatchewan to Mexico. The Hutterites who came to Manitoba and Alberta in 1918 made agreements with the provincial governments that prevented conflict. In British Columbia there was a renewed drive to segregate Chinese and Japanese children. But these attempts were sporadic and diffuse, and so far as the Chinese were concerned, the end of immigration in 1923 provided its own solution. The high level of achievement of Japanese children in the schools muffled opposition to their presence, but in the interwar years attempts were made to eliminate or control private part-time Japanese-language schools, which were said to be nurturing and disseminating Japanese nationalism among the school children. The greatest problem in British Columbia regarding education had to do with the Doukhobors, however. Conflict between Doukhobors and the educational authorities culminated in a series of school burnings by Doukhobors who were protesting the government's compulsory school laws and harsh penalties for those who did not comply.

In 1932 the Sons of Freedom Doukhobors attempted to focus attention on their cause by staging a series of nude marches. Over 600 were arrested and sentenced to three-year prison terms; 365 children who were either arrested with their parents or left without care were put in various institutions. Although bombings and burnings ceased when numerous members of this faction were imprisoned, it was evident that British Columbia had failed to Canadianize the Doukhobors. One educational authority at the time pointed out that Doukhobors did not oppose education *per se* but did oppose the content and rigidity of the provincial school system. "Insistence by the schools on dividing children into grades or using military drill, using competitive tests and comparative grading, on teaching history with military and political orientations, and refusing to allow the teaching of Russian did nothing to make schools more palatable."[21] The government refused to honour the promises of educational autonomy made to the Doukhobors when they first arrived, and the uncompromising nature of the Sons of Freedom sect led to an ongoing conflict that would erupt periodically over the next several decades.

In Montreal the major public issues related to the education of immigrant groups continued to concern the Italians and Jews. The 1920's and 1930's saw a decline in provisions by the Roman Catholic schools for teaching in the mother tongue in the first three years of school; Italians, Lithuanians, and Chinese had been among those benefiting from these provisions. By the 1930's more Catholic immigrant children were enrolled in the English sector of Montreal's Roman Catholic school system than in the French sector, as immigrant parents concluded that their economic destiny lay with the English-speaking majority of North America.

Meanwhile, the Jews in Montreal remained dissatisfied with the educational system: they had no representation on the Protestant School Board, and schools in which the student body was almost totally Jewish had no Jewish teachers. The Protestant board resisted attempts by Jews to gain equality on the grounds that this would undermine the Christian character of the Protestant system. Jews themselves were increasingly divided over whether they should continue to seek equality in the Protestant system or establish their own separate school system. Following lengthy court cases, in 1930 the Jews and Protestants worked out an agreement that established a number of rights for Jews within the Protestant system and pledged no discrimination against Jewish teachers. However, Protestants still refused to allow Jews to sit on the school board.

Private Schools

The activities of home missionaries, Catholic and Protestant, in setting up private schools among the immigrants slackened in the 1920's, but some groups continued to develop their own private supplementary schools. The decrease in bilingualism in the public schools and the advent of more highly educated immigrants, including trained and qualified teachers, led to increased interest in establishing such schools. Among Polish Canadians, for example, the strongly developed Polish community in the United States and the Polish government through its consular representatives in various cities provided support for private supplementary schools. The Federation of Polish Societies in Canada, founded in 1931, imported great numbers of textbooks, organized travelling lending libraries, and set up and supported a few schools in larger urban communities.[22]

Among the Ukrainians, the banning of their language from the public schools gave a strong impetus to the founding of part-time schools - by churches, adult education societies, reading clubs, and community centres - and the establishment of student hostels or institutes, where instruction in

Ukrainian language and culture was given. Swyripa describes these educational activities in Alberta:

> To ensure the survival of their language and culture, the Ukrainians organized *ridni shkoly* or part-time vernacular schools, and *bursy* or student institutes. The former could and did exist wherever there were sufficient pupils and a willing instructor. The latter emerged in the cities and larger towns of the prairie provinces. They not only guaranteed a Ukrainian linguistic and cultural environment for the student residents, thus cushioning the impact of urban life, but also facilitated education beyond the rural school.[23]

While full-time Hungarian schools emerged only in Saskatchewan, Hungarian supplementary schools existed in many areas of the Prairies and in central Canada.[24] In British Columbia by 1935 there were about forty Japanese supplementary schools with ninety teachers and more than 3,000 students.[25] Chinese schools existed in the 1930's and early 1940's in eleven locations across Canada; by 1941, they had about 1,500 students.[26]

The private schools had no easy time, especially during the depression years. Eager as parents were to pass on their language and culture, they had few means with which to do so. In some groups, including the German and Italian, they received financial aid from the governments in their homelands. The aid to the private schools carried an obligation to support the policies of the governments, which were at times at odds with Canadian policy or tradition. Since the private schools were not financed or supervised by Canadian authorities, however, there was little that could be done to prevent this.

SINCE WORLD WAR II

World War II, like World War I, led to an emphasis on the development of loyal, law-abiding Canadians and on stability and order. Nonetheless, it brought changes resulting in a place in the public school systems of most provinces for ancestral languages other than English and French, for other cultures than the British, and for multiculturalism. This has occurred without the disappearance of ethnic private schools and supplementary schools, which indeed have begun to receive public assistance. While the developments have not solved all the problems of immigrants and members of ethnic groups other than British and French in their relations with the schools, they have marked a new acceptance of pluralism in Canadian society.

The war, directed against a highly racist German regime, and post-war concern with human rights led to a new awareness of racism and ethnic discrimination in Canadian immigration policy and Canadian society. This awareness, and the vast numbers of immigrants entering the school systems, raised doubts about the policy of integration of immigrants and led to an examination of the linguistic and cultural obstacles to Canadianization. As well, Canadian-born members of various ethnic groups joined with educated immigrants in seeking new policies to meet the aspirations of established ethnic groups for cultural and linguistic retention.

Since the post-war immigrants flocked primarily to Toronto and, to a lesser extent, to Vancouver and Montreal, the school systems of these three metropolitan areas spearheaded the changes. In some residential areas many of the children were of the same language and culture, in others a variety of languages and cultures were represented in schools and individual class-rooms. In 1970 a survey conducted among teachers of new Canadian children in schools in the provinces of British Columbia, Alberta, Saskatchewan, Manitoba, and Ontario found that over thirty languages were spoken by children in English classes, and that as many as fifteen languages were represented in a single class.[27] Further, whether the classes were of one non-official language or of many, the numbers meant that children could not be left to learn the dominant language and culture on the playground and in the classroom without special programs.

From the point of view of school authorities, the first concern was the teaching of English (or French) to newcomers. In the major cities to which the immigrants went, the educational challenge and the financial burden were daunting. A study done in Toronto in 1962 showed that 15 per cent of the public school pupils were non-English-speaking, with Italian, German, Ukrainian, Greek, and Polish being the most common languages; the separate schools, that is, the publicly supported Roman Catholic schools, were at least as linguistically heterogeneous.[28] By 1975, 30 per cent of the public school students were born outside Canada and almost half did not have English as their first language.[29] To cope with the situation a variety of experimental ESL (English as a second language), subject upgrading, and bicultural-bilingual programs were introduced.

For the most part the children from recently arrived, non-English-speaking families performed well in the schools. A study of the students enrolled in the secondary schools of Ontario, both public and private, from 1959 to 1966, used two indices of performance: grade retention rates, that is, the number and percentage of students at each grade level who progressed successfully through school, and percentage of graduates, that is, the number of students who graduated from Grade 13 after five years in secondary school. On both indices, students from Yiddish-speaking homes were out-standing, and students from homes in which Ukrainian, German, Polish, Italian, Dutch, Slovak, and Hungarian were spoken had results similar to those from English-speaking homes. Toronto studies in the late 1960's showed that bilingual students who had learned two languages from an early age did better in school than their English-speaking unilingual classmates.[30]

Children of immigrants whose level of education was low did pose some problems, however. The Italians, among whom 72 per cent of participants in the labour force in 1961 had no schooling or elementary schooling only, and the Portuguese, whose formal education in the 1960's averaged 3.7 years for men and 2.8 years for women, drew special attention. Hence, concern about linguistic skills quickly became concern about "cultural deprivation," a lack in the home of attitudes and facilities conducive to achievement in the schools.

The implementation of changes in the classroom was aided by the growing ethnic diversity among teachers and other educational personnel. Prior to 1940 the members of the teaching profession and of school boards in English-speaking Canada were largely of British origin, but the shortage of teachers in the late 1940's, the 1950's, and the 1960's opened the schools to people of a variety of backgrounds, many of them recent immigrants. The increased heterogeneity of many communities also began to be reflected among school trustees.

In the 1970's, after proclamation of the federal policy of multiculturalism, the demand for the use of non-official languages in the public schools became pressing. One reason was to ensure that children did not fall behind in their schooling while they were learning one of the official languages; another, urged by members of established ethnic groups as well as by immigrants, was to teach children the language of their forebears. Classes in the heritage languages began as part of an extended school day, but increasingly these have been incorporated into the regular day. In Ontario in 1984-85 almost 91,000 children participated in the heritage language programs. Moreover, bilingual education in English and a heritage language has become possible in the three Prairie provinces: the Ukrainian-English and German-English programs in Edmonton, begun in the early 1970's, have been most notable. In 1984-85, total enrolments in the bilingual programs were 2,647 in Alberta, 1,691 in Saskatchewan, and 1,294 in Manitoba.[31]

The changes in immigration regulations late in the 1960's and the subsequent changes in sources of immigration brought to the schools children from the West Indies and from Asia, who not only differed from the majority in language, culture, or both but also in physical appearance. They made the schools not simply ethnically diverse but also multiracial to an unprecedented degree.

The West Indians have concentrated chiefly in Toronto and to a lesser extent in Montreal. Those belonging to the middle and upper classes dispersed throughout the city, and their children adapted easily to the schools. The working-class West Indians tended to concentrate in certain areas, where their children have presented problems related to language, culture, and minority status. In regard to language, school boards that had become accustomed to coping with different languages were slow to recognize that different dialects of English spoken by West Indians also presented obstacles, and in Montreal they failed at first to recognize that the Creole of the Haitians was not merely a dialect of French, or poorly spoken French, but a different language. They were also slow to recognize that moving from an authoritarian school system into a more permissive system and from a largely black society into a predominantly white one, together with the separation of children from parents for periods often extending to many years because of patterns of immigration, affected school deportment and achievement. An additional problem found among West Indians (but by no means limited to them) was the keeping of children out of school by illegal immigrants.

Immigrants from south, east, and southeast Asia have tended to have high levels of education, and the problems encountered by their children in the schools have been social rather than academic. Name-calling and brawling among schoolboys have intermittently drawn attention from school authorities and the media.

An issue that emerged in the Toronto area was the streaming of immigrant children of working-class backgrounds into technical or vocational programs or schools rather than academic programs or academic secondary schools. The parents, many of whom had high ambitions for their children, considered this to be a result of discrimination. Italian, Portuguese, and West Indian parents were prominent among those who complained. Authorities have denied any relationship between ethnicity or race and streaming, but the fact that among West Indians a much higher proportion of dark-skinned than light-skinned parents complained suggests that a relationship does exist.[32]

The province of Quebec, or rather the metropolitan area of Montreal, in sharing in the post-war immigration, received many Italians, Portuguese, and Greeks. It also received, especially in the 1960's and 1970's, considerable numbers of Jews from North Africa, Lebanon, and Egypt, and Haitians and Vietnamese; some members of each of these groups were French-speaking. In the 1950's and 1960's non-Catholics as a matter of course entered the English-language schools of the Protestant School Board; these schools were secular, or religiously plural, rather than Protestant in any narrow sense. For Roman Catholics whose language was neither French nor English - "allophones" - the issue remained regarding which of the sectors of the Catholic school system their children should be integrated into. Many of them saw the economic advantages of an education in English, and some even sent their children to Protestant schools to obtain those advantages. In the early post-war years the Montreal Catholic School Commission made some desultory gestures toward attracting allophone children by such means as offering evening classes in French to their parents. In 1968 the Ministry of Education established reception classes (*classes d'accueil*) for immigrant children who were to enter French-language schools, and in 1973 the ministry took over full responsibility for the classes. However, in the main, the children continued to gravitate to English-language schools for reasons that included the economic advantage of fluency in English and also the lack of welcome they felt within the French-language schools and the Francophone community.

With the Quiet Revolution and the drastic overhaul of the educational system, and with the growing awareness among Québécois of their declining birthrate in the 1960's, there came intense nationalist pressure to integrate immigrant students into the Francophone schools. Bilingual (French and English) and trilingual (French, English, and language of origin) schools within the French sector of the Catholic school system became an important issue, especially in the Italian-Canadian community of Montreal. By 1967 protests by Francophones against bilingual schools began to attract attention, and in 1968 in the Montreal suburb of St-Léonard the protests became violent. There a nationalist group, the Mouvement pour l'Integration Scolaire, gained control of the school board and voted for the replacement of a bilingual program by a unilingual French program. The parents, predominantly Italians but including also Hungarians, Germans, and Ukrainians, objected, and after demonstrations and counter-demonstrations some withdrew their children from the French school and placed them in private classes or even, on occasion, in the Protestant system. The incident led to Bill 63, which affirmed the right of parents to choose the official language in which their children would be schooled. But it also led to the Commission of Inquiry on the Position of the French Language and on Language Rights in Quebec – the Gendron Commission – and to the two language laws of the 1970's that first severely limited and then removed altogether the rights of immigrant children to English-language education in Quebec.

The first of these laws was Bill 22, passed in 1974 by the Liberal government. It decreed that only students who were of English mother tongue or who could show that they had sufficient knowledge of English to benefit from schooling in that language could enter English schools. Provision was made to test the proficiency in the English language of those who wanted to register in English schools and were not of English mother tongue. In addition, schools were to be allowed to increase instruction in English only if, in the opinion of the Minister of Education, the number of pupils whose mother tongue was English warranted the increase. Italian and Greek Canadians, unhappy with the bill, speedily established classes to prepare children for the language tests and later kept up a barrage of criticism of the tests and the manner in which they were administered. They received some support from French Canadians who wanted to enrol their children in English schools and could no longer do so.

Bill 101, passed in 1977 under the Parti Québécois government, was much more stringent. It made French the language of instruction in the kindergarten classes and in the elementary and secondary schools, except for:

> (a) a child whose father or mother received his or her elementary instruction in English, in Quebec; (b) a child whose father or mother, domiciled in Quebec on the date of the coming into force of this act, received his or her elementary instruction in English outside Quebec; (c) a child who, in his last year of school in Quebec before the coming into force of this act, was lawfully receiving his instruction in English, in a public kindergarten class or in an elementary or secondary school; (d) the younger brothers and sisters of a child described in paragraph c.

Children of parents who came to Quebec for a limited period were also eligible to attend English schools. In the main, however, all children of immigrants henceforth were consigned to French schools. The law met with some resistance: some English boards and teachers accepted "illegals" who should have gone to French schools. But inasmuch as Bill 101 did not give to the English the privileges they had retained under Bill 22, it was more

119

acceptable to the other ethnic groups. With the passage of time, more and more immigrants have been going to French schools: in 1982, 15 per cent of students in the Catholic schools of Montreal were of other ethnic origins, and the percentage would rise to 20 by 1984. A few of them also, beginning in 1978, have been provided with courses in their languages of origin, under the program known as PELO (*projet d'enseignement en langue d'origine*): in 1978-79 about 600 children were involved, and in 1984-85 enrolment was 3,449.[33]

Private Schools

The public and the separate schools were not alone in experiencing the shock of post-war immigration. The private ethnic schools multiplied and throve, and they increasingly received support from the federal government and from certain provincial governments. A few were regular all-day schools; most were supplementary schools.

Probably the first study of such schools was carried out under the auspices of the Royal Commission on Bilingualism and Biculturalism in the mid-1960's. It gathered data from sixteen ethnic groups. Only four of these sponsored full-time schools, the Mennonite, Jewish, Ukrainian, and Greek groups, but these schools had almost 9,000 students and were found in all provinces except those in the Atlantic region. The Mennonite schools were at the secondary and college levels, the Ukrainian schools at the secondary level, the Jewish schools chiefly at the elementary level, and the one Greek school also at the elementary level. Only in Quebec did they receive public support, and in the other provinces they suffered from financial difficulties that threatened to dilute the ethnic component in their programs.

Far more numerous were the supplementary schools. These operated for a few hours a week, after regular school hours or on Saturday, and attempted to pass on to the children as much of the language and culture as possible. The sixteen ethnic groups from whom data were obtained operated more than 500 such schools with an enrolment of close to 40,000, again, in all provinces except the four Atlantic provinces. They varied greatly in the degree to which their programs were structured and in their equipment and premises. They tended to share problems, however, such as the supply of appropriate textbooks, qualified teachers, and adequate funds.[34]

In the years that followed the survey, the private and the supplementary schools flourished. In Quebec, private schools had a larger place in education than in other provinces, and the drastic changes of the 1960's did not change this. From 1967 on, private schools following the core curriculum of the province and teaching the greater part of it in French have been subsidized by public funds. Many of the private schools are ethnic: twenty-three are Jewish, two are Greek, and two are Armenian. In Alberta and Manitoba also, private schools now receive public support. In Alberta, and to a greater extent in southern Ontario, the Dutch Christian Reformed Church has sponsored an important network of Christian schools. Members of various evangelical denominations have begun to enrol their children in these schools. In 1965 the number of students in Greek supplementary schools in Ontario was given as 900; in 1968 it was estimated at 1,200. The Report of the Royal Commission on Bilingualism and Biculturalism had no record of Chinese or of Portuguese supplementary schools in Ontario: in 1970, however, there were 302 pupils enrolled in a Chinese school in Toronto, in 1972 there were 621 in a Portuguese school in Toronto, and at about the same time there were 265 third-language schools in that city.

With the policy of multiculturalism, government assistance became available to supplementary heritage language schools under the Cultural Enrichment Program (CEP), one of seven sub-programs of the federal multicultural program. Grants were offered to help in "securing more adequate educational facilities, in attracting more qualified teaching staff, in purchasing badly needed teaching materials, and in meeting the administrative expenses incurred"; to assist in the training of teachers; and to help produce teaching aids. An evaluation of the CEP, carried out in 1983, indicated that from 1977-78 to 1980-81 the number of schools supported increased from 515 to 628, and the number of students enrolled in the schools grew from 78,014 to 92,189. In 1980-81, schools of thirty-eight groups, including native Indian and Scottish, received grants; Ukrainian, Jewish, German, Chinese, Greek, and Italian schools were most numerous. Approximately 45 per cent of the schools were in Ontario, 10 to 13 per cent in the Pacific region, Manitoba, and Alberta, and less than 8 per cent in Quebec, Saskatchewan, and the Atlantic region. Concerning the impact of the program, the evaluators reported:

> In the case of CEP, it is the Federal Government's act of giving rather than the gift itself that appears to have the most potent overall contribution to the achievement of Program objectives. In providing assistance to supplementary heritage language schools, the Federal Government has legitimated and raised the status of the schools and of heritage language learning itself. School representatives . . . frequently voiced the view the CEP failed to provide adequate funding under the three grant programs; but they also pointed out that the sheer fact of Federal Government funding gave their groups a lever to use in securing additional funds from the provincial government. Further, a number of school representatives suggested that the Federal support had helped mobilize support from the cultural community.[35]

By 1984-85, thanks to the CEP, about sixty languages were being taught in supplementary schools and the number of students was close to 118,000.[36]

In the 1980's the public schools offer instruction in an increasingly wide range of languages; use a number of languages in early grades to assist children while they are mastering one of Canada's official languages; and acknowledge the importance of various cultures and give them some place in the curriculum. In addition, they try, with varying degrees of finesse, to teach multiculturalism or the acceptance of ethnic diversity as an aspect of the

Canadian way of life. They do so through increasingly heterogeneous personnel. Private ethnic schools also flourish, although to a lesser extent than in the 1960's and 1970's because of the passing of the crest of the post-war wave of immigration, and they receive government aid. The view of the schools as bulwarks of British influence and Canadian Anglo-conformity is no longer accurate.

NOTES

1. For general discussions of education and ethnicity, see Cornelius Jaenen, "Canadian Education and Minority Rights," in Cornelius Jaenen, ed., *Slavs in Canada*, vol. 3 (Ottawa: Inter-University Committee on Canadian Slavs, 1971), pp. 191-208; Cornelius Jaenen, "Minority Group Schooling and Canadian National Unity," *The Journal of Educational Thought*, 7, 2 (1973), pp. 81-93, 136-37.
2. For discussions of the issues of Ukrainians and the school system, see Cornelius Jaenen, "Ruthenian Schools in Western Canada, 1897-1919," *Paedogogica Historica*, 10, 3 (1970), pp. 517-41; and Manoly R. Lupul, "Ukrainian-language Education in Canada's Public Schools," in Lupul, ed., *A Heritage in Transition*, pp. 215-43.
3. For discussions of pressures for Anglo-conformity, see Marilyn Barber, "Canadianization through the Schools of the Prairie Provinces before World War I: The Attitudes and Aims of the English-speaking Majority," in Martin L. Kovacs, ed., *Ethnic Canadians: Culture and Education* (Regina: Canadian Plains Research Center, 1978), pp. 281-94; Keith McLeod, "Education and the Assimilation of the New Canadian in the North-West Territories and Saskatchewan, 1885-1934" (Ph.D. thesis, University of Toronto, 1975).
4. For short summaries of the major trends, see M.R. Lupul, "Education in Western Canada before 1873," and "Educational Crises in the New Dominion to 1917," in J. Donald Wilson *et al.*, *Canadian Education: A History* (Scarborough: Prentice-Hall of Canada, 1970), pp. 241-89.
5. Barber, "Canadianization through the Schools"; McLeod, "Education and the Assimilation of the New Canadian"; Howard Palmer, *Patterns of Prejudice: A History of Nativism in Alberta* (Toronto: McClelland and Stewart, 1982), chapter 1.
6. C.J. Jaenen, "The Manitoba School Question: An Ethnic Interpretation," in Kovacs, *Ethnic Canadians*, pp. 317-32; Borislav Bilash, "Bilingual Schools in Manitoba, 1897-1916" (Winnipeg: Ukrainian Educational Services, n.d.); Stella Hryniuk and Neil McDonald, "The Schooling Experience of Ukrainians in Manitoba, 1896-1916," in Nancy M. Sheehan, J. Donald Wilson, and David C. Jones, eds., *Schools in the West: Essays in Canadian Educational History* (Calgary: Detselig Enterprises, 1986), pp. 155-73.
7. Francis, *In Search of Utopia*, pp. 161-83; Frank H. Epp, *Mennonites in Canada 1786-1920: The History of a Separate People* (Toronto: Macmillan of Canada, 1974), pp. 333-62.
8. Quoted in J.E. Rea, "My Main Line Is the Kiddies," in Wsevolod Isajiw, ed.,

Identities: The Impact of Ethnicity on Canadian Society (Toronto: Peter Martin Associates, 1977), p. 6.

9. McLeod, "Education and the Assimilation of the New Canadians," chapters 4-5.

10. Quoted in Palmer, *Patterns of Prejudice*, p. 47.

11. Peter Ward, *White Canada Forever: Popular Attitudes and Public Policy Toward Orientals in British Columbia* (Montreal: McGill-Queen's University Press, 1978), pp. 62-64; Mary Ashworth, *The Forces Which Shaped Them: A History of the Education of Minority Group Children in British Columbia* (Vancouver: New Star Books, 1979), pp. 54-73.

12. James W. St.G. Walker, *A History of Blacks in Canada: A Study Guide for Teachers and Parents* (Ottawa: Minister of State for Multiculturalism, 1980), pp. 109-15.

13. Patricia McKegney, "The German Schools of Waterloo County," Waterloo Historical Society, *Annual Report*, 1970.

14. Robert Harney and Harold Troper, *Immigrants: A Portrait of the Urban Experience, 1890-1930* (Toronto: Van Nostrand Reinhold, 1975), p. 110.

15. Stuart E. Rosenberg, *The Jewish Community in Canada* (Toronto: McClelland and Stewart, 1970), vol. 1, pp. 412-13.

16. Piniuta, *Land of Pain, Land of Promise*.

17. Arthur Chiel, *The Jews of Manitoba* (Toronto: University of Toronto Press, 1961).

18. John Lehr, "The Government and the Immigrant: Perspectives on Bloc Settlement in the Canadian West," *Canadian Ethnic Studies*, 9, 2 (1977), pp. 44-45.

19. S. Cipywnyk, "Multiculturalism and the Child in Western Canada," in *Multiculturalism and Education*. Proceedings of the Western Regional Conference, Canadian Association for Curriculum Studies, 1976, pp. 27-50.

20. Lubomyr Luciuk, ed., *Heroes of Their Day: The Reminiscences of Bohdan Panchuk* (Toronto: Multicultural History Society of Ontario, 1983), pp. 35, 37.

21. Ashworth, *The Forces Which Shaped Them*, p. 155.

22. Radecki, *A Member of a Distinguished Family*, p. 93.

23. Frances Swyripa, "The Ukrainians in Alberta," in Howard and Tamara Palmer, eds., *Peoples of Alberta: Portraits of Cultural Diversity* (Saskatoon: Western Producer Prairie Books, 1985), p. 237.

24. Dreisziger, *Struggle and Hope*, pp. 122-23.

25. Adachi, *The Enemy That Never Was*, p. 127.

26. Wickberg, ed., *From China to Canada*, pp. 170-71.

27. Mary Ashworth, *Immigrant Children and Canadian Schools* (Toronto: McClelland and Stewart, 1975), pp. 43-45.

28. Research Department in Cooperation with the Public School Principals' Association, *A Survey of Pupils Learning English as a Second Language in the City of Toronto Public Schools* (Toronto: The Board of Education for the City of Toronto, June, 1962).

29. Ramesh Deosaran, E.N. Wright, and Thelma Kane, *The 1975 Every Student*

Survey: Student's Background and Its Relationship to Program Placement (Toronto: The Board of Education for the City of Toronto, Research Department, 1976).

30. A.J.C. King, "Ethnicity and School Adjustment," *The Canadian Review of Sociology and Anthropology*, 5, 2 (1968), pp. 84-91; E.N. Wright, *Learning English as a Second Language: A Summary of Research Department Studies* (Toronto: The Board of Education for the City of Toronto, Research Department, 1970), p. 3.

31. Commissioner of Official Languages, *Annual Report 1985*, p. 199.

32. Subhas Ramcharan, "Special Problems of Immigrant Children in the Toronto School System," in Aaron Wolfgang, ed., *Education of Immigrant Students: Issues and Answers* (Toronto: Ontario Institute for Studies in Education, 1973), p. 103.

33. Commissioner of Official Languages, *Annual Report 1985*, pp. 198-99.

34. *Report* of the Royal Commission on Bilingualism and Biculturalism, Book 4, *Cultural Contributions of the Other Ethnic Groups* (Ottawa: Queen's Printer, 1970), pp. 148-59.

35. Res Policy Research Inc., "An Evaluation of the Cultural Enrichment Program," January 11, 1983, pp. 186-87.

36. Commissioner of Official Languages, *Annual Report 1985*, p. 196.

SEVEN

Religious Institutions

Religion has been a fundamental element of group identity. It binds together those who share certain beliefs and practices concerning the supernatural and sets them against those adhering to different beliefs and rites. Some religions are quite explicitly ethnic; others are, as new religions must be in the beginning, de-ethnicizing. Religions are often agents of social change; they are always subject to social change.

For many Canadian ethnic groups, especially before World War II, religion was an extremely important aspect of life. Some scarcely distinguished between religion and ethnicity, and attributed the survival of their people to religion and its organizations. Many had been sustained by religious faith in hardships preceding migration and saw the hand of God in their move to Canada. A few Asians had derived their first knowledge of Canada from Canadian missionaries serving in their homelands. On arrival, even those who had previously not been devout sometimes turned to religion, either because they sought solace or because they regarded religion as part of the Canadian way of life. Yet religious organizations brought to Canada by immigrants were often difficult to transfer, did not hold their adherents in the new land against the competition of sects and cults, and usually lost members of the second generation to older Canadian churches. Recently, the religious affiliations of the population have reflected the increased diversity of post-war Canada, and, in addition, the secularization accompanying modernization has had an impact on Canadians of all ethnic origins.

BEFORE WORLD WAR I

Early immigrants to Canada were virtually all Christians, but they represented a considerable range of denominations and religious organizations. During the French regime, the vast majority of settlers were Roman Catholic: Protestants and Jews were officially excluded, although they engaged in trade in the colony. With the ascendancy of the British, Protestants came not only from Great Britain and the American colonies but from Germany, Holland,

and Switzerland. In at least one case – the Germans brought to Halifax in 1750 and settled at Lunenburg in 1753 – Protestants were especially recruited to counterbalance Roman Catholic settlers of French origin. There were also Roman Catholics in small numbers from England and Scotland and in larger numbers from Ireland, as well as a small number of Jews.

Within Protestantism the Church of England had greatest state support and attempted to assimilate others. Lack of clergy and lack of funds exposed immigrant churches to its missionary efforts. In late eighteenth-century Halifax, for example, the Anglicans of St. Paul's first extended services to a German Lutheran congregation that did not have a pastor, then when a pastor was secured persuaded him to be ordained as an Anglican in order to receive a subsidy from the Society for the Propagation of the Gospel, and finally absorbed the Lutherans and their property.[1] In several parts of Upper Canada (Ontario) also the Church of England persuaded German Lutheran pastors to accept Anglican ordination in return for financial support; the pastors' success in bringing their flocks into the Anglican fold varied.[2] Churches less dependent on trained clergy, such as the German Mennonite churches, were not susceptible to proselytizing efforts; the Mennonites, of course, were also protected by their separatist views and their rural isolation. The Church of England itself in Nova Scotia, Ontario, and elsewhere proved slow to adapt itself to the New World, even with massive aid; it was not long in becoming one of many denominations adhered to by settlers of British origin, including among others the various branches of the Methodist, Baptist, and Presbyterian churches.

Sometimes missionaries were among the first representatives of their ethnic groups to come to Canada. Converting and "civilizing" the Amerindians had a strong appeal not only to French-Canadian priests and to missionaries of British origin but to other zealous preachers and teachers. Among Roman Catholics, the Italian, Father Francesco Bressani, was the pathfinder, the Slovene, Father Frederik Baraga, served with distinction among the Ottawa and Ojibway, and members of the Oblate order, including Belgian and Polish missionaries, also worked with the Indians and Métis.[3] A number of the missionaries, including Father Baraga, became interested in the languages of the Indians and contributed to the study of those languages.

The Jews were the first non-Christians other than the Native peoples to establish their religious structures in Canada. They brought both the Sephardic and the Ashkenazic rites. As early as 1768 a Sephardic congregation was founded in Montreal by Spanish and Portuguese Jews, to be followed in 1846 by an Ashkenazic congregation founded by English, Polish, and German Jews. The first congregation in Toronto, also Ashkenazic, was set up in 1856; from England and Germany, many were wealthy, mixed with the city's elite, and disappeared into the Christian community.

When immigration quickened in the last few decades of the nineteenth century, Roman Catholicism, Protestantism, and Judaism all received massive reinforcements from immigrants of various ethnic origins, and several

126

non-Christian religions became organized in Canada for the first time.

Many of the central and eastern European immigrants were devout Catholics, but were accustomed to rites and forms of organization different from those of the French Canadians and the Irish Roman Catholics already well entrenched in eastern and central Canada; some – for example, the majority of the Ukrainian immigrants – were Greek Catholics rather than Roman Catholics. For this reason, as well as for linguistic reasons, it was important for them to be served by priests of their own ethnic background. However, priests, like other educated people, were often reluctant to come to the New World. Also, in 1894 the Sacred Congregation for the Propagation of the Faith ruled that only celibate Ukrainian priests of the Greek Catholic Church should be allowed to minister in the United States and Canada. Married priests continued to serve in some ethnic groups, such as the Macedonian.

The immigrants had been accustomed to pay very little and only indirectly for the services of priests, who in the old country had belonged to churches that were established or richly endowed or both. In any case, in the first years of settlement funds were scarce. Dr. Oleskiw, in negotiating on behalf of Ukrainian settlers in 1896, proposed that the Canadian government should encourage priests to immigrate by providing a salary for them until the settlers were able to assume the financial responsibility; the government rejected the proposal, acting in accord with the principle of a thoroughgoing separation of church and state. Lacking state aid, it was often some time before an immigrant settlement could pay for the services of a priest or pastor. It had to make do with the services of whatever Roman Catholic or Protestant clergy were in the vicinity, or with an itinerant who served a number of missions. Shacks, log cabins, or community halls that also served for Saturday night dances were used until churches could be constructed, often by the parishioners themselves. The deprivation felt by some immigrants was expressed by a Ukrainian settler in Manitoba in 1899 in a letter published in the journal of the Basilian order in Galicia, *Misionar*:

> Dear Fathers,
> Life here is very good for our bodies, there is no physical deprivation, but what of that, when there are great deprivations of the soul. There is enough to eat, drink, wear. But our soul is poor, very poor. This is because it has nothing to eat, or drink, nothing from which to live, no roof to stand beneath. It can only shelter itself under strangers' roofs and listen to them, but it does not hear, and does not understand.[4]

The Ukrainian Greek Catholics received three priests and two nuns from Galicia in 1902, but the priests and parishes came under the jurisdiction of the Roman Catholic hierarchy. A Ukrainian Greek Catholic bishop arrived in 1912, and the following year the Ruthenian Greek Catholic Church was set up, incorporating the scattered parishes. However, Bishop Budka's pastoral letter in 1914 calling on Ukrainians to join the Austro-Hungarian army embarrassed his flock. In 1918 the Ukrainian Greek Orthodox Church of Canada was founded, mostly by dissenters from the Ukrainian Greek Catholic Church.[5]

In the West the distance between settlements meant that rural parishes could by no means replicate the densely concentrated ones in the homeland. Further, the parishes frequently brought together people and priests who had come from different communities, with different dialects and different customs. United effort could be maintained through the first years of settlement, but later the congregations were often torn by disputes. In almost all Christian denominations troubles arose; for example, German, Danish, Swedish, and Norwegian Lutherans on occasion found it impossible to dwell in harmony. In time, national or ethnic parishes developed, with priests to give leadership. The number of religious and secular societies founded in the parish depended largely on the priest, and in the 1900's and 1910's there usually were few of these since the priest might have four or five missions to serve as well as his parish.[6]

In the towns and cities Roman Catholic immigrants frequently found that their ethnically specific religious needs were ignored by Irish-Canadian and French-Canadian ecclesiastics. They were either absorbed quickly and lost their ethnic distinctiveness, or fought, often bitterly, to win a place for themselves and their ways. In the late nineteenth century Archbishop Langevin of St. Boniface, though zealous in trying to serve the new immigrants in his charge, saw no need for separate Ukrainian and Polish parishes in Winnipeg and urged Ukrainians to join the Polish Catholic Holy Ghost Church.[7] The Holy Ghost Church also served German, Hungarian, Slovak, and other Roman Catholics. In Coleman, Alberta, another Holy Ghost Church was set up to serve all Catholics of Slavic origin among the miners.[8] In Toronto, Polish and Ukrainian churches provided for the religious needs of Catholic Germans, Hungarians, Slovaks, and Czechs until they could establish their own churches. In Berlin (Kitchener), Ontario, a German Catholic parish provided facilities for Polish Catholics from 1865 until 1913, when a Polish church was built. In some instances, defections from the Roman Catholic Church occurred before the right to national or ethnic parishes was conceded. For example, the Polish National Catholic Church of the United States, independent of the Vatican, won a number of parishes in Canada, the first of them in Winnipeg in 1904, and still has churches – ten in 1973 – in Canada. However, by 1920 there were about fifty-two Polish parishes in Canada, of which forty-one were in Manitoba, Saskatchewan, and Alberta.[9]

In Montreal, the Roman Catholic Church was more willing to establish separate national churches. It was concerned with the preservation of French-Canadian culture and felt it would be dangerous for French Canadians to mingle with Italians, Poles, Ukrainians, Hungarians, Chinese, and Syrians in churches and parishes. The children of the immigrants were accommodated in the English-language schools, which had been set up to serve Irish immigrants.

Some priests met considerable anticlericalism. In the homeland, although the people had strong religious faith and attachment to the church as the armature of their rural communities, the priest had sometimes been reckoned among the oppressors of the peasantry. In Canada, the immigrants considered themselves free to criticize, especially since they had played a role in organizing the church and were still involved in its administration; they often took full advantage of this freedom. Even among Ukrainians, generally considered to have been deeply religious, anticlericalism appeared.[10]

Lack of clergy in Canada led some groups to receive itinerant priests or ministers from the United States. The result was that many religious organizations were made part of structures with headquarters outside Canada. In some instances eagerness for religious ministrations led communities to accept impostors or religious leaders of dubious moral standards. Bishop Seraphim of the All-Russian Orthodox Church, who from 1902 to 1908 created a scandal in Winnipeg by indiscriminate ordination of priests and building of a scrap-iron cathedral, was even said to display fits of insanity.[11]

The demands made on the priests who came were great. They had to seek out co-religionists in their ethnic group and motivate them to participate regularly in services they had been accustomed to getting along without for some time. Radecki wrote of Polish priests:

> The pioneer priests had to be hardy, without concern for comfort and personal well-being, and constantly on the move. They had to earn their own living, organize parishes, build and maintain churches or chapels, and retain the loyalty of the faithful under proselytization efforts of other churches. They had to be young, healthy, and dedicated to face the hardships, discouragement and poverty of their charges. The greatest problem for many of them was isolation from other priests. For months they travelled without the company of other clergy, without the consolation of retreats or encouraging words from their supervisors. Even those priests assigned to a parish often had responsibility for four or five missions. They had to travel, to divide their effort and attention between their parishioners and others without their own priests.[12]

Laymen who had struggled long and hard to build a church were frequently loath to leave all the decision-making to the priest, as they had done in the homeland. This was especially so when in the new land the priest was no longer the most learned member of the parish. Bitter conflict often ensued.

> The parishioners contributed heavily in time, effort, and funds to the building of *their* churches, and expected the parishes and the clergy to reflect not only religious traditions and beliefs but also Polish patriotic and other non-religious values. Since the parish and the clergy were dependent financially on their support, the parishioners hoped to have a voice, or at least be advised, on the distribution of parish funds. Some Polish clerics were not only willing to promote non-religious concerns, but were the instigators of such activities, but none were willing, or able,

because of the ecclesiastical rules, to share in the decision-making with their parishioners. These were persisting problems in a number of urban parishes which led on occasion to change in pastors, separation of a group, and formation of a new parish or a new church.[13]

Lack of clergy also exposed immigrants to the missionary efforts of the more established Protestant denominations. These regarded themselves as emissaries of a superior civilization in dealing not only with the Native peoples but with Roman Catholics and people from eastern, central, and southern Europe. The Methodists, Presbyterians, and Baptists in particular set up missions to "Christianize" and "Canadianize" immigrants. At times they competed fiercely for souls, shifting their missions from place to place in pursuit of the mobile immigrant workers. They tried to attract adherents and to implement the Social Gospel by providing English classes and social services as well as leadership in combatting social problems affecting the immigrants. Residential schools, in which young people living apart from their families were exposed to Anglo-Canadian Protestant values on a daily basis, and medical facilities were important parts of the missions. Sometimes the ministrations of the missionaries led to conversions; sometimes, as in the case of J.S. Woodsworth, they led the ministers into political activism that drew them out of their pulpits. Poles and Ukrainians were prime targets for Protestant missionaries, but few conversions resulted.

Some attempts at securing converts among immigrants were more elaborate and less straightforward than missions. These often were directed toward Catholic immigrants by Protestant clergy and church workers, who considered Catholics to be only nominal Christians. For example, the Presbyterian Church in 1904 helped set up the Independent Greek Church among Ukrainians. It had initial success with support from young men who espoused the tenets of the Radical party in Galicia and were intensely anticlerical. It failed when its connections with Presbyterianism became known. Most of its adherents returned to Greek Catholicism or Russian Orthodoxy: the remnants were absorbed into the Presbyterian Church in 1913.

There were some Protestant immigrants from mainly Catholic countries such as Poland and Hungary. They were able to set up churches in Canada but were largely excluded from ethnic community institutions. Like Jews from central and eastern Europe, they were included in census figures for a particular group, but were otherwise ignored by ethnic leaders.

The sects that settled in western Canada, such as Mennonites and Doukhobors, did not have problems of ministerial supply, since they did not have professional clergy. The Doukhobors did, however, have problems of leadership. The leader of the Doukhobor sect, Peter Verigin, was in exile in Siberia in 1899 when 7,400 of his followers immigrated to Canada; he himself did not come until 1902. In the meantime, many of the Doukhobors had progressed economically and had begun to ask for exemptions on religious grounds from the provisions of the Homestead Act and from regulations concerning marriage and the registration of births and deaths. Refused the exemption, they had begun the long series of conflicts with the Canadian government that led to the migration of many of them to British Columbia in 1908 and to the practice of nude parades and arson by a small number of the radical Sons of Freedom sect.

Among the immigrant groups, many of the sects were aided in maintaining themselves as religious groups by the fact that their members migrated in families. Ethnic groups in which the early arrivals were almost all men frequently did not experience a demand for religious services immediately. In logging, mining, and construction camps, Sunday was a time for washing clothes, writing letters, and performing other tasks for which the weekday's hard labour left little leisure. With the coming of women and the institution of families, however, the lack of religious ministrations became keenly felt. In the sectarian ethnic group no gap existed between settlement and organization of religious services.

The sects were, however, highly susceptible to fragmentation. Epp distinguished nine groups among the Mennonites of Dutch-North German origin and nine more among the Mennonites and Amish Mennonites of Swiss-South German origin in 1920.[14] The Doukhobors by then were also divided into a number of groups, notably the Independents, the Community Doukhobors, and the Sons of Freedom; they shared the essentials of their religion but differed in many other regards.

In addition to the larger sects, many smaller ones were brought to western Canada, some of them North American, others part of religious revivals sweeping through Europe. In Alberta the German Baptist Church of North America and the Evangelical Swedish Mission Covenant of America had established themselves by 1900, to be followed soon after by German-American Dunkards, Russian-German Seventh Day Adventists (who by 1921 had attracted Ukrainian and Scandinavian as well as British settlers), German-speaking Evangelical United Brethren, and Scandinavian-American Evangelical Free Church congregations. Those sects that had originated on the American frontier now found similar conditions in Canada.[15] Cults – that is, religious groups that were syncretic rather than fundamentalist like the sects – were commonly urban rather than rural, but among Hungarians in Bekevar, Saskatchewan, the Christian Spiritists' Society emerged before World War I and was the subject of great controversy. Its appearance is considered to have indicated a failure of the churches to meet spiritual and sociocultural needs, and it and its offshoots provided a variety of community services.[16]

The great influx of Jews from eastern Europe from 1880 until the war brought into being many Ashkenazi synagogues, especially in Winnipeg, Montreal, and Toronto. Establishing a synagogue was relatively easy, and there were few problems of religious leadership. However, Jews from different countries in many instances wanted different religious organizations. In Toronto before World War I separate synagogues developed for the English

131

and Germans, the Romanians, Poles, Russians, Galicians, Moldavians, and others; even within these groups, those from different regions sometimes split because of different customs.[17]

The Jews were the objects of proselytizers from the Christian churches. Missions to the Jews began early and continued long, without notable success. Such conversions as occurred were as frequently the result of intermarriage as of Christian evangelism. The Presbyterian Board of Home Missions opened a mission to the Jews of Montreal in 1892. It lasted only a few years, but another mission was started in 1915. In Toronto an interdenominational mission supported by wealthy individuals, the Toronto Jewish Mission, was set up in 1892, and a Presbyterian mission to the Jews began as early as 1898. Out of the Presbyterian efforts a Hebrew Christian Presbyterian Congregation emerged in 1913. Anglican activity began at least by 1903, but an Anglican mission, sponsored by Holy Trinity parish, did not open until 1912. Converts were leaders in much of the missionary activity, which included provision of medical services, rent subsidies, employment services, and parties for children. Most Christians were lukewarm about the efforts, and some Jews were roused to attack street preachers from the missions and in 1914 to form an Anti-Missionary League.[18] The Presbyterian Church started a mission to the Jews in Winnipeg in 1911 and an evangelical settlement house the following year.[19]

Of the non-Judeo-Christian religions, Buddhism was brought to Canada by Japanese immigrants. The first Buddhist temple was opened in Vancouver in 1905, and a priest was brought from Japan. The first Sikh temple or *gurdwara* was dedicated, also in Vancouver, in 1908: over $6,000 was collected for the building, and in addition much labour was contributed.[20]

Like the Jews, Asian non-Christians were the special targets of the missions. Proselytizing activity began among the Chinese in British Columbia as early as 1859; the first convert was secured in 1875, but he had few successors. In the West the Christian churches achieved little success among the Chinese until immigrants who were already Christian began to arrive. In central Canada, missionary work began in Montreal in the 1880's through the activity of the Presbyterian and Methodist churches. A Presbyterian minister of Chinese origin arrived in Montreal in 1894 and opened a mission three years later. Roman Catholics were less active, but a priest began religious instruction for Chinese children. According to oral tradition, about 1901 a Roman Catholic cleric attracted Chinese to his classes in English by playing his violin, and an American Jesuit, who after serving in Macao was able to preach in Chinese, baptized more than a hundred Chinese during a stay in Montreal from 1904 to 1906. The Presbyterians were more successful than the Roman Catholics because the former were more tolerant of customs brought from China.

There were also notable Chinese missionaries in Toronto at an early date. Among young people, such organizations as the YMCA and Young Men's Christian Institute attracted a number of Chinese Christians who rejected the authority of churches. In addition to attempting to convert the Chinese, the

132

missionaries offered language classes, medical services, welfare services, and support in fighting discrimination. Catholic and Protestant clergy joined to protest against special taxes on Chinese businesses, to deplore violence against Asians, and later to secure amendments to the draconian Chinese Immigration Act of 1923 and support demands for its repeal. Generally, however, the missionaries had little sympathy with the use of opium or with gambling, however much these might appear to be products of the male societies in which the Chinese were forced by Canadian immigration laws to live.

To the Japanese the missionaries offered English classes; the Methodists opened a school in Vancouver in 1912 that continued for twenty-two years. Proselytizing efforts beginning in 1892 employed Japanese Christians and resulted in a mission in Victoria and a Sunday school in Vancouver by 1906.[21]

World War I brought difficulties to all Germans in Canada and hastened the movement in their churches from the use of German to the use of English. The war was especially hard on the Protestant sects that had been granted exemption from military service, of which the largest was the Mennonite. While some Mennonites enlisted, the majority in both western and eastern Canada stoutly opposed all efforts to involve them in military service; nevertheless, they contributed generously to charitable projects and to the Red Cross and the Victory Loan campaigns.

The war also brought into prominence the temperance movement, with Manitoba, Saskatchewan, and Alberta, by referendums, all endorsing prohibition by December, 1916. The leaders in the movement were Protestants of British and Scandinavian origins, who had seen Catholic immigrants from eastern and central Europe as enemies. However, in each of the three Prairie provinces many Catholic immigrants saw the referendums as tests of loyalty and consequently voted for prohibition. By doing so they helped soften somewhat the hostility of the Protestant churches toward Catholicism.

BETWEEN THE WARS

In the West the religious organizations set up in various ethnic communities consolidated their positions during the 1920's. The period of explosive expansion of population was over and most of the best farm land was already occupied, but prosperity and modest increases in population strengthened existing churches and parishes and led to extension farther north. Some churches appointed special officers to concern themselves with immigrants. For example, in 1927 Polish Catholic priests, with lay assistance, set up an organization with headquarters in Winnipeg to advise new Polish arrivals on areas where farming conditions were favourable, other Poles were present, and Polish parishes or other organizations established.[22] The Norwegian Lutheran Church from 1927 to 1930 stationed a pastor in Winnipeg to serve as Director of Migration from Norway to Canada; the pastor reported, however, that the new arrivals showed indifference to the church.[23]

Among Ukrainians, the nationalistic fervour aroused by the brief establishment of a sovereign Ukrainian state gave impetus to the Ukrainian Greek Orthodox Church, which by 1924 was well organized, gaining adherents from the Independent Greek Church and the Russian Orthodox Church and among disaffected Greek Catholics. By 1931, 25 per cent of Ukrainians belonged to the Ukrainian Greek Orthodox Church as against some 58 per cent who belonged to the Greek Catholic Church, and the religious division was reflected in virtually every aspect of Ukrainian-Canadian life.[24] Protestant Ukrainian churches also had some success.

Among Mennonites, the departure of thousands of those who felt that church-directed schools were essential for their survival and the arrival of thousands of Russian Mennonites in the 1920's led to the dissolution of some congregations but the creation of many more. The increase was accompanied by continued fragmentation, although the *Russländer* (Russian Mennonites) contributed to the development of effective local, provincial, and interprovincial organizations.

The coming of the Hutterites to the western provinces in 1918 brought a new Protestant sect to Canada. Like the Mennonites, the Hutterites were pacifists. Their communal form of organization and extreme separatism formed a bulwark against assimilative influences, even though the Hutterites adopted advanced agricultural technology. The sect throve, in spite of opposition, and established many colonies.[25]

The smaller evangelical Protestant sects continued to proliferate. In Alberta, for example, the Church of God, an American "holiness" sect, entered in 1924 and attracted chiefly German-American settlers. In the same province William Aberhart began to use radio, in the 1920's an extremely popular medium, for evangelism on behalf of the Prophetic Baptist movement; soon after the Christian Missionary Alliance bought and began to operate a radio station. The rural audiences of the broadcasts were polyethnic. So also were the students attracted to the Bible schools, the first of which on the Prairies was begun at Three Hills, Alberta, in 1922. These schools thereafter multiplied.[26]

During the 1920's the leading Protestant churches were less active than previously in missionary work among immigrants. The Methodists and Presbyterians were caught up in the issue of union, out of which emerged the United Church of Canada in 1925. Many of their adherents in the West were also caught up in the agrarian revolt and the Progressive Party.

Missions to Jews did not cease. In 1929 a rabbi in Toronto had to protest against Presbyterian interest in converting Jews, and the Anglican Nathaniel Institute continued its work although its success was minimal. But the Jews had been able to establish their own institutional systems, and the churches "had come to see the intrusion of large numbers of Jews into Canada's Christian cities not as a problem of proselytizing and assimilating but one of neighbourliness and social adjustment."[27]

Of the Chinese, probably no more than 10 per cent were Christians by 1923, when immigration was cut off. Thereafter the proportion of Christians increased, since more non-Christians than Christians returned to China. In British Columbia, where the Chinese Canadians were concentrated, Christianity was less prevalent among the Chinese than in eastern Canada, where Presbyterian and United Church efforts were strongest and where barriers against social participation by the Chinese were lower than in Vancouver and Victoria.

The depression years were not good years for the denominations, including those that had been brought to western Canada by immigrants. Almost all suffered from a shortage of clergy and had to withdraw or amalgamate rural charges. In Alberta the Lutheran synods, the Russian Orthodox Church, and the Ukrainian Orthodox Church all had problems of ministerial supply. As people moved away from the drought area, many churches, missions, and parishes lost their ethnic character or ceased to exist. For example, the Norwegian Lutheran Church in 1920 had 140 congregations and preaching places in the Palliser Triangle; in 1945 it had seventy-five.

> In fact, the entire Norwegian Lutheran Church suffered heavy losses from 1929 to 1939. The total membership dropped from 14,108 in 1929 to 10,930 in 1939 exclusive of the membership in the coastal areas of British Columbia and exclusive of the smaller synods of the Lutheran Free Church and the Lutheran Brethren.[28]

Of the Norwegian Lutheran churches that remained, 60 per cent were receiving Home Mission Aid from the United States by 1936, and others had to be sent emergency aid.

The closing off of immigration during the depression brought special hardship to the Mennonites. Those who had come to Canada in the 1920's from Russia were keenly aware of the persecution of co-religionists, including relatives, in the Soviet Union, and worked feverishly to secure their admission to Canada. Their efforts brought meagre results: of between 13,000 and 18,000 Mennonites who were stranded in Moscow in 1929, the Canadian government allowed only 1,344 to enter between 1929 and 1932. Brazil, Paraguay, and the United States received many of the others.

During the 1930's the second generation was increasingly taking over in the ethnic communities, and for the second generation the old rituals and the ancestral language had less appeal than they had for the immigrant generation. The more "Canadian" churches gained: among Ukrainians, for example, between 1931 and 1941 members of the Ukrainian Catholic Church went from 58 per cent to 50 per cent of the population, and while the Greek Orthodox went from 24.6 to 29.1 per cent, the Roman Catholic, United, Anglican, Presbyterian, Lutheran, Baptist, and other churches all gained in Ukrainian membership. The United Church of Canada had a particular attraction as being "Canadian." Some churches tried to hold the young by switching from the ancestral language to English, and bitter controversy often ensued. On the one hand, members wanted to have the comfort and meaning of familiar words and phrases and to be able to confess their sins in their own language. On the other hand, leaders were concerned with the organization's competitive position in a society where another language dominated, and they saw advantages in switching to the use of English. In the Norwegian Lutheran Church of Canada, by 1940 only about 30 per cent of services were still in Norwegian.[29] In Dickson, Alberta, the oldest Danish community in the Prairie provinces, the shift from Danish to English occurred over a decade, but even so this change was disruptive:

> The agitation for change in the language within the church had started in the late 1930s by a body of young, second generation Danes who felt alienated so far as the older, native culture was concerned and who began seeking more of a Canadian identity. Specifically, they were looking for a shift from the use of Danish to English in the church. Many of them who scarcely knew Danish at all were being hauled to church each Sunday to sit through a service in a language they could not appreciate. Change was slow in coming, but shortly after World War II, the shift to English was all but realized. However, a large faction within the community continued to insist that the church was and should remain Danish. . . . The movement . . . literally tore the community in half.[30]

The denominations and the older sects also continued to feel a threat from the more evangelical sects and the cults. The newspaper advertisements, the leaflets, and the radio broadcasts served communities that were not being provided for by the hard-pressed churches, and their simple and graphic language was well within the grasp of those for whom English was not the mother tongue. The Bible schools, which continued to spring up in rural areas, offered young people opportunities for education at minimal cost and were "small enough, safe enough, short enough in duration, and flexible enough in terms of entrance requirements" to have a strong appeal. The attendance of Mennonite youth at non-Mennonite Bible schools led both in Ontario and in the West to a very considerable development of Mennonite Bible schools. Twenty-eight were founded in the 1930's.[31]

Even more disruptive in many religious organizations was a turning away from the churches toward political and economic movements of reform and, in a few cases, revolution. Although there had been Christian socialist movements among Catholics in Europe, in Canada the Catholic Church regarded socialism and communism as unmitigated evils, and the desperate people who embraced them therefore found themselves outside the church. In Protestantism, while many also abhorred socialism, some of its leading exponents were churchmen who came to their views out of the tradition of the Social Gospel.

The 1930's were extremely harrowing for Jews. Socialism and communism were not the only movements of the decade; fascism attracted followers in Canada as it did in Europe and the United States and gave the religious anti-Semitism of earlier decades a much more virulent form. At the same time, Canadian authorities refused to permit the entrance of Jews fleeing persecution abroad. The religious discrimination in the exclusion of Jewish refugees was clear: Czechoslavakian Jews who had been refused admission to Canada in 1938 reapplied as Christians and were given entrance visas, and in 1940 a senior immigration officer being lobbied to admit Polish Jewish children replied that Canada would accept "Roman Catholic Jewish children" but no others.[32]

DURING AND AFTER WORLD WAR II

The war did not ameliorate the situation of the churches in small towns and rural communities in the West. Securing priests and pastors from the homeland became impossible; young Canadian-born men went into the army or war industry rather than the church, or embarked on careers serving general congregations; the urbanization of the population led to the demise of many rural congregations.

In the larger towns and cities during the war there were some successes. Among Hungarians, for example, Roman Catholic parishes in both Toronto and Hamilton flourished, in Toronto under a non-Hungarian-speaking priest and in Hamilton under a member of the Sisters of Social Service. A Hungarian United Church congregation in Montreal also throve, moving from mission to self-supporting status and building its own church.[33]

The spirit of co-operation during the war and the emergence of umbrella organizations blunted some hostilities within ethnic groups that had been based on religion. For example, the Ukrainian Canadian Committee, founded in 1940, brought together representatives of Ukrainian Catholic and Ukrainian Greek Orthodox organizations, and also Ukrainian Protestant groups. While joint activities were regarded as temporary, they did have some lasting effects.[34]

The post-war immigration for many groups brought priests and ministers as well as many people who were desirous of pastoral care in their own language. Established ethnic churches and parishes were reinforced, and new ones were created. By 1975 there were thirty-three Catholic parishes in Toronto offering services in Italian; until 1956 there had been only three.[35] New Polish parishes were created in Toronto, Thunder Bay, and Montreal, and churches were bought or built in Vancouver, Calgary, Saskatoon, Sudbury, Woodstock, London, Brantford, and Ottawa.[36] Among Hungarians, in the affluent and optimistic late 1940's and early 1950's at least three ethnic parishes were organized in the tobacco district of southwestern Ontario. Roman Catholic churches were built or bought in four places, Greek Catholic churches in two, and Protestant churches in four.[37] The churches served as reception centres when refugees from the Hungarian revolution arrived, and they provided invaluable assistance to the newcomers.

The proportion of the Canadian population that was either Roman or Ukrainian Catholic rose steadily in the post-war period, and by 1981 was 47.3 per cent. While the major portion of Catholics were of French-Canadian and British Isles origins, there were also many Ukrainian, Italian, German, Polish, Hungarian, and Portuguese Catholics, and a number of Asian

TABLE 9

Population by Religious Group, Canada, 1921–81

	1921 %	1941 %	1961 %	1971 %	1981 %
Adventist	14,200 (0.16)	18,485 (0.16)	24,999 (0.14)	28,590 (0.13)	41,605 (0.17)
Anglican	1,410,632 (16.05)	1,754,368 (15.24)	2,409,068 (13.21)	2,543,180 (11.80)	2,436,375 (10.12)
Baptist	422,312 (4.80)	484,465 (4.21)	593,553 (3.25)	667,245 (3.09)	696,850 (2.89)
Buddhist	11,316 (0.13)	15,676 (0.13)	11,611 (0.06)	16,175 (0.075)	51,955 (0.22)
Christian Reformed	—	—	62,257 (0.34)	83,390 (0.39)	77,370 (0.32)
Christian and Missionary Alliance	283 (0.003)	4,214 (0.036)	18,006 (0.09)	23,390 (0.11)	33,895 (0.14)
Church of Christ Disciples	13,125 (0.15)	21,260 (0.18)	19,512 (0.11)	16,405 (0.08)	15,350 (0.06)
Confucian	27,185 (0.30)	22,282 (0.19)	5,089 (0.027)	2,165 (0.01)	(5)
Congregationalist	30,788 (0.35)	(1)	(1)	(1)	(1)
Doukhobor	12,674 (0.14)	16,878 (0.15)	13,234 (0.073)	9,170 (0.04)	6,700 (0.03)
Free Methodist	—	8,805 (0.08)	14,245 (0.078)	19,125 (0.09)	12,270 (0.05)
Greek Orthodox	170,069 (1.93)	139,845 (1.21)	239,766 (1.31)	316,605 (1.47)	314,870 (1.31)
Hutterite	(4)	(4)	(4)	13,650 (0.06)	16,530 (0.07)
Jehovah's Witnesses	6,689 (0.08)	7,007 (0.06)	68,018 (0.37)	174,810 (0.81)	143,485 (0.60)
Jewish	125,445 (1.42)	168,585 (1.46)	254,368 (1.39)	276,025 (1.28)	296,425 (1.23)
Lutheran	286,891 (3.26)	401,836 (3.49)	662,744 (3.63)	715,740 (3.32)	702,905 (2.92)
Mennonite	58,874 (0.67)	111,554 (0.97)	152,452 (0.84)	168,150 (0.78)	189,370 (0.79)
Methodist	1,161,165 (13.21)	(1)	(1)	(1)	(1)
Mormon	19,657 (0.22)	25,328 (0.22)	50,016 (0.27)	66,635 (0.31)	89,865 (0.37)
Pentecostal	7,012 (0.80)	57,742 (0.50)	143,877 (0.79)	220,390 (1.02)	338,790 (1.41)

Presbyterian	1,411,794 (16.07)	830,597 (7.22)	818,558 (4.49)	872,335 (4.04)	812,110 (3.37)
Roman Catholic	3,399,011 (38.69)	4,806,431 (41.77)	8,342,826 (45.74)	9,974,895 (46.25)	11,210,385 (46.55)
Salvation Army	24,771 (0.28)	33,609 (0.29)	92,054 (0.50)	119,655 (0.55)	125,085 (0.52)
Ukrainian Catholic	(2)	185,948 (1.61)(3)	189,653 (1.04)(3)	227,730 (1.06)(3)	190,585 (0.79)
Unitarian	4,943 (0.06)	5,584 (0.05)	15,062 (0.08)	20,995 (0.09)	14,500 (0.06)
United Church	8,739 (0.10)	2,208,658 (19.19)	3,664,008 (20.09)	3,768,800 (17.47)	3,758,015 (15.60)
Other	138,555 (1.58)	158,337 (1.38)	277,508 (1.52)	293,240 (1.36)	755,820 (3.14)
No Religion	21,819 (0.25)	19,161 (0.17)	94,763 (0.52)	929,575 (4.30)	1,752,385 (7.28)

1. Included with the United Church.
2. Greek Catholic and Greek Orthodox combined under "Greek Church."
3. Includes other Greek Catholic.
4. Included with "Mennonite."
5. Not listed separately.
SOURCE: Computed from *Census of Canada*, 1971 and 1981.

TABLE 10

Population by Selected Religions, Canada, Provinces, and Territories, 1981

Religion	Canada	Nfld.	P.E.I.	N.S.	N.B.	Quebec
Catholic[1]	11,402,605	204,465	56,450	310,725	371,245	5,618,365
Roman Catholic	11,210,385	204,430	56,415	310,140	371,100	5,609,685
Ukrainian Catholic	190,585	40	30	565	135	8,615
Protestant	9,914,580	352,695	61,175	487,255	295,785	407,075
Adventist	41,605	775	100	1,370	980	2,420
Anglican	2,436,375	153,530	6,805	131,130	66,260	132,115
Associated Gospel	7,895	—	—	65	20	130
Baptist	696,850	1,200	6,060	101,585	88,520	25,050
Brethren in Christ	22,260	365	225	420	240	570
Christian and Missionary Alliance	33,895	—	—	70	55	230
Church of God	10,040	10	30	60	30	475
Churches of Christ, Disciples	15,350	5	845	1,035	715	185
Church of the Nazarene	13,360	115	715	745	560	115
Doukhobors[2]	6,700	—	—	5	—	45
Evangelical Free Church	5,780	—	—	20	—	55
Hutterite	16,530	—	—	—	—	5
Jehovah's Witnesses	143,485	2,020	435	4,920	3,525	19,855
Latter Day Saints	89,865	200	140	1,570	810	2,150
Church of Latter Day Saints	82,060	200	140	1,570	815	2,125
Reorganized Church of Latter Day Saints	7,810	5	—	5	—	35
Lutheran	702,905	460	210	12,315	1,810	17,665
Mennonite	189,370	90	5	220	185	1,075

Methodist Bodies	47,840	55	55	300	135	1,615
Evangelical	19,030	5	45	65	30	915
Free Methodist	12,270	5	—	15	5	85
Missionary Church	7,940	15	25	—	—	5
Moravian	4,350	2,045	—	25	10	50
Pentecostal	338,790	37,450	1,315	10,695	21,450	17,420
Plymouth Brethren	8,060	35	155	225	40	895
Presbyterian	812,110	2,700	12,620	38,285	12,070	34,625
Reformed Bodies	104,175	5	240	915	100	495
Canadian Reformed Church	10,560	—	15	—	5	—
Christian Reformed	77,370	5	220	890	80	280
Salvation Army	125,085	45,120	315	4,900	1,965	1,440
Unitarian	14,500	35	50	325	285	1,325
United Church	3,758,015	104,835	29,645	169,605	87,460	126,275
Wesleyan	7,770	—	10	1,215	4,265	185
Worldwide Church of God	8,130	160	5	235	140	695
Other Protestant	245,550	1,490	1,170	4,995	4,165	19,925
Eastern Orthodox[3]	361,565	65	50	2,345	580	73,270
Greek Orthodox	314,870	50	40	2,020	535	62,265
Jewish	296,425	220	80	2,020	845	102,355
Eastern Non-Christian	305,885	680	230	3,030	1,175	34,325
Bahai	7,955	40	30	415	95	645
Buddhist	51,955	135	50	420	240	12,000
Hindu	69,500	315	75	1,025	475	6,690
Islam	98,165	100	70	790	315	12,115
Sikh	67,710	65	—	275	50	1,790

TABLE 10 (Continued)

Population by Selected Religions, Canada, Provinces, and Territories, 1981

Religion	Canada	Nfld.	P.E.I.	N.S.	N.B.	Quebec
Para-religious groups[4]	13,445	25	—	110	65	745
Non-religious groups[5]	1,788,995	5,605	3,240	34,335	19,685	132,935
Agnostic	10,770	15	10	220	110	420
Atheist	4,455	20	5	50	30	370
No religion	1,752,385	5,430	3,175	33,690	19,345	131,400
Total non-inmate population	24,083,495	563,750	121,225	839,800	689,370	6,369,070

Religion	Ont.	Man.	Sask.	Alta.	B.C.	Yukon	N.W.T.
Catholic[1]	3,036,245	318,815	310,010	613,930	538,435	5,595	18,330
Roman Catholic	2,986,175	269,070	279,840	573,495	526,355	5,470	18,215
Ukrainian Catholic	49,305	49,355	30,090	40,280	11,940	125	115
Protestant	4,418,960	573,420	557,315	1,240,000	1,484,925	12,310	23,670
Adventist	16,260	1,075	2,205	7,320	9,015	55	20
Anglican	1,164,315	108,220	77,725	202,265	374,055	4,665	15,295
Associated Gospel	5,760	105	970	565	280	—	—
Baptist	288,465	19,260	16,785	66,375	81,850	1,015	685
Brethren in Christ	15,535	490	845	1,040	2,525	5	—
Christian and Missionary Alliance	7,215	2,015	6,110	10,095	7,975	30	105
Church of God	3,435	440	1,000	3,065	1,500	—	—
Churches of Christ, Disciples	6,545	920	1,525	2,435	1,110	—	30
Church of the Nazarene	3,755	280	860	4,545	1,605	—	60

Doukhobors²	135	170	1,065	215	5,065	5	5
Evangelical Free Church	125	330	395	1,940	2,910	—	—
Hutterite	105	5,940	2,980	7,395	105	—	—
Jehovah's Witnesses	48,460	6,420	9,815	16,195	31,520	120	200
Latter Day Saints	20,095	1,840	3,075	42,980	16,740	160	105
Church of Latter Day Saints	14,505	1,775	2,565	42,190	15,925	160	100
Reorganized Church of Latter Day Saints	5,585	60	515	795	815	—	5
Lutheran	254,175	58,830	88,785	144,675	122,395	915	665
Mennonite	46,480	63,495	26,260	20,540	30,895	45	80
Methodist Bodies	25,360	2,085	4,430	7,360	6,345	60	40
Evangelical	5,460	1,375	2,240	5,430	3,415	20	20
Free Methodist	8,990	215	1,620	580	740	5	5
Missionary Church	6,000	85	150	1,395	260	—	—
Moravian	305	40	—	1,750	120	5	—
Pentecostal	119,535	15,825	16,435	41,485	55,095	520	1,570
Plymouth Brethren	3,270	610	310	550	1,960	—	5
Presbyterian	517,020	23,910	16,065	63,890	89,810	615	505
Reformed Bodies	66,910	2,300	515	17,880	14,785	—	35
Canadian Reformed Church	6,215	495	—	1,690	2,135	—	—
Christian Reformed	50,670	1,390	465	13,460	9,885	—	20
Salvation Army	45,065	3,695	3,050	7,020	12,275	150	100
Unitarian	6,120	800	325	1,210	3,955	45	25
United Church	1,655,550	240,395	263,375	525,480	548,360	3,310	3,725
Wesleyan	1,995	5	—	35	50	—	—
Worldwide Church of God	1,780	620	1,130	1,830	1,525	10	5
Other Protestant	89,160	13,215	11,125	38,460	60,845	585	420

143

TABLE 10 (Continued)

Population by Selected Religions, Canada, Provinces, and Territories, 1981

Religion	Ont.	Man.	Sask.	Alta.	B.C.	Yukon	N.W.T.
Eastern Orthodox[3]	167,325	21,135	22,495	49,275	24,640	195	195
Greek Orthodox	140,615	19,785	21,065	46,505	21,645	175	180
Jewish	148,255	15,670	1,585	10,655	14,685	20	65
Eastern Non-Christian	137,110	7,790	4,185	38,195	78,640	275	255
Bahai	3,250	165	465	775	1,815	125	135
Buddhist	18,595	2,015	985	6,200	11,190	75	50
Hindu	41,655	1,750	1,150	7,360	8,980	—	20
Islam	52,110	1,925	1,120	16,865	12,715	5	25
Sikh	16,645	1,685	220	5,985	40,940	45	10
Para-religious groups[4]	5,555	590	600	1,580	4,125	5	55
Non-religious groups[5]	620,815	76,285	60,255	260,015	568,170	4,680	2,970
Agnostic	3,995	595	140	1,520	3,660	50	20
Atheist	1,595	190	130	790	1,270	10	5
No religion	607,830	74,360	59,045	254,515	556,180	4,505	2,895
Total non-inmate population	8,534,260	1,013,705	956,440	2,213,650	2,713,615	23,075	45,540

1. Includes Roman Catholic, Ukrainian Catholic, and Polish National Catholic Church.
2. Includes both Orthodox and Reformed Doukhobors; the latter, however, constitute less than 1.2% of the total group.
3. Eastern Orthodox includes Greek Orthodox as well as a number of other nationally identified Orthodox Groups such as Antiochian, Armenian, Romanian, Serbian, Ukrainian, and Russian.
4. Para-religious groups include expressly identified groups such as Fourth Way, New Thought, Theosophical, Pagan, and a number of other diverse groups such as PSI, EST, The Farm, categorized as "Other Para-religious."
5. Non-religious groups include, in addition to Agnostic, Atheist, and No Religion, respondent entries that indicate no religious preference. This category also includes "Other (entries) not elsewhere classified."
SOURCE: *Census of Canada,* 1981.

and West Indian Catholics. The smaller and more scattered ethnic groups were accommodated in existing parishes, but national parishes also sprang up, with contributions from one ethnic group sometimes aiding another to establish its church.

The Protestant denominations, such as the United Church, the Anglicans, and the Baptists, gained especially from among both the native-born and immigrants from countries such as China, Japan, and Korea, where Protestant missionary activity had been intense. The denominations also had learned from the sects of the 1930's and adopted somewhat more flexible forms of organization. They had become multilingual: in the 1970's eight of the large denominations operated in at least twenty-seven European languages, in Arabic, several dialects of Chinese, Japanese, Korean, Vietnamese, and several other tongues.[38] However, their gains were chiefly among the English-speaking second and third generations. Of Ukrainians who belonged to the United Church in 1971, 52.1 per cent in the first generation, 39.6 per cent in the second generation, and 7.9 per cent in the third and later generations had Ukrainian as mother tongue, whereas of those who belonged to the Ukrainian Catholic Church the corresponding percentages were 82.5, 77.2 and 44.0.[39]

Some denominations that had had stern moral codes began to relax them, sometimes under influences from outside Canada. For example, among Lutheran Norwegian Canadians in western Canada, modernists from the United States have in recent years caused consternation by their tolerance, and even advocacy, of beer-drinking and dancing at church colleges:

> It was not without considerable conflict that a new American pastor of German descent, serving a congregation of Norwegian background, defended his beer drinking with the boys at the Legion, but also suggested that his council members could have a drink at the parsonage if they so wished. Another new pastor from the United States staged a wine and cheese party in order to get acquainted with the young adults of the congregation. He seemed shocked to learn that so many of the church members were opposed to social drinking. A third American pastor scheduled a "sock-hop" in the basement of the church for his large confirmation class. Unfortunately for him, he forgot to check this programme out in advance with his Board of Deacons who happened to be strongly opposed to staging dances in the church.[40]

The severing of institutional links with churches in the United States was one response to differences in standards. Among the Lutheran Norwegians this took place gradually from the 1940's on and was complete by 1967, when the Canada District of the American Lutheran Church became the Evangelical Lutheran Church of Canada.

Of the Protestant sects, the Hutterites were most able to maintain their religious commitment over time. Unbaptized young men sometimes left the colonies and behaved in ways contrary to the group's religious teachings, but they usually returned and became conforming members of the community.

Recently, however, small numbers of individuals and families have discarded the collectivistic orientation of Hutterite religion for the individualistic approach of evangelical Protestantism.

The Mennonites by the 1970's and 1980's ranged from Old Order Mennonites who maintained a separatist ideology to congregations that were difficult to distinguish from those of the United Church of Canada. Old Order Mennonites preserved rural life, plain dress, the use of the horse and buggy, the German language; they lost members to less strict groups, in some of which even enlistment in the armed services in time of war was not cause for excommunication.

Among Doukhobors, arson and dynamiting were directed by members of the Sons of Freedom against fellow Doukhobors they considered to have departed from the true path, as well as against the government and other economically or politically powerful organizations. In time, however, exposure to the larger society led to a degree of assimilation.

> It now seems likely that the Doukhobors will maintain their separateness merely as one of the many small and picturesque religious groups of Canada: their dietary rules less complex than those of the Orthodox Jews; their theological concepts no more unorthodox than those of the Mormons; their economic organization far less radical than that of the still communitarian Hutterites; their pacifism no more rigorous than that of the Quakers. Only the strange chants of the Living Book, like an unsevered umbilical cord, will unite them with their increasingly remote past in the steppes and mountains of Russia.[41]

Unlike the Hutterites and Mennonites, whose numbers continue to increase at each succeeding census, the number of Doukhobors has been declining, from 16,878 in the 1941 census to 6,700 in the 1981 census.

While many immigrants were Christian, other religions gained through immigration also, especially after 1967. Jews from various countries entered as the discriminatory policies of the past were discarded; included among them were Sephardic Jews from North Africa, who settled especially in Montreal, and ultra-orthodox Hassidic Jews, who formed their distinctive communities in both Montreal and Toronto. Asian immigrants included many Christians, but also many non-Christians who were intent on continuing their religious organizations in Canada. Among South Asians, Sikhism had already been well established in British Columbia, and by 1971 *gurdwaras* had been founded in Calgary, Edmonton, Toronto, and Montreal. Since then they have continued to proliferate. They act as multi-use community institutions and have played a vital part in the evolution of the Sikhs from a purely religious to an ethnic group. Similarly, Ismailis – South Asians, many of whom had settled in East Africa and who came to Canada as Ugandan refugees in the early 1970's – have set up places for worship (*jamat khanas*) that serve as community centres, and they, too, are evolving into an ethnic group. South Asians who have belonged to other religions, however, such as

Sunni Muslims, have united with those of other ethnic origins in the practice of their common religion.

Muslims, few before World War II, have entered in considerable numbers since the 1950's. Ethnically they have been chiefly Arabs and Pakistanis, but also Indians, Yugoslavs, Albanians, Bulgarians, and others.[42] Most are Sunnis, whose scripture is the Qur'an and whose prophet is Muhammed. The first mosque in Canada was erected in Edmonton in 1938; by the 1980's mosques were found from Halifax to Vancouver, and many Muslim organizations were associated in the Council of Muslim Communities in Canada, founded in 1972, which has among its aims seeking support for the implementation of certain Islamic laws in Canada and promoting good relations with Christians and Jews through dialogue.

Muslims suffered from the lack of *imams* as late as the 1970's. There were no Muslim seminaries in the Western Hemisphere:

> The Islamic community in Canada has not as yet been able to recruit any Arab or Indo-Pakistani young people to go to the Middle East to study for the imamate. (Three young blacks are studying in the Middle East.) Meanwhile, in the late 1970s, several Muslim organizations did not have an Imam at present including Vancouver, Windsor, Regina and Calgary.

Where *imams* were secured, they sometimes found a situation they were loath to accept.

> The organization of Muslim centers in Canada was initiated by the believers. . . . Because the congregations were supporting the mosque, the executive committees acquired inordinate powers, a situation not characteristic of Islam in Muslim countries.
>
> The executive committees developed constitutions that are "congregational" in character. Usually elected, these committees reserved the right to hire and dismiss the Imams who do not agree with their policies. Several of the Imams who came from the Middle East showed great reluctance to accept this division of power.

The Muslim communities in Canada have no unitary ethnic identity:

> The Muslim communities vary in national and geographical origin, mother tongue, racial and physical characteristics, consciousness of their heritage, their values, their primary identity, their recent experiences as a peoplehood and their emotional attachment to their roots.[43]

Islam claims to transcend the "tribalism" of language and race and to invite all people to participate in a commitment that would eradicate all ethnic, national, or cultural differences. However, ethnic differences in religious practice do exist among Muslims. Whether they will continue or whether discrimination will weld Muslims into a single unit is not yet evident.

Evangelical sects and syncretic cults continued to have appeal. Pentecostal groups, which steadily increased in numbers, drew especially those of Scandinavian and German ethnic origins. Cults in the 1960's and 1970's gathered in a small but conspicuous number of people, chiefly youths of Christian and Jewish backgrounds. The fact that they borrowed from Eastern religions – for example, Hare Krishna had its roots in Hinduism – meant that they played a part in the integration of various Asian groups into Canadian society.

Probably the salient feature of organized religion in the post-war years has been that it has declined in importance in the lives of Canadians. Industrialization and urbanization have been accompanied by secularism. The decline in religion in other parts of the world, including central and eastern Europe, preceded its decline in Canada. As late as the 1950's, some immigrants who had not had a religious upbringing on coming to Canada considered that religious affiliation was part of the Canadian way of life and consequently joined a church. The secularization of Canadian society has now proceeded so far in urban communities that such an opinion has become unlikely, although some new syncretic cults have enjoyed at least temporary popularity. Rural immigrant settlements, such as the Dutch Calvinist communities in Ontario, Alberta, and British Columbia, may retain a strong religiosity, but they are exceptional.

Secularism and the policy of multiculturalism have emboldened some non-Christians, chiefly but not solely among recent immigrants, to challenge the Christian assumptions underlying many Canadian practices and institutions. For example, the fact that Christmas and Easter are legal holidays whereas Rosh Hashannah and Yom Kippur are not has been cited as an example of bigotry. Increasingly, non-Christian holidays receive regular notice in the mass media and in some educational institutions. The reciting of the Lord's Prayer in the opening exercises of schools has been questioned, and in some school systems prayers from a variety of religions and silent meditation have replaced the use of the Lord's Prayer. Since the Constitution Act of 1982, the question has been raised whether the Lord's Day Act is consistent with clause 27, which states that the Charter of Rights and Freedoms should be "interpreted in a manner consistent with the preservation and enhancement of the multicultural heritage of Canadians."

An index of change is the growth in the number and percentage of the population professing no religion. At the time of the 1981 census over 90 per cent of the Canadian population professed to be Christian: that is, some 22 million, as compared to fewer than 300,000 Jews and just over 300,000 eastern non-Christians. On the other hand, the number of people professing no religion had risen from 95,000 in 1961 to 930,000 in 1971 and 1,800,000 in 1981. By 1981 those of no religion constituted more than 7 per cent of the population; in British Columbia they were almost 20 per cent of the population. By ethnic origin, British people bulked large among those of no religion, but so also did other northern Europeans (Germans, Dutch, and Scandinavians) and Asians (in 1971, 17 per cent of Japanese had no religion), and all of the numerically significant origin categories were represented. This rapid increase reflects the fact that it has become more respectable than in the past to list oneself as having no religion; the fact that since 1971 giving the information does not require face-to-face contact with a census taker probably also plays a part.

NOTES

1. Heinz Lehmann, *The German Canadians, 1750-1937: Immigration, Settlement and Culture*, ed. and trans. by Gerhard P. Bassler, chapter II, pp. 14-17.
2. *Ibid.*, chapter II, p. 37, chapter III, p. 55.
3. Spada, *The Italians in Canada*, pp. 29-31; Rudolf P. Cujes, "Contributions of Slovenes to the Socio-cultural Development of the Pre-Charter Canadians, The Canadian Indians," in *Slavs in Canada*, vol. 2 (Ottawa: Inter-University Committee on Canadian Slavs, 1968), pp. 117-26; Norris, *Strangers Entertained*, p. 96; Makowski, *History and Integration of Poles in Canada*, p. 39.
4. Stella Hryniuk and Roman Yereniuk, "Building the New Jerusalem on the Prairies: The Ukrainian Experience," in Ben Smillie, ed., *Visions of the New Jerusalem: The Story of Religious Settlement on the Prairie* (Edmonton: NeWest, 1983), p. 144.
5. Woycenko, *The Ukrainians in Canada*, pp. 78-80.
6. Radecki, *A Member of a Distinguished Family*, p. 146.
7. Paul Yusyk, "Religious Life," in Lupul, ed., *A Heritage in Transition*, p. 148.
8. Makowski, *History and Integration of Poles in Canada*, p. 162.
9. Rudolf K. Kogler, "The Polish Community in Canada," in Benedykt Heydenkorn, ed., *Topics on Poles in Canada* (Toronto: Canadian Polish Research Institute, 1976), p. 21.
10. Kostash, *All of Baba's Children*, pp. 113-27.
11. Yusyk, *The Ukrainians in Manitoba: A Social History*, pp. 72-73.
12. Radecki, *A Member of a Distinguished Family*, p. 146.
13. Henry Radecki, *Ethnic Organizational Dynamics: The Polish Group in Canada* (Waterloo: Wilfrid Laurier University Press, 1979), p. 63.
14. Frank H. Epp, *Mennonites in Canada, 1920-1940: A People's Struggle for Survival* (Toronto: Macmillan of Canada, 1982), p. 22.
15. W.E. Mann, *Sect, Cult, and Church in Alberta* (Toronto: University of Toronto Press, 1955).
16. M.L. Kovacs, "The Saskatchewan Era, 1885-1914," in Dreisziger, *Struggle and Hope*, p. 73.
17. Speisman, *The Jews of Toronto*, pp. 100-04.
18. *Ibid.*, pp. 131-44.
19. Marilyn Barber, "Nationalism, Nativism and the Social Gospel," in Richard Allen, ed., *The Social Gospel of Canada* (Ottawa: National Museums of Canada, 1975), p. 201.
20. Buchignani and Indra, *Continuous Journey*, p. 24.
21. Adachi, *The Enemy That Never Was*, pp. 110-12.
22. Radecki, *A Member of a Distinguished Family*, p. 145.
23. Loken, *From Fjord to Frontier*, p. 97.

24. Yusyk, "Religious Life," in Lupul, ed., *A Heritage in Transition*, pp. 152-57.
25. Hostetler, *Hutterite Society*.
26. Mann, *Sect, Cult, and Church in Alberta*, pp. 118-26.
27. R. Gruneir, "The Hebrew-Christian Mission in Toronto," *Canadian Ethnic Studies*, 9, 1 (1977), p. 26.
28. Loken, *From Fjord to Frontier*, p. 105.
29. *Ibid.*, p. 195.
30. Frank M. Paulsen, *Danish Settlements on the Canadian Prairies* (Ottawa: National Museums of Canada, 1974), p. 18.
31. Epp, *Mennonites in Canada, 1920-1940*, pp. 468-69.
32. Abella and Troper, *None Is Too Many*, pp. 1-2, 77-78.
33. Dreisziger, *Struggle and Hope*, p. 180.
34. Yusyk, "Religious Life," p. 158.
35. Father Ezio Marchetto, C.S., "The Catholic Church and Italian Immigration to Toronto: an Overview," *Polyphony*, 7, 2 (1985), pp. 107-10.
36. Radecki, *Ethnic Organizational Dynamics*, p. 89.
37. Dreisziger, *Struggle and Hope*, p. 198.
38. David Millett, "Religious Identity: The Non-Official Languages and the Minority Churches," in Jean Leonard Elliott, ed., *Two Nations, Many Cultures: Ethnic Groups in Canada* (Scarborough, Ontario: Prentice-Hall, 1979), pp. 185-86.
39. Warren Kalbach and Madeline A. Richard, "Differential Effects of Ethnoreligious Structures on Linguistic Trends and Economic Achievements of Ukrainian Canadians," in Petryshyn, ed., *Changing Realities: Social Trends Among Ukrainian Canadians*, p. 90.
40. Loken, *From Fjord to Frontier*, p. 206.
41. George Woodcock and Ivan Avakumovic, *The Doukhobors* (Toronto: Oxford University Press, 1968), p. 356.
42. Abu-Laban, *An Olive Branch on The Family Tree*, p. 139.
43. Yvonne Yazbeck Haddad, "Muslims in Canada: A Preliminary Study," in Coward and Kawamura, eds., *Religion and Ethnicity*, pp. 81-84.

EIGHT

Ethnicity and Politics

Studying the interaction of ethnicity and politics involves examining the values and political beliefs that immigrants brought to Canada, as well as the socio-economic conditions they came to. Some immigrants who came to Canada were refugees from the political struggles of their homelands and they often maintained a lifetime interest in their homelands, supporting political movements there and trying to influence Canadian foreign policy. At the very least they organized movements to keep alive their beliefs and perspectives and pass them on to their children. Even though these politically motivated immigrants constituted only a small portion of those who came to Canada, many of those who came for other reasons also brought with them political ideas and experiences that affected their adjustment to the Canadian political process. The political perspectives of their children and grandchildren were often coloured by the immigrant experience and by the socioeconomic conditions of the ethnic group in which they grew up.

The study of ethnic politics can be viewed in two ways: as internal politics within the ethnic group, and as political involvement in the larger Canadian society. Some groups developed a rich internal political life that did not spill over into the mainstream of provincial and national politics. For example, the Chinese, who in parts of the country were excluded by law from the Canadian political process, developed a large number of political organizations that represented different factions of homeland politics, as did other groups who were excluded in one way or another from full participation in Canadian politics.

The external political behaviour of a particular ethnic group includes its voting patterns, its organized lobbying activity, and its members' participation, as party officials or political candidates, in party politics. The political behaviour of the members of an ethnic group is related not only to their cultural and educational background and their previous political experience, but also to their status in Canadian society, their degree of geographical concentration, their economic circumstances, and the degree of discrimination or acceptance they experience. To understand the complex interplay of ethnicity and politics, one must also analyse the degree to which politicians see themselves as representatives of their ethnic groups and assess the degree to which the groups' views are taken into account by political institutions. Given the complexity of the issues and the lack of research on them, it should be stressed that we are just beginning to understand how these factors interrelate and when and why ethnicity comes into play in Canadian politics.

One obvious fact about ethnicity and politics is that, given the sizable numbers of immigrants in various regions of the country throughout the nineteenth and twentieth centuries, political parties have had to respond to their presence. Where they were numerous, immigrants became an important part of the political process. Since they had no roots or traditional loyalties in the Canadian system, their votes had to be actively sought in new ways. Consequently, political parties used a wide variety of techniques to recruit new immigrant voters and later their children. In addition, political parties had to take into account public attitudes toward immigrants and ethnic groups. Thus, the history of inter-ethnic relations in Canada and the history of ethnic politics are closely intertwined.

Because they are so closely tied to central questions of identity, status, values, and interests, ethnocultural issues have historically played a key role in public debate and in numerous elections and continue to do so in many parts of the country. Issues as diverse as the "schools questions," prohibition, foreign policy, and official bilingualism have aroused strong ethnic loyalties among the British and French as well as among the other ethnic groups. While the numerical superiority of the British and French has for the most part determined that they would decide the issues, nonetheless other ethnic groups have attempted to influence public policy and occasionally have had a significant impact.

Given the concerns of various ethnic groups to protect or enhance their status, close ties inevitably developed between many ethnic groups and politicians. Each tried to sway the other, the ethnic groups to ensure that their interests were looked after and the politicians to secure and hold the allegiance of particular groups. In time, ethnic groups also attempted to involve their own representatives in the political process and political parties began recruiting candidates from various ethnic groups. The speed with which this occurred varied with party, ethnic group, and region of the country.

Not all groups, however, have become active participants in the total political process. Some ethno-religious groups have wanted to stay aloof from Canadian politics: Hutterites, Hassidic Jews, and some Doukhobor and Mennonite groups believe that their need to be separate from "the world" precludes participation in the conventional political process. They have, however, involved themselves in issues directly concerning them, such as policies regarding immigration, education, taxation, exemption from military service, and landholding. Until the 1950's and 1960's, most Doukhobors rejected conventional or mainstream political activity. Nevertheless, their radical protest against many aspects of the Canadian state forms a significant chapter in the history of radical politics in Canada.

Although ethnicity has been important in the Canadian political process, its significance has varied over time. During certain periods, economic issues, regional interests, and class issues have taken precedence over ethnic issues. Even at such periods, however, ethnicity has often played a role in the decisions that were made. For example, the polyethnic character of the Prairies played an important part in the development of a sense of regional identity in the West. There were also significant variations between ethnic groups in their participation in the various protest movements that emerged in the West. The polyethnic character of the Prairies also played a crucial role in defining western attitudes toward such important national issues as bilingualism and multiculturalism.

THE PERIOD OF MASS MIGRATION, 1870-1920

From an early date, individual members of ethnic groups, such as Jewish politicians Ezekiel Hart in Quebec (elected in 1808 but not allowed to take his seat because of his Jewish background) and Henry Nathan from Victoria (first Jewish member of Parliament, elected in 1867) and Polish immigrant Alexsander Kierzkowski (also elected in 1867), played a part in the political process. However, they did so as individuals rather than as representatives of an ethnocultural group. They were middle class, well educated, and engaged in trade and commerce. On a group as opposed to an individual basis, the only ethnic groups of other than British or French origin numerous enough to interest politicians were Ontario and Nova Scotia blacks and Germans, and they were only rarely sought out. While immigration was a significant political issue in nineteenth-century Canada, the immigrant group that aroused the most controversy, both in central Canada and in the Atlantic region, was the Irish, whose history lies outside the scope of this chapter.

Maritimes and Central Canada
With the partial exception of Ontario's Germans, the political behaviour of people of other than British or French origin did not become an important part of the political scene in Canada until the period of large-scale settlement of the Canadian West. In the Maritime provinces, the question of relations between Acadians and the English-speaking majority overshadowed all other ethnic issues. By the 1870's, the sizable German group in Nova Scotia was largely assimilated since they had been in Canada for over a century. The blacks in Nova Scotia were still residentially and socially segregated and their poverty, isolation, and the prevailing racism of the larger white society kept them on the fringes of Nova Scotia's political life. Only among the immigrant coal miners and steelworkers in the Glace Bay/Sydney area of Cape Breton were newcomers concentrated enough to have an impact on local politics. During the first four decades of the twentieth century, many of the political cross-currents affecting "other ethnic groups" in other parts of the country had reverberations in industrial Cape Breton: Jewish, Croatian, and Ukrainian radicalism, Italian fascism, and the black nationalism of sup-

153

porters of Marcus Garvey and his "back to Africa" movement all found expression.

Until the 1930's the issues of immigration and the political potential of the other ethnic groups remained relatively unimportant in Quebec and Ontario. Nonetheless, immigration emerged as a public issue in Quebec in the period 1906-1911 as French-Canadian nationalist critics of Laurier such as Henri Bourassa and Olivar Asselin charged that the new immigrants arriving from continental Europe threatened the delicate ethnic balance in Canada between French and English and might adversely affect both the Canadian economy and social morality. The nationalists' opposition to Laurier had many other grounds, but the nativism they aroused contributed to the substantial erosion of support for the Liberals in Quebec in the 1911 federal election.

At the local level, by 1911 Montreal had the largest number of Jews and Italians of any city in Canada, but these groups were still too small, insecure, and working-class to have any significant impact on the political system. The prejudices of both French Catholics and English Protestants limited the political involvement of the new immigrant groups, although the Catholic Italians developed alliances with French-Canadian politicians, while the Jews worked more closely with English Protestants. Jews formed a large enough minority to elect their own representatives at both the provincial and federal levels beginning with Peter Bercovitch as a Liberal in the provincial legislature in 1916. But as a non-Christian and predominantly working-class group in Montreal, Jews were on the margins of society and had little political power. They attempted to use what influence they had to improve their legal and educational status, but throughout the early part of the twentieth century the community was divided between more established and financially secure Jews and more recent immigrants on the degree to which it was necessary for Jews to integrate into the larger society.[1]

In Ontario, from Confederation until the 1920's those of non-British, non-French origin made up approximately 10 per cent of the population. The Germans were by far the largest group but their percentage in the population declined at the same time that Jews, Italians, Finns, and central and eastern Europeans began to make their presence felt in the province's large urban centres and in the resource towns in northern Ontario. In the Berlin (Kitchener) area in the late nineteenth century, the Germans formed over three-quarters of the population and were courted by the main political parties. Those of German background included some descendants of the United Empire Loyalists, religious sectarians such as the Mennonites, and new arrivals from Germany. By the mid- to late nineteenth century, they had established cultural, social, and religious institutions and an active ethnic press. Berliners elected Hugo Kranz, a German immigrant, as their mayor in 1869, and as the first German-born member of Parliament in 1878.[2]

Over time, the Conservative Party came to represent the British in the area and the Liberals emerged as the dominant force among those of German background. These trends were heightened by the intense anti-German sentiment of World War I, as the British element in the population, supported by some Germans, forced the town to drop its German name and become Kitchener. Even so, people of German background continued to control the municipal government until the inter-war era. In the emotion-charged conscription election of 1917, ex-mayor W.D. Euler, a Liberal of German background, won handily through his outspoken defence of German Canadians.

By the late nineteenth century, German-speaking immigrants went in much larger numbers to the Canadian West, and Ontario gradually lost its pre-eminence as the centre of German culture in Canada. Though people of German background were the largest ethnic group in Canada after the French and British, they came from many different German-speaking areas of Europe, were divided between over a dozen different religious groups, were scattered across the country, and they arrived in at least ten different waves of immigration. Hence they did not have the cohesiveness to form a political force. The experience of being associated with the enemy in both world wars also led them to keep a low profile. Though Germans have comprised approximately 5 per cent of the Canadian population for much of the twentieth century, and over 10 per cent in Saskatchewan and Alberta, they have had very little impact on Canadian politics.

In Ontario the new immigrants from central, eastern, and southern Europe who came in the late nineteenth and early twentieth centuries were too few to play a significant role in the political process. They were concerned primarily with eking out a living and protecting themselves from discrimination. Nonetheless, the major political parties began to pay some attention to the newcomers: in Toronto, starting in 1907, the Conservative Party backed an Italian newspaper and in 1910 Conservative politicians helped organize a Hebrew Conservative Association. But prior to the 1920's immigrants in urban Ontario were largely seen as "foreigners" who were outside the political mainstream. New immigrants might concern themselves with local municipal issues but few ran for office, and fewer still were elected. Outside of municipal politics, the other ethnic groups were an insignificant factor in Ontario politics until after the Second World War.

Prairie Provinces

Even before the massive influx to the Prairies in the 1890's, the major political parties had tried to attract the new immigrants in the West. During the 1880's in Manitoba, for example, the Conservatives and Liberals had supported Icelandic-Canadian newspapers presenting their political points of view and encouraged participation in the political process. The editorial policy of *Heimskringla* (first published in 1886) was to favour the Conservative Party in Canada and the Democratic Party in the United States; *Lögberg* (begun in 1888) took the side of the Liberal Party. The two papers maintained their opposing positions through the years and split the Icelandic Canadians into two ideological camps.

Before the 1890's, however, the other ethnic groups on the Prairies were too few and too scattered to constitute a political force. Migrants from

Ontario dominated the political life of Manitoba and the Northwest Territories, and their main concern was to establish a British Ontario way of life on the Prairies. But by 1901 the non-British, non-French immigrants formed almost half the population. The West was growing, and winning its support was crucial to a political party's hopes of controlling the country as a whole.

As a new area of settlement, the Prairie region was a cauldron into which was thrown a great range of political ideas and perspectives: American populism, British labour socialism, British Toryism, European liberalism, socialism, anarchism, communism, and a variety of forms of utopianism. American and British immigrants contributed to the growth of the farmers' movement in Alberta and Saskatchewan during the 1910's and 1920's; urban British immigrants provided much of the leadership for trade unions, labour parties, and socialist parties in western Canada in the first three decades of the twentieth century.[3] The majority of central and eastern Europeans deferred to parties based on the perspectives of the Americans, the British, and the central Canadians. Conversely, a minority of central and eastern Europeans formed the backbone of the most radical political movements in western Canada from 1900 to 1940, including the Industrial Workers of the World, the One Big Union, and the Communist Party of Canada.

When large numbers of Germans, Scandinavians, and central and eastern Europeans arrived on the Prairies after 1896, the Liberals stood to gain the most. They invited the gratitude of the newcomers for allowing them into the country under their expansionist immigration policies. Clifford Sifton, the Minister of the Interior, was also the Liberals' chief political organizer in western Canada. Through a variety of means, including the establishment of ethnic newspapers, he attempted to appeal to the immigrants. Before the newcomers could vote, the Conservatives played upon public unease about the possible long-term social impact of central and eastern European immigration and the perceived threat to British values and Canadian identity that newcomers from continental Europe represented. The Conservative *Winnipeg Telegram*, for example, opposed Ukrainian immigrants as "ignorant and vicious foreign scum." Once the new settlers could vote, however, the Conservatives followed the Liberal lead by supporting ethnic newspapers and establishing political clubs for the newcomers. But a good deal of damage had already been done and the Liberals were able to quote the negative Conservative comments about central and eastern Europeans. The Conservatives' inability to win favour among the newcomers contributed to anti-immigrant sentiment, which further alienated ethnic voters. Tory frustration eventually led the government under Robert Borden to remove the vote of those who came from Germany and the Austro-Hungarian Empire under the Wartime Elections Act of 1917. This measure sealed the unpopularity of the Conservatives among the other ethnic groups on the Prairies and contributed to their weakness in this region until the 1950's.

The Liberals' success prior to World War I was based on their organizational strategies as well as on their policies, the economic prosperity of the country, their leadership, and Conservative mistakes. In addition to supporting existing ethnic newspapers or establishing new ones to reach new immigrants in their own language, the Liberals used a partisan civil service and political patronage. They cultivated influential people within the ethnic groups, at first as unofficial intermediaries with the group and later, in Alberta and Manitoba just before the war, as candidates for provincial political office. Brennan describes the successful efforts of the provincial Liberals in Saskatchewan to gain support among new immigrant groups:

> In districts with a substantial voting population whose mother tongue was not English, special proselytizing efforts were undertaken. A German Liberal Club was founded in Regina in 1908, for instance, and a close working relationship established with clergymen and other prominent representatives of the various ethnic groups in the province. Local men fluent in German, Ruthenian or other languages were recruited to address farmers' picnics, sports days and election rallies, and MLAS such as Gerhard Ens were also much in demand as speakers in "foreign" districts. The "Calder Machine" compiled detailed statistics concerning the ethnic composition of individual ridings and mailing lists facilitated the distribution of translations of government legislation and election propaganda.[4]

By the 1910's the growing proportion of other ethnic groups in the population and their bloc settlement made it possible for a few candidates of these groups to run for office. Given their recent arrival, their inexperience with the Canadian political system, their language difficulties, and discriminatory attitudes toward many of them, few of them were successful. In Alberta, for example, in the period from 1905 to 1921, whereas the Ontario-born in the population (15.37 per cent in 1911) made up 56.2 per cent of those elected, the European-born (12 to 16 per cent of the population) comprised only 5.7 per cent of the provincial legislators. But they had nonetheless begun to make an impact.

The Ukrainians were the most concerned with having their own representatives elected to office. There were enough of them, they were sufficiently concentrated, and their political perspectives were distinctive enough for them to field candidates and try to influence public policies through organized lobbying. One prominent Ukrainian newspaper, *Ukrainski Holos*, which had been established in Winnipeg in 1910 by well-educated immigrants, criticized both parties and urged Ukrainians to advance their interests by electing Ukrainian candidates.

When Ukrainian Liberals in Alberta became disenchanted with the failure of the provincial party to respond to their demands for a greater role for the Ukrainian language in the public school system, four of them ran as Independents in the 1913 provincial election. Though all four were defeated, a Ukrainian Liberal, Andrew Shandro, captured a seat and became the first Ukrainian MLA in Canada.[5]

The one exception to Liberal dominance on the Prairies was the period of Conservative rule in Manitoba from 1899 to 1916. Although the Conservatives had come to power partly by appealing to the prejudices of the dominant Anglo-Canadian group through their attack on the federal Liberals' immigration policy, they gradually gained support among the other ethnic groups through their defence of bilingual schools and their opposition to prohibition. The provincial Liberal Party became a vehicle for a reform movement among Anglo-Canadians who demanded the abolition of bilingual schools and the introduction of prohibition and women's rights. The reformers showed a scarcely concealed contempt for central and eastern European immigrants, whom they saw as abusers of both alcohol and women. Consequently, many central and eastern Europeans temporarily turned to the Conservative Party. But this support did not last long after the Conservatives' defeat by the Liberals in 1916, especially because of the unpopularity of measures taken by Conservatives at the federal level, such as the Wartime Elections Act and their harsh repression of the Winnipeg General Strike in 1919.

Ethnic Radicalism

Although in western and central Canada the other ethnic groups chiefly supported the mainline parties, a radical political movement emerged among a variety of new immigrant groups, particularly Jews, Ukrainians, and Finns. A minority of each group had brought with it strong Marxist ideals. Many Finnish loggers, miners, and tailors in British Columbia and Ontario, Jewish tailors and garment workers in Montreal, Toronto, and Winnipeg, and Ukrainian labourers, miners, and farmers in the three Prairie provinces shared a sense of exploitation and grievance. They dreamed that the emergence of a socialist society both in Europe and in Canada would right old wrongs and bring about a more just society. The abortive Russian revolution of 1905 led to the influx of political refugees who helped energize the left wing within each group. The high literacy rate, residential concentration, and political background of Jews and Finns facilitated radicalism; the radicalism of Ukrainians emerged not only because of their political background and concentration but also because of the intense discrimination and exploitation they experienced.

Finnish and Ukrainian workers both affiliated with the Socialist Party of Canada, but they broke with the SPC and in 1910 participated in the formation of the Social Democratic Party of Canada. Within the SDPC, Ukrainians, Finns, and Jews had their own branches but worked together in common causes, such as organizing unemployed workers in Winnipeg in 1915. Each group had its newspaper; *Robochyi narod*, for example, supported the Federation of Ukrainian Social Democrats, and the *Winnipeg Courier* was the voice of Jewish members of the SDPC. By 1915, the SDPC had 5,300 members, largely eastern Europeans and Finns; 20 per cent of the party members were in Winnipeg's North End, where Jewish and Ukrainian radicals were both prominent. However, the SDPC's opposition to conscription and its call for the overthrow of capitalism alarmed Canadian government officials and in 1918 the government banned the foreign-language affiliates and newspapers of the SDPC. Nonetheless, the radicals maintained an active network of organizations across the country. Indeed, government repression and popular hostility served to radicalize them further.[6] During the 1920's the newly constituted radical wings of each group, the Finnish Organization of Canada, the Ukrainian Labour-Farmer Temple Association, and the Labor League (later renamed the United Jewish People's Order), played key political roles through their support of the Communist Party of Canada.

The rivalry of left-wing groups inevitably led to conflict within ethnic groups. Many differences were also transplanted from the Old World: for example, Winnipeg's Jewish radical community included revolutionary Marxists, two varieties of left-wing Zionists (those who wanted a socialist homeland for the Jews wherever it might be, and those who sought to rein-state Palestine as the homeland for the Jews), and anarchists.[7]

The ethnically based left-wing groups such as the Ukrainian Labour-Farmer Temple Association (ULFTA) and the Finnish Organization of Canada (FOC) provided not only a political vehicle but also an array of social and cultural activities, which included co-operatives, dance groups, theatre groups, language schools, and, among the Finns, sporting groups. Left-wing groups also took up causes of immigrant workers in a variety of other ways. The Dominion Labor Party, for example, passed a resolution in December, 1919, condemning the persecution of Jews in eastern Europe.[8] Left-wing parties defended the immigrants' civil rights, condemning deportations, vote restrictions, and press censorship during World War I.

Three things must be remembered about the role of immigrants in the emergence of the left. First, left-wing parties were minority parties, some of them being only short-lived and attracting only a few thousand supporters. Second, such groups as the Ukrainians, Finns, and Jews were deeply divided politically, and only among the Finns did the majority of the ethnic group support the left. Third, support for the left varied from one immigrant group to another: while Jews, Finns, and Ukrainians who supported the left were attracted to Marxism, Scandinavian farmers favoured democratic socialism. Few Poles or Italians supported the left at all, although their socio-economic conditions were no better than those of the more radically inclined groups.

The immigrants' support for radicalism changed public attitudes toward immigration and coloured attitudes toward the political left. Central and eastern European immigrants came to be seen as dangerous revolutionaries rather than as cheap labour or hard-working farmers. A number of Canadians reasoned that class conflict was alien to Canada, where there was ample opportunity for all. Many left-of-centre parties were seen by the public as un-Canadian due to the amount of "ethnic" support they received.

Near the end of the war, government leaders worried about the increased support for radical organizations, particularly the Industrial Workers of the World and the One Big Union. Consequently, in 1918 Prime Minister Borden appointed C.H. Cahan, a Montreal lawyer, to the position of Director of Public Safety to investigate radical organizations. On the strength of his recommendations, the government banned several left-wing organizations with ethnic affiliations, suppressed a number of ethnic newspapers, and outlawed all meetings conducted in "enemy" or "bolshevik" alien languages.[9]

The connection between immigrants and radicalism was cemented in the public's mind by the Winnipeg General Strike, which had considerable support among Slavic and Jewish immigrant labourers. A series of strikes in Winnipeg in 1918 culminated in riots against non-British immigrants, who were blamed for fomenting radicalism and creating unemployment. The social unrest and revolutionary propaganda accompanying the June, 1919, strike aroused fears among some government leaders that Canada was on the verge of revolution. Opponents of the strike alleged that it was the work of aliens and demanded that immigrant radicals be deported. In Toronto, the press singled out Jews as radicals: *Saturday Night* magazine suggested that all Jews were Bolsheviks. The federal government responded with new laws that denied radicals entry into Canada and allowed the deportation of immigrant radicals. The "Red Scare" of 1919 brought to a culmination all the fears and anxieties that had developed concerning the political behaviour of central and eastern European immigrants.[10]

British Columbia and Asians

While the major political parties in the rest of Canada were beginning to appeal to immigrant voters, in British Columbia they took a different stand with regard to Asian immigrants. For decades the major parties and leading political figures led campaigns to limit or prohibit the entry of Asians, deny them the right to vote, and limit their ability to compete economically. Rather than competing for the Asian vote, the major parties tried to outdo each other in opposition to Asians.[11]

Anti-Asian sentiment was strong in British Columbia from the 1870's to the 1950's. Asians were regarded as alien, inferior, and unassimilable because of their race and their distinctive culture. Organized labour, a major force in British Columbia politics, alleged that they took jobs from white workers and lowered living standards. Veterans, patriotic groups, farmers, and small businessmen also demanded government restrictions on Asians.

Between 1878 and 1899 the British Columbia legislature passed twenty-six statutes aimed at restricting or preventing the settlement of Asians. When the federal government disallowed most of this legislation as unconstitutional, provincial politicians mounted a partially successful campaign to convince the federal government to pass restrictive immigration legislation of its own. While anti-Asian sentiment was most intense in British Columbia, it was present as well in other provinces; Quebec, Saskatchewan, and Nova Scotia also passed legislation prohibiting white women from working in restaurants, laundries, or other businesses owned by Chinese and Japanese.[12]

Excluded by law from participating in the political process, the Chinese, Japanese, and South Asians turned their attention to building their own community structures. Even in the provinces where they could vote, the Asians focused their attention on community and homeland politics. Political life in Canada's Chinatowns was particularly active, because developments were so profound and far-reaching in China and because the Chinese comprised a bachelor society in which men spent a good deal of time and energy in organizational competition. Contending Chinese political factions tried to gain support among Chinese Canadians and several leading Chinese politicians, including revolutionary leader Sun Yat Sen, made tours of Canada to elicit moral and financial support. Many Chinese Canadians hoped to see a strong and united China emerge out of the warring factions. They believed that a strong China, with world prestige, could further the interests of the Chinese in Canada. Because Japan was a world power and an ally of Great Britain until the 1930's, Japanese Canadians were not treated as harshly as were the Chinese Canadians by Canadian authorities, and the Chinese hoped that a strong China would be better able to protect their interests. The unsuccessful efforts of Chinese Canadians to stop the introduction of restrictive immigration laws showed their powerlessness.

The Chinese, Japanese, and South Asians in British Columbia (who between 1901 and 1931 made up from 8 to 10 per cent of the population) organized to protest the discriminatory treatment they faced. But the groups were as isolated from each other as from the larger white society, and they had virtually no white allies. Lacking the vote, they had to go cap in hand to politicians, pleading not only for respect and fairness, but for the right to make a living and to be united with their families. They considered the issue of immigration regulations particularly important. Some Chinese-Canadian and Japanese-Canadian organizations also fought discrimination in the workplace. The Chinese Labor Association used strikes and boycotts to fight discrimination. The mildly socialist Japanese Camp and Mill Workers Union, which was organized in 1920, advocated establishing ties with white labour. In 1927 it affiliated with the Trades and Labour Congress, which was becoming aware of the need to bring Asians within its ranks in order to achieve working-class co-operation and solidarity.

Though the smallest of the three Asian groups, the South Asians were the most organized and vociferous, demanding their rights as British subjects. Before World War I a nationalist movement among South Asians sought to remove discriminatory immigration restrictions and convert community members to Indian independence. The suspicions of the British and Canadian governments concerning the loyalty of local leaders drove many individuals into coalitions with the nationalists. The federal government countered with deportation or refusal to readmit those who had gone home to India to visit their families. By 1912 most of the leaders of the community were members of the Socialist Party and in 1913 they organized the revolutionary Ghadar Party to help bring about Indian independence and a socialist state in India. In response, British officials infiltrated the movement and used police informers to help crush it. Disillusioned with their treatment in Canada, and hoping to effect change in India, many of the leaders of the Ghadar movement returned to India.[13]

THE INTER-WAR YEARS

A variety of factors during the 1920's and 1930's contributed to the ideological polarization of a number of European ethnic groups, including Italians, Hungarians, Finns, Ukrainians, Croatians, Estonians, Latvians, and Lithuanians. These factors included the arrival of politicized newcomers, the attempts by foreign governments to gain support among their countrymen in Canada, and the reaction of the ethnic groups to the economic and social circumstances they faced in Canada. The depression most affected non-Anglo-Saxon immigrants in Canada because they were concentrated in the most insecure segments of the economy. Many were attracted to radical solutions for problems they faced. The strong divisions between the left and right were fed by a lively ethnic press in which newspapers engaged in fierce polemics. The attention of many groups was focused on events abroad, but there was a growing interest in the Canadian political scene on the part of groups that had been in Canada for a generation or more. The growing political interest of the Canadian-born coincided on the Prairies with the emergence of protest parties that were more open to non-Anglo-Saxons than the Conservative and Liberal parties had been. With the success of the protest movements, many more representatives of the other ethnic groups were elected to the provincial legislatures, and even a few to the federal Parliament.

However, the political power of the other ethnic groups had definite limits. Their significance as voters was being recognized, but those who were elected still represented "ethnic" ridings such as the predominantly Ukrainian riding of Vegreville in Alberta or heavily Jewish neighbourhoods in Montreal, Toronto, and Winnipeg. The influence of the MPs within their own parties was also limited. For example, although the first Ukrainian MP in Canada, Michael Luchkovich, supported an open immigration policy, his party advocated a restrictive policy. Even more strikingly, during the 1930's the views of the two Liberal Jewish MPs, Sam Jacobs from Montreal and Sam Factor from Toronto, on the question of refugees were ignored by the Liberal government.[14]

The limited influence of Jewish politicians on Canadian government policy suggests another important political issue of the 1920's and 1930's related to ethnicity. Nativist sentiments were far from dead, and both the provincial and federal governments had to deal with them. Anti-Japanese and anti-Chinese sentiment continued in British Columbia. Provincial politicians applied strong pressure on the federal government to stop all Chinese immigration, which it did in 1923, to reduce the number of Japanese immigrants to a token number, which it did in 1928, and to eliminate Japanese fishermen from the fishing industry. The depth of the hostility to Asians in British Columbia is indicated by the fact that the Liberals in the 1935 federal election campaign printed the CCF stand in favour of giving votes to Asians as anti-CCF propaganda. In Alberta, opposition to Mennonite immigration was so strong in 1929 that the provincial government refused a federal government request to allow more Mennonites to settle.[15] In Saskatchewan, opposition to Catholics, French Canadians, and immigrants was voiced by the Ku Klux Klan, which gained up to 20,000 members in the province in the late 1920's. Indeed, the Klan's tacit support for the Conservative Party helped bring down the Liberal government in the 1929 provincial election.[16]

During the depression, anti-radical nativism and anti-Semitism surfaced across the country. Immigrants were often blamed for unemployment, and politicians were pressed to deport immigrants both to reduce relief rolls in urban centres and to curb the growth of radicalism. In Montreal, Toronto, and Winnipeg, patterns of social discrimination were extended by right-wing groups into a vicious and sometimes violent anti-Semitism. In the 1930's, Prime Minister King felt the levels of anti-Semitism in Canada made admission of Jewish refugees unwise.

In the nationalistic atmosphere of the inter-war era, a number of European governments took an interest in immigrants from their countries to Canada and sought to influence their nationals abroad. For example, the Polish government began in the early 1920's to provide advice, literature, and funds to some political associations, and the Horthy regime in Hungary established special organizations designed to foster close ties between immigrants and the mother country.[17]

The German Nazi and Italian fascist consuls in Canada made strong efforts to gain support among their countrymen, with varying degrees of success. Between 1934 and 1939, the German government encouraged the formation of three different groups with varying links to the German Nazi party. The largest organization, the Deutscher Bund Canada, launched a national campaign to convince Canadians of the "truths of National Socialism" by means of films, rallies, speeches, and propaganda from Germany. However, the widely scattered and extremely diverse German community was far removed from an attachment to Germany and the Bund had little success: at its peak in 1937-38 it had a membership of about 2,000, mostly young recent immigrants. As one historian concludes, "by far the greatest majority of the Germans identified themselves as German Canadians, whose fate was tied to that of Canada."[18]

In contrast, fascism received a good deal of support among Italian Canadians in Montreal and Toronto, with some support in other centres. In the early 1920's newly arrived immigrants, including many war veterans, helped establish fascist clubs.[19] There was lively opposition to them within the Italian group, but through the consulates the fascists played a large part in the life of the communities. Support for Mussolini did not seem disloyal at a time when many English and French Canadians admired Mussolini, and the Pope's pacts with Mussolini seemed to give him the Church's blessing:

> Mussolini, the champion of the middle classes against Bolshevism, seemed to have won respect and approval for Italy in the world. His solution to the problem of the "red flaggers" and later, the Depression,

found support from part of the press in Canada and from many businessmen, academics, and veterans. Respectable Italo-Canadians, full of the patriotism of World War I, could, between 1922 and 1935, support Fascism with the full approval of their fellow Canadians. At last for the Anglo-Saxons, who had never understood the importance of Dante or Verdi, there was an Italian and an Italy to obliterate the image of ragged street musicians and cafoni track laborers.[20]

But support for the extreme right wing was limited. Canadian fascist parties, including the National Social Christian Party, the Canadian Union of Fascists, and the Canadian Nationalist Party, attracted some immigrants among the Italians, Germans, and Ukrainians because of their strong anti-communism and anti-Semitism. Pro-Nazi sentiments were also expressed in the Mennonite press in the 1930's because of Hitler's anti-communism and because of the Mennonites' German cultural roots, but the Mennonites' pacifism created an ambivalence toward Hitler's militaristic regime and Mennonite support for Hitler was limited and had no tangible results.[21] When Mennonites became involved politically in western Canada they were much more likely to be drawn either to the Liberals, who had allowed them into Canada in the 1920's, or to groups that emphasized a Christian message, such as Social Credit. In sum, the economic and social stress of the 1930's did not lead to strong right-wing views among the non-British, despite the efforts of both European governments and native-born Canadian fascists to attract them.

The political ideology that most worried Canadian authorities was communism. The Communist Party reached its peak among immigrant workers during the depression. It welcomed foreign-language affiliates, used foreign-language organizers, and helped establish newspapers in order to reach Bulgarian, Croatian, Finnish, Hungarian, Lithuanian, Polish, Russian, Slovak, Ukrainian, and Jewish workers in their own languages. It continued to be strongest among the Ukrainians, Finns, and Jews who had been radicalized before the war. The Finnish left was given added impetus at the end of World War I by the arrival of political refugees who had lost in the bitter civil war fought between "White" and "Red" Finns. Included were fifty Red Guard leaders who feared imprisonment or execution, among them the former socialist prime minister, Oskari Tokoi.[22] During the 1930's, among the Russians, left-wing clubs united in a Federation of Russian Workers and Farmers Clubs, which achieved its maximum expansion by 1935-36 with sixty clubs and about 2,500 members. By 1939 over one-tenth of the 16,000 strong CPC consisted of Yugoslavs, mainly Croats. At the end of the 1930's the left-wing press made up 38.5 per cent of total Finnish circulation, 41 per cent of Hungarian, 31 per cent of Ukrainian, and 13.8 per cent of Polish.[23]

The largest foreign-language group affiliated with the Communist Party was the Ukrainian Labour-Farmer Temple Association, which by 1939 had 201 branches across the country, 113 temples (halls), and 10,000 members. The ULFTA was strongest in urban and industrial areas and in resource-extraction communities, but was to be found also among marginal farmers in northern Alberta and Manitoba. The organization had a wide range of cultural activities, dramatic productions, insurance benefits, and an active social life. It gave strong support to strikes sponsored by the Communist-affiliated Mine Workers' Union of Canada and the Farmers' Unity League.[24] Though ULFTA was only a small segment of the Ukrainian community, it was well organized and vocal.

Though not as numerous in Canada as Ukrainians, the Finns were equally important in the Communist Party:

> During the first decade of its existence the Finnish Organization of Canada provided over half of the CPC's membership. Many Finnish Canadians had fought on the Communist side in the Finnish Civil War of 1918, and had a heightened sense of class consciousness. . . . At the Toronto Convention of the Workers Party of Canada (WPC) in 1922 the Finnish Organization of Canada was recognized as the Finnish Federation of the WPC; in effect, without losing their independence branches throughout the country also became branches of the WPC.
>
> The growth of the Finnish Organization of Canada in the 1920s far exceeded that of the CPC membership as a whole; by 1930 the organization (FOC) had seventy-four branches and membership of over 6,000. It also published a weekly newspaper . . . and maintained a variety of cultural and social programmes.[25]

Half of the Finns in Canada were in Ontario, with large concentrations in Fort William and Port Arthur, Sudbury, and Sault Ste. Marie. During the 1920's and 1930's many of them threw their energies into labour activities:

> Perhaps the Finns' most significant contribution to the Canadian labor movement was the organization of the northern Ontario bush workers into the Lumber Workers Industrial Union of Canada. The first of the major strikes in the Ontario lumber industry occurred in September 1926 when bushmen in the Thunder Bay area called a general walk-out, demanding higher pay and better camp conditions. For the next decade, there was at least one large strike involving several hundred Ontario lumber workers nearly every year. In the 1926 strike the workers won significant improvements in pay and conditions, and the Lumber Workers Industrial Union of Canada, under left wing leadership, emerged as the major union in the Ontario woods. The influence of Finns in this union was so strong that its minute books for the first decade were written in Finnish and the first two national secretaries of the union were Finns. Many Finns were also active in organizing the west coast fishermen as well as participating in attempts to organize the hardrock miners of northern Ontario.[26]

In spite of the close affiliation between the Communist Party and the ULFTA and the FOC, there was also tension. The Communist Party worried at times that the workers were more loyal to their ethnic organizations than to the party. In the late 1920's, the party tried to reduce the autonomy of the foreign-language affiliates and to stress working-class assimilation into the larger party:

> The internal strains caused by ethnic loyalties were especially acute after 1925 when the Communist International (Comintern) called for the Bolshevization of all national Communist movements; in Canada this meant a reduction in the influence and independence of ULFTA and the FOC. Between 1928 and 1931 the CPC was seriously disrupted by the issue of Bolshevization, and a number of leading members of ULFTA and the FOC were either expelled from the party or were severely censured.[27]

The growing class consciousness of many immigrant workers during the 1930's found expression in a wide variety of left-wing causes. Many supported strikes in industries including mining, lumbering, grain, and sugar beets. Some of the immigrants became part of the Mackenzie-Papineau battalion that left Canada in 1937 to fight on the Republican side in the Spanish Civil War.[28]

Those who participated in left-wing activities faced the constant threat of arrest and deportation. In 1931, the major Communist leaders were arrested on charges of sedition. After their prison terms, some of those who were not native-born (like Tomo Čačić, the editor of the left-wing Croatian newspaper *Borba*) were deported. Of the 400 Croatians who participated in a strike in Rouyn-Noranda mines in 1934, sixteen leaders were arrested and jailed and 100 others deported. About a hundred Finns were deported annually during the 1930's, as radicals or as indigents. Most of the Finnish Canadians who moved to the Soviet Karelia during the 1930's were members and supporters of the Finnish Organization of Canada.[29]

The Communist Party provided an important channel for immigrant grievances. Its few electoral successes were in predominantly central and eastern European immigrant neighbourhoods such as Winnipeg's North End. In 1926, William Kolisnyk, a leader in the ULFTA, became an alderman, the first Communist elected to public office in North America. Overall, North Winnipeg preferred more moderate candidates, like Jewish MP A.A. Heaps, who represented first the Independent Labour Party and later the CCF in Parliament during the 1920's and 1930's; nonetheless, the Communists were able to gain a substantial degree of support.[30]

Although the immigrants' support for the left was viewed with suspicion and hostility by Canadian authorities, it attracted even stronger opposition from conservative and nationalist organizations within their own groups, especially among Ukrainians. Part of the conflict derived from ideological and political disagreements about conditions in the Ukraine and the desirability of an independent Ukrainian state, but nationalists were also concerned that their being seen as "radical foreigners" would damage the public image of all Ukrainians. The same ideological division divided a number of other central and eastern European groups. Dreisziger assesses the significance of the left-right division for Hungarians in Canada:

> The spread of Communist influence caused problems for many Hungarian-Canadian organizations. In some cases the converts to revolutionary ideas simply left the existing conservative clubs. In others, they made attempts to gain control of their executives in order to turn them into organizations of the left, members of the growing federation of workers' associations. When frustrated in their plans, these people often resorted to obstructionism, and to slandering their opponents.[31]

Radical protest among immigrant workers in industrial and resource communities was parallelled by a growing farm revolt in the Prairie provinces. New farmer-based parties arose during the 1920's and 1930's to challenge the established political parties, banks, railways, and grain companies. But while support for the Communists made the immigrant workers subject to official harassment and discrimination, support for agrarian protest parties in the West brought the immigrants into the mainstream. In their quest for power, the new political movements realized the need to appeal to all voters. The United Farmers of Alberta (UFA) organized a "foreign-born committee" to act as an advisory council to its executive, printed its literature in several languages, and appointed "foreign-speaking" organizers to intensify its membership drive. In Saskatchewan, the Farmer-Labour Party, a predecessor of the CCF, in its first attempt at electoral politics in 1934, nominated a Ukrainian candidate in the Pelly constituency, printed pamphlets in several languages, and had speakers campaign in other languages than English.[32]

Although the UFA, the United Farmers of Manitoba, and the Farmer-Labour Party in Saskatchewan all made inroads, cultural barriers limited their support among central and eastern Europeans. The leaders of the farm movement were almost all of British background from Ontario, Britain, and the United States. The Progressive movement had also been closely allied with the Protestant churches and with prohibition and had generally been unsympathetic to bilingual schools or to an open immigration policy. It stressed common economic problems and a "melting pot" approach to community solidarity, and there were real limits to its ability to respond fully to or represent the immigrant groups. Some of the other ethnic groups on the Prairies preferred to stick with the Liberals throughout the 1920's and 1930's. Nonetheless, the new protest movements were more open to those of non-British origin than were the traditional parties. This was partly because they were new and did not have as many built-in traditions and cultural loyalties. They strongly emphasized democracy and egalitarianism and welcomed almost everyone.[33]

There were, of course, differences among ethnic groups in their support of the new movements. Scandinavians, with their background of co-operative movements in Scandinavia and involvement in populist politics in the American Midwest, were among the strongest supporters. The CCF took longer to win adherents among central and eastern Europeans in rural Saskatchewan because of the opposition of the Catholic Church to socialism, the anti-communism and anti-socialism of conservative members of the eastern European ethnic groups, and perhaps, as Lipset suggests, the conservatism of the desperately poor.[34]

The inter-war period, then, was, from a political standpoint, one of change and conflict for a number of groups. It was a period of new departures, of support for a variety of political movements of both the left and right, and of growing polarization within a number of groups. Many of these conditions changed with the outbreak of World War II.

WORLD WAR II

At the outbreak of World War II, European immigrants were far more aware of European issues than English or French Canadians. Several minorities from eastern Europe, including the Macedonians, Armenians, Slovaks, and Ukrainians, had developed strong organizations to support the liberation of their homelands. These groups hoped that somehow the events of the war might make possible the establishment of independent states for their groups. The war also gave Zionism a strong base of support, as Canadian Jewry became increasingly concerned about the plight of European Jewry and tried to convince the government to press Britain, which had a mandate over Palestine, to allow the migration of more Jews to Israel.[35]

Anti-immigrant sentiment was not as strong during World War II as it had been during the Great War. Many groups had been in Canada longer and had become more established and accepted. Several ethnic groups also achieved a new level of respectability during the war as many Canadians came to see their attachment to their homelands in a more positive light. For example, Polish and Chinese Canadians' support for their homelands now was seen as part of the war effort, rather than as disloyalty. Nonetheless, several political issues related to the other ethnic groups remained.

One had to do with Hutterite expansion. The Hutterites continually sought land for new colonies. They prospered during the war, and resentment against them as unfair competitors and as pacifists led in Alberta to legislation first in 1942 restricting their right to buy land and then in 1947 to restrictions on buying land within forty miles of an existing colony. In 1960 the forty-mile limit was removed, but a hearing before a community property control board and approval by the cabinet were imposed. The Communal Property Act was not repealed until 1972. In Manitoba an attempt to introduce similar restrictive legislation failed, but an informal agreement concerning the location of colonies was reached.[36]

The legacy of attempts by foreign governments during the 1930's to win support in Canada was the suspicion cast on ethnic groups from countries with which Canada was at war. The RCMP did not distinguish between staunch Nazis and working people who had suffered hardship from the depression and found support or consolation in three pro-Nazi organizations.[37] With the outbreak of the war, the police interned just over 300 Germans and German Canadians. Though there was some injustice in the internments, anti-German sentiment was much more limited than in 1914 and the RCMP were more careful in their roundups than they had been in the previous war. Unlike World War I, where the German enemy and German Canadians were merged in the public mind, the government and the bulk of public opinion made a distinction between Hitler and his followers, and the German people.[38]

Many Italian Canadians found themselves in a difficult position. Support for Mussolini had not seemed disloyal during the 1930's at a time when many English and French Canadians admired the Italian dictator. The Mussolini-Hitler pact in 1940 came at the same time as the thrust of German troops into Scandinavian and northern European countries. Considerable publicity was given to "fifth column" activity – aid furnished to the invading German army by German sympathizers. Consequently, there was a great deal of fear and hysteria in Canada. Responding to public pressure, the federal government in June, 1940, banned all Nazi, Italian fascist, and Canadian fascist groups. In addition, the federal government banned several left-wing ethnic organizations and closed down their halls and newspapers. Those banned included the ULFTA, Canadian Ukrainian-Youth Federation, the Finnish Organization of Canada, the Russian Workers and Farmers Club, and the Polish Peoples Association.[39] Leaders of left-wing ethnic organizations and Italian-Canadian fascist organizations were interned. The government justified the ban on the ground that from 1939 to 1941 the Communist Party in Canada had opposed the war effort. After Hitler attacked the Soviet Union in June, 1941, Communists in Canada supported the war effort, but the ban on left-wing organizations was not lifted until October, 1943.

While the government was crushing right- and left-wing ethnic organizations, it was at the same time encouraging the emergence of ethnic umbrella organizations, such as the Ukrainian Canadian Committee and the Polish Canadian Congress. Both the UCC and the PCC organized relief projects to help in the war effort. After the war they became involved both in helping refugee settlement and in attempting to influence Canadian foreign and immigration policies.

Unity within individual ethnic groups, however, did not come only through government prodding. The homelands of many ethnic groups had been occupied by foreign troops and their friends and families still at home needed food and clothing. At least temporarily, the war helped bring together groups that had very different ideologies: for example, despite the bitterness of the depression years, left-wing and right-wing Hungarians and Croatians co-operated temporarily in relief efforts.[40] Some traditional ethnic rivals, like the Serbs and Croatians, co-operated in wartime relief for Yugoslavia. Tension between the two main rivals in the Chinese community, the Chinese National League and the Chinese Free Masons, was also submerged in the war effort.[41] There were, of course, exceptions. Czech-Slovak tensions in Canada increased after the declaration of Slovakia's independence in 1939, which was supported by the main Slovak organization in Canada, the Canadian Slovak League.

While the loyalty of Germans, Italians, and even some eastern European minorities such as the Ukrainians was occasionally questioned during the war, the issue that was politically most explosive was the treatment of Japanese Canadians. Waves of intense anti-Japanese sentiment had swept British Columbia in 1937-38 when rumours circulated of illegal Japanese immigrants. After the outbreak of the European war, in the spring of 1940, rumours about Japanese subversion proliferated. British Columbia politicians demanded that Japanese and Chinese Canadians not be called up for military service lest it result in qualifying them for the vote. The most intense and violent wave of anti-Japanese sentiment was ignited by the Japanese assault on Pearl Harbor. In response to public pressure, the government on February 24, 1942, ordered all Japanese Canadians to abandon their homes, farms, and businesses and leave the Pacific Coast. Following the relocation of 22,000 Japanese Canadians from the coast, the government sold their property. Toward the end of the war the federal government, under intense pressure from British Columbia politicians, also encouraged the Japanese to seek voluntary deportation to Japan and after the war proceeded with its deportation plans. Civil rights groups finally secured the dropping of the deportation orders (1947), a partial compensation for property losses, and an end to the restrictions that prevented Japanese from returning to the coast (1949). The relocation, the confiscation of property, and the "repatriation" of Japanese Canadians, including those who were Canadian-born or Canadian citizens, constituted the harshest treatment ever meted out by the Canadian government to an ethnic group.[42]

A number of developments during and after the war served to undermine prejudices against various ethnic groups and enabled them to play a greater role in the political process. The revulsion against Hitler and Nazism extended to a reaction against the concept of a superior race and against public expressions of racism and anti-Semitism. Political support for discriminatory measures in Canada's immigration laws and in franchise restrictions began to crumble. Canada's signing of the United Nations charter in 1944 and the Universal Declaration of Human Rights in 1948 brought into glaring focus Canada's discriminatory policies.

Following intense lobbying by Asian groups and an increasingly sympathetic white public, South Asians and Chinese were given the vote in 1947 and Japanese in 1949. In 1947, after lobbying from a committee made up of both whites and Chinese, the Chinese Immigration Act was repealed. In 1951 the government allowed small quotas of immigrants from India, Pakistan, and Ceylon. More liberalized immigration and enfranchisement did not mean, however, that Asians would become an important political force. By the 1950's, as a result of relocation, the Japanese were widely scattered and the Chinese, with economic and social mobility, were also increasingly spread out across Canada.

ETHNICITY AND POLITICS, 1945-68

The liberalizing of attitudes toward Asian immigration was part of a more positive attitude to immigration that facilitated a new wave of immigrants in the post-war years. Business interests in English-speaking Canada considered that increased immigration would promote economic growth and that new sources of labour were needed. Unions, once opposed to large-scale immigration, now favoured it in order to develop a home market. In French Canada, the traditional hostility to immigrants decreased, even if it did not entirely disappear. Many ethnic and religious groups in Canada also exerted intense pressure on the federal government to respond to the plight of their countrymen and co-religionists in Europe.[43] The latter were often in desperate circumstances because of the forcible uprooting of populations during the war, economic distress, food shortages, and the threat of being repatriated to an area dominated by Communist forces.

As new and undecided voters, primarily in Canada's large urban centres, the immigrants played an important part in post-war politics. For example, during the 1950's, central, eastern, and southern Europeans (particularly Italians) came to form a sizable percentage of the voters in metropolitan Toronto and helped to determine election results in a number of key ridings.

Approximately 300,000 of the new immigrants were political refugees or displaced persons from central and eastern Europe. They played an important role in the re-emergence of anti-communism as a significant political force in Canada in the early 1950's. The political refugees from central and eastern Europe were mostly urban educated people fleeing the threat of Soviet occupation and Communist domination. They included many former government officials, members of army officer corps, and middle-class professionals as well as workers and farmers. They were highly politicized and willing to put a great deal of time and energy into their political concerns. They felt they had a unique perspective on world affairs since they had experienced communism first hand. They were determined to try to get the Canadian government to take up their causes.

These new immigrants set up a variety of organizations combining nationalism and anti-communism. Estonians, Latvians, Lithuanians, Ukrainians, Croatians, Slovaks, Macedonians, and Armenians all hoped not only that their homelands could be freed from Communist domination, but also that they would be independent. Their organizations, such as the League for the Liberation of the Ukraine or the Estonian Central Council, combined cultural and political activities and usually had youth affiliates through which the displaced persons tried to pass on their ideology to their children.

Many of these refugee organizations saw Canada as a temporary asylum from which they would return to their European home once conditions in Europe had changed.[44] Despite their efforts, the eastern European groups were unsuccessful in getting the government of Louis St. Laurent to take up the cause of the liberation of their homelands. For example, in response to requests by the Ukrainian Canadian Committee to "make mention of the

171

Ukrainians and a free Ukraine in international affairs and to give feasible support to the Ukrainian liberation movements and to the general movement to dismember imperialist Russia," the Department of External Affairs in 1952 warned Prime Minister St. Laurent to ignore this request since External Affairs regarded such a statement as interference in the internal affairs of the Soviet Union and left Canada open to questions of its treatment of French Canada. Ukrainian organizations achieved only one minor victory with External Affairs during the 1950's. Following intense lobbying by Ukrainian organizations and by John Decore, a Liberal Ukrainian MP from Alberta, the department agreed in 1951 to support the establishment of a radio program on the international service of the CBC directed toward Ukrainians in the U.S.S.R. External Affairs soon regretted its support for the broadcast: "External Affairs officers constantly tried to restrain programming they considered inflammatory, and out of step with the tone of Canadian foreign policy." Although the CBC and External Affairs wanted the Ukrainian section of the international service eliminated, neither the St. Laurent nor the Diefenbaker government "was predisposed to risk alienating a significant portion of the vote by ending it."[45]

Though their impact on Canadian foreign policy was limited, the arrival of right-wing anti-Communist refugees played a role in the decline of the ethnic left in the late 1940's and early 1950's. Bitter controversy raged between the newcomers and the left, which charged the newcomers with being Nazi collaborators, if not war criminals. But public opinion both in the larger society and within ethnic communities was running against the left, with the Cold War, the Gouzenko affair, and Canada's support for the Korean War. Some of the leaders of the Ukrainian and Jewish left also became disillusioned with Soviet communism during the 1950's because of Russification in the Ukraine and anti-Semitism in the Soviet Union, the Soviet invasion of Hungary, and Khrushchev's confirmation of the excesses of the Stalin era. Also, the economic prosperity of the 1950's took the edge off the radicalism of many immigrants who had been attracted to the left during the depression of the 1930's. Among the Yugoslavs, radicalism also declined because almost 2,000 pro-Tito Croatians, Serbs, and Slovenes returned to Yugoslavia at the end of the war to help establish a Communist state.[46]

One strong indication of changing currents of public opinion was the heated contest in Ontario in the 1955 provincial election between two Jewish politicians who represented different ends of the political spectrum: Allan Grossman, a Toronto city alderman who was running for the Conservatives, and the sitting MPP, J.B. Salsberg, a leader in the Communist movement in Canada.

> Grossman believed the campaign involved fundamental issues and was a contest between good and evil. Many others shared this view, and the campaign forced Toronto Jews to take sides with unprecedented frankness and passion. For Grossman, as for increasing numbers of his generation of Canadian Jews, the continuing presence of Joseph Sals-

berg as their representative in the Ontario legislature was a shame and humiliation; the campaign to defeat him was a solemn duty.[47]

With the strong support of anti-Communist Hungarians and Ukrainians, Grossman was able to defeat Salsberg and begin a political career spanning twenty years in the legislature and fifteen years as a cabinet minister. Grossman, as an intermediary between ethnic minorities and the provincial government, was able to keep the provincial Conservatives aware of the needs of immigrant voters and able to capture some support from them.

At the federal level, until the advent of John Diefenbaker in the late 1950's the Liberals had a number of advantages over the Conservatives in the postwar struggle for votes. Many groups had traditional ties with the Liberal Party because of its immigration policy and its defence of them during World War I and the depression against the nativism of the Conservatives (or, in Quebec, the Union nationale). The Liberals were once again in power during the relatively open immigration of the late 1940's and early 1950's; once they could vote, many newcomers showed their appreciation. Many immigrants also gravitated to the Liberals at the national level, since they felt that it made sense to have ties with the people holding the reins of power.[48]

Several prominent Liberal cabinet ministers with strong regional power bases, such as C.D. Howe in Port Arthur and Paul Martin in Windsor, had polyethnic ridings, which made them aware of the need to build a base of support among ethnic voters. For example, in C.D. Howe's riding in Port Arthur,

> by 1935 Mrs. Anna Koivu was delivering the Finn vote in the rural McIntyre Township and as "Log Cabin Granny" was writing a regular column in the Finnish newspaper *Canada Utiset*. The Styffe brothers, sons of a Norwegian American immigrant and consul, Oscar Styffe, were also heavily involved in the wartime federal Liberal organization. The Port Arthur Liberals had by all odds an impressive list of party workers reaching into every major ethnic group by the 1940s and on occasion [after 1944] even penetrated former strongholds reserved to the Communist party.[49]

Paul Martin was able to gain support among groups such as the Serbs and Italians in Windsor through establishing close ties with leaders and paying careful attention to individual immigration files. The Liberals' attempts to assert Canada's autonomy from Great Britain also won them support from non-British immigrants: for example, in 1947, the Liberals introduced a new Citizenship Act, which for the first time gave Canadians their own citizenship, separate from that of British subjects.

The Liberals were, however, vulnerable. The party did not reflect the ethnic diversity of Canada in its higher levels. By 1957 there were still no Jewish or Ukrainian cabinet ministers. Members of the other ethnic groups were also underrepresented as judges and senators and in the highest ranks of

173

the civil service. Individuals of Jewish, Ukrainian, and Icelandic background were appointed to the Senate during the 1950's, but groups such as the Italians and Poles were still campaigning in the late 1950's for their first Senate appointment.

By 1957 the federal Tories were in a position to make a major break-through among ethnic voters. Their opening came with the choice of John Diefenbaker as party leader in 1956. In the West, voters were tiring of the seeming futility of supporting third parties on the national scene. Diefenbaker's experience with a polyethnic constituency in Prince Albert made him sensitive to the feelings of discrimination and second-class citizenship that many ethnic groups in the West felt. His vision of One Canada, and his Bill of Rights, stressed the need for equal treatment and acceptance for all. In addition, Diefenbaker's strident anti-communism contributed to his success among central and eastern European ethnic groups. The displaced persons and other nationalist factions among them felt that at last they had a champion. In July, 1956, at the Ukrainian Canadian Congress, Diefenbaker expressed his sympathy for the liberation of the Ukraine from Russian Communist domination.[50]

The attempt by Diefenbaker and the Conservative Party to overcome decades of hostility on the part of many ethnic groups took a variety of forms. They enthusiastically recruited newcomers to the party. For example, Michael Starr, the former mayor of Oshawa, was appointed Minister of Labour in Diefenbaker's administration, thus making him the first Ukrainian-Canadian cabinet minister. Starr spoke in predominantly Ukrainian communities across western Canada and helped to swing many Ukrainians to the Conservatives. But Diefenbaker did not limit his appeal to central and eastern Europeans. In the 1957 federal election Douglas Jung ran successfully as a Conservative in Vancouver and became the first Chinese-Canadian member of Parliament. The Conservatives also courted the leaders of the ethnic press associations in Ontario and Manitoba. Through the office of the national director of the party, they encouraged Conservative candidates to cultivate parish priests and get what they called "ethnic co-operators" to do "undercover" work in ethnic groups.

In power, the Conservatives continued to court the ethnic vote. In 1962 the Conservative government changed Canada's immigration regulations to remove almost all elements of discrimination. Diefenbaker attended national celebrations, presented copies of the Bill of Rights to leaders of ethnic groups, and appeared at ethnic rallies on behalf of Conservative candidates.

But by 1962 Diefenbaker's support had begun to wane. The move in 1959 by the Conservative government to tighten the sponsorship system was interpreted by Italians as being directed against them. In 1959 and 1960, the government launched a crackdown on illegal Chinese immigration that included widespread raids on Chinese organizations; the extent and severity of the police operation and the damage to the reputation of the Chinese community alienated many Chinese.[51] The economic recession and growing unemployment further eroded support for the Conservatives. The constant reiteration of the anti-Communist theme, when combined with little concrete action, also began to diminish the enthusiasm in some ethnic groups for the Conservatives.

However, Lester Pearson, the Liberal leader, had difficulty capturing the hearts of ethnic voters, particularly in western Canada. Many of them saw Pearson as eastern, WASP, and remote; in addition, it was Pearson who set up the Royal Commission on Bilingualism and Biculturalism, whose terms of reference, activities, and recommendations they found offensive. The Commission, with its talk of two founding races and its focus on French Canadians, was widely perceived by Ukrainians and other central and eastern Europeans as relegating them to second-class status.

Another major development during the 1950's and early 1960's was the growing political importance of the other ethnic groups at the municipal and provincial levels. Several cities with large proportions of other ethnic groups in their population elected mayors from these backgrounds. Among prominent Ukrainian-Canadian mayors were Michael Starr, elected in Oshawa in 1949, William Hawrelak, elected in Edmonton in 1951, and Stephen Juba, elected in Winnipeg in 1956. During the 1950's and early 1960's, Toronto had two Jewish mayors, Nathan Phillips and Philip Givens, who had both been aldermen. All of these individuals tried not to be identified with a single ethnic group: Phillips, for example, referred to himself as the "mayor of all the people."

At the provincial level during the 1950's, Ukrainian, Jewish, and Scandinavian MLAs began receiving cabinet posts. For example, the first Ukrainian cabinet minister was appointed in Saskatchewan in 1952 (CCF), in Manitoba in 1955 (Liberal), in Ontario in 1958 (Conservative), and in Alberta in 1962 (Social Credit).[52] The variety of parties represented shows that Ukrainians were gaining political power by supporting the party in power in the province in which they lived. In addition to their growing representation at the cabinet level, the number of other ethnic groups in the provincial legislatures increased dramatically across the country, but particularly in the Prairie provinces, where those of Scandinavian, German, and Ukrainian origin were most heavily represented.

These political successes at the municipal, provincial, and federal levels reflected a variety of merging social and economic forces: the growing numbers of the other ethnic groups, their rising socio-economic status, and the maturing of a Canadian-born and educated second generation. The groups involved, particularly the Ukrainians, took great pride in elected officials as a sign of growing acceptance in the larger Canadian society and a sign that members of previously stigmatized ethnic groups could achieve the highest levels of public office.

THE COMING OF MULTICULTURALISM, 1968-1987

After the introduction of official bilingualism in 1969, the Liberals were made increasingly aware of the dissatisfaction among the other ethnic groups. The federal policy of multiculturalism within a bilingual framework, announced by the Trudeau government in October, 1971, emerged from a variety of political and policy considerations. Among these was the Liberal weakness in western Canada, where the federal policies of bilingualism had been seen as showing undue favouritism to French Canada and ignoring the western historical experience. In addition, the Liberals were well aware of the importance of the ethnic vote in urban Ontario, especially Toronto, and felt that multiculturalism could help them maintain this base of support.

Multiculturalism may indeed have softened opposition to official bilingualism: for example, in Manitoba in the early 1980's during the intense provincial debate over official bilingualism, the leaders of the other ethnic groups supported Franco-Manitobans and the provincial NDP government in their efforts to restore the language rights guaranteed under the original Manitoba Act of 1870. But the multiculturalism policy did not achieve a high profile in western Canada. Groups such as the Ukrainians continued to see Trudeau's policies as favouring French Canadians and his efforts at multiculturalism as half-hearted or insincere. Central and eastern Europeans also were alienated by Trudeau's efforts at *rapprochement* with the Soviet Union and what they saw as his refusal to show sufficient sympathy for Ukrainian dissidents in the Soviet Union.[53]

Though it did not achieve everything that was hoped, the policy of multiculturalism provided a focal point for ethnic politics throughout the 1970's and 1980's. Foreign policy and immigration policy continued to be of major concern to many organized groups, but the creation of a multiculturalism program within the Department of the Secretary of State (1971) and a Minister of State for Multiculturalism (1972) provided new programs and a lever for pressing the government to provide still more. The existence of the multiculturalism programs gave legitimacy to a wide range of ethnic activities and concerns that had previously been viewed with suspicion or indifference by many government departments and politicians. The federal government contributed to the establishment of national organizations for several groups, including the Chinese, Italians, and South Asians. In response to the multiculturalism policy, opposition parties began formulating their own policies for appealing to ethnic groups; in national election campaigns, the parties now routinely formulate policies in the area of multiculturalism. A government-appointed advisory body included many ethnic spokespeople who had been active in local party politics and gave them a sense of helping to shape government policies. The Minister of State for Multiculturalism also made his party aware of the concerns of ethnic groups and provided a focal point for Liberal and Conservative efforts to win crucial seats in cities with a large immigrant population, particularly Toronto. It is no accident that from 1972 to 1987 six of the ten ministers of multiculturalism represented Toronto ridings.

The introduction of multiculturalism as a policy at the federal level spurred several provinces to introduce similar programs, the three Prairie provinces and Ontario being the first to do so. Advisory councils in each of these provinces combine the functions of generating community input into the formulation of policy and rewarding or currying favour with ethnic leaders.

Although both Liberal and Parti Québécois governments in Quebec rejected the federal policy of multiculturalism, successive Quebec governments have had to deal with a diverse immigrant population in the post-war period, particularly in Montreal. The issue of the language of education for immigrants' children was particularly vexatious. Eventually the Parti Québécois passed Bill 101 (which is discussed in the chapter on education).[54] Despite initial resistance, most immigrant groups have gradually come to accept and live with the requirements of the legislation.

Though there were some in the PQ who thought it might be necessary to force immigrants to become part of French-speaking society, others saw that any hope for immigrant integration into a French-speaking society and immigrant support for an independent Quebec required a more tolerant and open approach. A Québécois was defined as anyone who learned to speak French and participated in a French-speaking culture as opposed to necessarily being of French origin. The PQ began making an effort to appeal to French-speaking groups such as the Haitians, Vietnamese, and North African Jews and also to groups such as the Spanish, Italians, Portuguese, and Latin Americans who fit into a Catholic culture in Quebec. Intellectuals and politicians in the PQ, including in particular the Minister of Immigration and Cultural Communities, Gérard Godin, developed their own policy of "interculturalism" that took into account ethnic diversity in Quebec and gave support to many of the same activities as the federal government's multiculturalism policy.[55]

By the early 1980's the PQ had begun to make inroads into several of the largest immigrant groups in Quebec – the Greeks, Italians, Portuguese, and French-speaking Sephardic Jews. The party appealed particularly to the younger Canadian-born generation who were eager to be accepted into the dynamic culture of Québécois nationalism and who felt that continuing identification with the minority English-speaking community in Montreal was a cultural dead end. In the absence of a viable New Democratic Party, the Parti Québécois also appealed to those, particularly among the Canadian-born, with social democratic connections. In the Italian and Greek communities these left-wing tendencies were promoted by ties with left-wing political movements in Italy and Greece and by concern over the plight of exploited workers in the garment and construction industries.

The varying responses of the provinces to multiculturalism reflected the ethnic composition and ethnic relations in different regions of the country. At the national level, the policy of multiculturalism demonstrated the growing political influence of the other ethnic groups, particularly Ukrainians, who had been among the strongest advocates of the policy. The policy itself contributed to the influence of ethnic groups through government funding of ethnic activities that gave further political legitimacy to ethnic organizations and leaders. One sign that supporters of the concept and policy of multiculturalism had been able to establish their position was the insertion in the Canadian Charter of Rights and Freedoms in 1982 of Article 27, which stated that the Charter "shall be interpreted in a manner consistent with the preservation and enhancement of the multicultural heritage of Canada."

The introduction of policies of multiculturalism at both the federal and provincial levels introduced a number of new elements to ethnic politics. One other major new element was the arrival of many new groups in the wake of the liberalization of Canada's immigration regulations in 1967. Over half of Canada's immigrants now came from the Third World, and they provided new political perspectives and a sense of relatedness to events in virtually every part of the globe, such as Chile, El Salvador, South Africa, Ethiopia, Uganda, the Punjab, and Vietnam. Refugees coming to Canada included all shades of the political spectrum. The bulk were still anti-Communist, including Czechs, Soviet Jews, Poles, and Vietnamese, but Canada also welcomed refugees from right-wing regimes, including Chileans, South Africans, Haitians, and Central Americans. Canadian immigration officials gradually became less worried about refugees with leftist ideas posing a threat to the Canadian state.

During the late 1960's the left-wing refugees included many young Americans who came to Canada as draft evaders and refugees from a society they considered repressive and militaristic. Their views, and those of the many American professors who came to Canadian universities at the same time, had a strong impact on young Canadians and influenced the views of a whole generation of college students toward the United States and American foreign policy. The American refugees are among the few who have been able to return home, though many in fact chose to stay in Canada despite an amnesty declared by the U.S. government in the late 1970's.

Besides providing a new perspective on world affairs, immigrants from the Third World gave a new impetus to and rationale for the federal policy of multiculturalism and helped shift the policy in new directions. The vast majority of Third World immigrants were non-white and were concerned about racism and discrimination. Consequently, they lobbied for more government emphasis on human rights and group understanding. In the early 1980's, the concern from the new "visible minority" groups about racism led to the establishment of a parliamentary committee, the report of which, *Equality Now* (1984), contained eighty recommendations, including several for affirmative action.[56]

Although Canada's new visible minorities are becoming organized and vocal at the national level, there have been few studies of their voting patterns. In most of the country, newcomers from Hong Kong and the Asian subcontinent have appeared to support the Liberal Party: it was in power when they came and they perceived Trudeau to be a strong leader who commanded respect internationally.

There were many regional variations to this pattern, however. In Alberta, for example, the newcomers were solidly absorbed into the Conservative

178

Party as the Filipinos, Chinese, Sikhs, West Indians, and Lebanese were anxious to play a part in shaping the course of Alberta politics. In 1985 party workers from these groups played an important part in choosing Don Getty as Conservative Party leader. The insecurity of these new groups was at the same time strikingly revealed by their desire to be on the winning side. The majority of political activists from these groups supported the front-running candidate Getty over Ukrainian lawyer Julian Koziak and Jewish lawyer Ron Ghitter, both of whom had been closely identified with their strong support for ethnic and human rights issues.

The growing concern about racism in Canada during the 1960's, 1970's, and 1980's had important implications for one of Canada's oldest ethnic groups, the blacks. Though attempts to form a continuing and stable national association for blacks have floundered for most of the twentieth century on the facts of dispersal, poverty, and regional differentiation, blacks across Canada were able to make tremendous political gains in these decades. Canadians became aware of the problems arising from racial discrimination through Canada being a member of the Commonwealth and a neighbour of the United States. The passage of human rights acts across Canada during the 1950's and 1960's came in part because Canadians felt both the injustice and the dangers of racism as exemplified in the United States. Growing political attention to Canadian blacks during the late 1960's came as much from fear about the possibilities of racial violence as from guilt over past injustices. Some blacks in Nova Scotia, who until the 1960's had been largely apolitical and had channelled their organizational life through their churches, began to look to assertive American models of black pride and black power. Young community leaders such as Rocky Jones challenged both the black community establishment and the white power structure and worked to free the black community from habits of deference and passivity. White politicians in Nova Scotia responded by providing support for new black organizations, such as the Black United Front, which promoted community development projects.

During the same time period blacks in Ontario also began to have more political influence. There had been occasional black politicians in the late nineteenth and early twentieth centuries. In Toronto, a Canadian-born black, W.P. Hubbard, a baker, was elected alderman in 1894 and was re-elected in thirteen consecutive elections. But examples of black political power were few and far between. During the 1960's and 1970's, aided by the arrival of American blacks, such as human rights activists Dan Hill and Wilson Head, and by the sizable influx of West Indian immigrants to Toronto, the blacks came to form a significant lobby group through organizations such as Toronto's Urban Alliance on Race Relations and community newspapers such as *Contrast* and *Share*. The growing political power of blacks was symbolized through the political career of black lawyer Lincoln Alexander, who was first elected as member of Parliament for Hamilton in 1968, appointed to the federal cabinet in the Clark government in 1979, and then chosen as Lieutenant-Governor of Ontario in 1985. Because of lack of numbers, outside of Nova Scotia and Ontario blacks have not been able to make the same political strides.

CONCLUSION

By the 1980's ethnicity has lost much of its political salience in the rural prairie regions where third, fourth, and fifth-generation Canadians were absorbed with regional issues, but it continued to play an important role in immigrant-receiving cities. Several long-established groups, such as the Jews and Ukrainians, continued to make their political muscle felt at all levels of government. Occasionally this political influence led to conflict between groups; the establishment of the Deschênes Commission in 1985 to inquire into the subject of war criminals in Canada helped turn the Jewish and Ukrainian communities against each other as long-standing prejudices and misunderstandings were compounded by continuing slights and slurs, real and imagined. The political influence of ethnic groups could also now be seen increasingly in the formulation of Canadian foreign policy as, for example, in the ill-fated undertaking by the Clark government to move the Canadian embassy to Jerusalem. Prominent public issues, such as the plight of Ukrainian and Jewish dissidents in the Soviet Union, continue to show that Canada is a polyethnic country, where developments in other parts of the world are watched intensely by many Canadians who have close ties with those areas. The history of ethnic groups has also begun to be politicized in some cases; the debate between the government and Japanese Canadians over the question of compensation for their treatment during World War II suggests a new stage in the development of ethnic politics in Canada.

The nature of the relationship between ethnicity and politics has changed significantly since the turn of the century. Political parties now strive for the support of non-whites rather than catering to racist public opinions. People of non-British, non-French origin can achieve the highest political offices in the land. Dave Barrett, premier of British Columbia from 1972 to 1975, David Lewis, the national leader of the NDP (1971 to 1975), and Joe Ghiz, elected premier of Prince Edward Island in 1985, two of them Jewish and one Lebanese Canadian, have shown that ethnic barriers to high public office are minimal. In 1986 Dutch-Canadian Bill Vander Zalm in British Columbia became the first immigrant of non-British origin to become premier of a province. The federal cabinet is also now thoroughly polyethnic. At the highest level of political symbolism, the choice of German-Canadian Ed Schreyer as Governor General in 1979 symbolized a reaching out to include people of non-British and non-French background. Schreyer, who had previously helped forge an ethnic coalition in Manitoba that brought the NDP to power in that province in 1969, used many languages in some of his official speeches to recognize the multicultural nature of Canadian society.

The political integration of the other ethnic groups has reached the point that only on rare occasions are individuals seen as representatives of individual groups. The needs and concerns of the other ethnic groups are increasingly a part of the consciousness of all government departments from External Affairs to the military. The provincial and federal civil services now more closely reflect the diversity of Canada's population than ever before.

During the twentieth century the non-British and non-French groups have significantly affected fortunes and policies of Canada's political parties and continue to do so. From the short-lived success of radical labour politics in the West to the strength of the protest parties in the Prairies during the 1930's and 1940's, to the weakness of the Conservative Party among those of non-British origin until the 1950's, to the long-standing strength of the Liberal Party throughout the twentieth century, ethnicity has affected the Canadian political process in myriad ways that historians and political scientists are just beginning to explore.

NOTES

1. Stuart Rosenberg, *The Jewish Community in Canada*, vol. 1 (Toronto: McClelland and Stewart 1970); Jack Jedwab, "Uniting Uptowners and Downtowners: The Jewish Electorate and Quebec Provincial Politics: 1927-1939," *Canadian Ethnic Studies*, 18, 2 (1986) pp. 7-19; Gerald Tulchinsky, "The Jewish School Question in Montreal from 1901 to the late 1920s," paper presented to the Canadian Ethnic Studies Association, Montreal, October 1985.
2. John English and Kenneth McLaughlin, *Kitchener: An Illustrated History* (Waterloo: Wilfrid Laurier University Press, 1983), chapters 2, 3, 4.
3. Anthony Rasporich, "Utopian Ideals and Community Settlements in Western Canada: 1880-1914," in H.C. Klassen, ed., *The Canadian West* (Calgary: Comprint, 1977), pp. 37-62; Nelson Wiseman, "Patterns of Prairie Politics," *Queen's Quarterly*, 88, 2 (1981), pp. 298-315; David Bercuson, *Fools and Wise Men: The Rise and Fall of the One Big Union* (Toronto: McGraw Hill-Ryerson, 1978); Paul Sharp, *The Agrarian Revolt in Western Canada* (Minneapolis: University of Minnesota Press, 1948); Ross McCormack, *Reformers, Rebels and Revolutionaries: The Western Canadian Radical Movement 1899-1919* (Toronto: University of Toronto Press, 1977).
4. J.W. Brennan, "Wooing the 'Foreign Vote': Saskatchewan Politics and the Immigrant, 1905-1919," *Prairie Forum* (Spring, 1978), p. 67.
5. O. Martynowych and N. Kazymyra, "Political Activity," in Lupul, ed., *A Heritage in Transition*, pp. 93, 95-96.
6. *Ibid.*, p. 98; Roz Usiskin, "The Winnipeg Jewish Community: Its Radical Elements, 1905-1918," *Historical and Scientific Society of Manitoba Transactions*, 3, 33 (1976-77), p. 22.
7. Usiskin, "The Winnipeg Jewish Community," pp. 12-18.
8. Mari Jalava, "Radicalism or a New Deal, the Unfolding World View of the Finnish Immigrants in Sudbury, 1883-1932" (M.A. thesis, Laurentian University, 1983); Henry Trachtenberg, "The Winnipeg Jewish Community and Politics: the Inter-War Years, 1919-1939," *Historical and Scientific Society of*

Manitoba Transactions, 3, 34-3, 35 (1977-78, 1978-79), p. 124.

9. Avery, *"Dangerous Foreigners,"* chapter 3.
10. Speisman, *The Jews of Toronto*, p. 320; Donald Avery, "The Radical Alien and the Winnipeg General Strike of 1919," in C. Berger and R. Cook, eds., *The West and the Nation* (Toronto: McClelland and Stewart, 1976), pp. 209-31.
11. Adachi, *The Enemy That Never Was*, p. 104.
12. Patricia Roy, "The Oriental Menace in British Columbia," in S.M. Trofimenkoff, ed., *The Twenties in Western Canada* (Ottawa: National Museum of Man, 1972); Wickberg, ed., *From China to Canada*, p. 152.
13. Buchignani and Indra, *Continuous Journey*, chapters 3, 4.
14. Palmer, *Patterns of Prejudice*, p. 114; Abella and Troper, *None is Too Many*.
15. Palmer, *Patterns of Prejudice*, pp. 118-20.
16. William Calderwood, "Pulpit, Press and Political Reactions to the Ku Klux Klan in Saskatchewan," in Trofimenkoff, ed., *The Twenties in Western Canada*, pp. 191-229; David Smith, *Prairie Liberalism* (Toronto: University of Toronto Press, 1975), chapters 4, 5.
17. Radecki, *A Member of a Distinguished Family*, p. 63; Dreisziger, *Struggle and Hope*, pp. 160-62.
18. Jonathan Wagner, *Brothers Beyond the Sea: National Socialism in Canada* (Waterloo: Wilfrid Laurier University Press, 1980); K.M. McLaughlin, *The Germans in Canada* (Ottawa: CHA Booklet, 1985), p. 38.
19. Roberto Perin, "Making Good Fascists and Good Canadians: Consular Propaganda and the Italian Community in Montreal in the 1930s," in Gerald Gold, ed., *Minorities and Mother Country Imagery* (St. John's: Institute of Social and Economic Research, 1984), pp. 136-58.
20. Robert Harney, "The Italian Community in Toronto," in Elliott, ed., *Two Nations, Many Cultures*, pp. 228-29.
21. Lita-Rose Betcherman, *The Swastika and the Maple Leaf: Fascist Movements in the Thirties* (Don Mills: Fitzhenry and Whiteside, 1975), p. 65.
22. Varpu Lindström-Best, *The Finns in Canada* (Ottawa: CHA Booklet, 1985), p. 5.
23. T.F. Jeletzky, ed., *Russian Canadians: Their Past and Present* (Ottawa: Borealis Press, 1983), chapter 11; Watson Kirkconnell, *Canada, Europe and Hitler* (Toronto: Oxford University Press, 1939), chapter 11.
24. John Kolasky, *The Shattered Illusion* (Toronto: Peter Martin, 1979); Helen Potrebenko, *No Streets of Gold: A Social History of Ukrainians in Alberta* (Vancouver: New Star, 1977); Kostash, *All of Baba's Children*.
25. Avery, *"Dangerous Foreigners,"* p. 120; for an authoritative account of Finnish-Canadian radicalism, see Edward Laine "Finnish Canadian Radicalism and Canadian Politics: the First Forty Years, 1900-1940," in Jorgen Dahlie and Tissa Fernando, eds., *Ethnicity, Power and Politics in Canada* (Toronto: Methuen, 1981), pp. 94-112.
26. Lindström-Best, *The Finns*, p. 12.
27. Avery, *"Dangerous Foreigners,"* p. 117.
28. Victor Howard, *The Mackenzie-Papineau Battalion: The Canadian Contingent*

in the Spanish Civil War (Ottawa: Carleton Library Series, 1986), p. 32.

29. Rasporich, *For a Better Life*, pp. 143-45; Ivan Avakumovic, *The Communist Party in Canada: A History* (Toronto: McClelland and Stewart, 1975), p. 33.

30. Donald Avery, "Ethnic Loyalties and the Proletarian Revolution: a Case Study of Communist Political Activity in Winnipeg, 1923-1936," in Dahlie and Fernando, eds., *Ethnicity, Power and Politics in Canada*, pp. 68-93; Trachtenberg, "The Winnipeg Jewish Community," p. 115; Elliot Katz, "The Participation of a Cultural Minority in Politics, Jewish Voting Preferences in Seven Oaks and River Heights, 1969 and 1973" (M.A. thesis, University of Manitoba, 1980), chapter 2.

31. Dreisziger, *Struggle and Hope*, p. 156.

32. Palmer, *Patterns of Prejudice*, p. 71; George Hoffman, "The New Party and the Old Issues: The Saskatchewan Farmer-Labour Party and the Ethnic Vote, 1934," *Canadian Ethnic Studies*, 14, 2 (1982), p. 8.

33. Andrew Milnor, "Agrarian Protest in Saskatchewan, 1929-48: A Study in Ethnic Politics" (Ph.D. thesis, Duke University, 1962).

34. Hoffman, "The New Party," p. 6; S.M. Lipset, *Agrarian Socialism* (Garden City, N.J.: Doubleday, 1968), chapter 8.

35. David Bercuson, *Canada and the Birth of Israel* (Toronto: University of Toronto Press, 1985), chapter 1.

36. H. Palmer, "The Hutterite Land Expansion Controversy in Alberta," *Western Canadian Journal of Anthropology*, II, 2 (1971), pp. 18-46.

37. Robert Keyserlingk, "Agents Within the Gates: The Search for Nazi Subversives in Canada during World War II," *Canadian Historical Review* (June, 1985), p. 223.

38. Robert Keyserlingk, "The Canadian Government's Attitude toward Germans and German Canadians in World War Two," *Canadian Ethnic Studies*, 16, 1 (1984), pp. 16-28; H. Palmer, "Ethnic Relations in Wartime: Nationalism and European Minorities in Alberta during the Second World War," *Canadian Ethnic Studies*, 14, 3 (1982), pp. 1-2.

39. J.A. Ciccocelli, "The Innocuous Enemy Alien: Italians in Canada During World War Two" (M.A. thesis, University of Western Ontario, 1977), p. 39; Palmer, "Ethnic Relations in Wartime," p. 7; Keyserlingk, "The Search For Nazi Subversives," p. 235.

40. Dreisziger, *Struggle and Hope*, chapter 6; Rasporich, *For a Better Life*, chapter 7.

41. Wickberg, ed., *From China to Canada*, chapter 14.

42. Ann Sunahara, *The Politics of Racism* (Toronto: Lorimer, 1981).

43. William Peterson, *Planned Migration* (Berkeley: University of California Press, 1955); Gerald Dirks, *Canada's Refugee Policy* (Montreal: McGill-Queen's University Press, 1977), chapters 6, 7.

44. Karl Aun, *The Political Refugees: A History of the Estonians in Canada* (Toronto: McClelland and Stewart, 1985), pp. 41, 81; Milda Danys, *DP: Lithuanian Immigration to Canada After the Second World War* (Toronto: Multicultural History Society of Ontario, 1986).

45. Bohdan Kordan and Lubomyr Luciuk, *A Delicate and Difficult Question:*

Documents in the History of Ukrainians in Canada, 1899-1962 (Kingston: Limestone Press, 1986); Bernard Hibbitts, "Ethnic Groups and Canadian Propaganda Policy in the 1950s," in Don Munton, ed., *Groups and Governments in Canadian Foreign Policy* (Toronto: Canadian Institute of International Affairs, 1985), pp. 101-03.

46. Rasporich, *For a Better Life*, pp. 176-79.

47. Peter Oliver, *Unlikely Tory: The Life and Politics of Allan Grossman* (Toronto: Lester & Orpen Dennys, 1985), p. 59.

48. For evidence of ethnic support for the Liberals in the post-war era, see, for example, John Wilson and David Hoffman, "Ontario," in Martin Robin, ed., *Canadian Provincial Politics* (Scarborough: Prentice Hall, 1972), p. 20; Harold Clarke *et al., Political Choice in Canada* (Toronto: McGraw Hill-Ryerson, 1980), pp. 77-78.

49. A. Rasporich, "Ethnicity in Lakehead Politics, 1900-1970," paper presented at the Canadian Ethnic Studies Association conference, Thunder Bay, October, 1983, p. 15; *Report* of the Royal Commission on Bilingualism and Biculturalism, Book IV, *The Cultural Contribution of the Other Ethnic Groups*, chapter 3.

50. Peter Stursberg, *Diefenbaker: Leadership Gained, 1956-62* (Toronto: University of Toronto Press, 1975), p. 95; Public Archives of Canada, Progressive Conservative Party Papers, Ethnic Files, 1957-1962; Ethnic Press Digest, 1957-1962.

51. Freda Hawkins, *Canada and Immigration: Public Policy and Public Concern* (Montreal: McGill-Queen's University Press, 1972), pp. 61-63; Wickberg, ed., *From China to Canada*, pp. 214-15.

52. Michael Marunchak, *The Ukrainian Canadians: A History* (Winnipeg: Ukrainian Free Academy of Sciences, 1970), p. 684.

53. M.R. Lupul, "The Political Implementation of Multiculturalism," *Journal of Canadian Studies*, 17, 1 (1982), pp. 93-102; H. Palmer, *Immigration and the Rise of Multiculturalism* (Toronto: Copp Clark, 1975), pp. 204-05; John Jaworsky, "A Case Study of the Canadian Federal Government's Multiculturalism Policy" (M.A. thesis, Carleton University, 1979).

54. Sheila Arnopoulous and Dominique Clift, *The English Fact in Quebec* (Montreal: McGill-Queen's University Press, 1980), p. 141; W. Coleman, "From Bill 22 to Bill 101: The Politics of Language Under the Parti Québécois," *Canadian Journal of Political Science*, 14, 3 (1981), pp. 459-85.

55. Pierre Anctil, "La Société québécoise face au multiculturalisme," paper presented to the Canadian Ethnology Society, Edmonton, May, 1986.

56. Report of the Special Committee on Visible Minorities in Canadian Society, *Equality Now* (Ottawa: Canadian Government Publishing Centre, 1984).

Montreal for a long time had Canada's largest Jewish community. The photograph is of a synagogue on St. Urbain Street in the early years of the twentieth century. (Notman Photographic Archives No. 10,760/McCord Museum of McGill University)

Synagogues in rural communities were more modest, as was this one in Sonnenfeld, Saskatchewan. (Public Archives Canada/C 27538)

Black churches, such as the African Methodist Episcopal Church in Edmonton (1921), played central roles in black communities. (Glenbow Archives)

Mennonites were among the earliest settlers in southern Ontario and in the West. Pictured are a group of Mennonite leaders in Coaldale, Alberta, in the late 1930's.

Reverend S. Nagatomi was the first minister of Raymond Buddhist Church.(Provincial Museum of Alberta Photograph Collection)

The Buddhist Church in Raymond, Alberta, was founded in 1929 in an attempt to halt the loss of Japanese culture. In post-war years the threat of loss has increased. (Provincial Museum of Alberta Photograph Collection)

The many ethnic groups who have settled in Canada have brought with them distinctive architectural styles. This is a Russo-Orthodox Church at Smoky Lake, Alberta. (Provincial Archives of Alberta/Photograph U.V. 16)

The church pictured was built in 1927 by German-Russian settlers who came to Alberta from Minnesota. (Provincial Museum of Alberta Photograph Collection)

In the family many ethnic rituals, especially religious rituals involving feasting or fasting, are celebrated. Here a rabbi and his children celebrate Passover.
(Public Archives Canada/PA 124945)

The post-war immigration led to the reinforcement of established ethnic churches and parishes and the creation of new ones. In 1963 a Serbian Orthodox Church was dedicated in Sudbury, Ontario. (Multicultural History Society of Ontario)

A Czech church in Chatham, Ontario, had a garden setting. (Ontario Archives/Multicultural History Society of Ontario Collection)

Ethnically based left-wing groups provided members with an array of social and cultural activities. Shown is the Ukrainian Labour-Farmer Temple Association, Saskatoon, 1928. (Public Archives Canada/PA 88636)

Post-war immigrants made anti-communism a significant political force in Canada in the early 1950's. The Byelorussian National Association demonstrates. (Ontario Archives/Multicultural History Society of Ontario Collection)

Greeks demonstrated in Toronto in the late 1960's against political events in their homeland. (Ontario Archives/Multicultural History Society of Ontario Collection)

Many saw the Green Paper on immigration (1975) as an attempt to reverse the trend toward a more open policy. A Toronto demonstration is pictured. (Public Archives Canada/PA 126346)

Voluntary associations were founded by ethnic groups to keep their traditions alive. The P. Mohyla Ukrainian Institute Drama Group in Saskatoon in 1919 is shown. (Public Archives Canada/PA 88603)

The year was 1921. The scene, Laurier street at Whitney Pier, as members of the city's Negro community paraded in support of a movement advocating, (as the banners indicate) "Africa for the Africans." The sizable brass band was one of a number organized within the city and residents who were around at that time recall that nobody ever had to march without the accompaniment of plenty of stirring martial music. Also noteworthy is the complete lack of sidewalks and paving. The photograph is from the album of Pier merchant Louis Mendelson. He's the white-shirted young man with the bicycle standing mid-right in the photo

Bands were also popular voluntary associations; this one was in the mining district of Cape Breton. (Beaton Institute Archives)

Youth groups, such as the Youth Group of the Armenian Canadian Union, Toronto Branch, were founded to try to keep young people in their ethnic communities. (Ontario Archives/Multicultural History Society of Ontario Collection)

Musical groups usually found appreciative audiences, as did the First Croatian Tamburitza Orchestra of Sudbury in the 1930's. (Multicultural History Society of Ontario)

Women's auxiliaries were expected to provide services for men's organizations and for youth groups. Men made the preparations for the formation of the Croatian Women's Club in Sudbury in the 1930's. (Multicultural History Society of Ontario)

After World War II ex-combatants' associations were among the many that were founded by immigrants. Shown is the Lithuanian Veterans' Guard Association in Sudbury. (Ontario Archives/Multicultural History Society of Ontario Collection)

The premises of voluntary associations helped to make ethnicity visible in large Canadian cities. (Photo by David Levine/Multicultural History Society of Ontario)

Members of visible minorities have frequently complained of being underemployed in the mass media. The photograph shows a Vancouver disc jockey of Chinese background in 1951. (Public Archives Canada/ PA 112783)

The vast and variegated post-war immigration resulted in an unprecedented growth of the ethnic press. The photograph is of a typesetter at German Publications, Scarborough, Ontario, 1969. (Multicultural History Society of Ontario)

Creating and maintaining communication within ethnic groups has been of intense concern to virtually all Canadian ethnic goups. Mr. Upeslacis, owner of Daina Press, is shown in Toronto, 1963. (Multicultural History Society of Ontario)

A newspaper's life is limited if Canadian-born generations lack fluency in the language in which it appears. Joshua Gershman edited the Yiddish paper Vochenblatt. *(Multicultural History Society of Ontario)*

Sports and athletics have been transplanted to Canada as part of the tradition of many ethnic groups. (Ontario Archives/Multicultural History Society of Ontario Collection)

Soccer teams have advertised their ethnic affiliations in their names, emblems, and colours. Shown are members of the Korean soccer team of Ontario, 1976. (Ontario Archives/Multicultural History Society of Ontario Collection)

Vera Cudjoe was founder and artistic director of Black Theatre Canada. (Multicultural History Society of Ontario)

Celebrations of Canadian holidays, such as Canada Day, since the 1960's have usually featured ethnic displays. (Beaton Institute Archives)

Filipino children celebrate a Canadian Christmas. (Ontario Archives/Multicultural History Society of Ontario Collection)

Two young Canadians play cowboy. (Thomas Bouckley Collection, Oshawa)

PART THREE

Other Institutions and the Maintenance of Identity

NINE

Ethnic Voluntary Associations

North American society, especially in its urban centres, is highly productive of clubs and associations of many kinds; Canada and the United States have been termed nations of joiners. Ethnic associations comprise a recognized category of voluntary associations, but not an especially large or significant one. In Canada the native-born are more likely to join voluntary associations than are immigrants, and it is the general associations of the community that they join; ethnic associations tend to be dominated by immigrants. The proportion of an ethnic group belonging to ethnic associations is likely to be small; for example, although Ukrainians have an image of being especially ethnically aware and dynamic, it was estimated that in 1971 of 580,000 Canadians of Ukrainian ethnic origin only between 30,000 and 60,000 belonged to ethnic organizations.[1] Nonetheless, the associations fill an important place in the lives of those who belong to them and also frequently represent the ethnic group to governments and to the rest of the outside world.

Soon after immigration, many peoples establish associations to meet wants related to settlement in the new country. These wants include services and information, and, perhaps most important, contact with others of their own language and background. Later, the immigrant associations may be supplemented or supplanted by ethnic associations, to meet wants that are shared by members of an ethnic group but not by the community at large. These objectives include the perpetuation of a particular language and culture, or needs that members of the ethnic group are prevented from meeting within existing voluntary associations by linguistic barriers, discrimination, high fees, or other obstacles. The initiative in starting the associations may be taken by individuals eager to rise to or to preserve white-collar status in their new country by serving an immigrant or ethnic clientele. With time, however, the appeal of ethnic associations often diminishes, especially for those whose principal occupational institutions come to lie outside the ethnic framework: wealthy businessmen, professionals, intellectuals, and unionized workers.[2] The associations then decline and die, or broaden their membership so that they cease to have an ethnic base. A new wave of immigration may then lead to the emergence of new associations.

BEFORE 1920

Although a few ethnic associations existed early in the history of Canada, with mass immigration at the end of the nineteenth century and the beginning of the twentieth century they proliferated. Immigrants who had come from rural communities, with some exceptions, were unaccustomed to participating in voluntary associations. They had been born into a family and a church, and around these, with the leadership of the clergy, all community social and ceremonial life had been centred. Under the auspices of the church, various societies had sometimes developed, but usually these were hardly voluntary: all members of the community of the appropriate age, sex, or marital status had been deemed to be members. When secular associations had emerged, especially those with nationalist aims or radical groups among the youth, they had been looked upon suspiciously or even suppressed by the government.[3]

Immigrants from urban areas in the homeland were more accustomed than their rural counterparts to organizational activity, some of it clandestine. In the years before World War I, however, the bulk of the immigrants attracted to Canada had peasant backgrounds, even though some of them might have had experience in cities as migrant labourers.

The Chinese were exceptional, in that even in rural areas they were used to forming voluntary associations, especially for raising short-term credit. In the towns of China various forms of voluntary associations had flourished among the rural-urban migrants. Thus Chinese immigrants brought considerable knowledge of associational principles with them.[4]

The Ukrainians also had some experience with associations. Members of populist and radical movements in Ukraine had organized reading clubs and national or community associations among the peasants to raise their educational and cultural level and arouse their national consciousness. The peasants, therefore, even when illiterate, had some acquaintance with organized efforts at adult education.[5]

Not only were most immigrants unaccustomed to voluntary associations, but their sense of group identity often only encompassed compatriots who were from the same town, village, or region in the homeland. Among the Chinese, for example, one type of association was based on surname, which was considered to connote kinship, and another on district or region; among the Italians, associations were often confined to the *paese* (district or village); and the Norwegians had *bygdelag* societies, bringing together those who had come from the same district in Norway. Many other ethnic groups also had *landsmannschaften*, associations of persons from the same local community. Only as proximity and shared experience in Canada took effect and as the benefits to be derived from larger associations began to be recognized did broader ethnic associations emerge.

The immigrants' lack of experience with voluntary associations was compensated to some extent by contacts with ethnic voluntary associations in the United States or, more rarely, in the European homeland. Only a few ethnic groups – the Macedonians were one – had their largest and best organized North American communities in Canada. The Norwegian *bygdelag* and Sons of Norway lodges, the Greek *Panhellenios Enosis*, the Icelandic chapters of the Independent Order of Good Templars, and chapters of the Slovak League of America are examples of Canadian associations with links to the United States.

Rural settlements were unlikely to have many voluntary associations other than churches and associations sponsored by the churches. The Icelandic immigrants, however, with an outstanding tradition of literacy, before the end of the nineteenth century had set up libraries and reading clubs, begun with books brought from home but later augmented by books in English; they had also established lodges of the Independent Order of Good Templars, other temperance societies, and at least one athletic club.[6] Reading clubs were set up in Ukrainian rural communities, not only under the auspices of the Catholic Church but also as secular organizations open to people of all religions and political persuasions. Later, many became associated with the Ukrainian Greek Orthodox Church.[7]

In the mining and construction camps and in the cities, the first ethnic voluntary associations were usually mutual-aid or benefit societies. In the old country, emergencies had been met with assistance from the immediate or extended family. In the New World, immigrants feared that unemployment, illness, or accident would prevent their earning a living, or that death among strangers would mean burial without the rites they considered essential. Sometimes it was a mine disaster or other tragic accident that led to the forming of a society. Among Germans a "Funeral Fee or Burial Society" was started in Halifax in 1753. The first Polish mutual-aid society was founded in Berlin, Ontario, in 1872, under the guidance of priests, and received its provincial charter in 1886. Italian mutual-aid societies were founded in both Montreal and Toronto well before the turn of the century. The first known association of Hungarian workers in Canada was the First Hungarian Sick-Benefit Society of Lethbridge, founded in 1901. Lithuanian mutual-aid organizations were begun in both Toronto and Montreal in 1905 and in Winnipeg seven years later. The burial society among the Chinese took the form of associations that shipped the bones of the dead back to China for burial. Such shipments occurred every seven years until 1932; unsettled political conditions prevented shipment in 1939.[8]

Where there were already settled and successful members of an ethnic group, they sometimes established philanthropic or charitable associations to assist newcomers and at the same time to preserve the reputation of the ethnic group. Such associations were among the "good works" in which women often took a leading part. The Jewish group was pre-eminent in philanthropic ethnic associations, because of the religious teachings of Judaism, the acute needs of many Jewish immigrants, and discrimination against Jews by some philanthropies. In Toronto, for example, by the time central and eastern European Jews began arriving in large numbers, both men's and women's philanthropic associations had been well launched by the predominantly English and German Jews who were already established.[9] Jews also participated in the charitable organizations of the general community.

In addition to mutual-aid and philanthropic associations, temperance societies, sports and athletic clubs, literary societies, musical groups, and theatrical associations appeared. Some of these societies reproduced homeland associations; others continued customs that in the homeland would not have required voluntary associations for their perpetuation. In the former cases, in cities as well as in rural communities, the associations were often branches of organizations in the homeland or in ethnic communities in the United States.

When barriers between the ethnic group and the rest of the community were not high, the voluntary associations tended to emulate those of the broader community. This was the case among Scandinavians in the West, where Icelanders in Winnipeg in 1916 founded a chapter of the Imperial Order of Daughters of the Empire, and also among the older Jewish residents in Toronto in the 1890's, where although it had exemplars in American Jewish communities, the Toronto Jewish Literary and Social Union affiliated with Holy Blossom Synagogue because the other literary societies in Toronto at the time had affiliations with churches. On the other hand, in highly segregated ethnic communities, instead of associations oriented to the wider Canadian community, branches of political parties in the homeland were formed: in Canadian Chinatowns the Kuomintang and the Empire Reform Association were active, and among South Asians the Hindustan Ghadar Party, the aim of which was the independence of India.

During the war years and those immediately following, some of the voluntary associations languished or disappeared. Their membership declined as people prospered, became engaged in war production or the armed services, or avoided association with groups whose loyalty might be questioned. They were under pressure to switch to using English in their meetings. Associations of those labelled enemy aliens, however unfairly, suffered most; some of them were outlawed. Some associations amalgamated as differences among them lost their significance.

On the other hand, for some groups concern for the people in their homelands led to increased activity and to the submergence of rivalries. Polish associations, for example, were especially active during the war. They were concerned with sending relief supplies to Poland through the Red Cross; with aiding recruitment for the Polish army being organized in France and the Polish army being organized in Niagara-on-the-Lake, Ontario, in 1917; and with clarifying the position of Poles in Canada who were defined as enemy aliens and securing the release of those who had been interned. To these ends, they formed special committees in major urban centres, held fund-raising drives, and wrote letters to newspapers. What Radecki found for the Poles was true for most ethnic groups:

> A common characteristic of all Polish organizations until 1920 was numerically small membership and lack of capable people able to assume positions of leadership or other offices. There were only a few organizers with some experience acquired in the Polish-American Associations which were established earlier, and a handful of others who participated in some organizational activity in Poland. Without experience and lacking organizers, the Canadian Poles drew heavily on the expertise and adopted models of lay organizations established by the Poles in the United States.[10]

UNTIL 1940

When immigration was renewed in the 1920's, the change in the average educational level of immigrants from many eastern and central European countries, the presence of some middle-class and upper-class immigrants, and the urban concentration of the newcomers made the prospects for associational structure much brighter. A number of the self-help, charitable, cultural, and sports organizations were revitalized.

However, because of the differences between the older arrivals and their children on the one hand and the newcomers on the other, associations were sometimes rent apart by bitter quarrels; in other instances new societies were created to serve different interests and wants. In particular, the political upheavals related to the war and the Russian Revolution had engaged many immigrants on one or the other side. New immigrants found their predecessors lacking in sophistication and interest concerning homeland politics. They therefore founded branches of old-country associations, including women's auxiliaries and youth groups. Among Ukrainians, for example:

> Some of the newcomers accepted the established forms of community life which they encountered here and joined one or other sectors of it. Quite a large number, however, were not satisfied with the already established "old forms" of organizational life and began to create new ones. They considered the older settlers and the Canadian born ones too Canadianized. Highly nationalistic and partisan in outlook, as far as their native land was concerned, with strong attachment to their old country national organizations, the newcomers began forming branches of these parent bodies and began publishing their periodicals. It was only natural that antagonism, friction and rivalry would develop between the old settlers and the new ones. This animosity within the group was particularly strong in the 1930's . . . .[11]

By the 1920's the linking of local associations into national associations became frequent, and a number of ethnic groups tried to establish umbrella organizations. The Canadian Jewish Congress was founded in 1919 and reconstituted in 1934; the Hungarian-Canadian Federation emerged in the late 1920's but was moribund by 1931, a victim of "quixotic planning, general apathy, and the Depression."[12] Among Ukrainians, three federations were established, the Ukrainian Labour-Farmer Temple Association, the Self-Reliance League of Canada, and the Ukrainian Catholic Brotherhood. Among Poles, also, several federations emerged, although discussions of co-operation and unification failed to lead to a single body.

The attempts at unification continued during the 1930's, but without notable successes. While in the cities associational life continued, in rural communities, especially in the West, associations foundered as farmers abandoned their land or sank into poverty and apathy. The cessation of immigration was to some extent countered in the cities by rural-urban migration. In most groups Montreal and Toronto became the nodes in the associational systems. Among Armenians, smaller centres played a larger role than Toronto.

The political organizations that had sprung up in the 1920's encountered difficulties in the 1930's when they espoused causes either on the far left or the radical right. The organizations in many cases involved homeland governments, which wanted to manipulate emigrants. Fascist consular officials created centres among Italian Canadians where the aims of Mussolini were glorified; National Socialist agents were at work among German Canadians; and the Soviets attempted to control some left-wing eastern Europeans. The results were violence and vandalism, antagonism on the part of many Canadians, and withdrawal of some immigrants from the organizations.

DURING AND AFTER WORLD WAR II

The war diminished differences between associations in many ethnic groups as strong common concerns for people in the homeland emerged. Raising funds for the defence of the mother country, for assistance to war victims, orphans, and prisoners of war, and for fighting men and their families became the paramount aim of most voluntary organizations. Bitter differences were transmuted into amicable rivalries in the amount of money sent overseas or invested in war bonds among such groups as the Hungarians, Croatians, and Poles.

The need to co-ordinate the war efforts was soon recognized. Special committees, composed of representatives of the various associations, were set up. Little more was needed to turn some of these into umbrella organizations, bringing together all but the Communist ethnic associations. Encouragement and aid came from the government, through the special advisory Committee on Co-operation in Canadian Citizenship (CCCC) created by the Department of National War Services.

One of the early umbrella organizations was the Ukrainian Canadian Committee:

Despite the intervention of non-Ukrainians, and, in particular, the

Department of War Services in Ottawa, and despite the fact that the alliance became possible through compromise, the Ukrainian Canadian community at large accepted the long awaited super-structure enthusiastically. It *had been* a long wait, and the Ukrainian top men had consistently pleaded for union. Everyone fervently hoped that the Committee would live up to expectations, thus, from the beginning it was morally and financially supported by a large segment of the organized community. Soon branches were formed across the country, and, for the first time many Ukrainians of diverse religious and ideological backgrounds, joined hands to plan and to work. When the first Congress was called by the Committee in Winnipeg in 1943, there were more than 700 accredited delegates from across Canada.[13]

The Canadian Polish Congress was established in September, 1944, with 115 affiliated organizations. Among Hungarians, however, after promising beginnings, the efforts of the cccc had little result beyond the formation of a few local co-ordinating committees.

After the war, the trend toward umbrella organizations continued. Some of the new immigrants began, as earlier arrivals had done, by centring their activities on family, kin, and friends and did not organize formally on an ethnic basis. Others were quick to set up formal associations, at first local associations related to regions in the homeland, then local associations for the ethnic group, followed by national associations and, finally, umbrella organizations to co-ordinate the efforts of their various national associations. Among umbrella organizations are the Canadian Arab Federation, the Byelorussian Canadian Co-ordinating Committee (founded in 1966), the Czechoslovak National Alliance (founded in 1942 and renamed the Czechoslovak National Association in Canada in 1960), the United Council of Filipino Associations across Canada, the National Japanese Canadian Citizens Association (founded in 1947), the National Congress of Italian-Canadians (founded in 1974), the Hungarian-Canadian Federation (founded in 1951), the Latvian National Federation of Canada (founded in 1949), and the National Council of the Lithuanian-Canadian Community (founded in 1952).

The need for co-ordination was the more apparent because of the vast elaboration of the associational structures of virtually all sizable ethnic groups. The numbers of post-war immigrants, their tendency to create new associations rather than to join existing ones, their varied educational levels and experience in organizations, and the wide range of their backgrounds, interests, and experiences have all led to the proliferation of ethnic associations. Economic associations, such as credit unions, business and professional associations, and associations of members of single occupations or professions (journalists, writers, artists, doctors, lawyers, engineers); learned societies; associations linked to political groups in the homeland or to Canadian political parties; ex-combatants' associations; sports and athletic associations – all have appeared in considerable numbers.

An indication of the variety of ethnic voluntary associations to be found in large ethnic groups in large cities is the list of participants in a metropolitan umbrella organization:

> In 1969 a start was made to organize an umbrella organization for Toronto Italia called FACI, *Federazione delle associazioni dai clubs italiani*. Among the organizations participating were many hometown and soccer clubs, the Italo-Canadian Automobile Club, Italo-Canadian Hunting & Fishing Club, Italian Club of the University of Toronto, Dante Society, Italian Philatelic Club, Italian Immigrant Aid Society, COSTI, Italo-Canadian Chamber of Commerce, and the Italian Society of Artists. The representatives of these organizations ranged from crusty old infighters of ethnic politics to hobbyists and social workers. They carried on their business in English and Italian.[14]

The difficulty of maintaining harmony within associations is indicated by an incident that occurred in the Italo-Canadian Recreation Club:

> It was about the mid-fifties that the Diocese of Toronto decided that they would give a gift to the Italo-Canadian Recreation Club, a gesture which almost ruined the store of goodwill which, up until then, had existed between the two major political factions that supported the club. When a gift from the Archbishop of Toronto, a gold crucifix, arrived at Brandon, the right-wing faction of the club was ready to have a celebration complete with bands and flags. The left-wing faction, however, stated loud and clear that either the initial agreement be kept (i.e., no religious affiliations), or they would demand that every cent contributed for the acquisition of the land and for the construction of the club be returned to them immediately. It was unthinkable. The ICRC would have gone bankrupt. They say that the metal in which the crucifix was cast became extremely shiny because of its endless comings and goings. The right-wing faction of the club maintained, "Either He stays or our money goes," while the left-wing faction stated, "Either He goes or our money goes." Meanwhile the crucifix glittered.
>
> They finally compromised. There would be no celebration and the crucifix would be placed in a seldom used room that functioned as a library.[15]

Changes in Canadian society lessened the need for some types of association that had previously been numerous. During the war years Canada had moved toward becoming a welfare state. The system of public social security programs expanded greatly with the introduction of unemployment insurance and family allowances, and it was to continue to expand. Some of the immigrants were accustomed to equally developed or more developed systems at home and were not reluctant to use them. Some of the ethnic mutual-aid and philanthropic associations founded by or for earlier immigrants were thus rendered unnecessary; some of them, in fact, had been transformed, formally or informally, into public institutions. Mutual aid remained one of the goals listed in the unrevised constitutions of associations, but no longer was this purpose stressed. On the other hand, immigrant aid societies, such as had long existed within the Jewish group, multiplied, with the important function of directing recent immigrants toward public sources of aid.

Since the 1960's concern about language has led to the development of public means of learning Canada's official languages and of maintaining ancestral languages. Language teaching therefore has become less important among the activities of ethnic voluntary associations. However, since language teaching is only one of the aims of supplementary schools, the associations whose purpose is the maintenance of such schools have continued to flourish.

Ethnic voluntary associations vary in the degree to which they are ethnically exclusive. Research carried out in the 1960's concerning the associations of Dutch, German, Italian, and Ukrainian Canadians indicated that only the German associations permitted some degree of membership of people of other ethnic groups.[16] A study of Polish organizations in Toronto in 1973 found that they were ethnically exclusive, the few non-Polish members being spouses of Poles.[17] In some groups bitter debate occurs over whether sons of women who marry out and thus do not have "appropriate" surnames can be members of credit unions and other ethnically exclusive associations.

Ethnic associations are usually composed of and led by immigrants. According to the research done in the 1960's, in only 8 per cent of Dutch associations, 11 per cent of German associations, and 23 per cent of Italian associations were more than 30 per cent of the members Canadian-born, and 56 per cent of Dutch associations had no Canadian-born members. Although at the time of the research close to 80 per cent of Canadians of Ukrainian origin were Canadian-born and there had been almost no Ukrainian immigration since the early 1950's, Ukrainian associations were largely made up of immigrants: only 41 per cent had more than 30 per cent of Canadian-born members. Immigrants comprised an even higher proportion of officers than of members. Eighty-nine per cent of the Dutch associations had no Canadian-born officers, and 82 per cent had none who had arrived in Canada before 1946; 64 per cent of German associations had no Canadian-born officers, and 39 per cent had none who had arrived before 1946; 39 per cent of Italian associations had no Canadian-born officers and 42 per cent none who had arrived before 1946; 36 per cent of Ukrainian associations had no Canadian-born officers and 43 per cent none who had arrived before 1946.[18] In Polish organizations in Toronto in the 1970's immigrants also predominated.

It is evident, therefore, that ethnic associations are by and large immigrant associations. Although some of them try to recruit the Canadian-born through such activities as scouting, camping, sports clubs, choirs, and dance groups, they have little success. The native-born in the majority of cases prefer activities that are not defined in ethnic terms.

The reliance of ethnic voluntary associations on immigrants for members and leaders appears to give them a limited lifespan. For example, the outlook for Polish organizations appeared to be bleak in the 1970's:

The present organizational membership is overwhelmingly composed of and led by the post-war and aging immigrants. . . . The organizers and leaders admit that they are not successful in recruiting members or participants in some organized body from among the Canadian-born individuals of any generation of Polish immigrants, nor from the comparatively smaller numbers of more recent arrivals from Poland. Should this condition continue it is likely that, with the death or retirement of the present membership, the organizational structure will cease to exist and the Polish group will lose its agencies devoted to maintaining Polish culture. This loss will also mean that the Polish-Canadian community will be without sources of reference and identification (now provided by the organizational complex) in the eyes of the other cultural groups in Canada.[19]

However, crises in Poland have renewed immigration in the early 1980's. The new immigrants have not joined existing organizations in large numbers but have created some new ones. What an observer has concluded about Alberta may be applied to Canada as a whole: "The future of Polish ethnic organizations will depend not on the children of the post-war refugees, who have integrated quickly and fully into Canadian society, but rather on immigrants who were educated in the Polish People's Republic and who arrived in Canada during the last two decades."[20]

The fact that ethnic associations are usually composed of and led by immigrants does not necessarily imply that ethnicity is an immigrant phenomenon. Members of the second and later generations may belong to the general associations of Canadian society and read the newspapers and watch and listen to broadcasts in the official languages, having lost fluency in their ancestral tongue; but they may be maintaining their identity in other ways. Exchanging visits with relatives in the homeland, observing special holidays in the home, retaining some parts of the ethnic cuisine – such activities may keep ethnic identity alive.

Government assistance has been given to ethnic voluntary associations for a long time, but it has become more publicized and larger since the institution of the policy of multiculturalism. Several of the programs of the federal government under such headings as cultural integration, intercultural communications, group development, and multicultural arts give grants to ethnic voluntary associations for various purposes; a number of provinces and municipalities also give financial or moral assistance to such associations. The fact that various levels of government recognize the contribution ethnic voluntary associations make to Canadian society has encouraged their formation and their continuance perhaps more than the grants themselves.

The adoption of a policy of multiculturalism in the early 1970's has had repercussions on the organizational life of ethnic groups. Among South Asians, for example, voluntary associations were few in 1971; now they are much more numerous:

In Metro Toronto alone there are at least sixty different South Asian organizations. There are another thirty or so in Montreal, forty in Alberta, twenty in Winnipeg, and another forty in the Vancouver area. Altogether, there are now perhaps 250 organizations in the country, with more being founded all the time. Virtually every local community of any size now supports some kind of an association and sometimes has several.[21]

Religious institutions are included; indeed, they predominate. Such groups as Sikhs and Ismaelis have, however, evolved or are evolving from religious into ethnic groups.

The repercussions of government aid are not all welcome in immigrant and ethnic communities. When there are competing voluntary associations, inevitably some are more successful in getting grants than others. The result may be the acrimonious exchange of charges and countercharges.

In spite of their limited membership, largely composed of the foreign-born, ethnic associations claim to speak for all those listed in the census as being in the appropriate origin category. Sometimes they even inflate the census figures to include the spouses of those who have married out of the group. Thus they wield considerable political power. In the 1980's the Ethno-cultural Council of Canada, composed of representatives of more than thirty ethnic organizations and funded by Multiculturalism Canada, has emerged as one of the most important pressure groups regarding multiculturalism.

NOTES

1. Ol'ha Woycenko, "Community Organizations," in Lupul, ed., *A Heritage in Transition*, p. 192.
2. Norris, *Strangers Entertained*, p. 41.
3. Henry Radecki, *Ethnic Organizational Dynamics: The Polish Group in Canada* (Waterloo: Wilfrid Laurier University Press, 1973), p. 44.
4. Wickberg, ed., *From China to Canada*, pp. 10-11.
5. Woycenko, "Community Organizations," pp. 173-74.
6. Lindal, *The Icelanders in Canada*, pp. 154, 177, 180, 196, 208.
7. Woycenko, "Community Organizations," pp. 174-75; H.W. Debor, "The cultural contributions of the German ethnic group to Canada," an essay prepared for the Royal Commission on Bilingualism and Biculturalism (n.d.), p. 61; Radecki, *Ethnic Organizational Dynamics*, p. 46; Robert F. Harney, *Italians in North America*, p. 12; Dreisziger, *Struggle and Hope*, p. 94; Gaida *et al.*, *Lithuanians in Canada*, Canada Ethnica 5 (Ottawa: Lights Printing and Publishing Co., 1967), pp. 267-68.
8. Wickberg, ed., *From China to Canada*, pp. 78, 175-76.
9. Speisman, *The Jews of Toronto*, pp. 56-75.
10. Radecki, *Ethnic Organizational Dynamics*, pp. 61-63.
11. Ol'ha Woycenko, "Ukrainian Contribution to Canada's Cultural Life," an

     essay prepared for the Royal Commission on Bilingualism and Biculturalism (1965), p. 14.

12.   Dreisziger, *Struggle and Hope*, p. 130.

13.   Woycenko, *The Ukrainians in Canada*, p. 210.

14.   Robert F. Harney, "The new Canadians and their life in Toronto," *Canadian Geographical Journal* (April-May, 1978), p. 25.

15.   Gianni Grohovaz, "See You at Brandon Hall. Oh! . . . I mean the Italo-Canadian Recreation Club," *Polyphony*, 7, 2 (1985), p. 102.

16.   David Sherwood and Allan C. Wakefield, "A Study of Voluntary Associations among Other Ethnic Groups in Canada," a study prepared for the Royal Commission on Bilingualism and Biculturalism (1968).

17.   Radecki, *Ethnic Organizational Dynamics*, pp. 122-23.

18.   Sherwood and Wakefield, "A Study of Voluntary Associations among Other Ethnic Groups in Canada."

19.   *Ibid.*, p. 3.

20.   Joanna Matejko, "The Polish Experience in Alberta," in Palmer and Palmer, eds., *Peoples of Alberta*, p. 296.

21.   Buchignani and Indra, *Continuous Journey*, p. 184.

TEN

The Media

The creation and maintenance of communications within ethnic groups and the treatment of immigration and of ethnic groups by the press, radio, and television have been of intense concern to virtually all Canadian ethnic groups. Within the group, getting and keeping in touch with one's fellows and with the institutions of the group, expressing one's feelings and interests in one's own terms, receiving news of the homeland and of members of the group in other lands, and obtaining information about Canada in a language and a context one can understand are among the motivations for supporting ethnic media. In addition, what the media of the society at large say or imply about the ethnic groups reflects and influences the treatment they as collectivities and their individual members will receive.

THE ETHNIC PRESS

At the time when the ethnic press began many immigrants had come from rural backgrounds and had little formal education. It is probable that in Canada, as in the United States, some became literate in order to read newspapers in their mother tongue. In some instances, for example, in Ukraine, Russia, Poland, and the Baltic states, the peasants had not been allowed to have books or newspapers in the language they were accustomed to speak, the vernacular that differed widely from the language of the educated classes. Other immigrants brought literacy and a custom of newspaper-reading to Canada: for example, the working-class Finns who came in the late nineteenth and early twentieth centuries were almost all literate, and they established a tradition of handwritten newspapers, the "fist press," that survived until World War II.[1]

Some immigrant groups had access to papers from their homelands or from the United States before they established publications of their own. Not only did Canadian settlers subscribe to such papers; they also contributed to them, telling about their experiences and encouraging others to join them or warning others to stay away. Further, when papers began in Canada, they often lacked enough reporters, writers, and editors to fill their pages, and consequently they resorted to reprinting articles from non-Canadian sources and thus reinforced and extended the influence of outside ethnic papers. However, newspapers from abroad did not contain information concerning the Canadian milieu, nor could they afford sufficient space for expression of one's hopes and fears in the new land and the longing for home. Hence they were only a stopgap.

When papers started in Canada, they found devoted readers. A Ukrainian-Canadian poet, Maria Adamowska, wrote of her father:

> . . . when Ukrainian newspapers began to be published, none of them escaped father's attention. Even if he had to go without food and live on water for a whole week, he found the money for newspaper subscriptions. Since there were several literate people in our community, they used to get together at our home on the long winter evenings, to read the papers and discuss their contents. Many a sunrise found these men, though weary from the previous day's hard toil, going without a wink of sleep to forge a happier lot for themselves and their children.[2]

The Canadian ethnic press has a history extending back to the eighteenth century when a German-language weekly was published for a short time in Halifax. It was followed by the weekly *Canada Museum und Allgemeine Zeitung*, in Berlin, Upper Canada, in 1835, and from then until World War I by scores of other German publications.[3] Other ethnic groups also produced publications, usually short-lived, soon after coming to Canada. For example, Icelanders who arrived in Manitoba in 1875 were served by a handwritten paper in 1876, *Framfari* from 1877 to 1880, and *Leifur* (named for the explorer Leif Ericson) shortly afterward for another three-year period.[4]

It was late in the nineteenth century, however, with the advent of large numbers of immigrants whose mother tongues were not English or French, that ethnic newspapers began to develop and multiply. The Icelandic-Canadian *Heimskringla* (The Round World) was established in 1886, and *Lögberg* (The Mount of Laws) in 1888;[5] the *Jewish Times* was begun in 1897; the Italian *Lo Stendardo* in 1898; the first printed Finnish-Canadian newspaper in 1903; the Polish-language *Glos Kanadyjski* in 1904; the *Chinese Times* in 1907; the first Arabic paper in 1908; the Slovak *Slovenske Slovo* (Slovak Word) in 1910; the Swedish *Svenska Canada Tidningen* in 1892 or earlier, *Canada Posten* in 1904, and *Canada Skandinaven* in 1911.[6]

In order to survive, the ethnic papers needed the support of organizations within the ethnic group. Some of the early publications, like those in English and French, were sponsored by churches, and waged vigorous war against the publications of other churches and against those of laymen considered liberal or anti-clerical within the ethnic group. The Roman Catholic Church supported papers in various languages. In the Polish paper, for example, the extension to Canada of the Polish National Catholic Church and of some other dissident Catholic movements from the United States was reflected in press polemics:

The Polish clergy waged a strong campaign against those movements and the *Gazeta Katolicka* was filled, until the first World War, with attacks against the 'national' clergy and their parishioners. The leaders of the laymen's camp, associated with the Polish Gymnastic Association 'Sokol' in Winnipeg, and later (from 1915) with the weekly *Czas*, defended the dissidents.[7]

Gazeta Katolicka was also aggressive against Protestant missions working among Poles and Ukrainians and called upon the Poles to participate actively in Canadian life. The Roman Catholic Church through the West Canada Publishing Company, directed by the Oblate order in Winnipeg, published four weekly journals, in English, German, Polish, and Ukrainian; by 1911 it had devoted more than $50,000 to the support of a Catholic press in the West.

In addition, some of the Canadian Protestant denominations, such as the Presbyterian Church and the Methodist Church, published or subsidized publications in the languages of various ethnic groups. This sponsorship was often clandestine and part of a campaign to gain converts; when it was revealed, the influence of the paper underwent abrupt decline. For example, the Ukrainian-language monthly *Ranok* (Morning) was published in Winnipeg from 1905 on as an organ of the Independent Greek Church, but it lost much of its constituency when its connections with the Presbyterian Church became known. It did survive, however: in 1920 it amalgamated with *Kanadyiets* (The Canadian), a struggling Ukrainian-language publication of the Methodist Church, and after the union of the Presbyterians, Methodists, and Congregationalists in 1925, the United Church continued to subsidize it until 1960.

Other publications had political parties as sponsors. These were sometimes Canadian; in other instances, sponsorship came from outside Canada. Among Ukrainians, for example, *Kanadiiskyi Farmer* was established by the federal Liberal Party and generally retained a Liberal orientation even after that party withdrew its direct financial support and the paper became a commercial enterprise; *Slovo* (1904-1905) was subsidized by federal Conservatives and *Kanada* (1913-1915) by Conservatives of Manitoba; *Chervonyi prapor* and *Robochyi narod* were socialist, and *Narodna hazeta* was one of many Communist papers. In addition, a number of publications were established to support Ukrainian national independence or a particular means of working toward it. Each of the three secular German-language weeklies in western Canada that continued publication after World War I broke out, *Der Nordwesten*, *Alberta Herold*, and *Der Saskatchewan Courier*, was owned by the political party in power in the province where it was published in August, 1914.[8] Like the church-sponsored papers, the political papers often engaged in fierce polemics with one another.

Ethnic publications were also commercial enterprises of businessmen. In some instances an individual published papers in a number of languages. For example, Františec Dojaček, a Baptist lay preacher of Czech origin, established National Publishers in Winnipeg, which published a number of papers in several European languages, including Ukrainian, Polish, Serbo-Croatian, and German. He was succeeded by his Canadian-born son, Charles Dojack. As a rule, the commercial publications have been blander than those with an ideological base; sometimes they have been advertising vehicles for railways, steamship companies, and other recruiters of immigrants; sometimes, like the Polish weekly *Czas* (Time), published by Dojacek, they have been taken over by sponsors, in the case of *Czas* by the Federation of Polish Organizations in Canada.

The number of ethnic publications and their circulation are hard to calculate. The publications often had a very short life; their editors and publishers had reason to exaggerate their circulation. According to a study for the Royal Commission on Bilingualism and Biculturalism, the number of ethnic publications grew from eighteen in 1892 to twenty-two in 1905 and thirty-seven in 1911, and the circulation from 45,500 in 1905 to 109,000 in 1911. German papers, twelve in number in 1911, were the most numerous and had by far the largest circulation, 43,000. Icelandic papers ranked second, with nine, but their combined circulation of 8,000 was exceeded by 18,000 for a single Ukrainian publication, 11,500 for two Swedish papers, and 9,000 for two Jewish papers.[9]

World War I dealt the German-language press in Canada a blow from which it has not recovered, and the war seriously hampered publications in a number of other languages. The foreign-language publications lost advertisers and subscribers who wanted to avoid any suspicion of disloyalty as long as the heated war atmosphere prevailed. Furthermore, the government exercised strict surveillance: possession of some newspapers could result in a jail term. Finally, in September, 1918, six weeks before the war's end, an order-in-council prohibited newspapers in German and a number of other languages. By the time the order was rescinded, interest in German-language publications had dwindled in central Canada; in the West, where settlements were more recent, four German newspapers revived, but these weathered the depression only with difficulty.[10]

Meanwhile, the number of publications in languages other than German increased. In the 1920's the number rose from thirty-four in 1921 (including four German) to forty-nine in 1931 (including eight German), and the circulation rose from 168,500 to 288,500. Many publications were founded as a result of the higher educational level and the various political ideologies of the immigrants of that period, but by no means all of them survived. The difficulties facing the Hungarian-Canadian press of the period also faced the presses of other ethnic groups:

> It is probably not unfair to say that, aside from the publications which managed to attain a subsidy, the Hungarian-Canadian press was in a sorry state. Part of the problem was atomization, which was particularly evident in the case of the religious press. Still another problem was the lack of experience and skill on the part of editors and publishers. Putting

out an ethnic newspaper was a small-scale yet complex undertaking that required the publisher to be a journalist, printer, editor, and businessman rolled into one. Few if any Hungarian Canadians combined all the necessary talents and skills. Contrary to what might be expected, the geographical dispersal of Hungarian Canadians was not always a negative factor; in fact a few of the newspapers benefited by it to some extent. It is noteworthy that while the *Canadian Hungarian News* and the *Little Newspaper*, serving the Canadian West and the Niagara Peninsula respectively, tended to prosper, no viable ethnic newspapers could come into existence in large, rather compact ethnic communities such as those in Montreal and Toronto. The fact was that a Hungarian Canadian residing in one of these cities needed an ethnic paper less than one living in the isolation of the prairie homestead or a southern Ontario small town. But when it came to having a paper that could serve the whole of Hungarian-Canadian society, Canada's huge size proved a disadvantage. It was simply not possible for a small team of men to be familiar with Hungarian-Canadian affairs both in the West and in the East. In fact, a paper published in Winnipeg could hardly command more interest in central Canada than one produced in New York or Cleveland. And there were many of these . . . . [11]

In spite of the depression in the 1930's, the number of publications had risen slightly by 1941, and the circulation increased substantially, to 341,500. The increase owed much to the efforts of far left and far right groups to publicize their causes. Among Italian Canadians, for example, three anti-fascist papers emerged in Toronto to counter the pro-fascist *Il Bollettino*; all were short-lived.[12] However, during the 1930's among the Canadian-born, ethnic publications increasingly faced competition from English-language newspapers. A Ukrainian Canadian who grew up in rural Saskatchewan wrote:

> The outside, non-Ukrainian world crept in only in the mid 1930's when such newspapers as the *Winnipeg Free Press*, the *Prairie Farmer*, the *Western Producer* and the Eaton's and Simpson's catalogues became more commonly available; those, in effect, became the 'bibles' for the people who could read English. That is when we really became more fully aware that there was an outside world that was very different from our own. We, the young people, read the letters to the editor published in these papers, and especially the comic strips, also in such papers as the *Chicago Herald* and *Tribune and Examiner*.[13]

During World War II the suppression of publications simply because of the language they employed did not occur. Pro-Nazi publications were banned, however, as were pro-Soviet publications before 1941. Voluntary shifts of language and other wartime pressures brought down the number of publications to forty-three by 1951.

Before the war, ethnic publications were almost entirely independent of each other and co-operated little. In 1942 the editors of western papers formed the Canada Press Club; the majority were ethnic papers, although the *Winnipeg Free Press* and the Winnipeg *Tribune* were also represented. In 1951 the Ethnic Press Association of Ontario was founded, and in 1958 the Winnipeg and Toronto clubs united to form the Canada Ethnic Press Federation. Four years later the Ethnic Press Association of British Columbia and the Ethnic Press Association of Quebec were formed. Not all eligible papers have joined the Canada Ethnic Press Federation, but it has become a powerful voice on behalf of anti-Communist ethnic groups and a lobby for immigration. During the 1950's two advertising agencies, New Canadian Publications and Lingua Ads Service, were established in Toronto to sell advertising space and supply translations of advertisements for members.

Meanwhile, the vast and variegated post-war immigration, with its notable inclusion of professionals and intellectuals in many ethnic groups, had begun to result in an unprecedented growth of the ethnic press, to which the improved organization contributed. By 1959 the number of publications reached 148, and by 1965 it reached 155; the number of subscribers by 1963 was 742,000.

The ethnically and racially open immigration after 1967 enabled many hitherto small groups to start newspapers. The result was that, by 1978, incomplete data revealed at least 275 "ethno-cultural publications," including seven that were "inter-ethnic." Thirty were Ukrainian, twenty-one Italian, eighteen German, eighteen Jewish, fourteen Greek, thirteen Chinese, twelve Arabic, eleven Dutch, eleven Polish, and ten South Asian (East Indian); there were also Byelorussian, Filipino, Korean, and black publications.

The existence of an ethnic newspaper is precarious: for example, by 1982 more than half of the Hungarian-language newspapers founded in Ontario after World War II had died.[14] A newspaper's life is usually limited because it loses its readers when immigration declines and a Canadian-born generation arises lacking fluency in the ancestral language and interest in the problems dealt with in the ethnic press. A survey carried out in 1973 of ten ethnic groups in five large Canadian cities found that language fluency greatly affected readership of the ethnic press, with almost three-quarters of the fluent respondents being readers of the ethnic press. Fluency varied widely from group to group but invariably was high in the first generation, dropped sharply in the second, and was almost non-existent in the third.[15] Without immigration, even editors, reporters, and technical personnel fluent in the ancestral language begin to disappear, as they age, retire, and die. Television, which does not demand fluency in English or French, competes with the press even in the immigrant generation.

The members of the second generation who have a strong consciousness of their ethnic origin sometimes know the language well enough to read ethnic papers, but they are alienated by what they consider an over-simplified treatment of issues or excessive attention to homeland politics. In addition, they are more accustomed to the aural and visual media. Thus, even a switch to bilingualism or to English (or, in Quebec, to French) may not save an ethnic publication.

Most ethnic publications have limited financial resources. The editor and frequently members of his or her family work long hours at multifarious tasks for small rewards in order to keep the publication alive. Apart from subscriptions, funds are usually raised by taking on commercial printing jobs and by having periodic campaigns for donations. Vagueness about circulation data makes much of the ethnic press unattractive to potential advertisers, interested though the latter may be in the buying power of the ethnic groups represented.

The need for funds leads ethnic publications to request government aid, and considerable assistance is given. Various governments distribute information to ethnic papers and give direct and indirect aid to the Canadian Ethnic Press Federation and provincial ethnic press associations in Ontario and Manitoba. Most important, however, is governmental advertising. All levels of government advertise in the ethnic press, and recently the amount of advertising has increased greatly. Before 1970 the federal government spent between $80,000 and $120,000; in 1977-78, the amount spent by federal departments, chiefly in the press but to some extent also in broadcasting, was $1,250,000;[16] in 1983 it was decided to spend a minimum of $2 million annually on federal government advertising in the ethnic media.

Another form of assistance is provided by the independent news service, Canadian Scene. A voluntary non-profit organization founded in 1951 to assemble articles on various aspects of Canadian life, translate them, and send them out to newspapers, it won accolades from ethnic journalists: "There are no words," wrote one editor, "that will fully express what this agency did to introduce newcomers to Canadian life, its customs and laws, its richness and beauty, its opportunities and its charm."[17] Its services have been extended to radio and television stations carrying ethnic programs.

THE MASS PRESS

At least as important to many members of various ethnic groups is the treatment they receive in the printed mass media. Such treatment is usually taken, on the one hand, as an expression of the attitudes of the dominant group or groups and, on the other, as a powerful force in shaping those attitudes. With some exceptions, such as occasional sympathetic treatment of Quebec's small Chinese population in *La Presse*, the French-language press until the 1950's was hostile or at best indifferent to immigration, and also to ethnic groups other than the French within Canada.

Alexis Gagnon, for instance, wrote a series of articles in 1946 for Montreal's influential *Le Devoir*. His articles were picked up in other French-language dailies. As Gagnon described it, dark and powerful forces in Canada were then conducting an intensive pro-immigration campaign in alliance with ethnic groups. Once in Canada these groups would become partners of the Anglo-Canadian elite. Their goal, he declared, was to perpetuate the majority British domination of the state through immigration.

This would, of course, thwart the impact of French Canada's high birth rate. The pro-immigration campaign, he concluded, had no economic motivation. It was a pure and simple conspiracy against French-Canadian survival.[18]

In particular, the French-language press tended to be anti-Semitic, convinced that immigrants were granted privileges and rights denied to French Canadians, and sure that the federal government discriminated against French and Roman Catholic immigrants.

By the 1950's, however, the French-Canadian press was less unanimous. For example, in 1952, while an editor of *Le Soleil* complained that French-speaking immigrants were few and not suited to Canadian methods of production, his counterpart in *Le Droit* advocated encouragement of immigration by the Quebec government to increase the province's population, and an editorial in *Le Devoir* advocated the reception of refugees and surplus populations.[19]

The next decade, that of the Quiet Revolution, brought the creation in 1965 of a Department of Immigration in Quebec and the inauguration of activity concerning the selection and reception of immigrants. The newspapers were generally favourable to these moves and repeatedly charged that the federal government discriminated against Quebec in matters of immigration. Their attitudes concerning various ethnic groups in Quebec were closely related to what they felt were the attitudes of members of the groups to Québécois nationalism.

By the late 1970's and the 1980's the French-language dailies generally welcomed immigrants and refugees as essential for the maintenance of the population of Quebec. They also had begun to publish articles on the various ethnic groups in population centres or the province as a whole, a practice long established in English-language newspapers.

The English-language press was less unanimous and less consistent than the French-language press. During the first great wave of immigration prior to World War I, much of the press welcomed immigration as necessary to fill the empty spaces of the West with producing farmers. But even then caution was sometimes called for, lest Canadian institutions, inherited from Britain, and Anglo-Saxon Canadians be submerged by foreign hordes, or immigrants destined for farms stop off in cities to create problems of congestion and of labour relations. Clifford Sifton, son of a newspaper administrator and himself principal proprietor of the *Manitoba Free Press* for many years, used the press freely, during and after his nine years as Minister of the Interior, to express his views concerning immigration and the potential of various ethnic groups; those who opposed him for bringing in non-British immigrants did so in many instances editorially.[20] Sifton's successor, Frank Oliver, was also a newspaper man adept in the use of the press.

An analysis of editorials concerning Ukrainians in Winnipeg newspapers 1896-1905 revealed that of the three daily newspapers, the *Manitoba Free Press*, the *Winnipeg Tribune*, and the *Nor'Wester Winnipeg Telegram*, the first was positive, the second somewhat negative, and the third strongly negative. Even the *Free Press* regarded Ukrainian settlers as second best, presumably to northern Europeans; but in contrast to the *Telegram* and the *Tribune*, which viewed the Slavs as undesirable, it considered them to be capable of rapid assimilation into the British way of life. All three papers resolutely opposed any policy that might hamper assimilation, such as bloc settlement.[21] In British Columbia, Chinese, Japanese, and South Asians suffered even more adverse treatment in the press, since they were considered unassimilable.

The rank order that emerged in immigration policy was evident in newspaper editorials. Asians, although they might be praised as interesting and even admirable visitors to Canada, were subject to vituperation when it was a question of their settling. In Vancouver papers, for example, during the period 1905-1914 Chinese, Japanese, and South Asians received far more attention than their numbers warranted, and almost all of it was unfavourable. On the other hand, Anglo-Canadians and British were portrayed positively, and other white groups seem to have gained from being on the same side of the colour line as the British:

> In addition to legitimizing the position of Anglo Canadians and the British born, [the] stigmatic press coverage of South Asians must also have ideologically benefited the non-British European population of Vancouver, for they had the status of 'white European' immigrants. It may also have served to warn these ethnically marginal individuals not to press their cultural and social claims too strongly.[22]

In any event, most Europeans ranked between the Anglo-Canadians and the British on the one hand and the Asian groups on the other; the exception was the Italians, who ranked lowest of all. At the same time newspapers and magazines published in Toronto, including such labour papers as the *Lance* and the *Tribune, Jack Canuck, Saturday Night*, and *Maclean's* all opposed Chinese immigration, usually vituperatively.[23]

The rank order continued during the 1920's and 1930's. However, with the coming of the depression in the 1930's the English-language press became antagonistic to immigration of any kind. The immigrants who had entered before the crash were seen as causing unemployment and as being dangerous radicals who should be deported.[24] Later, with the onset of war, immigrants were the target of suspicion as subversives. Still later, when the economy expanded after the war, English-language newspaper editors clamoured for immigration to relieve labour shortages.

One newspaper practice offensive to members of many ethnic groups was the mention of the ethnic affiliation of alleged malefactors. It was felt that this contributed to adverse stereotypes of ethnic groups. By the 1970's and

1980's the practice had ceased to be regular in metropolitan dailies. On the other hand, mention of the ethnic affiliation of heroes was demanded.

BROADCASTING

With the advent of radio and television the press has become only one of several means of communication, and sometimes not the most important. A considerable amount of broadcasting in languages other than English and French takes place. It began in the 1930's and 1940's but came under scrutiny only in the 1950's. In 1955 there were about sixty-two hours of third-language programs available per week on AM radio. By 1972-73, there were 320 hours per week on AM radio, 137 on FM radio, twenty-four on conventional television, and forty-five on cable television, a total of 526 hours. Much of this was on a small number of multilingual radio stations, in Montreal, Toronto, Winnipeg, and Vancouver.

In 1972 at least seventeen non-official languages were employed in broadcasting, including Italian, Greek, German, Ukrainian, Polish, Portuguese, Slavic, Dutch, Serbo-Croatian, Arabic, Lithuanian, Macedonian, Maltese, Russian, and Tagalog; the first three were most used. A decade later the influx of Asians had led to broadcasts in various Chinese and South Asian languages. The verbal content of programs was frequently matched or even exceeded by the musical content; modern music was emphasized as a means of attracting second-generation Canadians. Technological advances permitted live broadcasts of sports events from the homelands of many immigrants.[25]

In the survey carried out in 1973 of ten ethnic groups in Montreal, Toronto, Winnipeg, Edmonton, and Vancouver, 23.5 per cent of respondents did not know of any non-official language radio programs in their area. Greeks, Italians, and Portuguese generally were most likely, and Chinese, Hungarians, and Scandinavians least likely, to know of such programs. The fluent were more likely to know than those who had only some knowledge of the language. As for television, 46.3 per cent knew of no available programming. On the other hand, only 4.2 per cent were very interested and 6.3 per cent somewhat interested in listening to non-official language radio programs should they become available, while 13.6 per cent were very interested and 14.3 per cent somewhat interested in watching television programs. The Chinese and Hungarians were most interested in radio programs, the Ukrainians in television programs.[26] By 1985,

"ethnic broadcasting" [had] mushroomed into six fully fledged ethnic AM and FM stations, one television station (CFMT), a regional pay television network (Worldview) and two discretionary satellite-to-cable network services (Chinavision and Telelatino). As well, 52 conventional AM and FM stations provide 257 hours per week of third language programming and seven conventional TV stations in Ontario provide 102 hours per week. In addition, single language programming is offered on closed-circuit audio services on the cable FM band and ethnic special programming service channels exist in the Vancouver, Calgary and Montreal areas.[27]

With rare exceptions, broadcasts in languages other than English and French have been limited to the private stations and networks. The Canadian Broadcasting Corporation has interpreted its mandate as limited to the country's official languages. It has been under considerable pressure to change its policies: for example, the Royal Commission on Bilingualism and Biculturalism recommended that it participate, along with the Canadian Radio-Television Commission, in studies of broadcasting in other languages, and the Canadian Consultative Council on Multiculturalism, ethnic organizations, and groups of students have presented briefs in favour of multilingual broadcasting.[28] So far, however, the CBC has stood firm.

The pressure on the CBC is probably not intended to open the way for a major increase in broadcasting in the non-official languages so much as to force recognition of these languages by the public corporation. The symbolic value of recognition by the CBC is highly regarded, particularly by spokesmen for some Ukrainian organizations. Thus, the existence of abundant multilingual broadcasting on private stations by no means lessens the pressure on the CBC.

The CBC does carry network and local programs featuring the culture, history, current social conditions, and attitudes of ethnic groups and dealing with public issues affecting ethnic groups. It also, like the private networks, gives casual and informal recognition to the fact that Canadians are of many ethnic origins by the names listed in newscasts, sports reports, and other programs and in acknowledgements of those involved in production; by the accents in which speakers, although broadcasting in English or French, present their views; and by the titles and content of some of its programs, such as "Wojeck" and "The King of Kensington," both popular series in their time, and "Seeing Things," in the mid-1980's considered an especially successful series. Such acknowledgement of the varied ethnic origins of Canadians, although it is rarely mentioned by the spokesmen or advocates of ethnic groups, may be effective in shaping the image held of Canadians both inside and outside the country.

A 1982 study of the portrayal of visible minorities in prime-time television on three networks was carried out in Winnipeg. The three networks were the CBC, the private Canadian network CTV, and the American CBS network. The finding was that the CBC had the lowest level of discrimination and CBS the highest level, discrimination being measured by "comparing the percentage of visible minority characters who participate in valued facets of TV life with the percentage of Caucasian characters who so participate."[29]

On a number of occasions the portrayal of members of a particular ethnic group on radio or television has drawn protests from the group and from other Canadians concerned with racial and ethnic relations. In 1979, for example, the CBC broadcast a three-part program on organized crime in

Canada entitled "Connections." The program was considered to imply that Italian Canadians were disproportionately represented in organized crime and, when not criminal, were at least tolerant of organized crime. Italian-Canadian individuals and associations took strong exception to the program. Later in the same year, a public affairs program on a private television network, "Campus Giveaway," charged that foreign students were crowding Canadian students out of professional schools and focused on the faces of Chinese students when foreigners were discussed. All of the students shown were in fact Canadian citizens. Led by students, Chinese Canadians organized to protest against the program, held demonstrations in cities from coast to coast, and eventually force a public apology; the protests helped to unite a previously loosely knit community.[30]

Fear of protests sometimes inclines producers toward bland or idealized portrayals of ethnic groups. It is thought that including the kind of detail that humanizes and creates fellow feeling for characters will be interpreted as demeaning to the group. The fears are not groundless: a broadcast in the 1960's in which an Italian grandmother visiting a new apartment flushed a toilet to see if it was working, a natural gesture that only the oversensitive could interpret as indicating unfamiliarity with indoor plumbing, resulted in a storm of protest to the CBC.

MEMBERS OF OTHER ETHNIC GROUPS AS MEDIA PROFESSIONALS

Since the late 1960's, the issue of the employment of members of the visible minorities (blacks, Asians, and Native peoples) in the mass media has arisen periodically in centres such as Toronto. There has been concern about the scarcity of non-whites in advertising and in news, soap operas, situation comedies, and other programs: it is said that if members of the visible minorities are not shown, the media convey the message that they are not part of Canadian society. There has also been concern about stereotypical casting of non-whites when they are employed, in spite of the growing presence of members of the visible minorities throughout the society, as well as concern about perceived reluctance to use broadcasters with "non-Canadian" accents. Demands for greater use of non-whites in advertising have been precipitated by the increased employment of blacks in commercials on American television, much watched in certain regions of Canada, by the sudden increase in immigration of members of the visible minorities, and by allegations of discrimination on the part of advertising agencies. A review committee established by the Ontario Human Rights Commission reported in 1971 that "the proportion of visible minority group members who are employed as models or as performers is small indeed,"[31] and that the image of Canada being presented was of a country populated almost exclusively by whites.

During the 1970's, some advances were made in both print and broadcast media. A study commissioned by the Secretary of State in 1977 examined advertising over four Toronto and Hamilton television channels and in catalogues from major stores, national newspapers and magazines, and parts of the ethnic press. It reported that the situation had improved somewhat for blacks, although not for members of other visible minorities. The report concluded that only the government of Ontario appeared "to have made an effort, in their own advertising, to portray Canada as a country of diverse racial and ethnic groups and to promote the multicultural aspects of Canadian life." Nonetheless, Queen's Park received a number of complaints about its advertising in the next few years. Therefore, in 1981 the Ontario government established a task force on racial and ethnic diversity in government advertising; the task force recommended greater use of members of the visible minorities in advertising and found no practical obstacles to such use.[32] Similar recommendations were made at a federally sponsored conference on visible minorities and the media in 1982 and in *Equality Now! Report of the Special Committee on Visible Minorities in Canadian Society* in 1984. In 1983 a program for training a small number of members of visible minorities in broadcast journalism was initiated by the CBC's English radio and television networks.

By the 1980's in various cities Asian and black Canadians were regularly seen on news broadcasts. Nonetheless, it was still frequently claimed that the increase in the employment of members of visible minorities had not kept pace with the increase in their numbers in the population. The evidence marshalled in support of the claim, however, was not fully convincing.

THE ETHNIC MEDIA TODAY

The ethnic media operate primarily in the centres of immigrant population, of which Toronto is now the predominant one. In 1979, of approximately 170 newspapers in non-official languages – a far from complete total – 100 were published in Ontario and 80 per cent of these in Toronto, in at least twenty languages. Toronto also had two weeklies serving the black and West Indian populations. At approximately the same time, about 50 per cent of all third-language radio and television programming in Canada was produced and broadcast in Toronto; there were many sources, including four AM radio stations, one FM radio station, two conventional television stations, and the channels of six cable television systems. Among languages employed were Italian, German, Greek, Ukrainian, Polish, Serbo-Croatian, Hungarian, and Chinese.

Montreal, less of a centre for the ethnic press, in some ways pioneered third-language broadcasting. It was the first Canadian city to have a multilingual radio station, licensed in 1962, and by the early 1970's had broadcasts in non-official languages on AM radio, on FM radio (to a very small extent), on conventional television, and on cable television. It also had an unusual medium, cable radio: two cable radio stations distributed programs through the wire facilities of a television company, one in Italian and the other in Greek. Although the amount of broadcasting was large, only subscribers to the cable service could receive it.

Vancouver in the 1980's has three daily newspapers, some monthlies and magazines serving the Chinese community, four newspapers published by members of the East Indian community, three Greek newspapers, and a German and a Jewish newspaper; it has ethnic radio broadcasts on three stations, and television broadcasts on the community cable channel and on the multilingual commercial channel.

In the 1980's the ethnic press is in good health. Although every year many ethnic newspapers fail, new ones are always being born. Ethnic radio and television broadcasting is also flourishing and making use of the latest technological improvements in order to satisfy the wants of its audiences. It is just as important that representatives of various ethnic groups have begun to have an impact on the way in which ethnicity and race are dealt with in the general media and on the hiring practices of the communications industries.

NOTES

1. Varpu Lindström-Best, "'Fist Press': a Study of the Finnish Canadian Handwritten Newspapers," *Polyphony*, 3, 2 (1981), pp. 65-73.
2. Maria Adamowska, "Beginnings in Canada," in Piniuta, *Land of Pain, Land of Promise*, p. 73.
3. Herbert Karl Kalbfleisch, *The History of the Pioneer German Language Press of Ontario, 1835-1918* (Toronto: University of Toronto Press, 1968).
4. *The Multilingual Press in Manitoba* (Winnipeg: Canada Press Club, 1974).
5. *Heimskringla* and *Lögberg* amalgamated in 1959 as *Lögberg-Heimskringla*.
6. *The Multilingual Press in Manitoba*, pp. 89, 123-26; Victor Turek, *Polish-Language Press in Canada* (Toronto: Polish Research Institute in Canada, 1962), pp. 100-01; Joseph M. Kirschbaum, *Slovaks in Canada* (Toronto: Canadian Ethnic Press Association of Ontario, 1967), p. 282.
7. Turek, *Polish-Language Press in Canada*, pp. 66-67.
8. W. Entz, "The Suppression of the German Language Press in September 1918," *Canadian Ethnic Studies*, 8, 2 (1976), pp. 56-57.
9. *Report of the Royal Commission on Bilingualism and Biculturalism, Book IV, The Cultural Contributions of the Other Ethnic Groups*, Tables A-148 and 149, pp. 342, 343.
10. Kalbfleisch, *History of the Pioneer German Language Press*.
11. Dreisziger, *Struggle and Hope*, pp. 126-27.
12. Angelo Principe, "The Italo-Canadian Anti-fascist Press in Toronto, 1922-40," *Polyphony*, 7, 2 (1985), pp. 43-51.
13. Bohdan Panchuk, *Heroes of Their Day: The Reminiscences of Bohdan Panchuk*, ed. and intro. by Lubomyr Y. Luciuk (Toronto: Multicultural History Society of Ontario, 1983), p. 26.
14. Susan M. Papp, "The Hungarian Press in Ontario," *Polyphony*, 4, 1 (1982), p. 68.
15. K.G. O'Bryan, J.G. Reitz, and O.M. Kuplowska, *Non-Official Languages: A Study in Canadian Multiculturalism* (Ottawa: Supply and Services Canada, 1976), pp. 66-70.

16. Stanley Zybala, "Problems of Survival for the Ethnic Press in Canada," *Polyphony*, 4, 1 (1982), p. 27.
17. Benedict Heydenkorn, "The Immigration Policy of Canada," in J.M. Kirschbaum *et al.*, eds., *Twenty Years of The Ethnic Press Association of Ontario* (Toronto: The Ethnic Press Association of Ontario, 1971), p. 60.
18. Abella and Troper, *None Is Too Many*, p. 234.
19. David C. Corbett, *Canada's Immigration Policy: A Critique* (Toronto: University of Toronto Press, 1957), pp. 21-22.
20. Palmer, ed., *Immigration and the Rise of Multiculturalism*, pp. 44-45.
21. John C. Lehr and D. Wayne Moodie, "The Polemics of Pioneer Settlement: Ukrainian Immigration and the Winnipeg Press," *Canadian Ethnic Studies*, 12, 2 (1980), pp. 88-101.
22. Buchignani and Indra, *Continuous Journey*, pp. 6, 44; Dorcen M. Indra, "South Asian stereotypes in the Vancouver Press," *Ethnic and Racial Studies*, 2, 2 (1979), pp. 166-89.
23. K. Paupst, "A Note on Anti-Chinese Sentiment in Toronto," *Canadian Ethnic Studies*, 9, 1 (1977), pp. 54-59.
24. Palmer, *Patterns of Prejudice*, pp. 128, 137.
25. Canadian Radio-Television Commission Research Branch, *Multilingual Broadcasting in the 1970s* (Ottawa: Information Canada, 1974).
26. O'Bryan *et al.*, *Non-Official Languages*, pp. 68-73, 147-51.
27. An Analysis of CRTC, 1985-139, a Broadcasting Policy Reflecting Canada's Linguistic and Cultural Diversity.
28. *Report of the Royal Commission on Bilingualism and Biculturalism, Book IV, The Cultural Contribution of the Other Ethnic Groups*.
29. Gary Granzberg, "The Portrayal of Visible Minorities by Canadian Television During the 1982 Prime-time Season," *Currents*, 2, 2 (1984), pp. 23-26.
30. Anthony B. Chan, *Gold Mountain: The Chinese in the New World* (Vancouver: New Star Books, 1983), pp. 161-86.
31. Frederick Elkin, "The Employment of Visible Minority Groups in Mass Media Advertising," a report submitted to the Ontario Human Rights Commission, 1971, p. 18.
32. *Ontario Task Force on the Portrayal of Racial Diversity in Government Advertising and Communications* (1982).

ELEVEN

Ethnic Identity

In Canada it is common to reply to the question "Who are you?" in ethnic terms. Immigrants in the past were sometimes not aware of an ethnic identity when they arrived, seeing themselves only as coming from a village or at most a province, or as adherents of a particular religion. They became ethnically conscious as they were thrust into association with others who shared their language and culture or their physical traits or both, and were accorded a common label and common treatment. But they usually knew of some people from whom they sharply distinguished themselves. More recently, with the salience of ethnicity throughout the world and with the sophistication of many immigrants, people have had an ethnic identity on arrival, and an attitude toward it, either as a burden to be cast off or as a treasure to be passed on to their children. With the passage of time and of generations, both the content and the meaning of the immigrants' ethnic identities change. Whether they continue to consider themselves in the same way or begin to couple the word "Canadian" with the old label, or to call themselves simply "Canadian," the ethnic aspect of their selves and their lives is transformed. Their children and their children's children have a different sense of ethnic identity and manifest it in different ways.

The sense of ethnic identity is difficult to gauge. It is essentially subjective or internal, but it has external aspects that are frequently used as indices. It is for the external aspects that governmental aid is sought and recently has been frequently obtained. The relationship between the external and internal aspects of identity is extremely complex: the feelings of ethnic identity of individuals may or may not be in line with objective criteria defining ethnicity.

For white ethnic groups, among the most conspicuous external manifestations have been language, folklore, cuisine, and sports. Ancestral languages, however important or unimportant in the past, have recently been given primacy as ethnic symbols because of the salience of language in industrial and post-industrial societies and, in particular, the salience of language in Canada since it became officially bilingual in 1969. Languages have been considered to be inseparable from cultures, and linguistic transfer has been deemed to be loss of language and culture. Languages have played a crucial role in many of the white ethnic groups as vehicles for other elements of culture. They have served as means of unifying the groups: people who have spoken regional dialects have, through learning the standard version of their language, come not only to enlarge the number of those recognized as their ethnic fellows but also to identify with linguistically dependent aspects of the high culture of their homeland. Languages have been boundary markers, for unless they are world languages they are exclusive to the group.

The descendants of peasant immigrants with high rates of illiteracy, unaccustomed to give importance to linguistic matters, have become keenly interested in linguistic retention. Ukrainians are perhaps exceptional because of the perceived threat to their language in their homeland: their concern about their language in the schools and in the media has been unremitting. The abolition of bilingual schools in Manitoba and the punishment of children for speaking Ukrainian in Prairie schools have played a prominent part in the litany of grievances of Ukrainians against Canadian governments and society. The recent introduction of heritage languages into the curricula of the public schools and the introduction of bilingual Ukrainian-English education in the city of Edmonton have been viewed as triumphs.

Not only schools but families and churches have been crucial to the transmission of ancestral languages. The term "mother tongue" is often interpreted as indicative of the role of the family: the mother, because of her contact with the young child, is seen as having the duty to pass on the ancestral tongue. In an immigrant group, the myriad other duties devolving on the mother hamper her endeavours in regard to language teaching. One of the results of the mother's role in some groups, such as the Armenian and the Jewish, is that women have been allowed to teach language classes while being barred from many other occupations outside the home. In settled communities the old also play a role in transmitting language and culture, as storytellers to the young, but the absence of grandparents is another obstacle to the teaching of the ancestral language in many immigrant households.

The church has frequently regarded its well-being as tied to the traditional language. Sometimes this language is not in everyday use: through centuries, Hebrew was the language of Judaism, too holy for daily use, until it became the language of Israel; in some sects high German was the language of the religious texts and services while low German was used in other aspects of life; until the 1960's Latin was employed in many Catholic religious rituals. But churches have been among the most dedicated sponsors of language classes for children, and priests and pastors have been among the teachers of such classes.

However cherished the mother tongue is, among first-generation immigrants comprehension of one of the country's official languages and fluency in speaking it have been crucial for economic and social adjustment. Spokespeople for immigrants have been much concerned about opportunities to acquire knowledge of the official languages. They have pointed out that workers in segregated occupations and women in the home have often lacked such opportunities. It has been rare, though not unknown, that people have protested that the teaching of English and French has infringed on the rights of another language in Canada.

Knowledge of ancestral languages declines sharply from generation to generation. Research has shown that fluency in non-official languages is virtually confined to first-generation immigrants, and that in the third and succeeding generations the majority have no knowledge at all of the ancestral tongue. On the other hand, even in the third generation most people profess to be in favour of the retention of ancestral languages by their children. The chief reason all generations give for favouring retention is, however, not the keeping up of customs or traditions, nor communication with other members of one's ethnic group. Rather, it is the economic and cultural advantage of knowing more than one language.[1]

Linguistic transfer does not necessarily mean a renunciation of ethnic identity. The Canadian-born may claim the right to select their own symbols of identity and resist pressure from their elders to give primacy to language. How long and how intensely they retain identification with their ancestral group once they have adopted another language may vary greatly from group to group, but the linguistic versatility of Jews and the ethnic retention in spite of linguistic transfer of Scots and Irish indicate that language is not always essential.

One of the ways other than language that members of ethnic groups have had of displaying their ethnic identity has been by maintaining their folkloric heritage and transmitting it from one generation to another. Few belonged wholly to a folk culture or society before coming to Canada: even many eastern Europeans who came out during the Sifton era had been migrant labourers to industrial cities or had had contact with migrant labourers and thus with city ways. They often learned folk arts in Canada, as symbols of their heritage, rather than having retained them. So, among South Asians, music and folk dance have become important community phenomena; among Japanese Kabuki dance, flower arranging, and paper folding are taught and practised; Ukrainians have bandura orchestras and teach embroidery and the painting of Easter eggs. The intellectuals of the group often profess to scorn "red boots multiculturalism" and "dancing in church basements" as trivial or frivolous. Nonetheless, folklore has proved to be extremely persistent.

Several explanations can be given for this persistence. Folklore has great symbolic value:

> Generally, the folklore symbolizes an era in which the people, now in danger and in too much contact with others, were alone and showed their traditional culture in a more pure form. The heroes of lore are thought to have possessed the true virtues, the virtues that distinguish this people from others. The true German of folklore was unspoiled by foreign influences, whether Roman or Jewish. He was set up as a model

for the new, restored, true German. Something like this is happening in the Zionist movement, too, where a hardy, sometimes belligerent, athletic Jewish youth is set up both as the original and as the true model for the future.[2]

It is also eminently suited to display before those who do not belong to the ethnic group. Ethnic dancing and instrumental music in particular have become the stock in trade of ethnic or multicultural festivals. A study sponsored by the Multicultural Directorate of the Department of the Secretary of State in 1982 found that in a representative sample of approximately 6,000 folkloric performing arts groups from across Canada, most performances, while they mark special occasions or holidays of the group's own ethnic community, are for general audiences rather than the ethnic community only, and substantial numbers of performances are also for other people's festivals or galas and for special Canadian events and national days.[3]

Certain forms of folklore, such as music, dance, and theatre, have appeal to the young. The Multiculturalism Directorate's study indicated that passing the culture on to children and youth ranked high among reasons for participating in the performing arts. It also showed that in fact the performers tended to be concentrated among those under thirty-five years old. The folkloric performing arts thus are a means of transmitting some of the cultural symbols of the group to new generations so that social networks are established on an ethnic basis and chances of endogamous marriage are increased.

That the folklore thus transmitted is symbolic rather than part of a functioning folk culture is shown by periodic attempts to "purify" it or "make it more authentic." A functioning culture changes and adapts. Weeding out Canadian variants in favour of old country forms indicates that the folklore reflects only a museum culture.

One frequent type of change not resisted is the transmutation of elements of folklore into "high culture." Many immigrants have not been familiar with the high culture of their homeland: to southern Italian peasants, for example, Leonardo da Vinci, Michelangelo, Dante, and Verdi have meant little. But they and their children have learned of the homage the world pays to such immortals and have come to take pride in them. Immigrant and native-born artists in various fields who contribute to high culture have been cherished by their ethnic groups, and have on occasion incorporated the folk symbols of those groups into their work. The symbols have thus become part of a more universal heritage.

The same might be said for ethnic foods, whether everyday dishes or *haute cuisine*. They also have become symbolic and, likewise, are suited to sharing and to becoming part of wider Canadian custom. In Canada in the 1980's ethnic bakeries, food stores, and restaurants multiply and flourish. Members of many ethnic groups have not been able to maintain their dietary patterns in their homes for lack of ingredients or lack of time for preparation. They have had to limit their ethnic dishes to ceremonial occasions, or to indulge in them only in restaurants. There the general public shares in the dishes, and the dishes are modified to meet the more general tastes.

Foods, ways of cooking and serving them, and meals have been important experiences in the lives of all immigrants. Food, of course, is intimately related to the family. Fasting and feasting are also religious rituals of great importance. The familial and religious connotations of ceremonial meals, such as Christmas and Easter dinners, and of fasting, in Judaism and Islam as well as Christianity, result in memories of eating and drinking and fasting as part of a social group being among the most poignant recollections of childhood.

Ethnic entrepreneurs have taken advantage of the situation to establish businesses. Markets serving a particular ethnic group or groups from a particular region; bakeries; butchers at which the religious prescriptions of a group and the customs concerning kinds and cuts of meats and seasoning of sausages can be maintained; fishmongers; restaurants – all these have contributed to the rise of businessmen in the occupational and income structure. Bread was a staple for many European peoples and came to be endowed with rich cultural and religious symbolism; hence, bakeries have sprung up in most immigrant areas. In Toronto, for example, by 1912 there were ten small Jewish bakeries producing bread and rolls in the Ward, the area bounded by Yonge, University, Queen, and Dundas. In the 1920's, as the community spread out, so did the bakeries; they began also to serve non-Jewish immigrants from eastern Europe. In the 1930's the dispersion continued, the bakeries began to show some specialization along class lines, a variety of cakes and pastries began to be offered, and the clientele was extended beyond Jewish and eastern European immigrants to include Canadians of all origins. The war accelerated and accentuated these trends, and the 1940's and 1950's were a time of prosperity. They also brought competition, as more recent arrivals began to set up their own small family-run bakeries.

The Estonians were among those who quickly saw that the influx of continental European immigrants offered an opportunity to suppliers of European-type breads. A number of them established small bakeries in Toronto and Hamilton, and some of the bakeries soon grew into sizable enterprises. In the 1960's many new German and Italian bakeries were established, and these offered competition to the Estonian businesses; in the 1970's all the Estonian bakers retired except one.[4] Bakers often did not pass their businesses on to their children: in both the Jewish and the Estonian groups the children of bakers, though they worked in the shops in their youth, tended to go on to higher education and to enter professions.

Ethnic restaurants have ranged from "greasy spoons" to luxurious dining places. At one extreme are cafés and grills in which hamburgers, hotdogs, and sandwiches are served to the public but special soups and stews and sausages are prepared for the owner's family and acquaintances; at the other extreme are restaurants in expensive locations that advertise their exotic character in their service, menu, décor, and prices. In all cases the dishes on the menu have been modified, not simply by the unavailability of ingredients

216

(in the 1970's and 1980's, transportation and refrigeration have made most foodstuffs accessible everywhere), but by the necessity of appealing to the tastes of the public as well as those of the appropriate ethnic group.

The Chinese were early in making the restaurant business an ethnic specialty. For them, at the turn of the century, it was an alternative to the laundry business; it required somewhat greater initial outlay than a laundry but offered a larger return. As Chinese spread eastward from British Columbia they set up restaurants in small towns, where sometimes the restaurateur was the only Chinese, and in large cities. Usually they were inexpensive eating places serving Western-style foods, and their owners had to fight the discrimination visited upon Asians. For example, by-laws restricted them to certain areas and laws made it illegal for white women to work in Chinese restaurants. But they prospered nonetheless, and restaurants in Chinatowns serving Chinese-style food in the 1930's and 1940's began to enjoy a vogue that has continued to the present. Nowadays, not simply Chinese cookery but styles of cooking from various provinces of China are offered.

Macedonians also have made of restaurant-keeping something of an ethnic specialty in the Toronto area, where they have concentrated. It is said that during World War I a quarrel broke out between Canadian soldiers and a Greek restaurant owner, which led the soldiers to wreck a number of Greek-owned restaurants. After this incident many Greeks sold their restaurants, and large numbers of Macedonians who had been working in the restaurants bought them. A study of Macedonian restaurants in Toronto in the 1970's, while unable to establish the exact number of Macedonian-owned restaurants, refers to estimates ranging from 600 to two-thirds of all restaurants in Toronto.[5]

Before World War II, eating in restaurants was not a major aspect of Canadian life. With urbanization and industrialization, eating outside the home has become much more general. The burgeoning of ethnic restaurants in all large cities has led to emphasis on food as one of the prime areas of ethnic differentiation. French, Italian, Japanese, Korean, Vietnamese, Moroccan, and many other types of restaurants have come to enjoy great popularity. Sometimes a restaurant offers more than one ethnic cuisine, Chinese and Middle Eastern, for example, or Ukrainian, Polish, and German.

Although they are less often singled out as expressions of group identity than folklore or cuisine, sports and athletics have been important parts of the tradition of many ethnic groups and have been transplanted to Canada by early arrivals. Ethnic sports associations and athletic achievements for a long time attracted little notice because they lay outside the North American mainstream. Only a few outstanding individuals of non-British origin, such as Bobbie Rosenfeld, a Russian-born Jewish athlete whose many achievements included winning a silver medal at the 1928 Olympics, became household names. But sports were important within ethnic communities as means of holding the loyalty of the young, particularly the young men. Churches often recognized the role of sports and offered the use of their premises for gymnastics or sponsored basketball, baseball, and hockey teams. Political movements also saw the utility of sports, and a workers' sports movement throve in the 1920's and 1930's among Canadian Communists.[6]

Since World War II, the people who have immigrated from every corner of the earth have brought their sports traditions with them. Finns, Czechs, and Estonians have brought modern and rhythmic gymnastics, for example, the West Indians have revivified cricket, originally brought to Canada by upper-class Britishers, and the East Asians have made karate and tai chi popular. Above all, soccer has won a place as a Canadian sport, not so well publicized and patronized as hockey, baseball, and football, perhaps, but taught in the schools and played in leagues at a number of levels. Harney describes the ethnic aspect of soccer in the Toronto region in the 1970's:

> . . . in the Toronto and District Soccer League in the early 1970s, more than three-quarters of the seventy-eight teams had ethnic emblems, colours, and/or specifically national associations in their names. Among the teams were Panhellenic, First Portuguese, Croatia, Serbia White Eagle, Toronto Falcons, Hungaria and Heidelberg. Rivalries were along ethnic and sub-ethnic lines, and although sports should be either a substitute for or a mock and harmless form of warfare between nations, the National Soccer League had to stop its season prematurely in 1974 because of violence among players and fans of competing South Slav teams.[7]

In addition to supporting Canadian teams emblematic of their ethnic group, through television people are able to follow the soccer exploits of teams in their homelands. Italy's 1982 soccer victory in the World Cup occasioned an outburst of joy in the Italian community of Toronto, the largest in Canada, that has become legendary. It has been estimated that half a million people assembled on the streets to celebrate the victory.

However, sports and athletics are not simply expressions of group identity. Teams bearing ethnic designations have often selected players in terms of ability rather than ethnicity, so that matches that appear to be inter-ethnic actually pit polyethnic teams against one another. Similarly, in professional team sports, individuals of outstanding ability have been sources of pride for their ethnic group, but at the same time those individuals have been subject to de-ethnicization or ethnic transfer.

Most permanent external symbols of ethnic identity are physical traits. A person can change his or her behaviour, including linguistic behaviour; he or she cannot change skin colour, hair form, or other physical characteristics except by procedures that are often painful and costly. Thus it has been possible to single out members of the visible minorities for discrimination. Their numbers in the country were for long kept low by immigration regulations, and those who were admitted were denied full participation in Canadian society. Blacks, South Asians, Chinese, and Japanese developed their own communal structures and retained some of their distinctive behaviour patterns. They were given little opportunity to think of themselves as Canadians. Black Canadians whose ancestors came to Canada in the seventeenth and eighteenth centuries and Chinese, Japanese, and South Asian Canadians whose grandfathers or great-grandfathers immigrated in the late nineteenth century and early twentieth centuries complain of being asked where they came from.

However, visibility is not clear-cut. Sensitivity to physical differences and knowledge of the appearance of members of different ethnic groups vary. Some ethnic groups are considered at times to be and at other times not to be visibly distinguishable from the bulk of the population.[8] Individual members of some groups can "pass" as members of the dominant white groups. Further, intermarriage can decrease physical differences from the rest of the population: the high rates of intermarriage among Japanese Canadians have led to fears that, without renewal of immigration, they might disappear as a visible group. In addition, it is possible that in time the conception of a Canadian may be broadened and redefined so that black and Asian Canadians are not as frequently asked where they come from, as they now tend to be. As their numbers and their social and economic status increase they may become increasingly recognized as Canadians.

Ethnic self-identification is usually examined in terms of the survival of ethnic groups, and change of ethnic identity is seen as loss. It can instead be seen as transfer. In most cases, to cease to regard oneself as Polish or Greek or Danish is to begin to regard oneself as Canadian, or as both Canadian and a member of an ethnic group. In some cases, however, individuals may lose one identity without acquiring another: "I don't know what I am" is a complaint of some second-generation immigrants.

Efforts to probe the internal aspects of identity have usually centred on the question, "To what ethnic group do you feel you belong?" In a study of ancestral languages carried out in 1973, which included no one of British or French ethnic origin, people were asked how they usually throught of themselves and were given four options, ranging from an ethnic label to Canadian. In a sample, two-thirds of which was composed of immigrants and almost 20 per cent of which was composed of people who had been in Canada less than ten years, "17.3 per cent identified themselves with an ethnic label ('Chinese,' 'Dutch,' and so on), 44.5 per cent identified themselves with a dual label (Chinese-Canadian, or 'Canadian of Chinese origin,' and so on), and the remaining 35.4 per cent identified themselves simply as 'Canadians.' "[9]

A more recent study, conducted in Metropolitan Toronto between 1977 and 1979, used a sample of men and women between the ages of eighteen and sixty-five who were in the labour force or were students. It employed an Ethnic Identity Index, based on "(1) the respondents' self-definition in terms of the hyphenated or unhyphenated ethnic or Canadian label, (2) the importance the respondents place on their ethnicity, (3) the respondents' perception of closeness of one's ethnic ties." The range of index scores was from 3, indicating high ethnic identity, to 8, indicating low ethnic identity. The scores do not, of course, show the degree to which a strong Canadian identity has emerged. Of the groups surveyed in the first generation, the West Indians had a score of 3.94, the Chinese 4.35, the Italians 4.37, the Jewish 4.44, the Ukrainians 4.61, the English 5.12, the Portuguese 5.26, and the Germans 5.73.[10]

Generation is usually considered to be the chief factor affecting ethnic identity. First-generation immigrants often have cultural and linguistic badges they cannot shed even if they wish to; second-generation immigrants may still have, or feel they have, distinctive marks, but even more commonly have a feeling of being divided or being in transition; members of the third and later generations, unless they have visible characteristics linking them to their ancestral group, have a choice of identifying themselves with that group or simply being Canadian. In a study carried out in 1969-71 in eighteen ethno-religious bloc settlements in north-central Saskatchewan, all Hutterites favoured preservation of ethnic identity, but among Doukhobors, Ukrainian Catholics, Ukrainian Orthodox, Mennonites, Scandinavians, French, and German Catholics there was a steady increase from the first through the second and third generations in the proportion not favouring identity preservation.[11] In the Metro Toronto study, the indices for the groups that included three generations in all cases but one increased regularly. For Germans, the index in the second generation dipped to 5.57 but in the third generation this rose to 7.69, the highest index attained by any group.[12]

The significance of generation is made most evident among the Japanese, where different terms are used for the different generations. The immigrants are Issei, their children are Nisei, their grandchildren are Sansei. Since most immigration of Japanese to Canada before 1967 occurred from 1904 to 1914, the generational names also indicate roughly the age of the person and the outstanding historical events experienced.

Important as it is, generation is not the sole factor influencing ethnic identity. Through the years, questions in the Canadian census have given prominence to ethnic origin. Periodically efforts were made to remove the questions, or to allow people to answer Canadian or American. However, spokespeople for various ethnic groups fought against such efforts: in 1961 members of the Legislative Assembly of Quebec threatened to call upon French Canadians to boycott the census or answer Negro to the question about ethnic origin if Canadian and American were accepted as answers.[13] The question has continued to be asked, with the difference that in 1981 it no longer specified that origin should be reckoned on the male side. Having to claim an ethnic origin, and knowing that it was entered in official records, has accentuated ethnic consciousness. It is ironic that immigration statistics ceased to be kept regarding ethnic origin in the late 1960's when the Royal Commission on Bilingualism and Biculturalism had brought ethnicity to the forefront in Canada.

Surnames also have an effect. The bearers of surnames that are not of British origin are often asked what the origin of the name is and are approached for support by ethnic organizations that make assumptions about origin based on names. In 1986 it was revealed that "foreign-sounding" names on court dockets were routinely checked by immigration officers looking for illegal aliens. Researchers sometimes propose surnames as found in telephone directories or on voters' lists or assessment roles as the basis for sampling an ethnic group, or employ names as clues to the immigration and settlement of ethnic groups.

Names are, however, an uncertain guide to ethnic identity. They may be changed fairly easily. Sometimes in the past immigration officers simplified names or changed them completely for convenience; immigrants later also simplified or changed their surnames, especially (according to two studies of name-changing carried out in Ontario in the early 1960's[14]) Slavic immigrants. Such changes in many cases, but not all, reflect changes in ethnic identity; sometimes individuals or their descendants revert to the original family names.

Although the legal process of changing one's name by deed poll is easy, the psychological process may be extremely difficult. When attempts were made to Anglicize the names of the Armenian orphans known as the Georgetown boys in 1923, one boy said of another, ". . . do you see that boy sitting on the end of this row? He lost his father and mother, his home and country – everything that is dear to a boy's heart. All he has left of his past is his name. Please sir, you won't take that away from him, will you?" As a result the attempt at name-changing was abandoned.[15] In the case of one Italian immigrant, the Anglicizing of his name from Veltri to Welch has been blamed for his mental illness and early death.[16]

Discrimination based on name, appearance, or accent against members of various ethnic groups has heightened ethnic consciousness; it has also exerted pressure toward discarding an ancestral ethnic identity. The novelist John Marlyn has decribed how the protagonist of *Under the Ribs of Death*, Sandor Hunyadi, the Canadian-born son of a cultured Hungarian immigrant growing up in Winnipeg in the 1920's, was led by discrimination to turn away from the values of his father and to change his name to Alex Hunter so that nobody would be able to tell that he had ever been a foreigner.[17] The signal discrimination against enemy aliens, especially Germans, during World War I and against Japanese Canadians during World War II appears to have led in the first instance to many denials of reprobated ethnic origins and in the second to avoidance of ethnic communities and institutions and to intermarriage.

The policy of multiculturalism also has contradictory effects. It has been interpreted as encouraging retention of ancestral ethnic identity, culture, and language, and has been criticized either for attempting to do so or for doing so inadequately. At the same time, it involves programs designed to remove barriers to full participation in Canadian society and to promote interchange between different ethnic groups: thus, to the degree that it succeeds, it facilitates development of a Canadian identity. The contradiction reflects a paradox in the aims of ethnic groups. They want both to remain distinctive and to have equality, as collectivities and as individuals, with others. However, the question must be posed whether more than marginal differentiation, or symbolic ethnicity, is possible in an egalitarian pluralism. Critics of the policy of multiculturalism accuse it of ignoring issues of economic and political power in favour of cultural issues. They assume that the two kinds of issues can be separated. The assumption is erroneous: "Cultures . . . differ in nothing more than in the skill, work habits and goals which they instill into the individual."[18] Hard choices must be made whether stress will be put upon preservation of differences or equality; the choices will be made by individuals rather than by collectivities.

NOTES

1. O'Bryan *et al.*, *Non-Official Languages*.
2. Everett C. Hughes, *The Sociological Eye: Selected Papers* (Chicago and New York: Aldine Atherton, 1971), p. 186.
3. The Levy-Coughlin Partnership, "The National Survey of Folkloric Performing Arts Groups," Prepared for the Multiculturalism Program of the Government of Canada, 1982.
4. Aun, *The Political Refugees*, p. 58.
5. Harry Vjekoslav Herman, *Men in White Aprons: A Study of Ethnicity and Occupation* (Toronto: Peter Martin Associates, 1978), p. xiii.
6. Bruce Kidd, "The Workers' Sports Movement in Canada, 1924-40: The Radical Immigrants' Alternative," *Polyphony*, 7, 1 (1985), pp. 80-88.
7. Robert F. Harney, "Homo Ludens and Ethnicity," *Polyphony*, 7, 1 (1985), pp. 9-10.
8. Doug Daniels, "The White race is shrinking: perceptions of race in Canada and some speculations on the political economy of race classification," *Ethnic and Racial Studies*, 4, 3 (1981), pp. 353-56.
9. O'Bryan *et al.*, *Non-Official Languages*, p. 97.
10. Wsevolod W. Isajiw, "Ethnic Identity Retention," Ethnic Pluralism Paper No. 5 (Toronto: Centre for Urban and Community Studies, University of Toronto, 1981), pp. 47-49.
11. Alan Anderson and Leo Driedger "The Mennonite Family: Culture and Kin in Rural Saskatchewan," in Ishwaran, ed., *Canadian Families*, p. 166.
12. Isajiw, "Ethnic Identity Retention," p. 49.
13. *Globe and Mail*, 18 January 1961.
14. Canadian Institute of Cultural Research, *Ethnic Change of Name, Ontario – A Pilot Study* (Toronto: Canadian Institute of Cultural Research, 1965); Brenda Conway, "A Study of Factors Involved in Name Changing by Members of Ethnic Minorities" (M.A. thesis, University of Toronto, 1966).
15. Jack Apramian, "The Georgetown Boys," *Polyphony*, 4, 2 (1982), pp. 44-45.
16. John Potestio, "The Memoirs of Giovanni Veltri," *Polyphony*, 7, 2 (1985), p. 14.
17. John Marlyn, *Under the Ribs of Death* (Toronto: McClelland and Stewart, 1957).
18. Hughes, *The Sociological Eye*, p. 75.

TWELVE

Multicultural Canada

Canadian society no longer consists of a British mainstream and variegated tributaries: it is now essentially ethnically diverse. Its institutions, although based on British models, are uniquely Canadian, and within them people of many origins take their places without a sense of strangeness or inferiority. Discrimination still exists, especially against recently arrived groups, but there is an array of formal and informal means of combatting it, and few Canadians hesitate to employ those means. Canada has become multicultural.

For a long time, the assumption of the dominant British group in Canada was Anglo-conformity, that is, that immigrants admitted to the country or their descendants would assimilate to the British group. The reason for the isolation of the Native peoples on reserves and for the restriction or exclusion of blacks and Asians was that they were considered unassimilable; the south and central European groups whose admission was grudging were thought to be assimilable but only with difficulty. Anglo-conformity in time became untenable either as a description of Canadian society or as an ideal and was replaced by references to the Canadian mosaic – that is, a theory that ethnic groups contributed and should contribute to Canadian society and culture by keeping their ancestral cultures and traditions. However, although the mosaic was extolled in the speeches of politicians and other dignitaries, public policy continued to be governed by the notion of Anglo-conformity.

In the 1960's, with heightened concern about human rights and the emergence of ethnicity as a dominant theme in many parts of the world, a tumultuous nationalism developed in Quebec, which had as one of its outcomes the appointment in 1963 of the Royal Commission on Bilingualism and Biculturalism. The Native peoples, among whom ethnic consciousness was increasing, were not specifically mentioned in the terms of reference of the Commission, and it therefore decided not to deal with them. The "other ethnic groups" were included, however: the Commission was charged to take into account their "contribution . . . to the cultural enrichment of Canada and the measures that should be taken to safeguard that contribution." Spurred by

223

this, and by a reference to "the two founding races" that they felt was insulting to the non-British and non-French, the other ethnic groups showed a new assertiveness. Spokespeople for them, many of them politically sophisticated Canadian-born and post-war immigrants, seized on the concept of a "Third Force" capable of playing a mediating role between English and French. The idea was put forward by the Ukrainian Canadian Paul Yusyk in his maiden speech in the Senate, and Ukrainians took a lead in promoting it. The strength of the Third Force was usually estimated as being at least equal to all those listed in the census as being of non-British and non-French origins; often it was declared to be one-third of the population.

On the other hand, the sociologist John Porter was at the same time insisting that ethnic and cultural differences should be ignored in the interests of equality.[1] To Porter, the vaunted mosaic was simply a division of labour by means of which the British maintained a privileged position and relegated all others to inferior status. However, proponents of a Third Force were more impressed by his data showing the unequal ranking of various ethnic origin categories in the occupational and income hierarchies and the virtual exclusion of all but the British from the elites than by his prescription that differences be given no recognition. Spokespeople for the other ethnic groups used his work in lobbying for government support for ethnic and cultural differences, contending that only by this means could equality be achieved.

The fact that the government heeded the pressure of lobbyists for the other ethnic groups is an indication that those groups had already gained economic and political strength. While cynics hold that the government acted only in order to have a counterpoise to French-Canadian aspirations, the other ethnic groups would not have been seen as a potential counterpoise if they had not been strong. It had been possible in the past to ignore them. Now they included senators, members of Parliament, prominent and wealthy business people, academics, and public servants. Thus they received attention, and the new emphasis on human rights, on ethnicity as a resource, and on the dangers of racism throughout the world have made Canadians of British origin more responsive than they had been earlier.

The government's first response was to abandon the phrase "bilingualism and biculturalism" in favour of "bilingualism and multiculturalism." Next, the Royal Commission on Bilingualism and Biculturalism devoted Book IV of its *Report* to the other ethnic groups. It was both a description of the past and present role of Canadians whose origins were not British, French, or Native and an outline of a social policy concerning those Canadians, particularly such of them as wished to retain their ethnic identity and some of their cultural heritage. In addition, in 1967 the federal government completed the process begun in the late 1940's of eliminating the undeclared but *de facto* ethnic and racial bias from its immigration policy by introducing the nine-point program for the selection of immigrants.

On October 8, 1971, the federal government, as its response to Book IV of the *Report* of the Royal Commission on Bilingualism and Biculturalism, proclaimed a policy of multiculturalism within a bilingual framework:

The government will support and encourage the various cultures and ethnic groups that give structure and vitality to our society. They will be encouraged to share their cultural expression and values with other Canadians and so contribute to a richer life for us all. . . .

In implementing a policy of multiculturalism within a bilingual framework, the government will provide support in four ways;

First, resources permitting, the government will seek to assist all Canadian cultural groups that have demonstrated a desire and effort to continue to develop a capacity to grow and contribute to Canada, and a clear need for assistance, the small and weak groups no less than the strong and highly organized.

Second, the government will assist members of all cultural groups to overcome cultural barriers to full participation in Canadian society.

Third, the government will promote creative encounters and interchange among all Canadian cultural groups in the interest of national unity.

Fourth, the government will continue to assist immigrants to acquire at least one of Canada's official languages in order to become full participants in Canadian society.[2]

In the decade that followed, not only the federal government but most of the provinces were active in promoting multiculturalism. The federal government appointed a minister of state responsible for multiculturalism in 1972, and in the following year set up a consultative council to advise him. Through the Multiculturalism Directorate within the Department of the Secretary of State, it carried on liaison activities with ethnic communities and with the ethnic press, sponsored research, including major projects on non-official languages and ethnic attitudes to multiculturalism, and a series of histories of ethnic groups, aided the development of the Canadian Ethnic Studies Association, supported activities in the performing and the visual arts, and assisted programs of linguistic instruction. A number of provinces also proclaimed policies of multiculturalism and, often with federal subsidies, took initiatives in the spheres under their jurisdiction, notably education.

At the same time, several other significant pieces of legislation were passed. The Citizenship Act that came into effect in 1977 abolished the preferential treatment previously accorded to British subjects who applied for Canadian citizenship. The Canadian Human Rights Act, passed in 1977, outlawed discrimination on grounds of race, national or ethnic origin, or colour or a number of other factors within the federal area of legislative competence. The Immigration Act proclaimed in 1978 reiterated the principles of universality and non-discrimination.

Finally, the Constitution Act of 1982 contained two clauses designed to entrench both the individual and the collective aspects of the policy of multiculturalism:

15. (1) Every individual is equal before and under the law and has the

right to equal protection and equal benefit of the law without discrimination and, in particular, without discrimination based on race, national or ethnic origin, colour, religion, sex, age or mental or physical disability.

(2) Subsection (1) does not preclude any law, program or activity that has as its object the amelioration of conditions of disadvantaged individuals or groups, including those that are disadvantaged because of race, national or ethnic origin, religion, sex, age or mental or physical disability. . . .

27. This charter shall be interpreted in a manner consistent with the preservation and enhancement of the multicultural heritage of Canadians.

The proclamation of multiculturalism and its endorsement by all political parties did not mean either widespread knowledge of the policy or its acceptance by the public. A survey carried out between November, 1973, and March, 1974, revealed that only about one-fifth of the population knew of the policy. The same survey found a generally positive attitude toward multiculturalism, but throughout the 1970's criticism was directed at the policy on many grounds. Some of the leading intellectuals of Quebec decried it as destructive to the hard-won status of French Canadians as a charter-member group in the Canadian federation. Other critics saw it as backward-looking, or as designed to preserve the privileges of those of British origin by emphasizing cultural differences within the population. Still others, and perhaps the majority, regarded the policy as a cynical attempt to buy the chimerical ethnic vote.

On the other hand, spokespeople for some ethnic associations criticized the policy as insufficient. These tended to be from well-organized groups, who felt that their pressure had brought about the policy and that its main thrust was or ought to be linguistic and cultural maintenance. The ethnic groups for which they claimed to speak were white and European and had come to Canada before World War I, during the settlement of the West, and in the 1920's; they had received small but important additions from the displaced persons camps. They had endured discrimination and had not yet achieved full equality in Canadian society. But they were on their way, and hence did not see the issue of equal participation as pressing but as being amply looked after under human rights legislation, federal and provincial. These groups were, however, vitally concerned about the loss of their ethnic identities and their ancestral languages and cultures.

Their viewpoint was clear in the first annual report of the Canadian Consultative Council on Multiculturalism, which, for example, excoriated multicultural centres because all groups could participate in their programs "only through use of a common language, presumably either French or English."[3] It was also clear in the objections raised by the same Council when ministers responsible for multiculturalism from late 1975 on proposed giving greater attention to group understanding and the fighting of racism, even though they explicitly pledged to maintain support for heritage languages and folkloric activities.

Neither the proclamation of the policy of multiculturalism nor the human rights legislation in fact ended racial and ethnic discrimination. Some of the earlier targets had ceased to be victims, but newly arrived groups were subject to unequal treatment. In particular, groups whose presence had not been conspicuous at the time of the proclamation of the policy, members of the visible minorities, suffered from a variety of forms of discrimination, both individual and institutional. South Asians suffered verbal abuse, physical violence, and vandalism, especially in the mid-1970's in Vancouver and Toronto; Haitians encountered discrimination in employment and police brutality in Montreal; various groups complained of discriminatory behaviour by police. The visible minorities were at the time suffering not only from colour prejudice but from prejudice against recent immigrants, heightened by unemployment rates that were blamed on immigration. The association of unemployment and immigration is, of course, questionable: it can be argued persuasively that immigrants contribute to employment both as consumers and as entrepreneurs.

By the 1980's, however, the policy of multiculturalism and human rights legislation had gained ground. Entrenched in the constitution and extolled by prominent visitors to the country – including Queen Elizabeth II and John Paul II – they had begun to be regarded as uniquely Canadian characteristics and as a mainstay of the country's cohesion. They thus created an atmosphere in which ethnic groups could assert their pride in their origins and individuals could challenge discrimination.

It is notable that the discrimination against members of the visible minorities led to a large number of investigations by advocacy organizations and by governments, including reports on race relations in eleven Canadian cities commissioned in early 1982 and a report of a special committee of the House of Commons on visible minorities in Canadian society in 1984.[4] The findings of the investigations were well publicized; the effects are difficult to gauge. That the results were not negligible, however, is indicated by the eagerness of some groups that lack distinctive physical traits to be included among the visible minorities.

Also, some of the protests against discrimination have focused on exclusion not from the lower ranks of economic, political, and social structures but from the elites. Many elites have now been breached by members of hitherto disadvantaged groups, but not many people distinguishable from the majority by colour have achieved the top ranks in the socio-economic order. That exclusion from high ranks is being protested underlines the fact that not all members of the visible minorities have been forced into a lowly entrance status as early blacks, Chinese, Japanese, and Sikhs were. Their high levels of education, talents, and skills are often recognized not fully but in part in the receiving society.

Multiculturalism has not made possible the preservation of cultures and languages brought to Canada from all parts of the world. It could not: to do so even partially would require a degree of separation of ethnic groups within the country that no one would consider possible or desirable. Nor has multiculturalism brought about equality of opportunity for all Canadians, regardless of time of arrival, cultural and linguistic differences, and colour. But the policy would not have been proclaimed if Canada had not been moving away from its Anglo-conformist and racist past into a more egalitarian pluralism, and the policy has given impetus to that shift. It has made symbolic ethnicity a matter of pride, and it has given victims of discrimination arms with which to fight.

NOTES

1. Porter, *The Vertical Mosaic*.
2. Canada, *House of Commons Debates*, 1971, pp. 8545-46.
3. Canadian Consultative Council on Multiculturalism, *First Annual Report* (Ottawa: Canadian Consultative Council on Multiculturalism, 1975), p. 20.
4. *Equality Now! Report of the Special Committee on Visible Minorities in Canadian Society* (Hull, Quebec: Queen's Printer, 1984).

Bibliography

Abella, Irving, and Harold Troper. *None Is Too Many: Canada and the Jews of Europe, 1933-1948*. Toronto: Lester and Orpen Dennys, 1982.

Abu-Laban, Baha. *An Olive Branch on the Family Tree: The Arabs in Canada*. Toronto: McClelland and Stewart, 1980.

Adachi, Ken. *The Enemy That Never Was: A History of the Japanese Canadians*. Toronto: McClelland and Stewart, 1976.

Allen, Richard, ed. *The Social Gospel in Canada*. Ottawa: National Museums of Canada, 1975.

Anctil, Pierre. "La Société québécoise face au multiculturalisme," paper presented to Canadian Ethnology Society, Edmonton, May 17, 1986.

Anderson, Alan B., and James S. Frideres. *Ethnicity in Canada: Theoretical Perspectives*. Toronto: Butterworths, 1981.

Anderson, Grace M. *Networks of Contact: The Portuguese and Toronto*. Waterloo: Wilfrid Laurier University Press, 1974.

Anderson, Grace M., and David Higgs. *A Future to Inherit: The Portuguese Communities of Canada*. Toronto: McClelland and Stewart, 1976.

Arnopoulos, Sheila, and D. Clift. *The English Fact in Quebec*. Montreal: McGill-Queen's University Press, 1980.

Ashworth, Mary. *The Forces Which Shaped Them: A History of the Education of Minority Group Children in British Columbia*. Vancouver: New Star Books, 1979.

———. *Immigrant Children and Canadian Schools*. Toronto: McClelland and Stewart, 1975.

Aun, Karl. *The Political Refugees: A History of the Estonians in Canada*. Toronto: McClelland and Stewart, 1985.

Avakumovic, Ivan. *The Communist Party in Canada: A History*. Toronto: McClelland and Stewart, 1975.

Avery, Donald. *"Dangerous Foreigners": European Immigrant Workers and Labour Radicalism in Canada, 1896-1932*. Toronto: McClelland and Stewart, 1979.

———. "Ethnic Loyalties and the Proletarian Revolution: A Case Study of Communist Political Activity in Winnipeg, 1923-1936," in *Ethnicity Power and Politics in Canada*, edited by Jorgen Dahlie and Tissa Fernando. Toronto: Methuen,

229

1981, pp. 68-93.

——. "The Radical Alien and the Winnipeg General Strike of 1919," in *The West and the Nation*, edited by C. Berger and R. Cook. Toronto: McClelland and Stewart, 1976, pp. 209-31.

Bercuson, David. *Canada and the Birth of Israel*. Toronto: University of Toronto Press, 1985.

——. *Fools and Wise Men: The Rise and Fall of the One Big Union*. Toronto: McGraw-Hill Ryerson, 1978.

Betcherman, Lita-Rose. *The Swastika and the Maple Leaf: Fascist Movements in Canada in the Thirties*. Toronto: Fitzhenry and Whiteside, 1975.

Boissevain, Jeremy. *The Italians of Montreal: Social Adjustment in a Plural Society*. Studies of the Royal Commission on Bilingualism and Biculturalism, no. 7. Ottawa: Queen's Printer, 1970.

Bradwin, Edmund W. *The Bunkhouse Man: A Study of Work and Pay in the Camps of Canada 1903-1914*. Original edition, 1928; reprint, Toronto: University of Toronto Press, 1972.

Brandstaetter, Maureen. "A Study of Prairie German Canadian Newspapers during the First World War." M.A. thesis, University of Calgary, 1986.

Brennan, J.W. "Wooing the 'Foreign Vote': Saskatchewan Politics and the Immigrant, 1905-1919," *Prairie Forum*, 3, 1 (1978).

Breton, Raymond, Jeffrey G. Reitz, and Victor Valentine. *Cultural Boundaries and the Cohesion of Canada*. Montreal: Institute for Research on Public Policy, 1980.

Briant, Peter C., and Daniel Hadekel. "Ethnic Relations in the Construction Industy on the Island of Montreal." Report presented to the Royal Commission on Bilingualism and Biculturalism, 1966.

Buchignani, Norman, and Doreen M. Indra, with Ram Srivastava. *Continuous Journey: A Social History of South Asians in Canada*. Toronto: McClelland and Stewart, 1985.

Burnet, Jean, ed. *Looking into My Sister's Eye*. Toronto: Multicultural History Society of Ontario, 1986.

Calderwood, William. "Pulpit, Press and Political Reactions to the Ku Klux Klan in Saskatchewan," in *The Twenties in Western Canada*, edited by S.M. Trofimenkoff. Ottawa: National Museum of Man, 1972.

Campbell, Douglas, ed. *Banked Fires: The Ethnics of Nova Scotia*. Port Credit: The Scribblers' Press, 1978.

Canada. *Report of the Special Committee on Hate Propaganda in Canada*. Ottawa: Queen's Printer, 1966.

Canada, Royal Commission on Bilingualism and Biculturalism. *Report, Book IV: Cultural Contributions of the Other Ethnic Groups*. Ottawa: Queen's Printer, 1970.

——. *Report, General Introduction*. Ottawa: Queen's Printer, 1967.

Caroli, Betty Boyd, Robert F. Harney, and Lydio F. Tomasi, eds. *The Italian Immigrant Woman in North America*. Toronto: Multicultural History Society of Ontario, 1978.

Chan, Anthony B. *Gold Mountain: The Chinese in the New World*. Vancouver: New Star Books, 1983.

Chimbos, Peter D. *The Canadian Odyssey: The Greek Experience in Canada*. Toronto: McClelland and Stewart, 1980.

——. "Immigrants' Attitudes toward

their Children's Inter-Ethnic Marriages in a Canadian Community," *International Migration Review*, 5, 1 (1971), pp. 5-17.

Ciccocelli, J.A. "The Innocuous Enemy Alien: Italians in Canada During World War Two." M.A. thesis, University of Western Ontario, 1977.

Cipywnyk, S. "Multiculturalism and the Child in western Canada," in *Multiculturalism and Education*. Proceedings of the Western Regional Conference, Canadian Association for Curriculum Studies, 1976, pp. 27-50.

Clement, Wallace. *The Canadian Corporate Elite: An Analysis of Economic Power*. Toronto: McClelland and Stewart, 1975.

Clement, Wallace, and Dennis Olsen. "The Ethnic Composition of Canada's Elites 1951 to 1973," a report for the Secretary of State. 1974.

Coleman, W. "From Bill 22 to Bill 101: The Politics of Language under the Parti Québécois." *Canadian Journal of Political Science*, 14, 3 (1981).

Corbett, David C. *Canada's Immigration Policy: A Critique*. Toronto: University of Toronto Press, 1957.

Coward, Harold, and Leslie Kawamura. *Religion and Ethnicity*. Waterloo: Wilfrid Laurier University Press, 1978.

Curtis, James. "Voluntary Associations Joining," *American Sociological Review*, 36 (1971), pp. 872-80.

Dafoe, John W. *Clifford Sifton in Relation to His Times*. Toronto: Macmillan of Canada, 1931.

Dahlie, Jorgen. "Scandinavian Experiences on the Prairies, 1890-1920: The Frederiksens of Nokomis," in *The Settlement of the West*, edited by Howard Palmer. Calgary: Comprint Publishing Company, 1977, pp. 102-13.

Daniels, Doug. "The white race is shrinking: perceptions of race in Canada and some speculations on the political economy of race classification," *Ethnic and Racial Studies*, 4, 3 (1981), pp. 353-56.

Dawson, C.A. *Group Settlement: Ethnic Communities in Western Canada*. Toronto: Macmillan of Canada, 1936.

——. Introduction to *The British Immigrant: His Social and Economic Adjustment in Canada*, by Lloyd G. Reynolds. Toronto: Oxford University Press, 1935.

Debor, H.W. "The Cultural Contribution of the German Ethnic Group to Canada," an essay prepared for the Royal Commission on Bilingualism and Biculturalism.

Dégh, Linda. *People in the Tobacco Belt: Four Lives*. Ottawa: National Museum of Canada, 1975.

Dirks, Gerald E. *Canada's Refugee Policy: Indifference or Opportunism?* Montreal: McGill-Queen's University Press, 1977.

Donnelly, M.S. "Ethnic Participation in Municipal Government – Winnipeg, St. Boniface, and the Metropolitan Government of Greater Winnipeg," a study prepared for the Royal Commission on Bilingualism and Biculturalism.

Dreisziger, N.F., with M.L. Kovacs, Paul Bödy, and Bennett Kovrig. *Struggle and Hope: The Hungarian-Canadian Experience*. Toronto: McClelland and Stewart, 1982.

Dumas, Evelyn. *The Bitter Thirties in Quebec*. Translated by Arnold Bennett. Montreal: Black Rose Books, 1975.

Elkin, Frederick. "The Employment of

Visible Minority Groups in Mass Media Advertising," a report submitted to the Ontario Human Rights Commission, 1971.

Elliott, Jean Leonard. *Two Nations, Many Cultures: Ethnic Groups in Canada*. Scarborough, Ontario: Prentice-Hall, 1979.

Entz, W. "The Suppression of the German Language Press in September 1918 (with special reference to the secular German Language papers in Western Canada)," *Canadian Ethnic Studies*, 8, 2 (1976), pp. 56-70.

Epp, Frank H. *Mennonites in Canada, 1786-1920: The History of a Separate People*. Toronto: Macmillan of Canada, 1974.

——. *Mennonites in Canada, 1920-1940: A People's Struggle for Survival*. Toronto: Macmillan of Canada, 1982.

Francis, E.K. *In Search of Utopia: The Mennonites in Manitoba*. Altona, Man.: D.W. Friesen and Sons, 1955.

Gaida, Pr., S. Kairys, J. Kardelis, J. Puzinas, A. Rinkunas, and J. Sungaila. *Lithuanians in Canada*. Canada Ethnica 5. Ottawa: Lights Printing and Publishing Co., 1967.

Ganzevoort, Herman, and Mark Boekelman, eds. *Dutch Immigration to North America*. Toronto: Multicultural History Society of Ontario, 1983.

Gordon, Milton M. *Assimilation in American Life*. New York: Oxford University Press, 1964.

Granzberg, Gary. "The Portrayal of Visible Minorities by Canadian Television During the 1982 Prime-time Season." *Currents*, 2, 2 (1984), pp. 23-26.

Gray, James H. *The Winter Years: The Depression on the Prairies*. Toronto: Macmillan of Canada, 1966.

Gruneir, R. "The Hebrew-Christian Mission in Toronto," *Canadian Ethnic Studies*, 9, 1 (1977), pp. 18-28.

Hall, D.J. *Clifford Sifton*, vol. 2. Vancouver: University of British Columbia Press, 1985.

Hamelin, Jean, ed. *Histoire du Québec*. Toulouse: Privat, 1976.

Harney, Robert F. "Boarding and Belonging: Thoughts on Sojourners' Institutions," *Urban History Review/Revue d'histoire urbaine*, 2 (1978), pp. 8-37.

——, ed. *Gathering Place: Peoples and Neighbourhoods of Toronto, 1834-1945*. Toronto: Multicultural History Society of Ontario, 1985.

——. *Italians in North America*. Toronto: Multicultural History Society of Ontario, 1978.

——. "Men Without Women: Italian Migrants in Canada, 1885-1930," in *The Italian Immigrant Woman in North America*, edited by Betty Boyd Caroli, Robert F. Harney, and Lydio F. Tomasi. Toronto: Multicultural History Society of Ontario, 1978, pp. 79-101.

——. "The New Canadians and Their Life in Toronto," *Canadian Geographical Journal* (April/May, 1978).

——. "The Padrone System and Sojourners in the Canadian North, 1885-1920," in George E. Pozzetta, ed., *Pane e Lavoro: The Italian American Working Class*. Toronto: Multicultural History Society of Ontario, 1980, pp. 119-37.

Harney, Robert, and Harold Troper. *Immigrants: A Portrait of the Urban Experience, 1890-1930*. Toronto: Van Nostrand Reinhold, 1975.

Hawthorn, Harry B., ed. *The Doukho-bors of British Columbia*. London: J.M. Dent and Sons, 1955.

Helling, Rudolf A., Jack Thiessen, Fritz Wieden, Elizabeth and Kurt Wangenheim, and Karl Heeb. "They, too, Founded Canada: A Socio-Economic History of German-Canadians." Multilithed.

Helly, Denise. *Les Chinois à Montréal 1877-1951*. Québec: Institut québécois de recherche sur la culture, 1987.

Henripin, Jacques. "From Acceptance of Nature to Control: The Demography of the French Canadians Since the Seventeenth Century," in *French-Canadian Society*, vol. I, edited by Marcel Rioux and Yves Martin. Toronto: McClelland and Stewart, 1964, pp. 204-16.

Henry, Frances, ed. *Ethnicity in the Americas*. The Hague: Mouton, 1976.

Herman, Harry Vjekoslav. *Men in White Aprons: A Study of Ethnicity and Occupation*. Toronto: Peter Martin Associates, 1978.

Heydenkorn, Benedykt, ed. *Memoirs of Polish Immigrants in Canada*. Toronto: Canadian Polish Research Institute, 1979.

——, ed. *Past and Present*. Toronto: Canadian Polish Research Institute, 1974.

——, ed. *Topics on Poles in Canada*. Toronto: Canadian Polish Research Institute, 1976.

Hibbitts, Bernard. "Ethnic groups and Canadian Propaganda Policy in the 1950s," in *Groups and Governments in Canadian Foreign Policy*, edited by Don Munton. Toronto: Canadian Institute of International Affairs, 1985, pp. 100-04.

Hill, Douglas. *The Opening of the Canadian West*. Don Mills, Ontario: Academic Press, Canada, 1973; originally published in 1967.

Hoar, Victor. *The Mackenzie-Papineau Battalion: Canadian Participation in the Spanish Civil War*. Toronto: Copp Clark, 1969.

Hobart, Charles W. "Italian Immigrants in Edmonton: Adjustment and Integration," a research report prepared for the Royal Commission on Bilingualism and Biculturalism, vol. 1.

Hoffman, George. "The New Party and the Old Issues: The Saskatchewan Farmer-Labour Party and the Ethnic Vote, 1934," *Canadian Ethnic Studies*, 14, 2 (1982), pp. 1-20.

Hostetler, John A. *Hutterite Society*. Baltimore: The Johns Hopkins University Press, 1974.

Hughes, Everett C. *French Canada in Transition*. Chicago: University of Chicago Press, 1943.

Hughes, Everett C. *The Sociological Eye: Selected Papers*. Chicago: Aldine-Atherton, 1971.

Indra, Doreen M. "South Asian Stereotypes in the Vancouver Press," *Ethnic and Racial Studies*, 2, 2 (1979), pp. 166-89.

Isaacs, Harold R. *Idols of the Tribe: Group Identity and Political Change*. New York: Harper and Row, 1977.

Isajiw, Wsevolod, ed. *Identities: The Impact of Ethnicity on Canadian Society*. Toronto: Peter Martin Associates Limited, 1977.

——. "Ethnic Identity Retention." Ethnic Pluralism Paper no. 5. Toronto: Centre for Urban and Community Studies, University of Toronto, 1981.

Isajiw, Wsevolod W., and Norbert J. Hartmann. "Changes in the Occupational Structure of Ukrainians in Canada: A Methodology for the Study of Changes in Ethnic Studies," in *Social and Cultural Change in Canada*, vol. 1, edited by W.E. Mann. Toronto: Copp Clark, 1970, pp. 96-112.

Ishwaran, K., ed. *Canadian Families: Ethnic Variations*. Toronto: McGraw-Hill Ryerson, 1980.

Jaenen, Cornelius, "Canadian Education and Minority Rights," in *Slavs in Canada*, vol. 3, edited by Cornelius Jaenen. Ottawa: Inter-University Committee on Canadian Slavs, 1971, pp. 191-208.

——. "Minority Group Schooling and Canadian National Unity," *The Journal of Educational Thought*, 7, 2 (1973), pp. 81-93.

——. "Ruthenian Schools in Western Canada, 1897-1919," *Paedogogica Historica*, 10, 3 (1970), pp. 517-41.

Jalava, Mari. "Radicalism or a New Deal, the Unfolding World View of the Finnish Immigrants in Sudbury, 1883-1932." M.A. thesis, Laurentian University, 1983.

Jaworsky, John. "A Case Study of the Canadian Federal Government's Multiculturalism Policy." M.A. thesis, Carleton University, 1979.

Jeletzky, T.F., ed. *Russian Canadians: Their Past and Present*. Ottawa: Borealis Press, 1983.

Johnston, Hugh. *The East Indians in Canada*. Ottawa: Canadian Historical Association, 1984.

Joy, Richard J. *Languages in Conflict*. Toronto: McClelland and Stewart, 1972.

Kalbach, Warren E. *The Impact of Immigration on Canada's Population*. Ottawa: Dominion Bureau of Statistics, 1970.

Kalbach, Warren E., and Wayne W. McVey. *The Demographic Bases of Canadian Society*, second ed. Toronto: McGraw-Hill Ryerson, 1971.

Kalbfleisch, Herbert Karl. *The History of the Pioneer German Language Press of Ontario, 1835-1918*. Toronto: University of Toronto Press, 1968.

Karni, Michael G., ed. *Finnish Diaspora I: Canada, South America, Africa, Australia and Sweden*. Toronto: Multicultural History Society of Ontario, 1981.

Katz, Elliott. "The Participation of a Cultural Minority in Politics, Jewish Voting Preferences in Seven Oaks and River Heights, 1969 and 1973." M.A. thesis, University of Manitoba, 1980.

Kaye, V.J. "Three Phases of Ukrainian Immigration," in *Slavs in Canada*, vol. 1. Edmonton: Inter-University Committee on Canadian Slavs, 1966.

Keyserlingk, Robert. "Agents within the Gates: The Search for Nazi Subversives in Canada during World War II," *Canadian Historical Review* (June, 1985), pp. 211-39.

——. "The Canadian Government's Attitude toward Germans and German Canadians in World War Two," *Canadian Ethnic Studies*, 16, 1 (1984), pp. 16-28.

Kirkconnell, Watson. *Canada, Europe and Hitler*. Toronto: Oxford University Press, 1939.

Kirschbaum, Joseph M. *Slovaks in Canada*. Toronto: Canadian Ethnic Press Association of Ontario, 1967.

Kirschbaum, J.M., B. Heydenkorn, V. Mauko, and Rev. P. Gaida, eds. *Twenty Years of the Ethnic Press As-*

sociation of Ontario. Toronto: The Ethnic Press Association of Ontario, 1971.

Koch, Eric. *Deemed Suspect: A Wartime Blunder*. Toronto: Methuen, 1980.

Kogler, Rudolf, and Benedykt Heydenkorn. "Poles in Canada, 1971," in *Past and Present*, edited by Benedykt Heydenkorn. Toronto: Canadian Polish Research Institute, 1974, pp. 27-36.

Kolasky, John. *The Shattered Illusion*. Toronto: Peter Martin, 1979.

Kordan, Bohdan, and Lubomyr Luciuk. *A Delicate and Difficult Question: Documents in the History of Ukrainians in Canada, 1899-1962*. Kingston: Limestone Press, 1986.

Kos-Rabcewicz-Zubkowski, L. "Contributions Made by the Polish Ethnic Group to the Cultural Enrichment of Canada," an essay prepared for the Royal Commission on Bilingualism and Biculturalism.

Kosa, John. *Land of Choice: The Hungarians in Canada*. Toronto: University of Toronto Press, 1957.

Kostash, Myrna. *All of Baba's Children*. Edmonton: Hurtig, 1977.

Kovacs, Martin L., ed. *Ethnic Canadians: Culture and Education*. Regina: Canadian Plains Research Center, 1978.

Kralt, John. "Ethnic Origin in the Canadian Census, 1871-1981," in *Changing Realities: Social Trends Among Ukrainian Canadians*, edited by W.R. Petryshyn. Edmonton: The Canadian Institute of Ukrainian Studies, 1980, pp. 18-49.

LaViolette, Forrest E. *The Canadian Japanese and World War II*. Toronto: University of Toronto Press, 1948.

Lee, Carol. "The Road to Enfranchisement: Chinese and Japanese in British Columbia," *B.C. Studies*, 30 (1976), pp. 44-76.

Lehmann, Heinz. *The German-Canadians, 1750-1937: Immigration, Settlement and Culture*. Edited and translated by Gerhard P. Bassler. St. John's, Newfoundland: Jesperson Press, 1986.

Lehr, John C. "The Government and the Immigrant: Perspectives on Ukrainian Block Settlement in the Canadian West," *Canadian Ethnic Studies*, 9, 2 (1977), pp. 42-52.

Lehr, John C., and D. Wayne Moodie. "The Polemics of Pioneer Settlement: Ukrainian Immigration and the Winnipeg Press," *Canadian Ethnic Studies*, 12, 2 (1980), pp. 88-101.

Lindal, Walter J. *The Icelanders in Canada*. Canada Ethnica 2. Winnipeg: National Publishers, 1967.

Lindström-Best, Varpu. *The Finns in Canada*. Ottawa: Canadian Historical Association, 1985.

——. "'Fist Press': a Study of the Finnish Canadian Handwritten Newspapers," *Polyphony*, 3, 2 (1981).

Lipset, S.M. *Agrarian Socialism*. Garden City: Doubleday, 1968.

Loken, Gulbrand. *From Fjord to Frontier: A History of the Norwegians in Canada*. Toronto: McClelland and Stewart, 1980.

Lupul, Manoly R., ed. *A Heritage in Transition: Essays in the History of Ukrainians in Canada*. Toronto: McClelland and Stewart, 1982.

——. "The Political Implementation of Multiculturalism," *Journal of Canadian Studies*, 17, 1 (1982), pp. 93-101.

——, ed. *Ukrainian Canadians, Multiculturalism, and Separatism: An Assessment*. Edmonton: University of Alberta Press, 1978.

Lysenko, Vera. *Men in Sheepskin Coats: A Study in Assimilation*. Toronto: Ryerson, 1947.

Macdonald, Norman. *Canada: Immigration and Colonization 1841-1903*. Toronto: Macmillan of Canada, 1968.

Makowski, William Boleslaus. *History and Integration of Poles in Canada*. Niagara Peninsula, Canada: The Canadian Polish Congress, 1967.

Malliah, H.L. "A Socio-Historical Study of the Legislators of Alberta." Ph.D. dissertation, University of Alberta, 1970.

Mann, W.E. *Sect, Cult, and Church in Alberta*. Toronto: University of Toronto Press, 1955.

March, R.R. "Political Mobility of Slavs in the Federal and Provincial Legislatures in Canada," *Slavs in Canada*, vol. 2. Toronto: Inter-University Committee on Canadian Slavs, 1968.

Marunchak, Michael. *The Ukrainian Canadians: A History*. Winnipeg: Ukrainian Free Academy of Sciences, 1970.

McCormack, A. Ross. *Reformers, Rebels, and Revolutionaries: The Western Canadian Radical Movement 1899-1919*. Toronto: University of Toronto Press, 1977.

McEvoy, F.J. "A Symbol of Racial Discrimination: The Chinese Immigration Act and Canada's Relations with China, 1942-47," *Canadian Ethnic Studies*, 14, 3 (1982), pp. 24-42.

McLeod, Keith. "Education and the Assimilation of the New Canadians in the North-West Territories and Saskatchewan, 1885-1934." Ph.D. dissertation, University of Toronto, 1975.

McRae, Kenneth. "Language Policies as an Aspect of Cultural Policy," working paper prepared for Linguistic and Cultural Diversity, a Canada/Unesco Symposium, Ottawa, September 25-30, 1972.

Migus, Paul M., ed. *Sounds Canadian: Languages and Cultures in Multi-Ethnic Society*. Toronto: Peter Martin Associates, 1975.

Milnor, Andrew. "Agrarian Protest in Saskatchewan, 1929-48: A Study in Ethnic Politics." Ph.D. dissertation, Duke University, 1962.

Mitchell, Elizabeth B. *In Western Canada Before the War*. Saskatoon: Western Producer Prairie Books, 1981.

Morrison, Jean. "Ethnicity and Violence: the Lakehead Freight Handlers Before World War I," in *Essays in Canadian Working Class History*, edited by Gregory S. Kealey and Peter Warrian. Toronto: McClelland and Stewart, 1976, pp. 143-60.

Morton. W.L. *Manitoba, A History*. Toronto: University of Toronto Press, 1957.

The Multilingual Press in Manitoba. Winnipeg: Canada Press Club, 1974.

Newman, Peter C. *Bronfman Dynasty: The Rothschilds of the New World*. Toronto: McClelland and Stewart, 1978.

Norris, John. *Strangers Entertained: A History of the Ethnic Groups of British Columbia*. Vancouver: British Columbia Centennial '71 Committee, 1971.

O'Bryan, K.G., J.G. Reitz, and O.M. Kuplowska. *Non-Official Languages: A Study in Canadian Multiculturalism*. Ottawa: Supply and Services Canada, 1976.

Oliver, Peter. *Unlikely Tory: The Life and*

Politics of Allan Grossman. Toronto: Lester and Orpen Dennys, 1985.

Palmer, Howard. "Ethnic Relations in Wartime: Nationalism and European Minorities in Alberta during the Second World War," *Canadian Ethnic Studies*, 14, 3 (1982), pp. 1-23.

——. *Immigration and the Rise of Multiculturalism*. Toronto: Copp Clark, 1975.

——. "The Hutterite Land Expansion Controversy in Alberta," *Western Canadian Journal of Anthropology*, 2, 2 (1971), pp. 18-46.

——. *Land of the Second Chance: A History of Ethnic Groups in Southern Alberta*. Lethbridge: The Lethbridge Herald, 1972.

——. *Patterns of Prejudice: A History of Nativism in Alberta*. Toronto: McClelland and Stewart, 1982.

Palmer, Howard, and Tamara Palmer, eds. *Peoples of Alberta: Portraits of Cultural Diversity*. Saskatoon: Western Producer Prairie Books, 1985.

Papp, Susan M. "The Hungarian Press in Ontario," *Polyphony*, 4, 1 (1982), pp. 64-68.

Panchuk, Bohdan. *Heroes of Their Day: The Reminiscences of Bohdan Panchuk*. Edited and with an introduction by Lubomyr Y. Luciuk. Toronto: Multicultural History Society of Ontario, 1983.

Paris, Erna. *Jews: An Account of Their Experience in Canada*. Toronto: Macmillan of Canada, 1980.

Paulsen, Frank M. *Danish Settlements on the Canadian Prairies*. Ottawa: National Museums of Canada, 1974.

Paupst, K. "A Note on Anti-Chinese Sentiment in Toronto," *Canadian Ethnic Studies*, 9, 1 (1977), pp. 54-59.

Pearson, Lester B. *Mike: The Memoirs of the Right Honourable Lester B. Pearson*, vol. 3, *1957-1968*. Edited by John A. Munro and Alex I. Inglis. Toronto: University of Toronto Press, 1975.

Perin, Roberto. "Making Good Fascists and Good Canadians: Consular Propaganda and the Italian Community in Montreal in the 1930s," in *Minorities and Mother Country Imagery*, edited by Gerald Gold. St. John's: Institute of Social and Economic Research, 1984, pp. 136-58.

Peter, Karl A. "The Decline of Hutterite Population Growth," *Canadian Ethnic Studies*, 12, 3 (1980), pp. 97-110.

——. *The Dynamics of Hutterite Society: An Analytical Approach*. Edmonton: University of Alberta Press, 1987.

Peterson, Tom. "Ethnic and Class Politics in Manitoba," in *Canadian Provincial Politics: The Party System of the Ten Provinces*, edited by Martin Robin. Scarborough: Prentice Hall, 1972, pp. 78-97.

Peterson, William. *Planned Migration: The Social Determinants of the Dutch-Canadian Movement*. Berkeley: University of California Press, 1955.

Petryshyn, W.R., ed. *Changing Realities: Social Trends Among Ukrainian Canadians*. Edmonton: The Canadian Institute of Ukrainian Studies, 1980.

Piniuta, Harry. *Land of Pain, Land of Promise: First Person Accounts by Ukrainian Pioneers, 1891-1914*. Saskatoon: Western Producer Prairie Books, 1978.

Porter, John, "Bilingualism and the Myths of Culture," *Canadian Re-*

view of Sociology and Anthropology, 6 (1969), pp. 111-19.

——. *The Vertical Mosaic: An Analysis of Social Class and Power in Canada*. Toronto: University of Toronto Press, 1965.

Potrebenko, Helen. *No Streets of Gold: A Social History of Ukrainians in Alberta*. Vancouver: New Star, 1977.

Radecki, Henry. *Ethnic Organizational Dynamics: The Polish Group in Canada*. Waterloo: Wilfrid Laurier University Press, 1979.

Radecki, Henry, with Benedykt Heydenkorn. *A Member of a Distinguished Family: The Polish Group in Canada*. Toronto: McClelland and Stewart, 1976.

Ramcharan, Subhas. *Racism: Nonwhites in Canada*. Toronto: Butterworths, 1982.

Ramirez, Bruno, and Michele Del Balzo. "The Italians of Montreal: From Sojourning to Settlement, 1900-1921," in Robert F. Harney and J. Vincenza Scarpaci, eds., *Little Italies in North America*. Toronto: Multicultural History Society of Ontario, 1981, pp. 63-84.

Rasporich, Anthony W. "Ethnicity in Lakehead Politics, 1900-1970," paper presented at Canadian Ethnic Studies Association Conference, Thunder Bay, October, 1983.

——. *For a Better Life: A History of the Croatians in Canada*. Toronto: McClelland and Stewart, 1982.

——. "Utopian Ideals and Community Settlements in Western Canada: 1880-1914," in *The Canadian West*, edited by Henry C. Klassen. Calgary: University of Calgary Press, 1977, pp. 37-62.

Reid, W. Stanford, ed. *The Scottish Tradition in Canada*. Toronto: McClelland and Stewart, 1976.

Reitz, Jeffrey G. *The Survival of Ethnic Groups*. Toronto: McGraw-Hill Ryerson, 1980.

Richmond, Anthony H., and Warren E. Kalbach. *Factors in the Adjustment of Immigrants and Their Descendants*. Ottawa: Minister of Supply and Services, 1980.

Rose, Albert, ed. *A People and Its Faith*. Toronto: University of Toronto Press, 1959.

Rosenberg, Stuart. *The Jewish Community in Canada*, vol. 1. Toronto: McClelland and Stewart, 1970.

Roy, Patricia. "The Oriental Menace in British Columbia," in *The Twenties in Western Canada*, edited by S.M. Trofimenkoff. Ottawa: National Museum of Man, 1972, pp. 243-58.

Ryder, N.B. "The Interpretation of Origin Statistics," *Canadian Journal of Economics and Political Science*, 21, 4 (1955), pp. 466-79.

Sack, B.G. *History of the Jews in Canada*. Montreal: Harvest House, 1965.

Schermerhorn, R.A. *Comparative Ethnic Relations*. New York: Random House, 1970.

Sharp, Paul. *The Agrarian Revolt in Western Canada*. Minneapolis: University of Minnesota Press, 1948.

Sherwood, David, and Allan C. Wakefield. "A Study of Voluntary Associations among Other Ethnic Groups in Canada," a study prepared for the Royal Commission on Bilingualism and Biculturalism, 1968.

Smillie, Ben. *Visions of the New Jerusalem: The Story of Religious Settlement on the Prairies*. Edmonton: NeWest, 1983.

Smith, David. *Prairie Liberalism*. Toronto: University of Toronto Press, 1975.

Smith, David. *The Regional Decline of a National Party: Liberals on the Prairies*. Toronto: University of Toronto Press, 1981.

Spada, A.V. *The Italians in Canada*. Canada Ethnica 6. Montreal: Riviera Printers & Publishers, 1969.

Speisman, Stephen A. *The Jews of Toronto: A History to 1937*. Toronto: McClelland and Stewart, 1979.

Stone, Leroy D. *Urban Development in Canada*. Ottawa: Dominion Bureau of Statistics, 1967.

Sturino, Franc. "Family and Kin Cohesion among South Italian Immigrants in Toronto," in *The Italian Immigrant Woman in North America*, edited by Betty Boyd Caroli, Robert F. Harney, and Lydio F. Tomasi. Toronto: Multicultural History Society of Ontario, 1978, pp. 288-311.

Stursberg, Peter. *Diefenbaker: Leadership Gained 1956-62*. Toronto: University of Toronto Press, 1975.

Sunahara, Ann. *The Politics of Racism*. Toronto: Lorimer, 1981.

Tarasoff, Koozma J. "Russians of the Greater Vancouver Area," *Slavs in Canada*, vol. 1. Edmonton: Inter-University Committee on Canadian Slavs, 1966, pp. 138-47.

Thompson, John Herd. *The Harvests of War: The Prairie West, 1914-1918*. Toronto: McClelland and Stewart, 1978.

Thompson, John. "The Prohibition Question in Manitoba, 1892-1928." M.A. thesis, University of Manitoba, 1969.

Timlin, Mabel F. "Canada's Immigration Policy, 1896-1910," *Canadian Journal of Economics and Political Science*, 26, 4 (1960), pp. 517-32.

Trachtenberg, Henry. "The Winnipeg Jewish Community and Politics: The Inter-War Years, 1919-1939," *Transactions of the Historical and Scientific Society of Manitoba*, 3:34-3:35 (1977-78, 1978-79).

Troper, Harold. *Only Farmers Need Apply*. Toronto: Griffin House, 1972.

Trudel, Marcel. *Initiation à la Nouvelle-France, Histoire et institutions*. Montréal: Holt, Rinehart and Winston, 1968.

——. *L'Esclavage au Canada français, Histoire et conditions de l'esclavage*. Québec: Les Presses Universitaires Laval, 1960.

Turek, Victor. *Poles in Manitoba*. Toronto: Polish Research Institute in Canada, 1967.

——. *Polish-Language Press in Canada*. Toronto: Polish Research Institute in Canada, 1962.

Usiskin, Roz. "The Winnipeg Jewish Community: its Radical Elements 1905-1918," *Transactions of the Historical and Scientific Society of Manitoba*, 3:33 (1976-77).

Vaugeois, Denis. *Les Juifs et la Nouvelle France*. Trois-Rivières: Boréal Express, 1968.

Wagner, Jonathan. *Brothers Beyond the Sea: National Socialism in Canada*. Waterloo: Wilfrid Laurier University Press, 1980.

Walker, James W. *A History of Blacks in Canada: A Study Guide for Teachers and Parents*. Ottawa: Minister of State Multiculturalism, 1980.

Wangenheim, E.D. "The Social Organization of the Japanese Community in Toronto – A Product of Crisis." M.A. thesis, University of Toronto, 1956.

Ward, W. Peter. *White Canada Forever*:

Popular Attitudes and Public Policy Toward Orientals in British Columbia. Montreal: McGill-Queen's University Press, 1978.

Wardhaugh, Ronald. *Language and Nationhood: The Canadian Experience*. Vancouver: New Star Books, 1981.

Weinfeld, M., W. Shaffir, and I. Cotler, eds. *The Canadian Jewish Mosaic*. Toronto: John Wiley & Sons, 1981.

Wickberg, Edgar, ed. *From China to Canada: A History of the Chinese Communities in Canada*. Toronto: McClelland and Stewart, 1982.

Wilson, J. Donald, Robert M. Stamp, and Louis-Philippe Audet, eds. *Canadian Education: A History*. Scarborough: Prentice-Hall of Canada, 1970.

Wilson, S.J. *Women, the Family and the Economy*. Toronto: McGraw-Hill Ryerson, 1982.

Winks, Robin W. *The Blacks in Canada: A History*. Montreal: McGill-Queen's University Press, 1971.

Wiseman, Nelson. "Patterns of Prairie Politics," *Queen's Quarterly*, 88, 2 (1981), pp. 298-315.

——. *Social Democracy in Manitoba: A History of the CCF/NDP*. Winnipeg: University of Manitoba Press, 1983.

Wolfgang, Aaron, ed. *Education of Immigrant Students: Issues and Answers*. Toronto: Ontario Institute for Studies in Education, 1975.

Woodcock, George, and Ivan Avakumovic. *The Doukhobors*. Toronto: Oxford University Press, 1968.

Woodsworth, James S. *Strangers Within Our Gates or Coming Canadians*. Original edition, 1909; reprint, Toronto: University of Toronto Press, 1972.

Woycenko, Ol'ha. *The Ukrainians in Canada*. Canada Ethnica 4. Ottawa: Trident Press, 1967.

——. "Ukrainian Contribution to Canada's Cultural Life," an essay prepared for the Royal Commission on Bilingualism and Biculturalism. 1965.

Young, Charles H. *The Ukrainian Canadians: A Study in Assimilation*. Toronto: Thomas Nelson & Sons, 1931.

Yuzyk, Paul. *The Ukrainians in Manitoba: A Social History*. Toronto: University of Toronto Press, 1953.

Zybala, Stanley. "Problems of Survival for the Ethnic Press in Canada," *Polyphony*, 4, 1 (1982), pp. 15-29.

Index

Aberhart, William: 134
Abu-Laban, Baha: 61, 66
Adamowska, Maria: 198
Africans: 14
Albanians: 147
Alberta Department of Education:
    106
Alexander, Lincoln M.: 179
Alvensleben, Gustav Constantin
    Alvo von: 63-64
American Civil War: 19
American Revolutionary War: 15,
    16, 17, 18, 26, 109
Amerindians: 3, 4, 13, 14, 15, 16,
    17, 18, 19, 20, 25, 126; *see
    also* Native peoples
Amherst, Jeffery, first Baron: 16
Anderson, Alan: 99
Anderson, Grace M.: 96
Anderson, J.T.M.: 112
Ann: 17
Anticlericalism: 128-29, 130
Anti-Missionary League: 132
Anti-Semitism: 38, 62, 67, 72,
    163, 164, 172, 204
Arabs: 147, 198; Canadian Arab
    Federation, 191
Arcand, Adrien: 38
Armenians: 30, 59, 61, 120, 168,
    171, 190, 213, 221
Asians: 31, 37, 38-39, 41, 44, 54,

58, 59, 70, 71-72, 76, 88, 98,
    103-04, 117, 118, 125, 132-
    33, 137, 148, 160-61, 209;
    see also Chinese, Japanese,
    Koreans, South Asians, Viet-
    namese
Asselin, Olivar: 154
Assimilation: 3, 98, 103, 104, 105,
    107, 112, 153, 166, 205; *see
    also* Canadianization
Associations and organizations: 26,
    66, 76, 97-98, 114-15, 132,
    151, 160, 161, 163, 164,
    169-70, 171, 172, 179, 185-
    96; Montefiore Club, 76;
    Primrose Club, 76; lands-
    mannschaften, 186-87;
    mutual-aid societies, 187,
    192-93; philanthropic socie-
    ties, 187-88, 192; reading
    clubs, 193; temperance socie-
    ties, 187, 188; *see also*
    Umbrella organizations
Austrians: 14

Balts, *see* Estonians, Latvians,
    Lithuanians
Baraga, Father Frederik: 126
Barcz, Dominik: 14
Barrett, David: 180

Basques: 112
Bata, Thomas: 77
Bekevar, Saskatchewan: 131
Belgians: 22, 27, 59, 68, 94, 126
Belzberg family: 77
Bengali: 13
Bercovitch, Peter: 154
Berlin (Kitchener), Ontario: 128, 154-55, 187, 198
Bernard, Hans: 13
Bible schools: 134, 136
Bilingualism: 8, 9, 152, 153, 175-76
Bill 101, Province of Quebec: 119-20, 177
Bill 63, Province of Quebec: 119
Bill 22, Province of Quebec: 119
Birthrate: 90, 91, 96, 97, 118
Blacks: 14, 17-18, 19, 21-22, 27, 32, 37-38, 44-45, 72, 100, 103, 108-09, 153, 179-80, 209, 218-19, 227; see also Visible minorities
Black United Front: 179
Bloc settlement: 9, 25, 26, 27, 30, 112, 205
Boarding houses: 61-62, 86-88, 95
Borba (The Struggle): 166
Borden, Sir Robert: 156, 159
Bourassa, Henri: 154
Bradwin, Edmund W.: 32, 58, 86
Brandeau, Esther: 14
Brantford, Ontario: 137
Brennan, J.W.: 157
Bressani (Bresciani), Father Francesco Giuseppe: 13, 126
British North America Act: 104
Bronfman family: 76, 77
Buddhism: 12, 132
Budka, Bishop Nykyta: 33, 127
Bukovynians, see Ukrainians
Bulgarians: 59, 68, 86, 147, 164
Button, Thomas: 11
Byelorussians: 20, 69; Byelorussian Canadian Co-ordinating Committee, 191

Cabot, John (Giovanni Caboto): 12
Čačić, Tomo: 166
Cahan, C.H.: 159
Calgary, Alberta: 27, 38, 39, 76, 98, 137, 146
Canada Ethnic Press Association: 202, 203
Canada Museum und Allgemeine Zeitung: 198
Canada Posten: 198
Canada Press Club: 202
Canada Skandinaven: 198
Canadian Bill of Rights (1960): 72, 174
Canadian Broadcasting Corporation (CBC): 172, 207-08, 209
Canadian Consultative Council on Multiculturalism: 207, 225, 226
Canadian Ethnic Studies Association: 225
Canadian Human Rights Act (1977): 225
Canadian Hungarian News: 201
Canadianization: 89, 106, 110, 111-12, 113, 115, 130
Canadian Jewish Congress: 189-90
Canadian Nationalist Party: 164
Canadian Pacific Railway (CPR): 21, 25, 27, 29, 31, 59, 60, 63
Canadian Scene: 203
Canadian Ukrainian-Youth Federation: 169
Canadian Union of Fascists: 164
Cartier, Jacques: 12
Census, Canadian: 5, 22, 28, 44, 195, 220
Central Americans: 178
Champlain, Samuel de: 12
Charter-member groups/founding peoples: 3, 13, 54, 224
Charter of Rights and Freedoms (1982): 72, 148, 178, 225-26
Chervonyi prapor (Red Flag): 199

Chicago Herald: 201

Chileans: 21, 41, 53, 178

Chinese: 12, 21, 31, 37, 44, 52, 53, 59, 63, 65, 71-72, 76, 83, 88, 98, 107-08, 110, 113, 114, 115, 121, 128, 134-35, 151, 160-61, 162, 168, 170, 174, 176, 179, 186, 187, 188, 198, 205, 206, 208, 217, 218-19, 227

Chinese Free Masons: 169

Chinese Immigration Act (1923): 37, 94, 133, 170

Chinese Labor Association: 161

Chinese National League: 169

Chinese Times: 198

Christianity: 125-31, 132-36, 137-46, 147-48

Christian Missionary Alliance: 134

Conquest: 15

Churches: 17, 111, 120, 125-50, 186, 198-99, 213, 217; All-Russian Orthodox Church, 129; Baptist Church, 130, 135, 145; Congregational Church, 199; Christian Reformed Church, 120; Church of England (Anglican Church), 17, 111, 126, 134, 135, 145; Lutheran Church, 6, 17, 98, 126, 128, 133, 135, 136, 145; Evangelical Lutheran Church of Canada, 145; Methodist Church, 111, 130, 132, 133, 134, 199; Presbyterian Church, 111, 132, 134, 135, 199; Greek Catholic Church, 33, 127-28, 130, 137; Independent Greek Church, 130, 134, 199; Polish National Catholic Church, 128, 198-99; Roman Catholic Church, 6, 8, 13, 14, 15, 17, 19, 28, 103-05, 125, 126, 127, 128, 129-30, 132, 133, 136-37, 198-99; Russian Orthodox Church, 130, 134, 135; Ukrainian Greek Catholic Church, 127, 134, 135, 137; Ukrainian Greek Orthodox Church, 128, 134, 135, 187; United Church of Canada, 134, 135, 145, 199

Churchill, Manitoba: 11

Citizenship Act (1947): 173; (1977), 225

Clark, Charles Joseph: 179-80

Class: 19, 41, 57-59, 61, 62, 69, 74, 75-77, 82, 117, 118, 126, 154, 159, 166, 185, 216; elites, 75-77, 227

Clement, Wallace: 75, 76, 77

Columbus, Christopher: 11

Commission of Inquiry on the Position of the French Language and on Language Rights in Quebec (Gendron Commission): 119

Commission of Inquiry on War Criminals (Deschênes Commission): 180

Committee on Co-operation in Canadian Citizenship (cccc): 190-91

Common School Act, Ontario: 109

Communal Property Act: 168

Communism: 136, 171, 174, 190, 218

Communist Party of Canada (cpc): 156, 159, 164, 165, 166, 167, 169, 172-73

Conservative Party: 27, 154, 155, 156, 157, 158, 162, 172, 173, 174, 175, 176, 178, 181, 199

Constitution Act of 1982, *see* Charter of Rights and Freedoms

Contrast: 179

Co-operative Commonwealth Federation (ccf): 162, 167, 168, 175

Co-operatives: 66

Cordasco, Antonio: 63
Credit unions: 66, 69, 191;
    Ukrainian Credit Union of
    Toronto, 69; St. Stanislaus and
    St. Casimir Credit Union, 69
Crequy, Leonard: 13
Croatians: 12, 20, 21, 59-60, 69,
    153, 162, 164, 166, 169, 171,
    172, 190
Crow's Nest Pass: 59
Cuisine: 212, 215-17
Cults: 125, 131, 136, 147-48;
    Christian Spiritists' Society,
    131; Hare Krishna, 148
Cultural Enrichment Program
    (CEP): 121
Culture: 6, 7, 8, 9, 16, 89, 100,
    103, 104, 106-07, 110, 111,
    115, 116, 212-13, 226, 227-
    28
Czas (Time): 200
Czechoslovaks: 68; Czechoslovak
    National Alliance, 191
Czechs: 22, 27, 33, 128, 169-70,
    178, 199-200, 218

Dafoe, John W.: 106
Dahl, Peter: 20
Danes: 11, 26, 27, 28, 36, 68, 69,
    128, 136
Debartch, Pierre Dominique: 14
Decore, John: 172
De Grassi, Philip: 19
De Meuron regiment: 16, 20
Deportation: 33, 38, 68, 69, 159,
    166, 170
Der Nordwesten: 199
De Teive, Diogo: 11
Deutscher Bund Canada: 163
Dickson, Alberta: 136
Diefenbaker, John George: 173,
    174-75
Discrimination: 7, 8, 18, 19, 21,
    31, 32, 37-38, 41, 58, 63, 65,
    67, 69, 72-73, 76, 99, 107-

08, 115, 136-37, 147, 151,
    160-61, 163, 170, 174, 179,
    188, 218, 221, 223, 224, 226,
    227-28
Displaced persons, see Refugees
Divorce: 83, 96
Dojaček, Františec: 199-200
Dojack, Charles: 200
Domestics: 61, 73-74, 84, 86
Dominion Labor Party: 159
Dominion Lands Act (Homestead
    Act): 29, 30, 130
Donegani, Francesco: 16
Donegani, Giovanni: 16
Donegani, John: 16
Donegani, William: 16
Don Valley: 19
Doukhobors: 6, 29, 33, 34, 86, 99,
    103, 104, 108, 113-14, 130-
    31, 146, 152; Sons of Free-
    dom, 108, 113-14, 131, 146
Dreisziger, Nandor F.: 167
Drieger, Leo: 99
Dualism, Canadian: 8, 103
Dunkards: 19, 131
Dutch: 15, 19, 21, 27, 28, 37, 41,
    52, 53, 57, 68, 69, 89, 91, 94,
    98, 99, 120, 148, 193

Eastern Townships: 16
Economic conditions: 32, 34, 38,
    64, 65, 66-70, 77, 88, 90-91,
    95, 135, 172, 174
Edmonton: 27, 28, 39, 76, 96,
    117, 146
Education, see Schools
Eleniak, Wasyl: 28
Emigration: 5, 6, 7, 32
Empire Reform Association: 188
"Enemy aliens": 33, 34, 64, 69,
    106, 107
Epp, Frank: 131
Equality Now!: 178, 209, 227
Ericson, Leif: 11, 198
Esterhazy, Count Paul: 29

Estonians: 4, 27, 41, 69, 162, 171, 216, Estonian Central Council, 171, 218
Ethnic businesses: 62, 63, 65, 73, 216-17
Ethnicity: ethnic group defined, 4-5; ethnic origin, 5, 6; ethnic identity, 5, 8-9, 34, 81, 100, 125, 186, 212-22, 226
Ethnic press: 154, 155, 156, 157, 158-59, 162, 164, 166, 173, 179, 197-203, 209-10; ethnic press associations, 174; Ethnic Press Association of British Columbia, Ethnic Press Association of Ontario, Ethnic Press Association of Quebec, 202; *see also* Media of communication
Ethnocultural Council of Canada: 195
Euler, W.D.: 155
Exploitation of immigrants: 65-66, 177
Exploration: 11-13, 22
External Affairs, Department of: 172, 181

Factor, Sam: 162
Family: 81-102, 131, 213
Farmers' Unity League: 165
Fascism: 37, 136, 153, 163-64, 169, 190, 201
Federation of Polish Societies in Canada: 114, 200
Federation of Russian Workers and Farmers Clubs: 164, 169
Federazione delle associazioni dai clubs italiani (FACI): 192
Feltz, Charles Joseph de: 14
Fernandes, João: 11
Filian-Dubois, Thérèse: 14
Filipinos: 53, 179; United Council of Filipino Associations across Canada, 191

Finnish Organization of Canada (FOC): 159, 165-66, 169
Finns: 27, 33, 37, 38, 58, 60, 63, 64, 68, 69, 73-74, 84, 89, 154, 158-59, 162, 164, 166, 173, 197, 198, 218
Folklore: 212, 214-15, 227
Fort William, Ontario: 60, 165
Framfari (Progress): 198
Franklin, Selim: 22
French: 11, 13, 59, 68, 94
Frontier College: 32
Fuca, Juan de: 12

Galicians, *see* Ukrainians
Garon, André: 15
Garvey, Marcus: 154
Gazeta Katolicka: 199
Generations: 45, 98-99, 100, 125, 145, 175, 180, 194, 202-03, 213-14, 220
"Gentlemen's agreements": 31, 37, 83
Germans: 6, 11, 13, 14, 15, 16, 17, 18, 19, 20, 21, 22, 26, 27, 28, 29, 32, 33, 38, 41, 52, 53, 57, 58, 63-64, 67, 68, 69, 70, 96, 99, 105, 109, 115, 121, 128, 131, 133, 134, 137, 148, 153, 154-55, 156, 157, 163-64, 169, 170, 175, 180, 187, 190, 193, 216; *see also* Mennonites
Getty, Donald Ross: 179
Ghadar Party: 161, 188
Ghermezian family: 77
Ghitter, Ronald: 179
Ghiz, Joseph: 180
Gilbert, Sir Humphrey: 11, 12
Gimli, Manitoba: 26
Givens, Philip: 175
Glace Bay, Nova Scotia: 153
Globensky, Auguste France: 16
Glos Kanadyjski (Canadian Voice): 198

Godin, Gérard: 177
Gold rushes: British Columbia, 20, 21, 22; Yukon, 27
Gordon, Milton M.: 4-5
Gouzenko affair: 172
Grand Trunk Pacific Railway: 31, 63
Grauer, Jacob: 21
Gray, James: 67
Great Depression: 38, 66-69, 77, 90-91, 135, 162, 163, 173, 201, 205
Greeks: 12, 30, 44, 45, 53, 60, 61, 74, 98, 99, 119, 120, 121, 177, 206, 217
Grossman, Allan: 172-73
Group settlement, *see* Bloc settlement
Gzowski, Casimir: 19-20

Haitians: 45, 53, 117, 118, 177, 178, 227
Halifax, Nova Scotia: 15, 17, 126, 187, 198
Hamilton, Ontario: 36, 53, 76, 137, 179
Harney, Robert F.: 110
Hart, Aaron: 16, 20
Hart, Arthur Wellington: 20
Hart, Ezekiel: 153
Hawaiians: 21
Hawrelak, William: 175
Head, Wilson: 179
Heaps, Abraham Albert: 166
Hebrew Society of Montreal: 27
Heimskringla (The Round World): 155, 198
Helgesen, Hans: 22
Helmcken, Dr. John Sebastian: 21
Heritage languages: 117, 121, 227
Hesse-Heynan Regiment: 16
Heydenkorn, Benedykt: 5
Higgs, David: 96
Hill, Daniel G.: 179
Hindus: 31

Hitler, Adolf: 164, 169, 170
Homes for the aged: 97-98
Hong Kong: 21, 178
Honour: 82, 88
Howe, Clarence Decatur: 173
Hubbard, William Peyton: 179
Hudson, Henry: 11
Hudson Bay: 11, 12
Hudson's Bay Company: 4, 21, 25, 67
Hungarian-Canadian Federation: 190, 191
Hungarian revolution: 41
Hungarians: 12, 27, 28, 29, 32, 33, 35-36, 38, 43, 59, 62, 68, 69, 89, 91, 98, 99, 115, 128, 131, 137, 162, 164, 169, 187, 190, 191, 206, 221
Hutterites: 6, 30, 34, 36, 86, 97, 99, 103, 113, 134, 145-46, 152, 168

Icelanders: 25-26, 98, 105, 111, 155, 188, 198
Il Bollettino: 201
Illegal immigrants: 6, 73, 118, 170, 174
Immigrant aid societies: 193; Italian Immigrant Aid Society, 63
Immigration policy: 8-9, 13, 25, 32, 33, 34, 37-38, 41, 44, 65, 70, 89, 94, 95-96, 115, 117, 161, 167, 170, 173, 174, 176, 178; Immigration Act (1976), 96; Railway Agreement, 34
Imperial Order of Daughters of the Empire: 188
Indians: 45, 147; *see also* South Asians
Industrial Workers of the World: 156, 159-60
Intermarriage: 5, 14, 16, 30, 88-89, 95, 98-100, 195
Ismailis: 146, 195
Italians: 6, 12, 13, 16, 20, 30, 32,

37, 41, 44, 45, 52, 53, 59, 60, 62, 63, 68, 69, 70-71, 76, 83, 86, 88, 94-95, 96, 98, 99, 110, 114, 115, 116, 118, 119, 121, 126, 128, 137, 154, 162, 163-64, 169, 170, 173, 174, 176, 177, 187, 190, 193, 198, 201, 206, 207-08, 215, 216, 221; National Congress of Italian-Canadians, 191
Italo-Canadian Recreation Club: 192

Jacobs, Sam: 162
Japanese: 31, 38-39, 44, 59, 64, 69, 71-72, 83, 88, 98, 100, 107, 108, 113, 115, 148, 160-61, 170, 180, 205, 214, 218-19, 220, 227; National Japanese Canadian Citizens Association, 191
Japanese Camp and Mill Workers Union: 161
Jewish Colonization Association: 27
Jewish Times: 198
Jews: 5, 6, 12, 14, 15-16, 20, 22, 27, 30, 33, 37, 38, 41, 52, 53, 59, 61, 62, 67, 68, 70, 71, 75-76, 77, 87, 88, 98, 99, 103, 110, 111, 114, 118, 120, 121, 125, 126, 131-32, 134, 136-37, 146, 148, 152, 153, 154, 158-60, 164, 168, 173, 175, 177, 179, 180, 188, 193, 198, 213, 216
Jones, Coleman Burnley ("Rocky"): 179
Juba, Stephen: 175
Jung, Douglas: 174

Kanadiiskyi Farmer (Canadian Farmer): 199
Kanadyiets (The Canadian): 199

Kashubs: 20
Khrushchev, Nikita: 172
Kierkowski, Alexander: 153
King, William Lyon Mackenzie: 39, 163
Kogler, Rudolf: 5
Kolisnyk, William: 166
Komagata Maru: 31, 32
Koreans: 53
Korean War: 53
Kosiak, Julian: 179
Kranz, Hugo: 154
Kruger, Theodore: 21
Ku Klux Klan: 163
Kuomintang: 188

Labor League (United Jewish People's Order): 159
Labrador: 11, 12
Langevin, Archbishop Adélard: 128
Language: 6, 7, 8, 30, 52-53, 89, 90, 100, 103, 104, 105-07, 108, 109, 111, 113, 114, 115, 116, 118-20, 121-22, 128, 135-36, 145, 193, 194, 200, 202, 203-04, 206-07, 209, 210, 226, 227-28; *see also* Bilingualism, Heritage languages
L'Anse aux Meadows, Newfoundland: 11
La Penha, Daniel S. de: 12
La Penha, Joseph de: 12
La Presse: 203
La Salle, René-Robert, Cavalier de: 13
Laskin, Bora: 77
Latin Americans: 177
Latvians: 4, 41, 89, 94, 162, 171; Latvian National Federation of Canada, 191
Laumeister, Frank: 21
Laurier, Sir Wilfrid: 27, 154
Laurier-Greenway compromise

(1896): 105
League for the Liberation of the Ukraine: 171
Lebanese: 30, 52, 179
Le Devoir: 204
Le Droit: 204
Leifur: 198
Le Jeune, Olivier: 14
Le Soleil: 204
Lethbridge, Alberta: 100, 187
Lewis, David: 77, 180
Liberal Party: 27, 106, 107, 119, 154, 155, 156, 157, 158, 162, 164, 167, 172, 173, 176, 177, 178, 181, 199
Lindström-Best, Varpu: 73-74
Lingua Ads Service: 202
Lipset, Seymour Martin: 168
Lithuanians: 4, 41, 59, 69, 110, 114, 162, 164, 171, 187; National Council of the Lithuanian-Canadian Community, 191
Little Newspaper: 201
Lögberg (The Mount of Laws): 155, 198
London, Ontario: 137
Lo Stendardo: 198
Louisbourg, Nova Scotia: 17
Luchkovich, Michael: 162
Lufti, Ameen: 61
Lunenburg, Nova Scotia: 17, 57
Lysenko, Vera: 74

Macedonians: 30, 59, 62, 83, 86, 90, 127, 168, 171, 187, 217
Mackenzie, William Lyon: 18-19
Mackenzie-Papineau battalion: 166
Maltese: 44
Manitoba Free Press: 106, 204, 205; *see also Winnipeg Free Press*
Marlyn, John: 221
Maroons: 18

Marriage: 82-83, 91; "picture" brides, 84; war brides, 94; *see also* Intermarriage
Martin, Paul: 173
Media of communication: 156, 158-59, 160, 172, 194, 197-211; *see also* Ethnic press
Mennonite Colonization Association: 36
Mennonites: 6, 19, 25-26, 27, 30, 33, 34, 36, 57, 86, 99, 103, 105-06, 111, 113, 120, 126, 130, 131, 133, 134, 135, 136, 146, 152, 154, 162-63; Amish, 19, 131
Mercenary soldiers: 14-15, 16, 17, 20
Métis: 20, 25, 126
Mexicans: 21
Miners: 59, 60, 68; Mine Workers' Union of Canada, 165; mining camps, 21, 58-59
Minister of State for Multiculturalism: 176, 225
Minority ethnic groups: 4, 6-7
Misionar: 127
Missionaries, missions: 22, 111, 114, 125, 126, 130, 132-33, 145
Mitchell, Elaine Allen: 3-4
Montenegrins: 68
Montreal: 8, 14, 15, 16, 20, 30, 32, 36, 38, 39, 41, 52, 56, 63, 71, 75, 76, 96, 98, 99, 114, 116, 126, 128, 131, 132, 146, 154, 209, 227
Montreal Catholic School Commission: 100, 118
Montreal Protestant School Board: 110, 114, 118
Monts, Pierre Du Gua de: 17
Moravians: 19
Mouvement pour l'Integration Scolaire: 119
Multiculturalism: 9, 115, 117, 121-22, 148, 153, 175-78,

194, 214, 221-22, 224-28;
Multiculturalism Directorate,
195, 215, 225
Multilingualism: 112
Munk, Jens: 11
Muslims: 147; Council of Muslim
Communities in Canada, 147
Mussolini, Benito: 163, 169, 190

Narodna Gazeta (People's
Gazette): 199
Nathan, Henry, Jr.: 22, 153
Nationalism: 6, 35, 111-12, 113,
153, 154, 161, 163, 166, 171,
177, 186, 204, 223
Nationality: 6-7
National (ethnic) parishes: 128,
137
National Socialists (Nazis): 163,
164, 168, 169, 170, 190;
National Social Christian
Party, 164; Deutscher Bund
Canada, 163
National War Services, Depart-
ment of: 190-91
Native peoples: 4, 9, 12, 13, 22,
45, 223, 224; *see also* Amer-
indians, Métis
Nativism: 34, 162, 163, 173
New Canadian Publications: 202
New Democratic Party (NDP): 176,
177, 180
New France: 13-14, 15, 16
Niagara, Ontario: 18
Niagara-on-the-Lake, Ontario:
188
North Africans: 41
Norwegians: 11, 20, 22, 26-27,
28, 30, 33, 36, 68, 84, 89,
128, 136, 145

Occupations: 13, 14, 15, 16, 17,
20, 21, 22, 28, 31, 41, 57, 62-
63, 65, 70-71, 73, 76-77,

185-86, 191, 213-14; wom-
en's occupations, 86, 90, 95,
213
Okinawans: 31
Oleskiw, Dr. Joseph: 28-29, 127
Oliver, Frank: 205
Olsen, Dennis: 77
Onderdonk, Andrew: 21
One Big Union: 156, 159-60
Ontario Department of Education:
109
Ontario Human Rights Commis-
sion: 208
Oppenheimer, David: 22
Oppenheimer, Isaac: 22
Oshawa, Ontario: 174
Ottawa: 25, 137

Pakistanis: 45, 99-100, 147; *see
also* South Asians
Pandosy, Brother Peter: 22
Parmenius, Stephen: 12
Parti Québécois: 117, 119
Pearl Harbor: 170
Pearson, Lester Bowles: 175
Peddling: 59, 61-62, 66
Phillips, Nathan: 175
Pining, Diedrich: 11
Poles: 5, 6, 12, 14, 16, 20, 28, 29-
30, 33, 35, 41, 53, 62, 64, 65,
66, 67, 68, 69, 71, 83, 87, 88,
91, 94, 96-97, 98, 99, 105,
110, 114, 126, 128, 129-30,
133, 137, 164, 168, 187,
188-89, 190, 193-94; Cana-
dian Polish Congress, 169,
191
Polish Peoples Association: 169
Political parties: 152, 199; *see also*
Communist Party of Canada,
Conservative Party,
Co-operative Commonwealth
Federation, Liberal Party,
New Democratic Party, Parti
Québécois, Union Nationale

Port Arthur, Ontario: 37, 60, 165, 173
Porter, John: 75, 76, 77, 224
Port Royal: 17
Portuguese: 11, 12, 44, 45, 53, 96, 98, 116, 118, 121, 137, 177, 206
Pothorst, Hans: 11
Prairie Farmer: 201
Priests: 35, 58, 127, 128-30, 132, 174, 213
Prince Albert, Saskatchewan: 174
Progressive movement: 134, 167
Prohibition: 133, 152, 167
Projet d'enseignement en langue d'origine (PELO): 120
Prophetic Baptist movement: 134
Protest marches: 68-69; On-to-Ottawa Trek, 69
Pylypiew, Ivan: 28

Quebec City: 13, 15, 16
Quiet Revolution: 118, 204

Racial groups: 7, 32, 104, 117-18; *see also* Visible minorities
Racism: 22, 38, 115, 153, 170, 178, 179, 180, 224, 226; *see also* Discrimination
Radecki, Henry: 129, 189
Radicalism: 33, 38, 64, 68, 69, 136, 152, 153, 156, 158-60, 161, 164, 166-67, 172, 177, 181
Radio: 134, 172, 206-10
Ranok (Morning): 199
Rasminsky, Louis: 77
Rebellion of 1837: 16
Refugees: 38, 41, 52, 74, 94, 137, 151, 162, 163, 164, 171, 172, 178, 226
Regina, Saskatchewan: 69
Regionalism: 8, 66
Reichmann family: 77

Reisman, Simon: 77
Religion, *see* Churches, Cults, Sects
Return migration: 39
Richter, Francis Xavier: 22
Roblin, Sir Rodmond Palen: 105
Robochyi narod: 158, 199
Romanians: 28, 29, 30, 33, 38, 66, 68
Rosenfeld, Bobbie: 217
Ross, George: 109
Rouyn-Noranda: 166
Royal Canadian Mounted Police (RCMP): 69, 168-69
Royal Commission on Bilingualism and Biculturalism: 4, 13, 120, 121, 175, 200, 207, 220, 223-25
Royal Commission to Inquire into the Immigration of Italian Workers to Montreal and Alleged Fraudulent Practices of Employment Agencies: 63
Russian Revolution: 36, 189
Russians: 28, 29, 33, 36, 38, 59, 68, 98, 99, 131, 164; *see also* Doukhobors
Ruthenians, *see* Ukrainians
Ryder, Norman: 5
Ryerson, Egerton: 109

St. Laurent, Louis: 171-72
St. Nicholas Day: 91
Salsberg, Joseph B.: 172-73
Saturday Night: 160
Sault Ste. Marie: 37, 165
Scandinavians: 6, 11, 26-27, 28, 36-37, 52, 54, 58, 66, 73, 84, 98, 99, 131, 148, 167-68, 175, 206; *see also* Danes, Icelanders, Norwegians, Swedes
Schermerhorn, Robert A.: 4
Schmid, Jean Lucas: 14
Schools: 9, 64, 76, 85, 89, 103-24; bilingual schools, 105-06,

107, 114, 117, 167, 213; denominational schools, 103-05, 110, 116; private schools, 106, 108-09, 111, 114-15, 120-22, 193
Schreyer, Edward Richard: 180
Schubert, Augustus, 21
Secretary of State, Department of: 176, 208, 225
Sects: 6, 25-26, 34, 86, 125, 131, 133, 134, 136, 147-48; Church of God, 134; Evangelical Free Church, 131; Evangelical Swedish Mission Covenant of America, 131; Evangelical United Brethren, 131; German-Baptist Church of North America, 131; Seventh Day Adventists, 131; *see also* Hutterites, Mennonites, Doukhobors
Secularization: 125, 148
Segregation: 16, 18, 19, 107-08, 153, 188, 214
Self-Reliance League of Canada: 190
Selkirk, Thomas Douglas, 5th Earl of: 20
Seraphim, Bishop: 129
Serbs: 59, 68, 169, 172, 173
Seven Oaks, battle of: 20
Seven Years' War: 14
Sex ratio: 83-84, 88, 91-94
Shandro, Andrew: 157
Share: 179
Sifton, Sir Clifford: 27, 30, 31, 156, 204-05, 214
Sikhs, Sikhism: 31, 59, 66, 132, 146, 179, 195, 227
Simcoe, John Graves: 19
Singh, Gurdit: 31
Slavery: 14, 17-18, 19, 22
Slovaks: 27, 33, 59, 98, 99, 128, 164, 168, 169-70, 171, 198; Canadian Slovak League, 170
Slovenes: 12, 69, 126, 172

Slovenske Slovo (Slovak Word): 198
Slovo (Word): 199
Soccer: 218
Social Credit Party: 164, 175
Social Democratic Party of Canada: 158-59
Socialism: 136
Socialist Party of Canada: 158, 161
Sojourners: 13, 32, 60, 63, 86, 90
South Africans: 178
South Asians: 31, 53, 76, 83, 88, 97, 146-47, 160-61, 176, 188, 194-95, 205, 214, 218, 227; *see also* Indians, Pakistanis
Soviet Union: 135, 176, 180
Spanish: 12, 18, 20, 177
Spatial distribution of ethnic groups: 9, 45-54
Spencer, Andreas: 13
Sponsored immigration: 44, 94-96, 174
Sports and athletics: 212, 217-18
Starr, Michael: 174, 175
Stelli, George: 22
Strikes: 60, 68, 161, 165, 166; strikebreakers, 68
Stronach, Frank: 77
Sudbury, Ontario: 37, 69, 137, 165
Sun Yat Sen: 161
Supplementary schools, *see* Schools, private
Surnames as indicators of ethnic identity: 220-21
Svenska Canada Tidningen (Swedish Canada News): 198
Swedes: 26, 27, 28, 30, 36, 68, 128, 198
Swiss: 15, 19, 20, 21, 68
Swyripa, Frances: 115
Sydney, Nova Scotia: 153
Sylvester, Frank: 22
Synagogues: Sephardic, 126, 146; Ashkenazic, 126, 131-32;

Hassidic, 146; Holy Blossom
   Synagogue, 188
Syrians: 30, 59, 61, 110, 128

Taber, Alberta: 100
Teachers: 64-65, 112-13, 114, 117
Television: 202, 206-10, 218
Third force: 9, 224
Third World: 75, 178
Three Hills, Alberta: 134
Thunder Bay, Ontario: 53, 98, 99,
   137
Timmins, Ontario: 37, 64, 69
Tokoi, Oskari: 164
Tonty, Henry de: 13
Toronto: 8, 30, 36, 37, 38, 39, 41,
   44, 53, 62, 63, 76, 94, 96-97,
   98, 116, 117-18, 121, 126,
   128, 131-32, 137, 146, 171,
   227
Toronto Jewish Literary and Social
   Union: 188
Trades and Labour Congress: 161
Tres Reyes: 12
Tribune and Examiner: 201
Trois-Rivières: 16, 20
Troper, Harold M.: 110
Trudeau, Pierre Elliott: 176, 178
Turek, Victor: 87
Turks: 59
Tyrkir: 11

Ukrainian Canadian Committee:
   137, 169, 171-72, 190-91
Ukrainian Canadian Congress:
   174
Ukrainian Catholic Brotherhood:
   190
Ukrainian Labour-Farmer Temple
   Association (ULFTA): 159,
   164-65, 166, 169, 190
Ukrainians: 5, 7, 20, 26, 28, 29-
   30, 33, 34-35, 41, 53, 58, 59,
   62, 64-65, 66, 67-68, 69, 71,
74, 84, 85, 86, 88, 89, 96, 98,
   99, 103, 105, 106, 110, 111,
   112-13, 114-15, 120, 121,
   127-28, 130, 131, 134, 137,
   145, 153, 156, 157, 158-59,
   162, 164-67, 168, 170, 171-
   72, 173, 174, 175, 179, 180,
   185, 186, 189, 190-91, 193,
   198, 200, 205, 206, 207, 213,
   214, 224
Ukrainski Holos: 157
Umbrella organizations: 137, 169,
   189, 190-91
Union Nationale: 173
Unions: 60, 63, 156, 160, 161,
   165, 171
United Empire Loyalists: 15, 17,
   19, 154
United Farmers of Alberta: 167
United Nations charter: 170
United States: 5, 7-8, 18, 21-22,
   25, 26-27, 29, 32, 33, 34, 44-
   45, 129, 135, 145, 178, 187
Universal Declaration of Human
   Rights: 170
Urban Alliance on Race Relations:
   179
Urbanization: 36, 82, 137, 148,
   217

Vancouver: 8, 12, 22, 37, 39, 44,
   62, 63, 69, 76, 98, 108, 116,
   132, 133, 137, 174, 210, 227;
   riots of 1907, 31, 32
Vander Zalm, William: 180
Vaugeois, Denis: 15
Veddar, Volkert: 22
Vegreville, Alberta: 162
Verazzano, Giovanni da: 12
Verigin, Peter: 13
Victoria, British Columbia: 21, 22,
   63, 107-08, 133
Vietnamese: 41, 53, 118, 177, 178
Vikings: 11
Vinland: 12

Visibile minorities: 7, 44, 99-100, 178, 207, 208, 218-19, 227

Walker, James W.: 109
War of 1812: 16, 18, 19
Wartime Elections Act (1917): 156, 158
Waterloo, Ontario: 57
Watteville regiment: 16
Welland, Ontario: 36
West Canada Publishing Company: 199
Western Producer: 201
West Indians: 6, 18, 38, 45, 53, 74, 98, 117-18, 145, 179, 218; *see also* Blacks, Visible minorities
Windsor, Ontario: 36, 173
Winnipeg: 8, 26, 28, 30, 62, 67-68, 76, 87, 98, 128, 131, 132, 188
Winnipeg Courier: 158
Winnipeg Free Press: 201, 202

Winnipeg General Strike: 30, 33, 66, 158, 160
Winnipeg Telegram: 156, 215
Winnipeg Tribune: 202, 205
Wolf, Andreas: 13
Woodstock, Ontario: 137
Woodsworth, James Shaver: 32, 87, 130
World War I: 28, 32-33, 35, 63-64, 69, 106-07, 133, 154-55, 159, 168-70, 173, 188-89, 200
World War II: 7, 38, 69, 91, 115-16, 137, 180, 201
Woycenko, Ol'ha: 35

York Factory: 20
Young, Charles: 85
Yugoslavs: 68, 147; *see also* Croatians, Serbs, Slovenes
Yukon: 8, 21, 27, 100
Yusyk, Paul: 224